S0-BZJ-552

# NETWORK PROFESSIONAL'S LIBRARY

# WINDOWS NT

# Windows 98 Networking

# NETWORK PROFESSIONAL'S LIBRARY

# WINDOWS NT

# Windows 98 Networking

**Bradley F. Shimmin**

**Steven P. Klingler**

Osborne/**McGraw-Hill**

Berkeley   New York   St. Louis   San Francisco
Auckland   Bogotá   Hamburg   London   Madrid
Mexico City   Milan   Montreal   New Delhi   Panama City
Paris   São Paulo   Singapore   Sydney
Tokyo   Toronto

Osborne/**McGraw-Hill**
2600 Tenth Street
Berkeley, California 94710
U.S.A.

For information on translations or book distributors outside the U.S.A., or to arrange bulk purchase discounts for sales promotions, premiums, or fund-raisers, please contact Osborne/**McGraw-Hill** at the above address.

### Windows 98 Networking

Copyright © 1999 by The McGraw-Hill Companies. All rights reserved. Printed in the United States of America. Except as permitted under the Copyright Act of 1976, no part of this publication may be reproduced or distributed in any form or by any means, or stored in a database or retrieval system, without the prior written permission of the publisher, with the exception that the program listings may be entered, stored, and executed in a computer system, but they may not be reproduced for publication.

1234567890 AGM AGM 90198765432109

ISBN 0-07-882551-2

**Publisher**
   Brandon A. Nordin
**Editor-in-Chief**
   Scott Rogers
**Acquisitions Editor**
   Gareth Hancock
**Project Editor**
   Ron Hull
**Editorial Assistant**
   Debbie Escobedo
**Technical Editor**
   Eric Hammond

**Copy Editor**
   Ralph Moore
**Proofreader**
   Stefany Otis
**Indexer**
   Irv Hershman
**Computer Designer**
   Jani Beckwith
   Michelle Galicia
**Illustrator**
   Brian Wells
**Series Design**
   Peter F. Hancik

Information has been obtained by Osborne/**McGraw-Hill** from sources believed to be reliable. However, because of the possibility of human or mechanical error by our sources, Osborne/**McGraw-Hill**, or others, Osborne/**McGraw-Hill** does not guarantee the accuracy, adequacy, or completeness of any information and is not responsible for any errors or omissions or the results obtained from use of such information.

# ABOUT THE AUTHORS

**Bradley F. Shimmin** is Editor for *LAN Times*. He produces, manages, and writes the portion of the *LAN Times* Web site dedicated to software components. His seven years of experience include everything from systems administration to online development.

**Steven P. Klingler** is the Marketing Services Director for Tomax Technologies, Inc. He serves as Vice Chairman of the Board of the Association of Online Professionals, and he has authored many articles and reviews for *LAN Times*.

# NETWORK PROFESSIONAL'S LIBRARY

# AT A GLANCE

# NETWORK PROFESSIONAL'S LIBRARY

# CONTENTS

### Part II

### Working with Windows 98

**Part III**

**Managing Windows 98 Clients**

## Part IV

### Appendices

# INTRODUCTION

This book is all about networking with Windows 98. Computer networking used to be an expensive and complicated undertaking, but not any more. It has become an integral part of everyday life for nearly all computer users.

At the office, your computer is likely attached to a Local Area Network (LAN) that connects it to all other computers in your workgroup, department, or throughout the whole office. If the company you work for has more than one office, all locations are likely to be networked together over a Wide Area Network (WAN). And most corporate LANs are also connected to the Internet. We've come a long ways since the early days when networks were simple and generally isolated.

Today most home PCs are also networked, but they don't often use the same Network Interface Cards (NICs) and Ethernet cabling that is typical in the corporate environment. Instead, home users participate in the global network that is the Internet. They use dial-up modems and ISDN adapters to connect with Internet Service Providers (ISPs) and corporate remote access servers. Sometimes serial cables or infrared ports are used to network two PCs together on a temporary basis, or for simple LAN functionality such as exchanging files, sharing printers, or playing multi-player computer games.

Whether you're a home user or a corporate network administrator, this book will teach you how to network with Windows 98.

As a network administrator, you are faced with the unique challenge of integrating PCs that are running several different operating systems on your corporate network that is likely to include both Windows and NetWare file servers. You're also expected to deploy the latest operating system upgrades and Internet client software. This book was written specifically for you. It covers everything you need to know to plan, install, configure, and manage Windows 98 in a corporate network environment.

Home users will also find everything they need to know to install, configure, and manage Windows 98 for access to the Internet or corporate networks using the dial-up networking that is built into Windows 98. In fact, home users can benefit from nearly everything in this book, with the possible exception of Chapters 4 and 5, which concern Networking in Windows NT and NetWare environments; and Chapters 15 and 16, which address corporate deployment and management issues.

As e-mail and the Web have become a part of everyday life, it is now impossible to talk about networking without talking about the Internet, Web browsing, and Web publishing. Not to worry, we'll teach you how to connect to the Internet, exchange e-mail and browse Web pages. Then we will take you to the next level by teaching you how to install and run the Windows 98 Personal Web Server and to publish your own Web content.

# WHAT IS NETWORKING

In simple terms, networking is the act of communicating between two or more computers. In practical terms, it is the ability to share and exchange information, data, programs, or resources such as printers, modems, and backup devices.

There are several distinct types of networks, including Local Area Networks (LANs), Wide Area Networks (WANs), the Internet, Intranets, and Extranets. Let's take a brief look at the differences.

# Local Area Network

As the name suggests, a LAN is a local network. All computers on the LAN reside in the same location and are usually closely associated with each other by their function, the users' job responsibilities, workgroup, department, or location.

# Wide Area Network

When two or more LANs are connected together the resulting network is known as a WAN. Historically, WANs have been extremely expensive and complicated to install and operate, but the Internet has changed all that. You can now use the Internet to establish a global WAN by connecting each LAN to the Internet over inexpensive local connections with properly configured firewalls or other security mechanisms.

# Internet

The Internet is often misunderstood. Many have described it as being the computers that are connected together by the global TCP/IP network. In reality, the Internet is the global TCP/IP network. When you connect an individual PC to the Internet over a dial-up modem connection, or connect every computer in your office through a gateway on your LAN, your computers do not become the Internet, they are simply connected to it.

# Intranet

To many, the word Intranet is nothing more than marketing hype, a new buzzword that simply describes the LAN. But there is a subtle difference. LANs can be based on any networking protocol and they are limited to the local network. Like the Internet, Intranets are based on the TCP/IP protocol and are not confined to the limitations of a single location. They take the best attributes of LANs, WANs, and the Internet and combine them for the benefit of the organization's internal purposes. By definition, an Intranet is not accessible to the general public or to customers, suppliers, or business partners.

# Extranet

The only difference between an Intranet and an Extranet is who can access it. The name Extranet is a fairly new term that has come to describe the part of your network that is accessible to the public or to customers, suppliers, and business partners over the Internet.

# WHY NETWORK WITH WINDOWS 98

There are just as many reasons why companies decide to network their computers as there are ways to do it. In the end, it all comes down to two basic functions that networks make possible:

▼ Access to shared resources

▲ The ability to communicate with others

## Access to Shared Resources

In the early days of networking, computer hardware was very expensive and networking was seen by many organizations as a way to save money by reducing the amount of hardware that they had to buy. Instead of buying costly tape backup devices or CD-ROMs for every workstation, they could buy one or two and share them with all users on the network. Now computer hardware is cheap, but companies have learned that the value gained by being able to access shared network resources goes beyond simple cost savings.

The most commonly shared resources on a network include

▼ Hard drives

■ CD-ROMs

■ Program files

■ Data files

■ Printers

■ Fax services

▲ Backup services

There was a time when the ability to share resources was considered a luxury. Today it is essential. Business applications depend on the ability to share common data files, program files can be centrally managed and updated, and centralized backup procedures protect against costly data loss.

## The Ability to Communicate with Others

It's no secret that workers are more productive when they have timely and reliable access to the information they need to do their jobs. Networks help by providing the communications infrastructure necessary to communicate with each other:

▼ Internet access

■ E-mail

■ Chat

■ Whiteboard

▲ Collaboration

Interest in and use of the Internet has driven the development of these technologies at an increasingly feverish pace over the past few years. It's a trend that will continue in the foreseeable future, resulting in more useful and productive ways to communicate and collaborate with co-workers, customers, and suppliers, no matter where they may be. This book will teach you how you and the people in your organization can use these tools with Windows 98.

# WHAT'S INSIDE

This book contains practical information you can really use. We will help you install, configure, use, and manage Windows 98 in a networking environment. Then we discuss and explain how to use it in Windows 98, Windows NT, NetWare, and TCP/IP (Internet, Intranet and Extranet) network environments; give you specific details on how to use the built-in networking applications and utilities to communicate with others and access, create, and publish information on the Web; and introduce you to the powerful tools that will help you deploy and manage Windows 98 on your network.

# HOW TO USE THIS BOOK

If you're new to Windows 98, we suggest you start at the beginning and read the whole book to the end. However, if you already have a basic understanding of how to use Windows 98 in a network environment, you may want to use it as a reference manual instead, and jump straight to the chapters that interest you.

NETWORK
PROFESSIONAL'S
LIBRARY

# PART I

# Networking Basics

# CHAPTER 1

# Introducing Windows 98

## What's ahead:

- What is Windows 98?
- What's new in Windows 98?
- Who should use Windows 98?

*"But the fruit that can fall without shaking
Indeed is too mellow for me."*

—Lady Mary Wortley Montagu, *The Answer*

Throughout this book, our emphasis is on teaching you, the network administrator or interested user, how to get the most out of Windows 98 when used in a networked environment. To really appreciate how easy and powerful Windows 98 is, you have to first understand what it is, how it is a better operating system than its predecessors, and why you want to use it. So, before we get lost in the wonderful world of networking with Windows 98, let's talk a little bit about the operating system itself and why it's a good choice for networking applications.

Historically, most personal computer users didn't give much thought to the operating system installed on their PC, as long as it worked when they turned on their computer. They stuck with whatever version of DOS was installed on their computer when they bought it. That's partly because users were often insulated from the DOS command line interface by menu systems or third-party shell programs, while the operating system ran quietly behind the scenes.

That began to change as users were required to upgrade their operating systems in order to take advantage of new hardware innovations and applications software. The line between the operating system and the shell, or user interface, became more and more blurred with each new release of Microsoft Windows. Even though Windows ran on top of DOS and was not really an operating system, it functioned as one by providing Application Programming Interfaces (APIs) that other applications were dependent on.

# WHAT IS WINDOWS 98?

When Microsoft released Windows 95, the distinction between Windows and the operating system became irrelevant. As far as most users were concerned, Windows 95 was the operating system. The truth is that Windows 95 still ran on top of and required DOS, but the DOS and Windows installation programs were integrated to the point that users could think of them as one and the same. One reason for the confusion is because Windows NT, Microsoft's other 32-bit Windows platform, was a real operating system and did not rely on DOS to run.

In many ways, Windows 95 fit squarely between Windows 3.x and Windows NT. It was similar to Windows 3.x in terms of its relation to and dependence on DOS and support for DOS and Windows 3.x device drivers. But from an application programming perspective, Windows 95 was a lot like Windows NT and most programs written for Windows 95 run unmodified on Windows NT but won't run on Windows 3.x at all.

Windows 98, formerly code-named "Memphis" during its development cycle, is the successor to Windows 95. It moves even closer towards the Windows NT platform with advances such as the Win32 Driver Model, which provides a framework for creating common device drivers for Windows 98 and Windows NT. But like its predecessor, Windows 98 still sits on top of DOS and can use DOS device drivers. The result is an almost ideal upgrade path for home and corporate users that are still running DOS, Windows 3.*x*, or Windows 95 but that aren't yet ready to make the jump to Windows NT.

Windows 98 builds on the foundation that was laid by Windows 3.1 and Windows 95 to provide a lot of powerful features that boost productivity and enhance the user's computing experience. Users are most likely to appreciate features they can see and interact with, such as Windows support for descriptive long file names, consistent and familiar menus and window controls, and such interface behaviors as right-clicking with the mouse to access context-sensitive menus and property sheets.

Many of Windows' most powerful features are easily taken for granted because they are unseen, which is how it should be. Plug and Play makes it easy for even novice users to install and configure new hardware or use docking stations without concern for conflicts with IRQ, I/O, DMA, or Memory Address settings. Its 32-bit protected-mode architecture provides preemptive multitasking and multithreading of 32-bit applications, cooperative multitasking of 16-bit applications, and the ability to manage applications that crash or are terminated without the need to reset the whole system.

Perhaps the most compelling feature in Windows 98 is its built-in networking. Support for file and printer sharing, messaging, faxing, Web browsing, collaboration, and content publishing is all built-in, as is connectivity over Network Interface Cards (NICs), dial-up modems and ISDN adapters, and direct cable or infrared connections. A PC running Windows 98 can participate in the Network Neighborhood, Internet, or intranet, acting as both a client and as a server on the network at the same time.

As the title suggests, this book is about networking with Windows 98. Before getting into the details of what you can do with Windows networking and how to do it, this chapter takes a look at what's new in Windows 98 and talks about who should use it.

# WHAT'S NEW IN WINDOWS 98?

When Microsoft set out to create Windows 98, their basic objective was to enhance Windows 95 in six key areas:

- ▼ Easier to use
- ■ More reliable
- ■ Faster
- ■ Better integrated with the Web
- ■ More entertaining
- ▲ More manageable for corporations to install, maintain, and support

Windows 98 is often described as Windows 95 with Internet Explorer 4.0 built-in. But if you look a little bit closer, you find that there are actually quite a few important enhancements that prove beneficial to all Windows users, whether they are connected to the Internet or not.

# Ease of Use

Windows 98 has been enhanced in several ways that make personal computers easier to use for both new and experienced users alike. As with most ease-of-use enhancements, business users will benefit from reduced training and support costs while home users will appreciate the ability to do more on their own with less dependency on others for technical support.

While changes to the user interface and online help systems are readily apparent to anyone that uses Windows 98, there are also several innovations that make it easier to manage and to configure the hardware devices connected to your PC.

## User Interface

The Windows 98 user interface has been given a face-lift by integrating Internet Explorer with both the desktop and with Windows Explorer (see Figure 1-1). This unifies the Windows user interface with the common look and feel of the Web browser. The Windows 95 user interface is still available for users that prefer the old look and feel, but there are some advantages to the new Web browser interface. Some of the enhanced features include single-click application launching, icon highlighting, forward and backward buttons, and a Start menu that can be customized with a variety of toolbars.

Windows integration with the Web is discussed in more detail later in this chapter, in the section entitled "Web Integration."

## Online Help

The online help system in Windows 98 has been enhanced with additional content and a new user interface that is based on Internet Explorer. This makes the online documentation and context-sensitive help systems easier to navigate and more familiar because the interface looks and works just like the Web browser (see Figure 1-2).

## Hardware Innovations

While enhancements to the user interface and online help system are readily apparent, some of the most important ease-of-use enhancements in Windows 98 are unseen.

Support for the Universal Serial Bus (USB) gives it a more powerful device-detection mechanism, supporting the next generation of Plug and Play hardware. USB devices can be connected to and removed from your computer without restarting the system. At the time this book was written, there were already dozens of USB devices available with lots

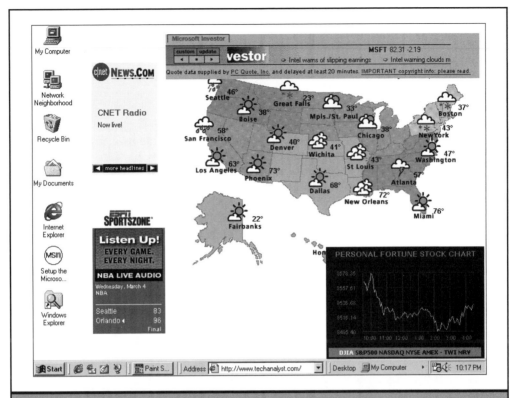

**Figure 1-1.** Windows 98's Active Desktop lets you put Web content right on the desktop

more on the way. Supporters of the standard envision a time when all peripherals will be connected to your PC through the USB interface, eliminating interrupt, DMA, and address conflicts.

**RESOURCE:** The USB News Web site is a great place to look for more information about USB, including a comprehensive listing of available products that support the USB standard. Just point your Web browser to http://www.usbnews.com.

Multi-monitor support gives you the ability to connect up to eight different monitors to your computer at the same time, providing more room to run specialized applications or for playing multi-monitor games. All monitors can be configured the same way, or each one can be configured to run at a different resolution.

Enhanced power management, supported through the Advanced Configuration and Power Interface (ACPI), provides better battery performance on new mobile PCs and provides easier device management on new PCs.

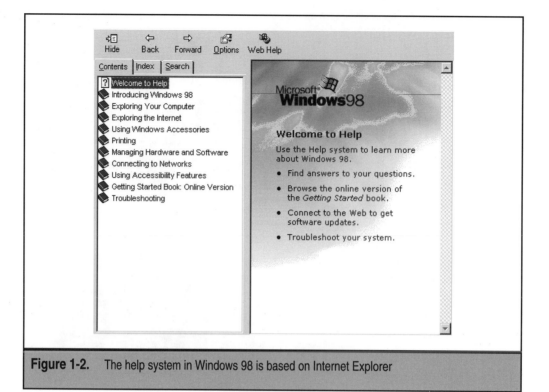

**Figure 1-2.** The help system in Windows 98 is based on Internet Explorer

# Reliability

When you talk about the reliability of an operating system, you're really talking about two different things. First and foremost, you're talking about the stability and dependability of the operating system itself. Does it lockup or crash? The second thing to consider is how well the operating system protects against and reacts to hardware failures.

Even though Windows 95 was a pretty reliable operating system by most accounts, there was still plenty of room for improvement.

## Bug Fixes

Although there are quite a few enhancements in Windows 98, much of the operating system is unchanged from Windows 95. In this sense, you can think of Windows 95 as a massive three-year-long beta test program for Windows 98. During that time, Microsoft never stopped collecting bug reports from end users and developers.

Windows 98 includes all of the bug fixes that Microsoft has made to Windows 95 since its original release, plus many others that were never available before. The result is a more stable and dependable operating system that is less likely to lockup or crash.

## Software Updates

With Windows 95, there really wasn't any way for end users to obtain software updates. The only way to get an updated copy of the operating system was to buy a new computer. That was unfortunate because it meant that most users had no access to the bug fixes and interim enhancements that Microsoft produced.

Fortunately, this has changed with Windows 98. The Start menu now includes a direct link to Windows Update, a Web-based resource site that is continually updated with the latest drivers and operating system files (see Figure 1-3). Connecting to the Web site automatically launches an Update Wizard that searches for new components on the Microsoft Web site. Installing new components is as simple as clicking on the ones you want.

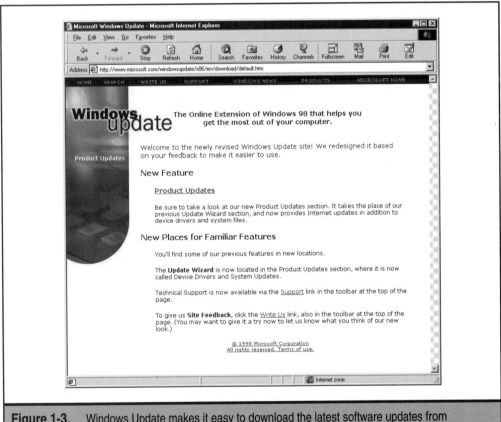

**Figure 1-3.** Windows Update makes it easy to download the latest software updates from Microsoft's Web site

## Data Integrity

The Windows 95 Plus Pack included a System Agent that was useful for specifying a regular schedule for the system to execute the scandisk and defrag disk maintenance utilities, or any other task you wanted to automate on a regular basis. Windows 98 includes a similar program, called the Task Scheduler, as a standard feature.

In addition to scanning the hard drive for errors and optimizing the physical layout of data on the disk, Windows 98 also has the ability to verify the integrity of your Windows configuration files, including the Windows Registry.

## Backup and Restore

No matter how good an operating system is, it can't prevent hardware failures from happening. Proper backup procedures are absolutely essential to ensure that valuable data can be restored if necessary.

The backup and restore utilities in Windows 98 have been enhanced with support for more backup devices than before. The operating system even has built-in support for SCSI tape drives.

## The Year 2000

Over the past few years, Year 2000 (Y2K) compliance has become one of the industries' hottest topics. Companies are scrambling to ensure that every operating system and business application they use has been Y2K certified. Even though there probably weren't any Y2K problems with Windows 95, Microsoft has officially certified Windows 98 as Y2K-compliant.

# Performance

Windows 95 was generally considered to be a good performer once it was up and running, but it was also known for being unreasonably slow during system startup, shutdown, and when launching applications. Windows 98 includes many strategic performance improvements in key areas, including:

▼   System startup

■   Application launch

■   System shutdown

■   Memory management

■   FAT32 file system

▲   General system usage

Even though some of these enhancements require new hardware, such as a QuickBoot BIOS or DMA-capable hard drive or CD-ROM, most of the enhancements provide real performance improvements on even the most basic hardware. In fact, older, slower machines, with very little RAM memory and slow hard drives, will benefit the most from enhancements that have been designed to use memory more efficiently and to minimize disk access.

## System Startup

Today's computers may boot faster than their slower ancestors, but they still seem to take way too long from the time you turn on the power until Windows 95 is finally loaded and ready to use. Windows 98 employs a variety of techniques to minimize the amount of time required to boot up your computer and load the operating system.

To fully appreciate the improvements in Windows 98, you need to first understand the various tasks and activities that take place during the boot process. Once a computer is turned on, the BIOS performs a power on self test, known as the POST. During POST, memory is counted and tested, disks spin up, option ROMs perform diagnostics, SCSI adapters enumerate the SCSI bus, the Video BIOS scrubs video memory and displays logos, floppy disks are checked, and Plug and Play hardware is configured. Following POST, the operating system is loaded from disk and device drivers must be loaded and initialized.

Windows 98 includes support for the Simple Boot Flag Specification for QuickBoot BIOS for OnNow PCs. In a nutshell, under the OnNow initiative, each device has settable power states to allow the PC to effectively hibernate, then instantly wake up on request, thereby eliminating the usual startup time required for devices to power up and initialize. The Simple Boot Flag on machines equipped with a QuickBoot BIOS allows Windows 98 to execute many activities that would normally take place during POST. The seemingly simple act of deferring these tasks until Windows is initialized actually results in pretty significant time savings. This is because Windows can perform these tasks simultaneously in the background while loading, instead of waiting until after the POST routine performs them one at a time.

**RESOURCE:**    Details of the OnNow specification can be found at http://www.microsoft.com/hwdev.

Other performance improvements have been made in Windows' own startup and initialization code, to eliminate unnecessary delays and optimize load times.

Windows 95 pauses for two seconds during startup, after displaying the "Starting Windows 95" message, to give the user an opportunity to press F4, F5, or F8 to access different boot options. To speed system startup, the two-second delay has been removed from Windows 98. The boot menu is now accessed by holding down the CTRL key during POST.

The time required to load and initialize drivers has been optimized through a series of simple changes. Windows 95 blindly loads some drivers whether they are actually needed or not, but Windows 98 ensures that only necessary drivers are actually loaded.

## Application Launch

Windows 98 includes a collection of tools that work together to minimize the time necessary to launch applications. At the heart of the process is a small monitoring program called TASKMON.EXE that performs a disk trace when applications are launched and records that activity in a log file. The next time DEFRAG.EXE (also called Windows Tune-Up Wizard) is executed, it reads that log file and uses the information it finds there to reorganize files as necessary in order to minimize the number of disk seeks required to load the application (see Figure 1-4).

Microsoft has taken great care to ensure that TASKMON.EXE does not interfere with applications as they load. It may slow execution slightly the first time each application is launched after being installed, but not significantly, and the performance gained as a result is well worth it.

The only catch is that you have to set up your hard disk with 4K clusters, available with the FAT32 file system, in order to fully realize the performance gains possible in Windows 98.

## System Shutdown

One of the biggest complaints people had with Windows 95 was that it took a long time to shut down, and sometimes it seemed to hang during the shutdown process. This was because Windows unnecessarily uninitialized and unloaded drivers during shutdown.

Uninitializing and unloading drivers isn't necessary in most cases because after shutdown, the computer is either turned off or rebooted, causing devices to be reinitialized before they are used again anyway.

Windows 98 has been changed so that it only unloads those drivers that have specifically requested shutdown notification. All others are left alone, resulting in a much faster system shutdown.

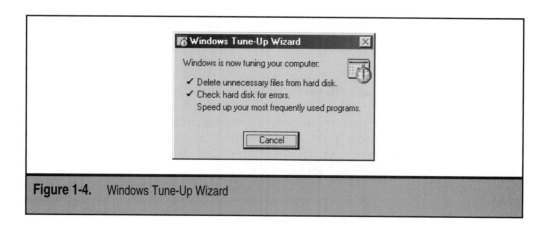

**Figure 1-4.**   Windows Tune-Up Wizard

## Memory Management

By combining a new MapCache feature with the new WinAlign utility program, the memory management system in Windows 98 has been made significantly faster and more efficient than it was in Windows 95. Everything your computer does depends on the memory management system provided by the operating system, including all networking services. So even though this isn't specifically a networking enhancement, it does improve the user's networking experience.

In Windows 95, executable and DLL code could occupy two pages in memory at the same time, one in the cache and another in the processes virtual address space (VAS). In Windows 98, MapCache ensures that all code pages that are aligned on 4K boundaries occupy only one page in memory. It accomplishes this by loading code pages from disk into the VCache, then storing a pointer to the 4K VCache page in the processes VAS instead of making its own copy, thereby saving nearly 4K of memory and the time required to copy the code page into the second location.

The VCache is managed by sophisticated algorithms that ensure that the most frequently used code pages remain in memory as long as possible, and that code pages are never stored on disk in a Windows swap file. Instead, they are simply discarded and reloaded from the original EXE or DLL file as needed. Doing so reduces the amount of overhead typically required to reload code pages from disk.

Besides being faster, another nice side effect is that less memory is used to store code pages, which improves overall system performance and reduces dependency on the swap file. You can do more on a system running Windows 98 than you can on the exact same system running Windows 95, before the swap file is even activated. Unlike some of the other performance enhancements in Windows 98 that primarily benefit new systems, this one is of greatest value to older, slower machines, that are equipped with less memory, because these PCs are more likely to be dependent on the swap file.

Because this feature was designed to work with 4K code pages, Microsoft has also created a utility called WINALIGN.EXE that can realign just about any EXE or DLL file on 4K boundaries. This typically results in a slightly larger file on your hard disk, but that's a small price to pay for better performance.

WinAlign automatically runs after Windows 98 is installed and it is added to the Task Scheduler to be run once every month. You can also run it directly from the Task Scheduler, where it is listed as "Tune-up Application Start," any time you want to and it is accessible by selecting "Windows Tune-up" from the System Tools program group, found under Accessories on the Windows Start menu.

There are certain files that should not be realigned, specifically signed binaries and Windows NT system binaries, but WinAlign knows how to recognize these files and automatically skips them. For every file that WinAlign modifies, it also stores information in the Registry that can be used to reverse the process by simply running WinAlign again, with the "-r" parameter.

## FAT32 File System

The FAT32 file system, which was first introduced in the OSR2 release of Windows 95, holds the key to some of the most significant speed improvements available in Windows 98. This is because FAT32 facilitates 4K cluster sizes, which corresponds to the 4K code segments used by MapCache and the application launch optimizations made possible when DEFRAG.EXE physically rearranges EXE and DLL files to correspond with actual disk reads as recorded by TASKMON.EXE.

Because disk space is always allocated one cluster at a time, the 4K cluster sizes made possible with the FAT32 file system also uses disk space more efficiently than the larger cluster sizes used by FAT16 when working with small files. Even the smallest of files can use up 8K, 16K, or 32K of disk space on a drive formatted with the FAT16 file system. The difference between the actual file size and the space allocated for the file is known as the *slack*. 6K or 12K of slack may not sound like much, but if you multiply that by hundreds or even thousands of files, it begins to add up to a lot of disk space.

The conversion from FAT16 to the FAT32 file system is fairly quick and reasonably safe because only a small amount of data is actually moved during the conversion process, as necessary to make room for the larger FAT tables (see Figure 1-5). During the conversion, a new FAT table is created without disturbing the active FAT table. Then the

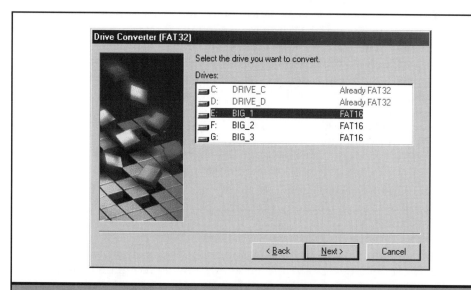

**Figure 1-5.**    Drive Converter makes conversion to FAT32 quick and easy

actual switchover takes place very quickly when the master boot record signature is changed to indicate that the volume uses FAT32. Finally, the boot record is changed to a FAT32 boot record.

**CAUTION:** FAT32 is not compatible with Windows 95 or Windows NT 4.0. If you convert your file system to FAT32, it is not readable by any other operating system and you will lose the ability to Dual Boot or access your hard disk when booting from a DOS system disk or Windows 95 Startup Disk. If you convert your file system to FAT32, be sure to create a new Windows 98 Startup Disk.

## General System Usage

Windows is a preemptive multitasking operating system. This means that it can execute multiple processes at the same time, but only if those processes can be preempted. If any process performs a lengthy operation without yielding, all other processes have to wait, and appear to run slower. The short delay, known as *latency*, usually isn't a big deal, and you aren't likely to even notice it happening while running traditional business applications such as word processors and spreadsheets. But latency does become very important when working with streaming media, such as audio and video feeds.

Microsoft found that one of the primary causes of latency in Windows 95 was coming from routines in the VFAT. Specifically, the problem is exhibited when the VFAT has to walk a long path that is contained entirely in the cache, because this process executes a lot of code and examines a lot of data without ever yielding to the multitasker. Although much of the code in the VFAT can't be preempted safely, they were able to add preemptive code in a few key spots where it was safe to do so.

For systems equipped with IDE Direct Memory Access (DMA) chipsets and ATAPI DMA-compatible hard drives and CD-ROMs, Windows 98 can actually allow the device to control data transfers instead of requiring the CPU to copy individual data packets. Using DMA does not increase transfer speeds, but it does reduce the amount of CPU utilization required when reading from the disk. This primarily benefits multimedia applications, such as games, that require a high level of CPU utilization while reading data from the CD-ROM at the same time.

**CAUTION:** Some hard drives and CD-ROMs report that they support DMA when in fact they do not. Enabling DMA on these drives can result in data corruption. For this reason, the Windows 98 upgrade disables the new DMA option by default, but you can turn it on by checking the DMA check box on the device property sheet in Windows Device Manager. Most OEM vendors perform stress tests to ensure that their equipment can safely support the DMA option; consequently the DMA option is typically enabled on new machines.

Additional performance gains have been achieved by optimizing handling of the Windows Registry. It is now stored in a more compact form when loaded in memory, so that it uses less memory and has better locality of key nodes. It is automatically compacted whenever it contains an excessive amount of unused space, leading to faster load times at system startup. And registry updates are recorded faster because only those registry blocks that actually change are ever written back to disk.

# Web Integration

Millions of computer users configured their own computers for networking and connected with the world's largest computer network without even realizing what they were doing. In their own minds, they were simply "surfing the Web," but in fact they were participating in the global network known as the Internet.

Over the course of just a few years, the Internet has changed computing and networking more than any other technology or event in the history of computers. It's not surprising that Web integration has been one of the most highly promoted features of Windows 98. Windows 95 supported the TCP/IP protocol, and the Internet Explorer Web browser has been available for several years now. But Windows 98 takes Web integration to the next level by fully integrating Internet communications and Web browsing with the core operating system.

## Internet Connectivity

All communications over the Internet are based on the TCP/IP protocol. Although TCP/IP was included in Windows 95, it wasn't installed by default. Windows 98 is much more Internet focused and TCP/IP has become the default communications and networking protocol when the operating system is installed.

Getting your Windows PC connected to the Internet used to be a complicated and time-consuming process. Fortunately, Microsoft has made it easier by enhancing Windows Dial-Up Networking and creating an Internet Connection Wizard. Windows Dial-Up Networking now has the ability to link and synchronize multiple modems and includes an ISDN Connection Wizard that makes it easier than ever to configure your ISDN hardware. The Internet Connection Wizard (see Figure 1-6) simplifies the task of configuring the proper dial-up settings for connecting to your Internet Service Provider (ISP) and accessing the Internet. These enhancements were available for Windows 95 as part of the Internet Explorer 4.0 upgrade, but are included as standard features in Windows 98.

On PCs that are equipped with TV tuners, Windows 98 also has the ability to receive Internet content through the television broadcast signal. This opens the door to a lot of exciting possibilities down the road as broadcasters begin to use the technology to integrate Web content with their television programs.

TCP/IP and Dial-Up Networking are discussed in Chapters 6 and 7.

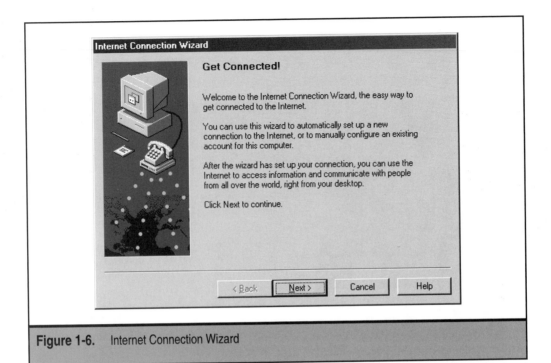

**Figure 1-6.**    Internet Connection Wizard

## Web Browser

Internet Explorer 4.0 is not only bundled with Windows 98, it has become the fundamental user interface of the operating system. The Active Desktop and the Windows Explorer are both based on the Internet Explorer Web browser engine and are capable of displaying Web content without opening a separate Web browser. This provides a single, unified user interface for accessing local, Internet and intranet content from the desktop.

Channels provide a way for end users to subscribe to Web sites of interest and let the Web browser automatically download new content according to a prescribed schedule. This provides the benefit of being able to browse that content very quickly because it has already been downloaded to your local hard disk, and allows you to access it offline, while not connected to the Internet (see Figure 1-7).

Additionally, Microsoft has publicly committed that the Internet Explorer Web browser will always run faster on the Windows 98 and Windows NT operating systems than it will anywhere else.

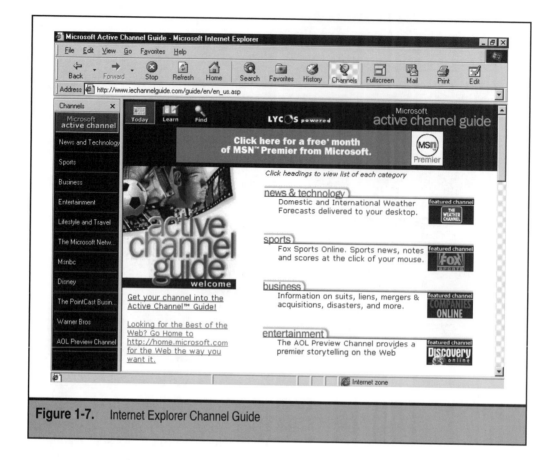

**Figure 1-7.** Internet Explorer Channel Guide

Internet Explorer, the Active Desktop, Channel Subscriptions, and Windows Explorer are discussed in Chapters 8, 9, and 12.

## E-Mail

Despite the popularity of the Web, e-mail is still the most widely used Internet application there is. Many people who don't have direct access to the Internet can exchange Internet e-mail through corporate e-mail systems or dial-up BBSs that are equipped with Internet mail gateways.

The Outlook Express e-mail client and collaboration tool is included with Windows 98 (see Figure 1-8). This application provides the ability to send e-mail messages with Simple Message Transport Protocol (SMTP), to retrieve e-mail messages with Post Office Protocol 3 (POP3), and access to Internet newsgroups with Network News Transfer Protocol (NNTP).

Outlook Express is discussed in Chapter 10.

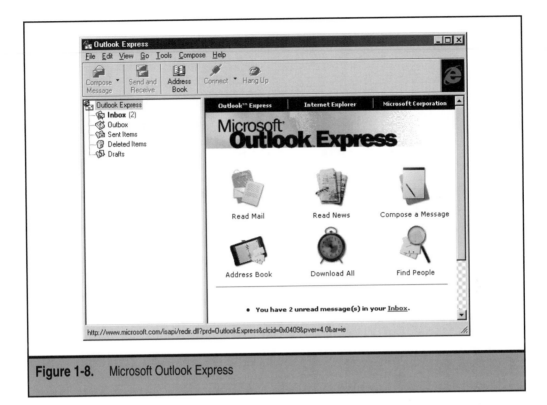

**Figure 1-8.**   Microsoft Outlook Express

## Collaboration

For real-time collaboration over the Internet, Microsoft has included NetMeeting with Windows 98. NetMeeting provides a shared white board, text chat, voice chat, video conferencing, and application sharing (see Figure 1-9).

NetMeeting is discussed in Chapter 11.

## Streaming Audio and Video

NetShow is Microsoft's networked multimedia software for on-demand streaming audio and video. You can use it to listen to audio recordings and live radio broadcasts or to watch music videos, movie trailers, and live television shows over the Internet (see Figure 1-10).

NetShow is discussed in Chapter 11.

## Web Publishing

Windows 98 also includes applications that make it easy to create and publish your own Web pages, including the FrontPage Express personal Web-page editing tool and Microsoft's Personal Web Server (see Figure 1-11).

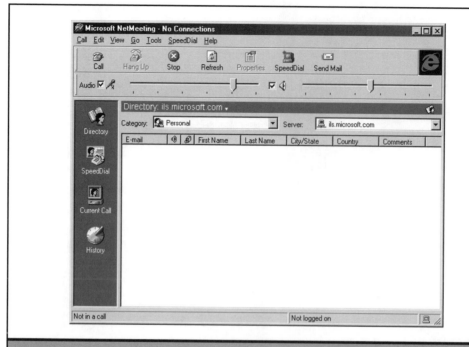

**Figure 1-9.** Microsoft NetMeeting

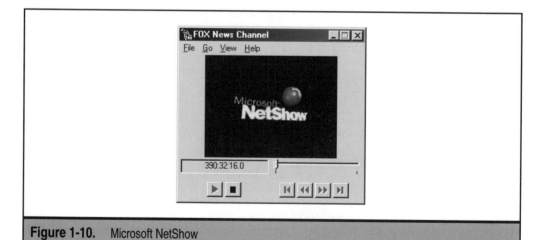

**Figure 1-10.** Microsoft NetShow

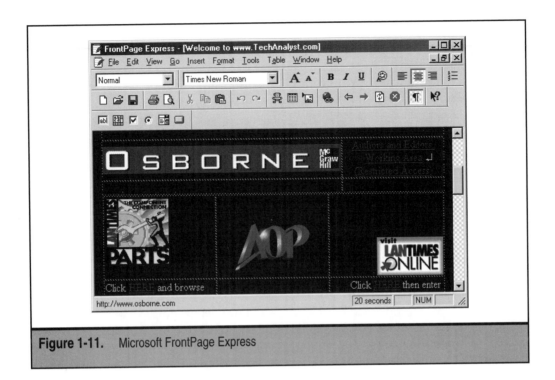

**Figure 1-11.**    Microsoft FrontPage Express

See Chapters 13 and 14 for more details on Web publishing with Windows 98.

## Entertainment

Entertainment has always been one of the primary driving forces behind the development of multimedia technologies that enhance the user's computing experience. When we speak of entertainment, computer games immediately come to mind. But the value of entertainment goes well beyond gaming. The business and education markets benefit from entertainment technology through more captivating and effective computer-based training, timely information delivery with streaming audio and video, and the ability for people in different locations to work together through video conferencing, group collaboration, and application sharing.

Some of the specific entertainment-related enhancements in Windows 98 include:

▼ Support for Digital Video Disc (DVD) and digital audio to deliver high-quality digital movies and audio directly to your TV or PC monitor

■ Support for the IEEE 1394 bus provides an industry-standard interface to control VCRs, stereos, and other consumer electronic devices from a Windows 98 PC

■ DirectX APIs provide graphics and video performance that exceeds console game systems, and support for forced-feedback joysticks to enhance the gaming experience

■ The ability to watch TV on your PC and to review and search for television programs with the built-in Program Guide

▲ Support for Enhanced Television, which combines television and HTML content to facilitate the creation and delivery of new entertainment possibilities

# Manageability

Deploying and maintaining Windows on a large number of PCs can be a pretty daunting task. Fortunately, Windows 98 has a few new features that help to make the task easier and more manageable.

Windows 98 improves manageability in the key areas of installation and configuration, diagnostic information, and the use of a common device driver model.

## Installation and Configuration

The Zero Administration Kit (ZAK) for Windows 98 is part of Microsoft's Zero Administration Initiative. ZAK lowers the total cost of ownership by making it easy to deploy and centrally manage the Windows operating system and selected application programs such as Microsoft Office.

The ZAK client can be configured to deploy Windows 98 in either AppStation or TaskStation configurations. The AppStation configuration is typically deployed for knowledgeable users that need to operate several different business applications, while being prevented from accessing configuration settings or installing other applications. The TaskStation configuration is intended for use by task-oriented workers that only need to access a single application, with no access to the operating system or any other applications.

Users that are already running the Windows 95 or Windows 3.x operating systems will appreciate the Windows 98 Upgrade Wizard. The Upgrade Wizard provides a smooth migration path by making it possible to upgrade to Windows 98 while preserving your configuration settings.

## Diagnostic Information

Troubleshooting a hardware conflict or software failure can be frustrating. The most useful and valuable tool you could have is accurate information about how the PC is equipped and what the software was doing at the time it failed.

Windows 98 provides two utilities that can help. The System Information Utility helps identify hardware problems by providing a wealth of information about the PC's hardware configuration and resource conflicts, as well as a record of all device drivers that are currently loaded and a detailed history of device changes and driver updates (see Figure 1-12). The Dr. Watson utility program is designed to help you understand

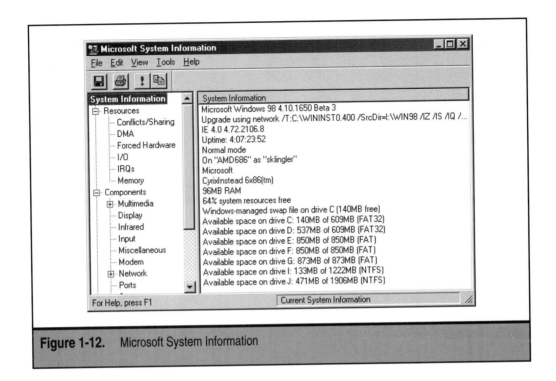

**Figure 1-12.**   Microsoft System Information

software failures. Whenever an application fails, Dr. Watson creates a log file containing critical information about the program at the time of the crash.

### Common Device Drivers

One of the biggest hassles any system administrator faces when upgrading their organization to a new operating system is the task of locating the latest working device drivers to support the various hardware components installed on their PCs. In the past, this was further complicated by the need to use different device drivers to support the very same hardware on identical PCs running Windows 95 and Windows NT.

Relief may be just around the corner. Both Windows 98 and Windows NT 5.0 support Microsoft's new Win32 Driver Model. Device drivers that are written to the new specification will work with both operating systems.

## WHO SHOULD USE WINDOWS 98?

Microsoft has worked hard to position Windows 98 as the platform of choice for the consumer market, while promoting Windows NT for corporate users and mission-critical applications. In reality, Windows 98 is a very capable operating system that is well-suited for use by both home and business users.

# Home Users

For more than two years, Windows 95 has reigned as the undisputed standard operating system for home computer users, a position that will surely belong to Windows 98 before very long. The number of hardware vendors shipping new PCs with Windows 98 pre-installed, combined with the number of end users that will rush to buy and install the operating system upgrade, will lead to quick adoption in the home user marketplace.

Even users that never bothered to upgrade from DOS or Windows 3.x to Windows 95 will find the Windows 98 upgrade attractive because many of the enhancements included in this new release are designed to improve system performance, especially when running on ill-equipped, low-end PCs. Such features include better Web integration, improved memory management, and faster system startup, shutdown, and application launching. Inexperienced users appreciate how easy it is to add or upgrade components with Windows support for Plug and Play.

Another important factor, especially for home users on a limited budget, is the large number of affordable software titles that are available for the Windows platform. There are literally thousands of low-cost business applications, educational programs, and games from which to choose.

# Corporate Users

Windows 95 is currently widely used in the workplace, despite Microsoft's efforts to convince corporate users that Windows NT is a better platform for running mission-critical business applications. Windows 98 gives business users even more reasons not to upgrade to the more expensive Windows NT platform.

One of the basic factors that has prevented corporations from adopting Windows NT is its hardware requirements. Even though the typical new PC is well-equipped to run NT, corporations still have lots of PCs that aren't. In fact, a surprising number of businesses are still running Windows 3.x on many of their PCs, either because they can't run Windows 95 without expensive hardware upgrades or because they simply haven't been convinced that there's any benefit to be had by upgrading to a new operating system. Windows 98 may overcome these objections because it provides more functionality and better performance than Windows 95 did, especially when running on older, ill-equipped PCs. And it doesn't hurt that nearly every new computer sold today comes with Windows 98 already installed.

Another factor that corporations can't overlook is that nearly all business applications that are currently available or under development are designed for the Windows 98 and Windows NT platforms. With all of the concern and attention that has been focused on Year 2000 (Y2K) issues, businesses are being forced to look for new or upgraded software that is certified Y2K-compliant. In the process, many will be forced to upgrade their operating systems to Windows 98 or NT.

There are better reasons for corporations to upgrade their operating systems to Windows 98, such as lower training and support costs and higher productivity. Training costs are lower and employee productivity is higher in part because employees that run

Windows 98 on their home PCs are already familiar with the user interface. Support costs are reduced as a result of such innovations as the Win32 Driver Model, which allows you to use the same device drivers for both Windows 98 and Windows NT.

One of the reasons that Windows 95 and Windows 98 have been accepted so well in the business environment is its integrated networking support. A PC running Windows 98 can participate on the corporate network as a client workstation with access to network resources, no matter what operating system the network servers are running. It also has the ability to take on the role of a file or print server, by providing shared access to files and printers on the local PC.

# COMING UP

Networking with Windows 98 is the focus of this book. So far, we've introduced you to the operating system and discussed many of the enhancements that make Windows 98 easier to use, more reliable, faster, better integrated with the Web, more entertaining, and more manageable than its predecessor, Windows 95. Our focus for the remainder of the book will be on how to install, configure, manage, and use Windows 98 so as to get the most out of it when used in a network environment.

In the next chapter, we discuss how to plan for your Windows 98 installation, show you how to install the operating system, and review basic configuration settings.

NETWORK
PROFESSIONAL'S
LIBRARY

# CHAPTER 2

# Installing Windows 98

**What's ahead:**

- Workstation and networking considerations
- Pre-installation checklist
- Installation walk-through
- Setting up Windows 98

*"The man who said 'The harder the toil,*
*the sweeter the rest,' never was profoundly tired."*

—John Muir, *An Adventure with a Dog and a Glacier*

Thought before action. In no situation is this maxim more important than in the installation of an operating system (OS). Before beginning to install Windows 98, you should follow this chapter closely. Even though this OS can automatically lead you through the installation process, the steps it executes to do so are not trivial. Windows 98 is not a Windows application; it does not "ride" upon DOS. It is its own OS. After installation, when you boot up your computer, DOS will not load—only Windows 98 loads. Therefore, you should thoroughly prepare for your installation, because an OS, unlike a simple program, can leave your workstation unusable if it is not installed correctly.

After reading this chapter, you should have a good understanding of the Windows 98 installation process from many different perspectives. You should be able to determine whether or not your current PC can support a successful installation. You should also have an understanding of the different options available to you during the installation process. Most importantly, you should be able to quickly and easily install Windows 98 from a floppy disk, CD-ROM, or network. And you should be able to configure your Windows 98 machine, once it has been installed, creating printer definitions, defining maintenance schedules, and customizing the appearance of Windows 98.

# INSTALLATION PROCEDURES

Microsoft Windows 98 boasts a novel installation because it is modular. When you install Windows 98, you actually complete four different procedures, or modules. Those procedures are:

▼ Collecting information about your computer

■ Copying Windows 98 files to your computer

■ Restarting your computer

▲ Setting up hardware and finalizing settings

Although Windows 98 seems like it could install itself, you must ensure that the appropriate environment exists for the OS to not only install correctly but operate correctly as well. First, you must determine whether or not you have a workstation that can support the OS. This includes such items as hard disk space, memory size, and Central Processing Unit (CPU) type.

Once you have authenticated these variables, you must take a close look at your current OS. Do you have MS-DOS? Do you have Windows 3.1? Or, do you even have an

OS? If you do have an OS, what do you want to do with it after Windows 98 is installed? Do you want to maintain it, or would it be better to discard it?

The third and perhaps the most important area you should survey is the network upon which you intend to install Windows 98. First, you should find out if Windows 98 supports your network. Then you should assess how you want to install the Windows 98 workstation upon that network. For example, you must ask yourself the following questions:

▼ Do I have to modify my workstation configuration in order to communicate with the network after installation?

■ Do I need to have a network client installed before I install Windows 98?

▲ What steps do I need to take to ensure security for my workstation and my network?

# WORKSTATION CONSIDERATIONS

The best place to start in considering whether or not to install Windows 98 is your workstation. If your workstation's hardware and software cannot support Windows 98, there is no sense in mulling over network support for Windows 98 until you can accommodate the necessary requirements.

## Hardware Requirements

The hardware required to install Windows 98 should be your first consideration. Only install Windows 98 if your workstation meets the following criteria.

### Disk Space Requirements

In order to run Windows 98, you should reserve at least 195MB of disk space. Depending upon your system configuration, this number can span from 120MB all the way up to 295MB. If this seems too demanding, just compare Windows 98 with its companion OS, Microsoft Windows NT, which requires roughly the same amount of disk space.

**CAUTION:** If you install Windows 98 on a hard disk other than C:\, reserve at least 25MB of disk space on drive C:\. Windows 98 requires that much to install its configuration, system, and log files, which are used during the installation process.

The same is true for the Santa Cruz Operation Inc.'s SCO Open Desktop or Sun Microsystems Inc.'s Solaris. Although many developers would disagree with this current OS trend toward mammoth disk space requirements, such prerequisites are brought on by the enormous demands made upon OSs. For example, preemptive multitasking, built-in network support, mini application suites, and similar features, are common in today's 32-bit desktop OS, all of which require disk space.

## CPU Requirements

The 32-bit file and processing system of Windows 98 requires a 32-bit machine architecture. The inability to run Windows 98 on a lesser system, such as an AT 286 machine, stems not from the lack of speed or processing power, but rather from the inability to process the Windows 98 code. Microsoft recommends that you use at least a 486 Intel CPU running at least 66 MHz.

## RAM Requirements

Because most Microsoft Windows-based machines already contain between 8 and 16MB of RAM, you will most likely not be burdened by the fact that Windows 98 requires at least 16MB of RAM. However, we recommend that you run Windows 98 with at least 32MB of RAM. It will hit the disk much less often and therefore provide much better performance.

# Your Current Workstation

There are no definitive OS software requirements for installing Windows 98. You can have MS-DOS 2.*x*, IBM Corp.'s OS/2, Windows 95, or Windows for Workgroups 3.11 installed on your system. Windows 98 will either work with or replace whatever OS you possess. However, there are some repercussions depending upon the method you choose in dealing with any existing OSs.

Because your current workstation most likely contains an OS, data, and programs you use from day to day, you should carefully think out your plan of action when installing Windows 98. If you have, for example, a Windows 3.1 OS and a number of communications packages, and you choose to install Windows 98 alongside the Windows 3.1 program, you will be forced to manually create all references to these programs and data on your computer. Conversely, if you choose to install Windows 98 over your current installation of Windows 3.1, you forfeit all chances of running standard Windows 3.1 without uninstalling Windows 98 and reinstalling Windows 3.1. Windows 98 allows you to run alongside other OSs such as Windows NT, a topic explored further in this section.

Therefore, choose your course of action carefully. Think through your current and future needs. For example, ask yourself: "Do I need to run an OS such as Windows NT in addition to Windows 98? And if I do, what hard disk storage space requirements will I incur, and how will I boot to each system?" In this regard, you should consider each application's ability to dual boot to another OS.

## No OS

If you do not have an OS, do not worry. Windows 98 does not require MS-DOS or the Microsoft Windows OS in order to install, boot up, or run the Windows 98 workstation. During its installation, if the setup program detects no OS, it automatically creates a mini Windows system and installs Windows 98 on top of it.

## MS-DOS

If you have MS-DOS and no other OS, you also need not worry. Although Windows 98 requires the Windows OS in order to be installed, it has the ability to creatively sidestep an absence of Windows. During installation, if the Windows 98 SETUP.EXE file is executed from MS-DOS, it automatically attempts to find an installed copy of Windows. If it cannot find one, it asks you if you want it to install a miniature version of Windows from which it automatically installs Windows 98.

Of course, keep in mind that if you have only MS-DOS and you want to maintain its inherent capabilities, Windows 98 lets you dual boot to a limited MS-DOS 6.22 configuration or to Windows 98. During the boot up process, you can simply press the F4 key and you will be left at an MS-DOS prompt.

## Windows 3.1

If you have Windows 3.1, you have basically two choices. First, you can install Windows 98 over your current Windows 3.1 OS. This is recommended because in upgrading Windows 3.1 to Windows 98, all of your program and program group icons automatically migrate to the Windows 98 interface. Of course, if things go sour during the installation, you may have to scrub the Windows 3.1 OS anyway, which is yet another good reason to fully back up your entire hard disk before installing Windows 98.

The second installation alternative if you have Windows 3.1 is to install Windows 98 in a separate directory. With this choice, you can dual boot to MS-DOS 6.22 and then run Windows 3.1. As mentioned earlier, if you want to do this, you need only press F4 during the booting process.

## Windows 3.11

If you have Windows 3.11, you have the same choices as you would with Windows 3.1. You can install Windows 98 directly over Windows 3.11 or you can install them side by side. If you rely upon the peer-to-peer networking capabilities of Windows 3.11, you may want to perform the latter of the two choices. In that way, any incompatibilities between Windows 98 and Windows 3.11 will not preclude you from working effectively in both environments.

## Windows 95

You can simply run SETUP.EXE from the command prompt or with the Run application from the Start menu. Windows 98 automatically brings all of your application settings forward during the upgrade.

## Windows NT

If you have Windows NT, either advanced server or standard edition, you can boot between it and Windows 98, but only if you have installed Windows NT on a FAT volume. If you have installed Windows NT on a high-performance Windows NT File System (NTFS) volume, Windows 98 will not run under multiboot mode. To take advantage of Windows NT and Windows 98, you must first install Windows NT (on a FAT volume) with its dual-boot capability enabled. You can then boot to MS-DOS and install Windows 98. This allows you to boot Windows NT (Server or Workstation), Windows 98, or MS-DOS 6.22.

## OS/2

If you have IBM Corp.'s OS/2 OS and you want to use both it and Windows 98 from the same partition, you are out of luck because both OS/2 and Windows 98 replace MS-DOS—both cannot reside on the same bootable partition. You can, however, install OS/2 on a primary partition, boot to a secondary MS-DOS partition, and then install Windows 98. In this way, you can take advantage of OS/2's powerful boot manager program to set different partitions as the active, boot partition. This allows you to make either the OS/2 partition or the Windows 98 partition the active boot partition. The main directive here is to install OS/2's boot manager and OS/2 first, and then install Windows 98.

# NETWORK CONSIDERATIONS

Because one of Windows 98's strongest capabilities is its networking feature set, you will most likely not need to spend an excessive amount of time preparing for this portion of your installation. However, there are some salient points you should consider for your Windows 98 installation within a network environment that are specific to each type of network (for example, within Microsoft networks or third-party networks). Third-party networks are those belonging to vendors other than Microsoft. However, because Novell NetWare integrates well with Windows 98, you should consider it as you would a Microsoft network.

With a third-party installation, you must take into account whether or not your network is supported by Windows 98, you must consider whether or not your network's protocol stack is supported by Windows 98, and you must assess these two areas in conjunction with the chance that you will be utilizing more than one type of network.

With Microsoft networks, you will not be presented with many network integration problems because Windows 98 can seamlessly work with Windows NT, Windows for Workgroups 3.11, and Windows 98 networks. Within this environment, the only items of importance encompass security decisions. With the addition of user-level security to Windows 98, you must decide how to best implement both file-level and user-level security measures before you install your Windows 98 workstation.

Security, however, does not apply to Microsoft networks alone. With all network configurations, the question of how best to control and defend your data should be the final (and most important) decision you make prior to installation. Without security, not only is the data on your workstation at stake, but the data of your entire company is at stake.

# Networking Benefits

Before continuing on to the network-specific installation considerations, it is helpful to understand some of the features Microsoft Windows 98 possesses regarding network installation, management, and use. In many ways, these improvements will make your task of selecting and utilizing a network service (both third-party and Microsoft networks) quite simple. Some of Windows 98's features follow:

▼ *A 32-bit networking architecture, which includes a 32-bit network client, 32-bit file and printer sharing software, 32-bit network protocols, and 32-bit network card drivers.* Of course, to take advantage of these powerful networking features, you must have a computer that supports 32-bit network access through either an extended industry standard architecture (EISA) or a Peripheral Component Interconnection (PCI)-compatible computer and a network interface card (NIC). The most noticeable differences between a 32-bit architecture and a 16-bit architecture is speed, because data can pass between your network adapter card and the Windows 98 OS at twice the speed as 16-bit architectures.

■ *Support for multiple redirectors, multiple protocols, and network card drivers.* Through either Open Data-Link Interface (ODI) or Network Driver Interface Specification (NDIS) drivers, you can load multiple protocols simultaneously. You do not need to supply anything to take advantage of this feature if you are going to utilize Transmission Control Protocol/Internet Protocol (TCP/IP), Internet Packet Exchange (IPX), or NetBIOS Extended User Interface (NetBEUI). Basically, if your network supports one of these three protocols, you can immediately begin networking with your Windows 98 workstation.

■ *Extended workstation management features through Simple Network Management Protocol (SNMP) and Desktop Management Interface (DMI).* With these two standards, you can manage your Windows 98 workstation from a network interface such as Hewlett-Packard Corp.'s OpenView.

■ *Extended support for Novell's NetWare through a 32-bit Windows 98 client capable of attaching to both NetWare 3.x, NetWare 4.x, and NetWare 5.0 (in either bindery emulation or NetWare Directory Services (NDS) mode) and peer-to-peer resource sharing under NetWare peer-to-peer networking (Personal NetWare).* For the first time, users can access NetWare's advanced directory service (NDS) through Windows 98-only software. Before, in order to achieve true NDS connectivity, users had to adopt NetWare's third-party client software.

■ *Built-in systems management utilities that let you administer Windows 98 workstations, including your own.* Powerful auditing tools and a user security monitoring interface let you control how others use your workstation.

■ *Improved remote network access, in which you can connect to remote Microsoft network servers, Novell NetWare servers, and UNIX servers through the remote access protocols: Point-to-Point Protocol (PPP) and Serial Line Internet Protocol (SLIP).* If your company has direct access to the Internet, you can use these two protocols to access over 2.17 million networked computers.

▲ *Improved network printing.* This improvement enables you to select a printer through a common syntax. In this way, you can select a printer just as you would any other network service, such as a network drive or program.

# The Windows 98 Network Client

The built-in 32-bit client software and Microsoft's Plug and Play architecture solve a number of network installation problems. The type of NIC and protocol to use are resolved during the installation process. This built-in client makes the network portion of your Windows 98 installation relatively painless because, although planning for network integration under Windows 98 requires you to know what type of network you are going to connect with, the built-in client does not in most situations require you to obtain networking software for that network. The usefulness of the network client software within Windows 98 becomes apparent when you consider the following network installation scenario in which a Windows 98 client is being installed upon a Novell NetWare 4.1 network.

First, assume that the workstation already has client software installed (IPX ODI drivers). When you install Windows 98, you can choose whether you load the ODI drivers already on your workstation or the NDIS drivers shipped with Windows 98. If you choose to use your ODI drivers, you do not have to perform any additional configuration tasks. When you reboot the workstation, it simply uses the ODI drivers. Similarly, if you choose the NDIS drivers, Windows 98 automatically loads and configures the appropriate drivers for your network adapter. You won't have to lift a finger in order for Windows 98 to accomplish this task. It loads the drivers in the background during the installation process.

Second, assume that the workstation does not have any client software installed. When you install Windows 98, it detects your NIC and loads the appropriate NDIS drivers for your network. You need only reboot the workstation to take advantage of the network. No configuration is required on your part. It all occurs automatically during installation.

## Windows 98 Client Capabilities

In addition to the ease with which you can install and use the built-in Windows 98 network client, there are many features that make it a viable option when you consider how to connect your workstation to a network. If you install Windows 98 on a Novell NetWare network, for example, and you choose to utilize the built-in 32-bit client, you are able to take advantage of the following features:

▼ **High performance**   The Windows 98 client can be 200 percent faster than a Windows 3.1 OS running a NetWare Virtual Loadable Module (VLM) client.

■ **No conventional memory footprint**   Because the Windows 98 client replaces NetWare's real-mode 16-bit drivers with protected-mode 32-bit drivers, you can save tremendous amounts of memory for MS-DOS programs.

■ **Auto-reconnect**   When a connection is lost, the Windows 98 client does not lock up your workstation. It simply tells your applications to wait a moment until the connection is reestablished. If it is not reestablished, the client simply notifies the affected applications.

■ **Packet burst protocol support**   This is also supported in the standard NetWare client. It basically allows you to transmit data at a higher rate by transmitting multiple packets at one time. Normal protocol communications requires a response for each packet.

■ **Client-side caching**   Requests can be cashed within the client before being sent across the wire. This is an important feature when you enter the world of preemptive multitasking applications in which vast amounts of data can be sent to the NIC at one time.

■ **Plug and Play**   As mentioned previously, the Windows 98 client can automatically interrogate your hardware and configure its drivers to comply with that hardware during installation.

■ **Fully integrated with the Windows 98 interface**   This simply means that you do not have to load your network drivers outside of Windows 98. Loading, unloading, and configuring drivers takes place within the Windows 98 graphical user interface (GUI).

■ **Graphical logon/logoff capability**   With the Windows 98 client, you can log on or log off a NetWare 3.*x* and 4.*x* server without having to exit Windows 98 and type in the applicable commands from an MS-DOS prompt.

■ **User-level security using "pass-through" bindery or NDS**   This means that in order to share information with other Windows 98 workstations, NetWare's security system must be used to authenticate identification.

▲ **Point and Print support**   After you enable a printer, you can simply point to a file and print it with a click of the mouse.

Although some of these are specific to Novell NetWare networks, many are present on all computer networks, such as the no-memory footprint, auto-reconnect, client-side caching, Plug and Play, Windows 98 integration, protocol independence, and Point and Print services. Additionally, the Windows 98 client provides protection against aberrant Windows programs by running within a protected memory space, away from other applications. In this way, a crashed program cannot affect your network connection within other programs.

### Multiprotocol Support

A second advantage, aside from excellent network OS integration, is that the Windows 98 network client has the ability to simultaneously load multiple drivers through NDIS.

This is a trait common to many network clients. However, such a task is made easy with the Windows 98 client. If you want to switch between ODI and NDIS drivers, or if you want to load TCP/IP instead of IPX protocol, you can simply specify such through a Windows 98 Control Panel. Through the same panel, you can even choose to load them simultaneously. To activate these changes, you then reboot the computer. That's it. You will not have to modify the PROTOCOL.INI or NET.CFG files again.

# INSTALLING WINDOWS 98

Now that you have analyzed the general requirements and considerations involved in the installation of Windows 98, the next step is the actual installation. In most situations, the process should progress quite smoothly. The automatic hardware detection and configuration frees you from most compatibility questions. The fail-safe installation even makes corrective procedures much easier—it also makes it easier to return to your initial system should an unrecoverable error occur. However, although these and many other features place the intricacies of installation entirely upon Windows 98, there are some duties and preparations you should perform before running the installation program. Then, you will be able to install your new OS easily and assuredly.

This section addresses the preparations and tasks involved in properly installing Windows 98 on your workstation and your network. This discussion begins with the steps you should take before you install Windows 98, such as the proper configuration of your workstation, the creation of a safety disk, and so forth. Next, the many stumbling blocks you may encounter with different configurations are discussed, such as Personal Computer Memory Card International Association (PCMCIA) cards and disk partition configurations. Following this, the installation of Windows 98 from a number of different perspectives is presented, such as installation from CD-ROM, floppy disk, and a network. The installation of network support under Windows 98 is discussed next and, finally, the steps required to finalize and clean up the installation process are presented.

Before you run SETUP.EXE and install Windows 98, there are some necessary steps you should take. By following these guidelines, you should be able to configure your system for a smooth installation and avoid any installation tragedies.

## Safety Procedures

The first task involves the procurement of an insurance policy that allows you to restore your original system configuration should things go wrong during the installation process. By protecting the single most tangible element of your computer system, namely the installed software, you can quickly recover from any sort of mishap, such as a driver failure or file corruption. This involves two important steps: system backup and the creation of a backup diskette.

## System Backup

Any time you make changes to your computer, you should back up the data stored on its hard disk. There are many methods available to do this. You may already utilize an automated backup program such as 5th Generation's FastBack or Microsoft's backup utility, which is included with MS-DOS 6.0 and later. Because your workstation is most likely connected to a network, your network administrator may even have a backup program installed, like Palindrome's The Network Archivist, which will let you back up your hard drive to the network.

If you have an automated backup program, you should immediately follow the necessary steps to completely back up your hard drive. Make sure in doing so, however, that your backup program copies all of the hidden and system files that may be on your system. For example, your Windows 3.1/3.11 swap disk file, which is marked both hidden and system, must be restored to your hard drive along with the rest of the Windows files. If this file is not restored, you will receive a recoverable, albeit unfriendly, error message the first time you start Windows.

## Alternative Backup Procedure

In case you do not own an automated backup program, do not worry. There are other methods available for you to back up your data. The first and easiest method is to obtain a file-compression program that can both compress your data and back it up to a safe place. An excellent shareware compression/backup program called PKWare PKZip can be obtained from many Internet Web sites and very likely from your network administrator. The best versions of this program are 3.0 or later. Although there are many older versions available, the newer versions allow you to back up data across many floppy disks. This is most helpful if you do not have a larger media such as a network drive, tape drive, or read/write optical disk available for data storage.

For example, a PKZip backup routine utilizing a hard drive labeled C: and a floppy disk labeled A: should be followed like this: Make ready sufficient floppy disks to back up your entire hard drive. An easy way to assess your needs is to run CHKDSK.EXE on your hard drive and divide the total amount of used disk space by the capacity of your floppy disk drive. Of course, through compression, the number of disks needed will be far fewer than the number required to contain all of your data; however, because not all files compress with the same efficiency, you should ready a number of disks nearing the entire size of your hard disk.

Next, run the PKZip program. Your command line should look like this:

```
PKZIP -&sc a:\backup.zip
```

The "-&" means to back up your entire disk, "sc" indicates that you want to back up your disk labeled C:, and "a:\backup.zip" represents your target drive and the file name you want to store your data in. Most likely, you will perform this task across your network, storing your data on a network drive or some other backup medium. If you're backing up to a network drive, your command line should look like this:

```
PKZIP -sc z:\backup.zip
```

## Backup "Boot" Diskette

After you have secured all of your data, you should create a backup diskette. This disk, which should contain your system's precious configuration information, can be used to restore your workstation to its original state from a complete system failure. The way it works is quite simple. By duplicating the information your computer uses to boot up from your hard disk and a floppy disk, you should be able to boot from either medium. This diskette should be used not just for the installation of an OS such as Windows 98, but for any situation in which your hard drive may become unbootable. You may accidentally delete your COMMAND.COM file; you may overwrite your AUTOEXEC.BAT file; you may even format your hard drive. In all of these situations, a backup diskette can save the day.

This diskette should contain a number of files. First, it should be able to boot up your system. To accomplish this, you need to format a disk with the "/S" option. This copies the system and COMMAND.COM files to the diskette. You should copy your AUTOEXEC.BAT and CONFIG.SYS files to your floppy diskette. Once you have done this, you may need to edit those files to do away with any device drivers (lines beginning with "DEVICE=" in your CONFIG.SYS file) that are not pertinent to the functionality of your computer. Also, within your AUTOEXEC.BAT file, you may need to remove any commands that load programs such as Windows or a network client. Of course, you have to copy the files referenced by your CONFIG.SYS and AUTOEXEC.BAT to the A: drive, so be spartan about your choices.

Other files you should place on this floppy disk, if you are currently using Windows 3.1, Windows for Workgroups 3.11, or Windows 95, include these important .INI files:

```
C:\WINDOWS\WIN.INIC:\WINDOWS\SYSTEM.INIC:\WINDOWS\PROTOCOL.INI
(for Windows for Workgroups)
```

Optionally, you can include the following files on the floppy diskette:

```
C:\WINDOWS\*.GRPC:\WINDOWS\CONNECT.DATC:\WINDOWS\*.PWLC:\WINDOWS\*.INI
```

If you do not or cannot copy these files to your floppy diskette, make sure that they are at least backed up.

## Drastic Measures

Usually, you do not need to take such drastic measures for the installation of most software products, such as a spreadsheet, a word processor, or even Microsoft Windows 3.1. However, because Windows 98, as a true replacement for an OS such as MS-DOS, changes the way your hard disk boots, all of the data on that hard disk is subject to corruption.

# Machine Preparation

The second most important step you can take in preparing to install Windows 98 is to prepare your machine for installation. This includes making sure that you have enough disk space, analyzing your current system configuration, and removing any devices that may cause incompatibility problems.

Before you install, you should gather as much information about your system as possible. Although Windows 98, through its hardware detection capabilities, should be able to take you through the installation without requiring any information on your behalf, it is a good idea to maintain system information in the unlikely event that there are compatibility problems between devices or support problems between a device and Windows 98. For example, you should obtain the name and type of video card your computer has. If you are using a Simple Computer Systems Interface (SCSI) hard drive, you should obtain its interrupt number, Direct Memory Access (DMA) channel, and Input/Output (I/O) address.

Similarly, you should obtain this information for your NIC. If you are unsure about its configuration (for example, if it uses a soft-set configuration capability in which you cannot see its jumper settings), simply look either in the PROTOCOL.INI (for NDIS drivers) file or NET.CFG (for ODI drivers) file. They should contain all of the information you need in a readable format. It would be a good idea to print these files for later reference.

# Last Minute Tasks

There are basically two things you need to do before you install Windows 98. First, you should check your hard disk for any errors. If you are using MS-DOS 6.0 or later, execute either CHKDSK.EXE or SCANDISK.EXE. These programs prompt you to fix any problems that may exist, such as cross-linked files or bad sectors.

The second task involves ensuring that your network client software and hardware are installed and operating properly. To ensure the functionality of your workstation, simply log into an available server. At a less obvious level, you should ensure that within your AUTOEXEC.BAT file's PATH statement is contained a reference to the directory in which you have installed your network client.

If you are using Novell ODI drivers, ensure that the NET.CFG configuration file resides in the same directory in which your LSL.COM and network device driver files are located.

If you are utilizing the older IPX.COM network driver configuration, in which you generate the IPX.COM from the Novell utility WSGEN.EXE, you should replace it with either ODI or NDIS drivers. Windows 98 provides support for the IPX.COM drivers; however, because they are not extremely reliable, it would be worthwhile to adopt the newer drivers.

## Pre-Installation Checklist

The following list is a quick reminder of the primary tasks you should perform before you install Windows 98:

- ▼ Back up your system.
- ■ Create a boot disk.
- ■ Gather system hardware information.
- ■ Decide whether or not to install Windows 98 over your existing Windows OS.
- ■ Ensure that your compressed drive has enough space outside of the compressed volume.
- ■ Correct any problems with multiple configurations within your CONFIG.SYS.
- ■ Check for incompatibilities between your PCMCIA interface and Windows 98.
- ■ Check your hard disk for any errors.
- ▲ Ensure that your NIC is properly installed and functioning.

# INSTALLATION WALK-THROUGH

The remainder of this chapter focuses on the actual steps involved in the installation of Windows 98. If you like, you can follow this section while installing your new OS. For the most part, installing Windows 98 from floppy disk, CD-ROM, or network drive requires the same steps. Of course, if you use floppy disks, Windows 98 asks you to insert and remove disks. The only real difference comes in using a network connection to install Windows 98. There, you must ensure that Windows 98 can re-establish the network connection upon rebooting.

## Getting Started

To install Windows 98, you need to run SETUP.EXE. This program first checks to see if you have Windows (3.1 or 3.11) installed. Of course, if you have Windows installed, you should execute the SETUP.EXE program from within Windows.

*CAUTION:* Remember, you cannot install Windows 98 from within Windows NT. You must first reboot with MS-DOS and install Windows 98 on a separate hard drive or disk partition.

If you do not have it installed, you see a message indicating that Windows 98 is copying the necessary files to your hard disk. It then creates a miniature Windows program, from which it executes the remainder of the installation as though you had Windows installed on your system.

## Installing from Floppy Disk

The SETUP.EXE program is located on the first of your Windows 98 installation disks. To execute the program, simply place the floppy diskette in either your A: or B: drive, change to that drive, and type **setup**.

## Installing from a Network Drive

Make sure that your network card and drivers are installed and functioning normally, as mentioned previously. Log in to your network and change to the drive containing Windows 98. Of course, the methodology you use to reach the installation directory will be different for each network OS; consult your network administrator before you begin searching for Windows 98. The administrator can tell you the exact directory in which the SETUP.EXE program will be and how to get to that file. On a Novell NetWare network, for example, you should follow these steps:

1. Log in to the file server containing Windows 98. If you are on a NetWare 4.*x* network, you may need to issue a change of context command with the CX utility.

2. Map a drive, if necessary, to the volume containing the Windows 98 installation files. For example: MAP X:=KRITEN/SYS:.

3. Change to the appropriate drive and find the Windows 98 directory (or the directory created by your network administrator).

4. Change directories to the installation subdirectory and execute the program labeled SETUP.EXE.

You can follow similar steps with any Windows network (such as Windows for Workgroups, Windows 95, or Windows 98). Just ensure that you choose to reconnect your newly mapped drive. That allows your computer to reconnect to the server after rebooting in order to finish the installation process.

## Installing from a CD-ROM Drive

Because your system administrator most likely copied the Windows 98 installation CD-ROM directly to the network for the previous installation routine (installing from a network drive), you should execute the SETUP.EXE file from the installation subdirectory. However, instead of mapping a network drive before you execute the installation program, you need only access the CD-ROM drive, which is usually D: or E:. If you're installing Windows 98 from MS-DOS, you'll have to first install your CD-ROM drivers to access the CD-ROM from MS-DOS.

# Collecting Information

After you have executed the SETUP.EXE program, Windows 98 presents you with a screen like the one shown in Figure 2-1.

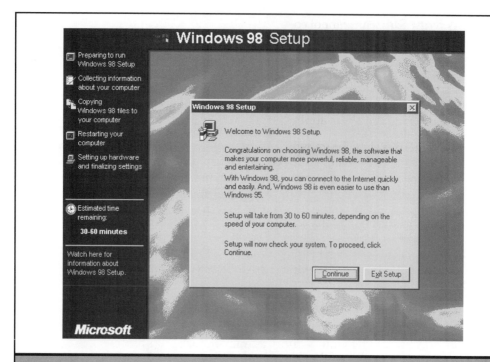

**Figure 2-1.**   Windows 98 installation welcome screen

This screen is present during much of the installation routine. If you want to exit from the installation process at any time, simply click on the button labeled Exit Setup in the lower right-hand corner. However, be aware that after you begin copying files, you may need to reboot your system with the backup boot disk you created previously and re-create the MS-DOS system files on your hard drive.

**RESOURCE:**   If your computer locks up at any time during this phase of the installation process, consult Appendix C, where you learn how to recover from a failed installation process.

Windows 98 then scans your computer's hardware to make sure that it is safe for you to install it on your system. If your system contains any OS/2 system files, or if you're running Windows NT, the installation routine gives you the option to exit. If you have simply forgotten to remove the hidden and system files from a previous OS/2 installation, don't worry. Just select Continue. Only do this, however, if you are sure that you do not have OS/2 installed on the active partition. Because both operating systems boot directly at startup, both cannot coexist. If you install Windows 98 on the same active partition as OS/2, your OS/2 operating system will not boot. If all is okay, it creates the Windows 98 Setup Wizard (see Figure 2-2), through which the remainder of the installation process takes place.

If you are running any other Windows or DOS programs from a current version of Windows (3.1, 3.11, or Windows 95), you are given the option of either quitting the installation or closing the active application, as shown here:

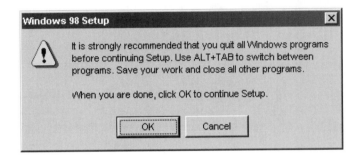

By failing to close any open applications, you may cause the Windows 98 installation process to fail, risking data corruption or loss. Therefore, if you have an application open, simply use the ALT-TAB key sequence to change to each open application, which you can safely close, and then return to the installation program. After Windows 98 scans your computer's hardware, it presents you with a welcome screen. At this point, Windows 98 asks you to read through and agree to the Microsoft license agreement before continuing. After you read the text, just click on the radio button that indicates that you accept the terms of the agreement and click on the Next button. After you enter your license number, Windows 98 then goes through a number of preparatory operations. It scans your system, creates a registry database, checks for installed components, and ensures that there is enough disk space available (see Figure 2-2).

One very nice feature of Windows 98 is its ability to recover from an installation failure. If your machine locks up, you can always reboot it, and Windows 98 recovers your information. But to help things along, when Windows 98 asks you to save your system files, ensure that you select Yes (see Figure 2-3).

This creates a mirror image of your existing OS, which can be recovered later on. But be prepared: Doing so requires as much as 50MB of disk space.

*CAUTION:*  Because Windows 98 comes with a fail-safe installation program that detects a previous installation attempt, if you exit from the Windows 98 installation prematurely, you are presented with a screen asking whether or not you want to verify and update files or run a full setup routine. Choose to restart the installation process regardless of the situation because it gives you the opportunity to correct any system problems *during* the installation instead of *afterward.*

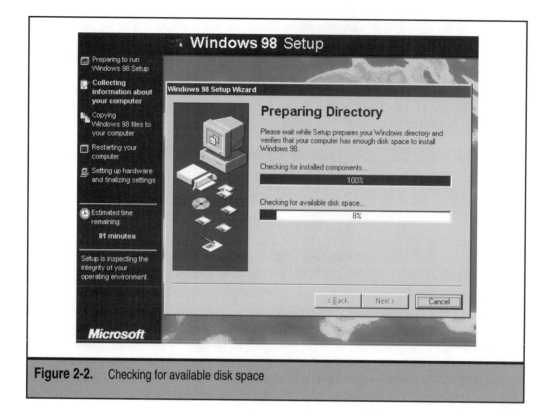

**Figure 2-2.** Checking for available disk space

Windows 98 then opens a dialog box, asking you to establish a geographical location. Here, just click on the name of the country in which you reside, and click on the Next button.

In order to recover from system problems after installation, Windows 98 gives you the opportunity to create a system disk, from which you can boot your machine should something go wrong (e.g., you can't boot Windows 98). With Windows 95, you had the choice of creating or not creating a system disk, but with Windows 98, the process has become mandatory. Windows 98 simply gives you the opportunity to put a floppy disk in your A: drive before it begins copying system files to the floppy. When prompted to do so, just insert your floppy disk and click on the OK button. Windows 98 erases the disk and copies the files necessary to boot Windows 98 from a floppy disk. When the process is done, take the disk out and click on the OK button to continue the installation process.

**SHORTCUT:**   You need not insert a formatted floppy disk. Windows 98 just overwrites the disk's contents. Consequently, it is important that you ensure that the floppy you choose does not contain any important information.

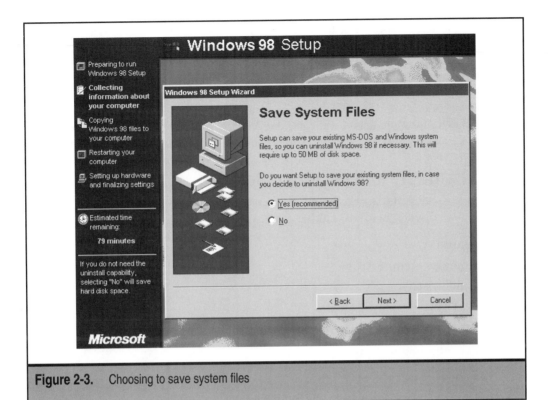

**Figure 2-3.**   Choosing to save system files

## Copying Windows 98 Component Files

Windows 98 is now ready to begin copying files to your hard disk. When prompted to start copying files, click on the Next button. Windows 98 takes complete control of the installation process, letting you know the percent of files copied and how many minutes remain until the installation process is complete. You need only watch for any signs of trouble.

*CAUTION:*   Actually, you should listen for signs of trouble. Often your computer appears to be doing nothing. The clock may be stopped; the screen may appear frozen. But as long as you can hear your hard disk, you can feel confident that the installation is continuing.

## Restarting Your Computer

This is the easiest part of the installation process. All you have to do is let Windows 98 automatically reboot. It then starts Windows 98 and enters the final phase of the installation process. Although this is the easiest phase, it is also the most dangerous. The problem applies only to those who install Windows 98 from a network drive. As mentioned earlier, if you want to install Windows 98 from a remote drive across a network, you must ensure that when Windows 98 restarts, it can re-establish a network connection. If it can't re-establish the connection, it asks you to insert either a Windows 98 floppy disk or the Windows 98 CD-ROM before it can continue. If this happens, you can click on the Cancel button and restart the installation process after connecting to the remote drive containing Windows 98. Or, you can click on the Cancel button, establish a connection to that remote drive, and copy the Windows 98 installation files to your hard disk.

## Setting Up Hardware and Finalizing Settings

Once Windows 98 restarts, it automatically enters the fourth phase in the installation process, where it sets up various entities, such as:

▼ Control Panel

■ Programs on the Start menu

■ Windows Help

■ MS-DOS program settings

■ Tuning up application start

▲ System configuration

When Windows 98 has been properly configured, you are prompted to remove all floppy diskettes (if you installed Windows from floppy disk), after which your machine reboots under the new Windows 98 OS. Do not be alarmed if it takes a few moments to load. Windows 98 merely needs some extra time to configure your computer. The next time you boot up your machine, things will go much more quickly.

*CAUTION:*  If your machine fails to shut down properly, do not worry. After waiting to make sure that the hard disk is not still operating, you can simply reboot your machine. It then continues as before with no interruption.

Once you see the background image for Windows 98, you are prompted to enter a login name and a password. Because this is the first time you will have logged onto Windows 98, you can specify any name and password you choose. However, if you are utilizing pass-through security from either your NetWare or Windows NT server, you should enter the appropriate name and password just as though you were logging directly into either of those network OSs. If the password is new, you are asked to retype it for verification.

## Windows 98 Welcome

Once you enter a user name and password, Windows 98 builds a driver information database of all your hardware devices. It then quickly updates your system to establish

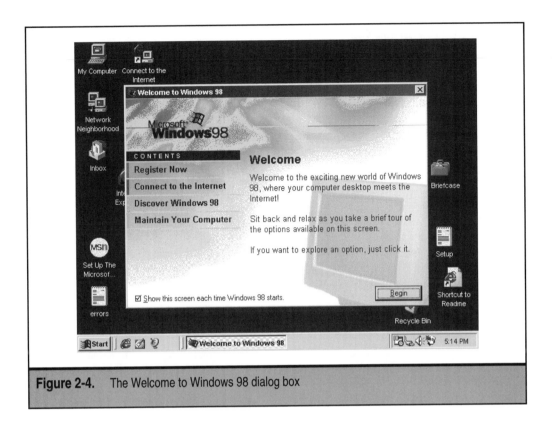

**Figure 2-4.**    The Welcome to Windows 98 dialog box

your personal settings. The only step left is to go through Windows 98's welcome program (see Figure 2-4).

Called Welcome to Windows 98, this dialog box is a multimedia tool designed to help you find out more about Windows 98 and finish any last-minute configuration tasks. From its main dialog box, you can select one of the following tasks:

▼   Register Now

■   Connect to the Internet

■   Discover Windows 98

▲   Maintain Your Computer

The important thing to note about these tasks is that you don't have to complete all of them before you use Windows 98. You can simply click on the × button in the top-right corner of the window and begin working with Windows 98. The Welcome to Windows 98 dialog box simply restarts the next time you reboot your machine. Conversely, you can let the dialog box guide you through the steps one-by-one, or you can click on a task to complete it right away. Either way, you can progress through these tasks at your own pace.

## Registering Windows 98

Though you don't need to complete the first task (Register Now) in order to use Windows 98, we recommend that you do so, as it gives you and your users immediate access to online support from Microsoft's Web site. Just click on the Register Now text to start the Microsoft Windows 98 Registration Wizard and follow the suggested steps. Don't worry if you mistakenly choose this item. You can always click on the Register Later button from the Registration Wizard to return to the Welcome to Windows 98 dialog box.

**RESOURCE:** To get the latest information on Windows 98 support and features, point your Web browser to http://www.microsoft.com/windows98/.

When you return to the Welcome dialog box, Windows 98 lets you know that you've completed the Register Now option by placing a check mark next to the option.

## Connect to the Internet

In order to fully utilize Windows 98's networking potential, it should be linked to the Internet. Click on the item labeled Connect to the Internet to get started. This opens the Internet Connection Wizard (see Figure 2-5).

It does not matter whether or not that takes place through a corporate firewall or via a local Internet Service Provider (ISP). You need only tell Windows 98 how you want to hook up with the Internet. The Internet Connection Wizard gives you three connection options:

▼ Create a new ISP account through the Microsoft Network (MSN)

■ Create an Internet connection through an existing ISP account or a LAN

▲ Use the existing ISP or LAN connection

This wizard leads you step-by-step through the tasks required to complete each option. If you click on the first option, Microsoft walks you through the installation of its MSN client. For more information on this feature, read through Chapter 9. If you click on the second option, Windows 98 helps you set up a TCP/IP and PPP connection to the Internet. To see more about setting up a TCP/IP connection, read Chapter 6. For more information on creating a PPP connection, read through Chapter 7. If you click on the last option, Windows 98 closes the Internet Connection Wizard and returns you to the Welcome dialog box without modifying any of your network settings.

## Discover Windows 98

The Discover Windows 98 option is not required. If you click on it, Windows 98 opens a multimedia presentation from the installation CD-ROM that talks about the many benefits of Windows 98. You can instruct your users to go through the presentation. However, it will not teach them anything about the day-to-day operation of Windows 98.

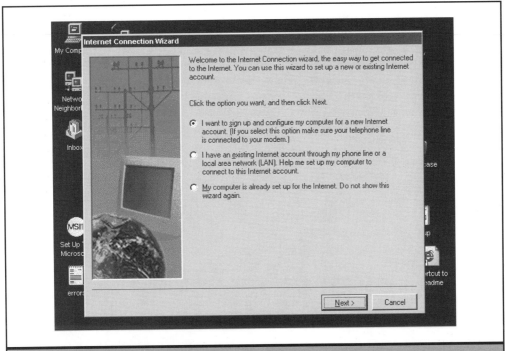

**Figure 2-5.**   The Internet Connection Wizard

## Maintain Your Computer

Click on Maintain Your Computer in order to set up Windows 98's automated system maintenance. As shown in Figure 2-6, the Maintenance Wizard helps you configure Windows 98 to run programs faster, provide more disk space, and ensure that system performance is optimal.

Windows 98 accomplishes these tasks by speeding performance of frequently used applications, checking your hard disk for errors, and deleting any unnecessary files from your hard drive.

In setting up system maintenance, you've got two options: express and custom. If you choose the Express radio button, you only need to tell Windows 98 when you want it to perform system maintenance (nights, days, evenings, or a custom time). Unless you have specific requirements—if you're using a laptop computer, for example—we recommend that you use the express option. After selecting Express, just click on the radio button on the ensuing dialog box that represents the time of day you wish Windows 98 to perform system maintenance.

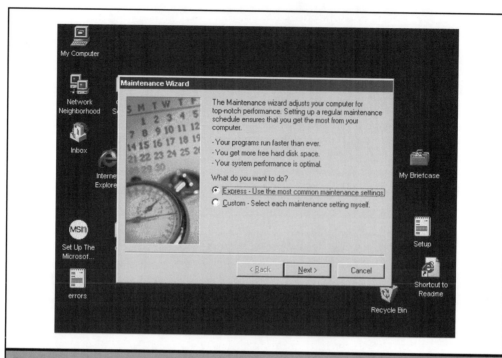

**Figure 2-6.** The Windows 98 Maintenance Wizard

**SOAPBOX:** Don't worry about losing control of Windows 98 in setting up these tasks. It checks to make sure that the OS has been idle for some time before beginning maintenance tasks. Also, you can preempt system maintenance while it is running without doing any harm to your OS.

If you click on the Custom radio button, you'll be able to choose the same time frames for maintenance with a few additions. You get to specify a custom time at which Windows 98 should perform system maintenance. You get to specify which applications start up with Windows 98 (this can be used to increase boot-up speed). Whether or not you choose to use the express or custom settings, just follow the wizard's prompts to go through the available options. When you're done, you can choose to either return to the Welcome dialog box or run the performance tasks right away. We recommend that you choose the former option and return to the Welcome dialog box as your machine will most likely not to do any performance tuning at this time.

When you return to the Welcome to Windows 98 dialog box, notice how the button labeled Begin now says "Exit." If you are ready to leave the dialog box, and you don't wish to return, just deselect the check box at the lower portion of the screen and click on the

Exit button. If you don't clear the check box, you'll return to the dialog box the next time you reboot your machine. That's all there is to installing and configuring Windows 98.

# COMING UP

We've covered a lot of territory in this chapter, from anticipating installation troubles to implementing the installation process. In doing so, we've shown you how to install Windows 98 on your computer. In the next chapter, we'll dig into the nitty-gritty elements of networking with Windows 98. We'll show you how to install the Microsoft network client, adapter drivers, protocols, and networking services.

NETWORK
PROFESSIONAL'S
LIBRARY

# CHAPTER 3

# Networking with Windows 98

## What's ahead:

- Why network with Windows 98?
- Preparing to network with Windows 98
- Using Windows 98 as a server to share files and printers
- Using Windows 98 as a client to access shared files and printers

*"Happy am I; from care I'm free!*
*Why aren't they all contented like me?"*

—Ludwig Minkus, *Opera of La Bayadhre*

Networking is an integral part of Windows 98. It comes complete with all the software you need to participate in traditional server-based and peer-to-peer networks. In a traditional server-based network, client workstations log in to dedicated network servers and all shared resources, such as files and printers, reside on those network servers. In contrast, all computers that participate in a peer-to-peer network can function as both workstations and as network servers.

In Chapters 4 and 5, we discuss how to use Windows 98 in server-based Windows NT and Novell NetWare networks. Throughout the rest of this chapter, we focus on how to use Windows 98 in a peer-to-peer network with other computers that are also running Windows 98.

# PREPARING TO NETWORK WITH WINDOWS 98

Successful, trouble-free networking begins with proper planning and preparation. Even though Microsoft has made networking extremely simple in Windows 98, it's still important to understand a little about how it works and how to install and configure the necessary software components before you get started.

## Planning

The first step is to make a plan. This plan involves asking yourself such questions as:

- ▼ How will your computer be connected to the network?
- ■ What networking protocols should you use?
- ▲ How is access to shared resources controlled and secured?

The answers to these questions will help when you put your plan into action.

### Network Connection

Windows 98 ships with support for several types of network connections, including traditional Network Interface Cards (NICs), dial-up connections over modems and ISDN adapters, direct serial cable connections, and infrared ports. In keeping with the theme of this book, this discussion focuses on NIC cards and the dial-up adapter.

**NETWORK INTERFACE CARD (NIC)**    The Network Interface Card is commonly referred to as a NIC. It is the most popular and commonly used type of network connection in the corporate environment. The NIC card plugs into one of the expansion slots in your computer and has a connector on the back plane for connecting to your network cabling. The NIC card also determines whether your computer uses Ethernet, Token Ring, or ArcNet to exchange data with other computers on the network.

As the Internet and TCP/IP have gained wider use and acceptance, IEEE 802.3 Ethernet has become the de facto standard for networking over 10Base-T or 10Base-2 wiring. 10Base-T uses unshielded twisted pair (UTP) wiring with RJ-45 connectors. 10Base-2 uses coaxial cable with BNC connectors. For the purposes of this chapter, it is assumed that you are working with an Ethernet NIC, but because Windows does not care what type of wiring you use, we don't either.

At the time of this writing, 10 megabit Ethernet and 100 megabit Fast Ethernet are both readily available and widely used. 10 megabit Ethernet is generally run to the desktop and 100 megabit Fast Ethernet is common for server-to-server and backbone communications. The Gigabit Ethernet (1000 megabit) standard is just emerging and even though there are several products available, they're still too expensive for all but the most demanding applications. As hardware prices continue to fall and high-bandwidth multimedia applications become more common, Fast Ethernet to the desktop will become more common, driving the need for Gigabit Ethernet for server-to-server and backbone communications.

**DIAL-UP ADAPTER**    Windows 98 also ships with a dial-up adapter. It basically emulates the functionality of a NIC card in software and routes all network traffic through your modem or ISDN adapter. Dial-up adapters are particularly useful for mobile and home-based users where it is not practical or possible to connect to the network through a traditional NIC card.

As telecommuting and high-bandwidth Internet applications have become more popular, users have found that they need more bandwidth than a single modem can provide. Windows 98 solves this problem with special support for linking multiple dial-up connections and treating them as a single very fast connection, and with enhanced support for ISDN adapters.

*JARGON:*  ISDN stands for Integrated Services Digital Network. Although it uses the same copper wiring as analog phone lines, ISDN connections are digital from end to end, which eliminates the digital-to-analog conversions that are necessary when using modems over analog phone lines. The term modem is symbolic of the digital-to-analog modulation that takes place when a modem sends data and the analog-to-digital demodulation necessary when a modem receives data (*modulation/demodulation*). Because ISDN adapters are digital to begin with and do not use modulation, they are not modems.

See Chapter 7 for more information on how to configure and use dial-up networking with Windows 98.

## Protocol Selection

Windows 98 ships with the following protocols:

▼ NetBIOS (Network Basic Input/Output System)

■ NetBEUI (NetBIOS Extended User Interface)

■ IPX/SPX (Internetwork Packet Exchange/Sequenced Packet Exchange)

■ ATM (Asynchronous Transfer Mode)

■ DLC (Data Link Control)

▲ TCP/IP (Transmission Control Protocol/Internet Protocol)

If this list looks a bit ponderous, don't worry. Windows 98 really does not need all of these protocols to connect with other Windows 98 computers. On the contrary, you can get by with just NetBEUI or just TCP/IP. However, this is not to say that these protocols can be used interchangeably. Each was designed to perform very specific networking tasks with very specific applications and operating systems. For instance, IPX/SPX was built by Novell to give users a client/server connection to their Network Operating System (NOS), NetWare. With IPX/SPX, NetWare users can print to a network printer or open files stored on a NetWare server. TCP/IP was built by the same folks who created UNIX and the Internet to give users peer-to-peer connectivity over Wide Area Networks (WANs). With TCP/IP, users can connect to another machine halfway around the world and work on that machine as though it were sitting in the same room.

NetBEUI sits between these two protocols in functionality. You can use it to print from or store files on another Windows 98 machine. Or you can use it to log on to a Windows 98 machine and execute remote applications as though they were local. However, you can't use it to access any IPX/SPX- or TCP/IP-centric applications or services. For example, unless someone built a Web server that used NetBEUI as a transport protocol, you couldn't use NetBEUI to browse pages on a Web server. The other protocols listed in this section are not customarily used with Windows 98, although they can be. For this reason, these other protocols are discussed in more appropriate chapters and the current discussion is confined to NetBEUI, TCP/IP, and IPX/SPX.

The magic of networking with Windows 98 is that you don't have to really choose between these three protocols. You can simply use them all because Windows 98 can assign more than one protocol to a single NIC. However, before you dump all of the protocols you've got on your Windows 98 machine, consider carefully your connectivity needs. Each protocol requires processing time. Add protocols indiscriminately, and you'll end up with poor network performance.

**NETBEUI** NetBEUI, in short, is a quick, lightweight protocol designed for efficient client/server connections within the confines of a Local Area Network (LAN). It wasn't built to route over WANs, or any network with more than one network segment, for that matter. If you intend to connect to a remote Windows 98 computer (even one in another department in the same company), NetBEUI is not the protocol for you. What NetBEUI can do for you, however, is provide ubiquitous connections within a predominantly Windows shop. If you've got perhaps 50 or so machines running on a LAN Manager, Windows for Workgroups, Windows 98, or Windows NT single-segment LAN, NetBEUI gets you connected to all parties involved quickly and easily.

**NETBEUI FUNCTIONALITY**   With NetBEUI as your sole network protocol, you are able to connect to Windows NT machines, log into those machines, and manipulate files thereupon. In short, you can perform virtually any Windows NT task. It is suggested, therefore, that you use NetBEUI as a base protocol, to which you add a secondary protocol, depending upon your needs. You'll find it quite useful regardless of what applications you run, as Windows 98, Windows NT, and Windows 95 use it to compile a list of available computers on a network. That is, when you open your Network Neighborhood dialog box, it is NetBEUI that Windows 98 uses to present you with a list of available servers.

**TCP/IP**   By far, of the two choices as secondary protocols for NetBEUI, TCP/IP is the most useful for most networking environments. This robust protocol is as old as the Internet. It was designed to provide UNIX users with peer-to-peer networking services. Because the Internet grew out of the UNIX-based college milieu, today you can use a peer-to-peer TCP/IP application such as FTP to log on to any one of the millions of machines on the Internet to download, upload, or manage files. However, TCP/IP's real fame and usefulness stems from its adoption by Tim Berners Lee in the early 90s as the Web's protocol of choice. If you're browsing the Web in any way, shape, or form, you're doing it via Hypertext Transport Protocol (HTTP), which rides only across TCP/IP.

**TCP/IP FUNCTIONALITY**   The best part about TCP/IP's success on the Internet is that it has translated to the world of LANs and WANs as well. When you install Windows 98, Windows NT, or virtually any other operating system, your basic, default protocol is now TCP/IP. In this way, TCP/IP has become the lingua franca of networking. Everyone understands it.

**RESOURCE:**   For more information on network protocols, refer to Appendix B.

**IPX/SPX**   Novell's flagship protocol, IPX/SPX, is a well-rounded, complete protocol designed to provide users with fast file and print services. It is built into the Novell NetWare NOS as its basic protocol, though recently Novell has expended considerable effort porting IPX/SPX services to TCP/IP. Unlike NetBEUI, IPX/SPX is a complete protocol. It does not need anything more to provide connectivity. It can also function over more than one LAN segment. However, unlike TCP/IP, it cannot provide very good WAN services, placing its optimal-sized network somewhere between what is manageable with TCP/IP and NetBEUI.

**IPX/SPX FUNCTIONALITY**    Because it is a complete protocol, if you choose, you can use just IPX/SPX to connect with other Windows 98 machines. All you need to do is ensure that you have the Client for Microsoft Networks service installed (more on that in a minute) on your client and IPX/SPX installed on the other Windows 98 machine (because it is not typical Windows 98 protocol, as are NetBEUI and TCP/IP). So why install it? Well, if you are working in an environment that contains NetWare servers, the decision to use IPX/SPX is an easy one. You might, for example, have Novell NetWare Directory Services (NDS) installed on a Windows NT machine, for which IPX/SPX on the client becomes a requirement. Also, you might be migrating to Windows from NetWare. Here, you could use IPX/SPX to facilitate that migration because both operating systems support it.

**PROTOCOL RECOMMENDATIONS**    To put all of this protocol talk into perspective, it is recommended that you install a combination of these three protocols based upon the following criteria:

▼    For Windows for Workgroups or LAN Manager environments, run NetBEUI.

■    For Internet connectivity or an environment with UNIX workstations, install TCP/IP along with NetBEUI.

▲    For a Novell NetWare environment, install IPX/SPX and NetBEUI.

Of course, if you are working in an environment that meets more than one of these criteria, it is suggested that you simply install those protocols required to connect to the machines in use, keeping in mind that NetBEUI requires IPX/SPX or TCP/IP for full functionality. For example, if you have a NetWare environment with LAN Manager servers, install NetBEUI with IPX/SPX. Conversely, if you have a Windows NT environment and Internet connectivity, install both NetBEUI and TCP/IP.

## Access Controls and Security

Whenever files and printers are shared, you need to be concerned about security—who can access those devices and how. Windows 98 provides two access control methods. User-level access control provides the strongest security available, but it requires a Windows NT Domain Controller on the network to do it. If you don't have one, you can still password-protect network shares with the Share-level access control option.

In either case, keep in mind that like its predecessor, Windows 95, the access controls in Windows 98 do not control access to the hard disk by local users; it only restricts access via the network. Anyone with physical access to the computer can always log on as a new user, or Cancel from the Windows logon dialog box, and still gain full access to the local resources, including unrestricted access to all the files on your hard disk.

# Installing the Network Adapter and Protocols

Now that we understand how our computer will be connected to the network and which networking protocols we want to use, the next step is to install and configure the necessary software for Windows 98. We'll start with the network adapter and protocols.

First, we need to open the Network Control Panel. Click on the Start button from the Windows 98 desktop, select the Settings option, and click on the Control Panel selection. This opens Windows 98's Control Panel, which contains a collection of system configuration utilities (see Figure 3-1).

Double-click on the Network icon to open the Network Control Panel. If this is the first time you have opened the Network Control Panel since Windows 98 was installed, you should see a message similar to the following, which notifies you that the network is not complete and asking if you want to continue.

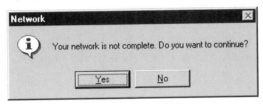

Answer yes.

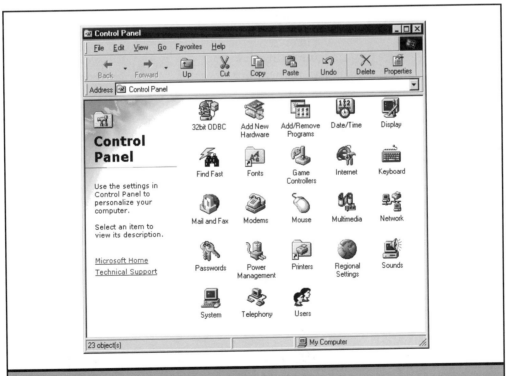

**Figure 3-1.**   Windows Control Panel

The Network Control Panel should now be open on your desktop. Notice in Figure 3-2 that only a dial-up adapter and a NIC (in this case, an Artisoft AE-2 or AE-3) are listed as installed network components.

Normally when you install Windows 98, it auto-detects your network adapter and modem and installs the TCP/IP protocol stack. Because we are going to install all three protocols (TCP/IP, IPX/SPX, and NetBEUI), we've simply deleted the default TCP/IP protocol to get a fresh start.

## Installing the Network Adapter

If Windows 98 did not auto-detect your NIC card, you will need to run the Add New Hardware Wizard from the Control Panel. If it does not find your NIC card and install the proper drivers for it, you can click on the Add button in the Network Control Panel and manually select your network adapter.

## Installing Protocols

With the network adapter installed, you're ready to begin installing network protocols. Click on the Add button and the dialog box shown in Figure 3-3 should appear.

Highlight the Protocol entry and click on the Add button. This opens another dialog box entitled Select Network Protocol (see Figure 3-4). In the window titled Manufacturers, click on the Microsoft entry to display a list of network protocols provided by Microsoft.

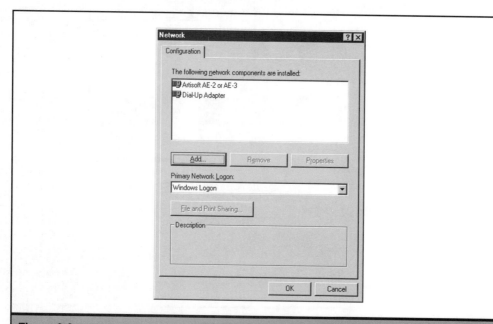

**Figure 3-2.**    Network Control Panel Configuration dialog box

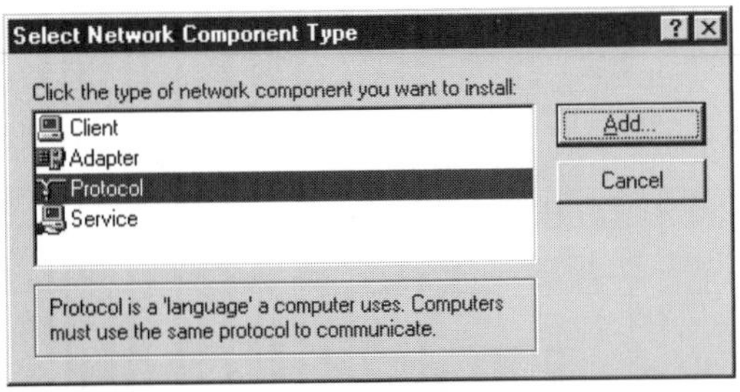

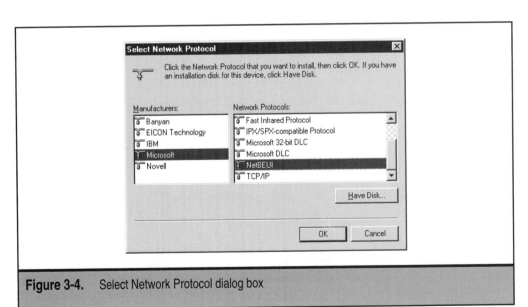

**Figure 3-3.**    Select Network Component Type dialog box

Locate and click on the NetBEUI protocol, then click on the OK button. You are returned to the Network Control Panel window, but now the NetBEUI protocol is listed as an installed protocol (see Figure 3-5).

Repeat the process two more times to install the TCP/IP and IPX/SPX protocols. When you're done, your screen should look very similar to Figure 3-6.

As you can see, every protocol you add is automatically bound to all installed network adapters. If you do not need to use every protocol with every adapter, you can conserve resources and speed up your machine by removing the entries that are not needed. For example, if you only plan to use the dial-up adapter for Internet access, there's no point leaving NetBEUI or IPX/SPX bound to it. You can remove those entries by clicking on them once, then clicking on the Remove button.

**Figure 3-4.**    Select Network Protocol dialog box

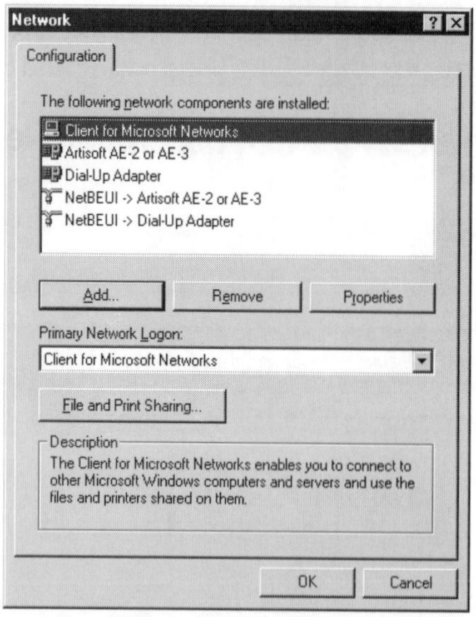

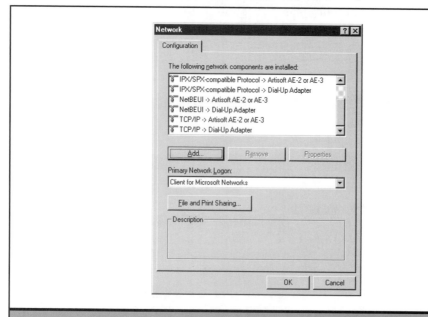

**Figure 3-5.** NetBEUI protocol is installed

**Figure 3-6.** All protocols installed

You will also notice that Windows 98 added the Client for Microsoft Networks to the list of installed components. Just ignore that entry for now. It is discussed in detail later in this chapter in the section titled "Client-Side File Sharing and Shared Printers."

## Installing File and Printer Sharing for Microsoft Networks

Even though file and printer sharing is addressed later in this chapter, it's a good idea to install the service now, before we proceed to configure our installed network protocols.

If File and Printer Sharing for Microsoft Networks is not already listed in the Network dialog box as an installed component, click on the Add button, then select Service from the Select Network Component Type dialog box. When the Select Network Service dialog box opens, click on Microsoft in the Manufacturers window, then click on File and Printer Sharing for Microsoft Networks in the Network Services window and click the OK button to dismiss the dialog box and install the service.

How to configure and use this service is discussed later in this chapter, in the section titled "File and Print Services." For now, we're satisfied that it is listed as an installed network component.

## Setting a Default Protocol

Windows 98 can communicate with other computers using any of the protocols that are installed and configured on both computers. To ensure that it does not have to work harder than necessary to identify a supported protocol, it is a good idea to specify the default protocol yourself. When using the Client for Microsoft Networks you can specify either NetBEUI or TCP/IP as your default protocol, depending on which is used by most of the computers you will be communicating with on your network.

To specify NetBEUI as your default protocol, simply click on the NetBEUI entry that is associated with your NIC card, click on the Properties button, select the Advanced tab, and click the check box labeled *Set this protocol to be the default protocol* (see Figure 3-7). Now, click on the OK button to close the dialog box and return to the Network Control Panel.

## Configuring NetBEUI

Of the three protocols we installed, NetBEUI is by far the easiest to configure. All you have to do once you've selected either it or one of its partner protocols as a default protocol is ensure that it is bound to the right network component. That is, you must ensure that it is going to talk to both the Client for Microsoft Networks and the File and Printer Sharing for Microsoft Networks service.

**SHORTCUT:**   Actually, you don't need to bind all of your protocols to the File and Printer Sharing for Microsoft Networks service. You can just bind one of them, perhaps IPX/SPX alone or NetBEUI and TCP/IP together, to this service and remove the bindings from the other protocols using the same procedure as setting up bindings. Again, just as when you removed protocols from unnecessary devices (a modem), this helps your computer run faster.

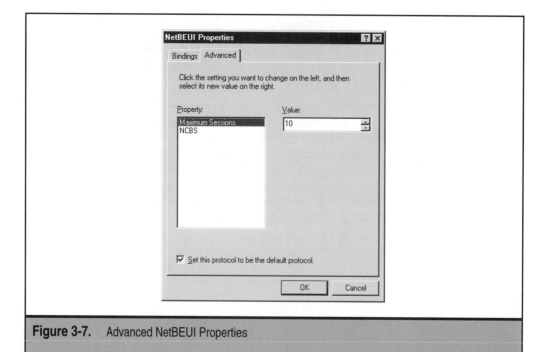

**Figure 3-7.** Advanced NetBEUI Properties

To ensure that NetBEUI is bound properly, select it from the Configuration tab in the Network dialog box and click on the Properties button. Once there, select the Bindings tab and look to make sure that both the service and the client are selected.

*CAUTION:* When you install protocols such as NetBEUI, Windows 98 automatically binds them to all available services (NICs, modems, and so forth). You should take care not to leave NetBEUI bound to all services. Only bind NetBEUI to the services you need. For example, if you won't use it over a modem, ensure that NetBEUI does not bind to that service. The more services a single protocol is bound to, the greater the system load will be and the slower your machine will perform.

## Configuring IPX/SPX

Going up the scale of difficulty one notch from NetBEUI is IPX/SPX. Here, you of course need to first check to see that it is bound to the appropriate client and service, as stated previously. Second, however, you need to apply your knowledge of the types of applications running on your network to decide whether or not to enable NetBIOS over IPX/SPX. You see, some applications, especially those built to run over Novell, LAN Manager, and IBM OS/2 networks, use NetBIOS as their main session layer protocol. So, if you have one of these networking environments or applications built for these environments running between your computer and another Windows 98 machine, you must run NetBIOS over IPX/SPX. To do this, click on the Configuration button as you did with NetBEUI and select the NetBIOS tab. Here, just click the check box, and you're good to go.

*CAUTION:*  Like any protocol, NetBIOS requires system resources. Therefore, choose to use it judiciously. If you don't think you need it, don't install it. Your machine will run better.

The last thing you need to do with IPX/SPX is set your frame type. Actually, the Microsoft-supplied IPX/SPX protocol does default to an automatic setting that "supposedly" detects your frame type. But it is better to set it manually, just to be on the safe side.

*JARGON:*  A frame type defines the structure of data as it passes over an Ethernet network. As you might imagine, different NOSs use different frame types, which is why you need to select a frame type appropriate to your NOS.

Once you have the IPX/SPX Properties dialog box open, click on the Advanced tab and select Frame Type. Then click on the Value pull-down menu and select the appropriate Frame Type. Just as a reminder, here are the available Frame Types and the type of network(s) they are associated with.

▼ Ethernet II: Used by DEC systems and AppleTalk Phase I networks

■ Ethernet 802.2: Used by Novell NetWare 4.x networks

■ Ethernet 802.3: Used by Novell NetWare 3.x networks

▲ Ethernet SNAP: Used by AppleTalk Phase II networks and TCP/IP networks

There are also two additional types: the Token Ring and Token Ring SNAP. These are used, as you might suspect, strictly with a Token Ring network infrastructure. If you've got such a network infrastructure, you'll know it.

## Configuring TCP/IP

The most difficult protocol to configure is TCP/IP. You've got to know a lot of information in order to properly configure this protocol. But before getting to the hard stuff, first open the TCP/IP Properties dialog box just as you did with NetBEUI and IPX/SPX and check your bindings. Once that's done, click on the NetBIOS tab. Notice that if you selected to run NetBIOS over IPX/SPX previously, you won't be able to specify it here, over TCP/IP.

Here's the hard part. Before you can connect to other Windows 98 computers using TCP/IP, you must first know the following information:

▼ Either the IP address of your machine, or leave the IP address blank if you will receive a dynamically allocated IP address using the Dynamic Host Configuration Protocol (DHCP).

■ If you are not using DHCP, and you have no IP address, you must know the IP address of your Windows Internet Naming Service (WINS). If you are using DHCP, this information is configured automatically.

■ If you are not using DHCP, and if your network connects to a disparate network, such as the Internet or a WAN, you need to know the IP address of that network's gateway. If you are using DHCP, this information is configured automatically.

▲ If you are not using DHCP, you need to know the IP address and domain name for your Domain Name System (DNS) server. If you are using DHCP, this information is configured automatically.

Of these, two are crucial: Your IP address and your DNS server. Without these two, you won't be able to see or be seen by any other TCP/IP-based machines. If you are the administrator of your network, you most likely have all of these at your fingertips; but if you're a power-user, setting up your system all on your own, you definitely have to go to a higher source for this data. There's no room for error here.

Once you have your TCP/IP data together, the rest is easy. You simply have to plug the numbers into the appropriate fields under the appropriate tabs, including IP Address, Gateway, WINS Configuration, and DNS Configuration, as shown in Figure 3-8.

The values you enter into these fields depends on how your network is configured. If you do not know what addresses and other settings to use, you should check with your network administrator or information services (IS) department before proceeding.

Be careful to enter this information correctly. Entering the wrong IP Addresses can have far-reaching consequences. Not only will you be unable to access the network correctly, you could also interfere with other computers on the network.

## Identification

The last step you need to take before you can begin networking with Windows 98 is setting up the identification and authentication information on your computer. In essence, you need to tell the world who you are and that you wish to participate in a network. To accomplish this, you must first set up your computer's identity. Click on the Identification tab from the Network dialog box, and enter the name of your computer. The actual name is not important. You could use something like Memphis. However, it is important that your computer's name be unique to prevent your computer from being mistaken for another computer. Then you must specify a group of computers or a domain to which you will belong under the field entitled Workgroup. You should get this name

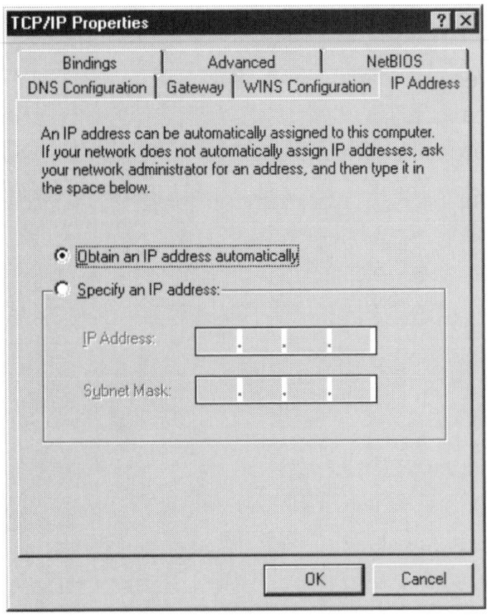

**Figure 3-8.** TCP/IP Properties dialog box

from your systems administrator, as it must match exactly the Workgroup name used by other members of the immediate network in which you want to work.

**SHORTCUT:** The most typical Workgroup name, believe it or not, is "workgroup."

The last thing to do here is enter a quick description of your computer. A good idea is to enter your full name and department (if applicable). Other computers use this field to get more information about your computer than what might be available from the computer name alone. When you're done, the Identification tab should look like the one in Figure 3-9.

Of course, you can use any computer and workgroup names you wish, but the computer name should be unique within the workgroup.

# SERVER-SIDE FILE SHARING AND SHARED PRINTERS

The basic idea behind peer-to-peer networking is that all "peers" act as both clients and servers. This means that every computer can elect to grant others access to its local files

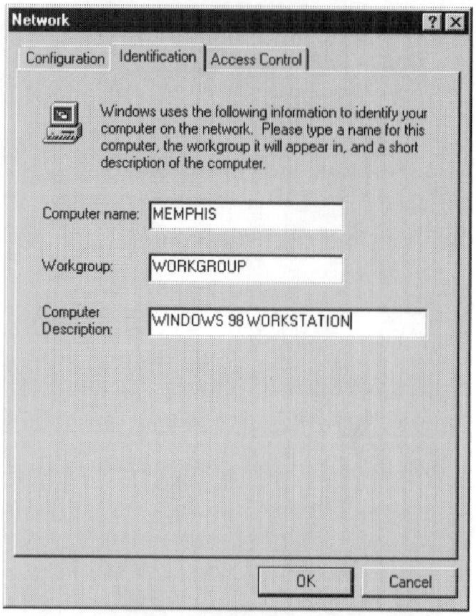

**Figure 3-9.** Identification panel of the Network dialog box

and printers and can also connect to and use the files and printers that have been shared by other computers.

Windows 98 ships with all the software you need, but it's up to you to install and configure the appropriate services and access controls and specify which devices to share.

# File and Print Services

File and printer sharing in Windows 98 is facilitated by the File and Printer Sharing for Microsoft Networks service. The service is installed and configured through the Windows Network dialog box, which can be opened by double-clicking on the Network icon in Windows Control Panel.

## Installing the Service

The service can be installed using the same technique used earlier, by clicking on the Add button and selecting the file and print sharing service. However, there is an easier way to do it. Just click on the File and Print Sharing button in the Network dialog box to open this dialog box:

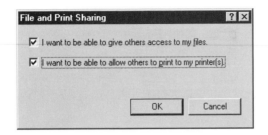

This technique works whether or not the service is already installed. If it is installed, you can view or change the current settings. If it is not installed, both settings are cleared, but the service is automatically installed if you enable either one.

Enabling file and printer sharing is as simple as clicking on the appropriate check boxes in the dialog box. If you enable one or both options, and the File and Print Sharing service was not already installed, it is installed automatically when you click on the OK button to close the File and Print Sharing dialog box.

### Configuring the Service

Like other network components, the File and Print Sharing service can be configured through the Properties dialog box, but it isn't necessary to do so when networking with other Windows 98 computers in a peer-to-peer environment. Unless you have a specific reason to do so, such as the need to control whether workstations announce themselves when they are active or to prevent them from competing for the role of browser master, do not change any of the configuration settings in the Properties dialog box.

## Access Controls

Before actually sharing any files or printers, you have to first decide which access control method to use. If the Network dialog box is not already open, open it now by selecting the Network icon from the Windows Control Panel, just as you did before.

Switch to the Access Control settings by clicking on the tab labeled Access Control (see Figure 3-10). On this screen, you can see that there are two options available: Share-level access control and User-level access control.

As previously discussed, user-level access control requires a Windows NT Domain Controller. Because we're working in a Windows 98 peer-to-peer environment, you should select the share-level access control option, which allows you to use passwords to control access to your shared files and printers.

## Sharing Files

The next step is to tell Windows which drives and directories you wish to share. This can be accomplished from either the My Computer dialog box or the Windows Explorer. For

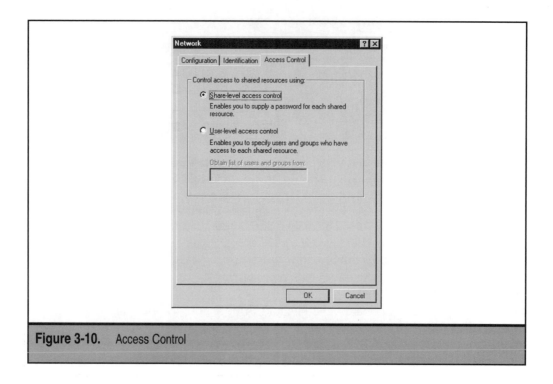

**Figure 3-10.** Access Control

the sake of discussion, let's start by double-clicking the My Computer icon (see Figure 3-11) on your Windows desktop.

Choose a local drive you wish to share, then right-click on the icon and select Sharing from the pop-up menu. This opens the Drive Properties dialog box shown in Figure 3-12 and sets focus to the Sharing tab.

Click on the Shared As radio button to enable sharing. When you do, Windows 98 provides a default Share Name, which you can change if you want to use a more descriptive name. The Comment field is used to provide additional information about the share, which can be helpful to describe the contents of the drive.

The next thing you need to do is to specify the access type and passwords. Our choices are Read-Only, Full, and Depends on Password. Specifying Read-Only access and entering a Read-Only Password allows users with the proper password to read files, but prohibits anyone from writing to the drive. The Full option allows you to specify a single password for granting full access to the shared drive. The third option, Depends on Password, allows you to specify separate Read-Only and Full-Access passwords, for granting selective access to the shared drive.

Of course, you don't have to share the entire drive if you don't want to. You can perform the exact same procedure from any subdirectory level you wish. Just specify a unique share name for the directory and other computers on the network see it just like any other shared drive.

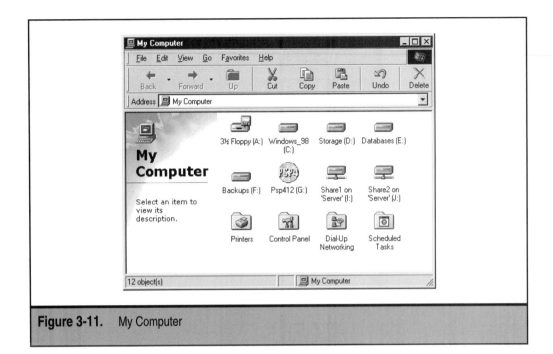

**Figure 3-11.** My Computer

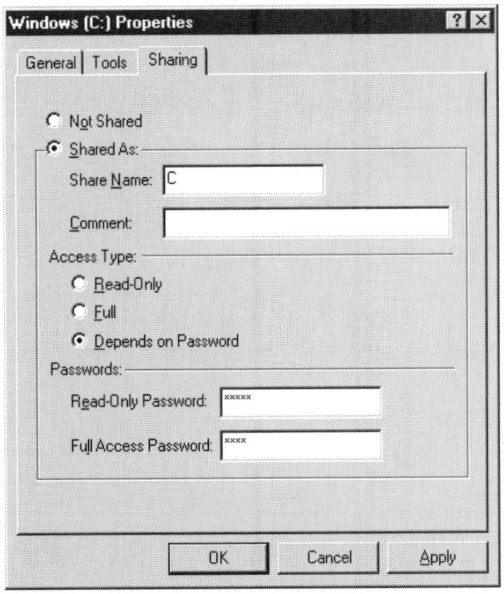

**Figure 3-12.** Drive Sharing

**NOTE:**   Also refer to Chapter 13 for a discussion of installing and using Web and FTP services on Windows 98.

## Sharing Printers

The procedure for sharing printers is almost identical to that of sharing files. Start by opening the Printers dialog box. You can do this by either double-clicking on the Printers icon in the My Computer window or click on the Windows Start button and select Settings and then Printers. The Printers window is shown in Figure 3-13.

Right-click on the printer you wish to share and select Sharing from the pop-up menu. This opens the printer's Properties dialog box and sets focus to the Sharing tab (see Figure 3-14), which you should recognize as being very similar to the Drive Properties dialog box.

To share the printer, you need to select the Shared As option and enter a name for the printer, or accept the default share name. You can also specify a descriptive Comment and control use of the printer by specifying an optional password. You can only share local printers. Windows 98 does not allow you to re-share a network printer.

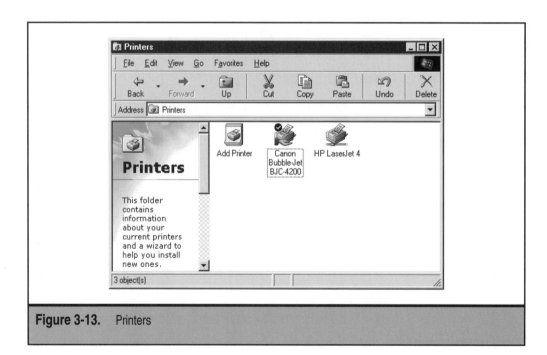

**Figure 3-13.**   Printers

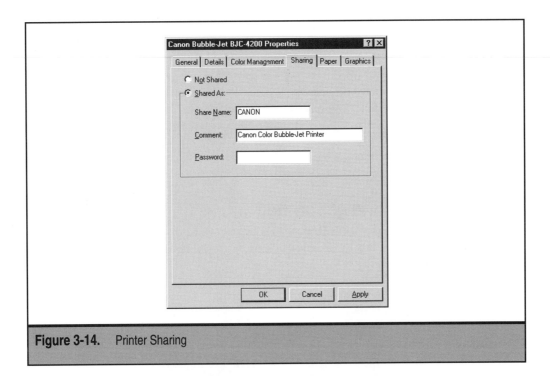

**Figure 3-14.**  Printer Sharing

# CLIENT-SIDE FILE SHARING AND SHARED PRINTERS

The Client for Microsoft Networks service allows Windows 98 to access files and printers that have been shared on other computers. The first step is to make sure the service is installed and configured.

## Installing the Service

Make sure the Networking dialog box is open and has focus. If it is not, you should open it now by double-clicking the Network icon in the Control Panel. The Client for Microsoft Networks service was automatically installed earlier, when you installed the networking protocols, so it should already be listed as an installed component. If it is not, click on the Add button now and select the Microsoft File and Print Service.

## Configuring the Service

Select the "Client for Microsoft Networks" service, then click on the Properties button. The Properties dialog is sectioned into two areas. The top section, titled "Logon Validation" is used in conjunction with a Windows NT domain controller and is discussed in Chapter 4.

The lower portion of the window, titled "Network Logon Options," contains two options: Quick Logon or Logon and Restore Network Connections, as shown in Figure 3-15.

If you choose the second option, Windows 98 restores your mapped network drives and printers every time you boot. Because it takes a little time to restore drive mappings, you should choose the Quick Logon option if you don't need to restore mapped drives every time you boot. Printer mappings are still remembered, but won't be connected until they are needed. In either case, you can always map additional drives, or re-map commonly used drives, whenever you want to do so.

That's it. Now you're ready to access other computers on the network.

## Browsing the Network Neighborhood

The best way to get familiar with Windows 98 networking is to browse the Windows Network Neighborhood. Start by double-clicking on the Network Neighborhood icon on your desktop.

The Network Neighborhood automatically displays all computers in your work-group (see Figure 3-16). To browse the file and printer shares available on any listed computer, just double-click on its icon.

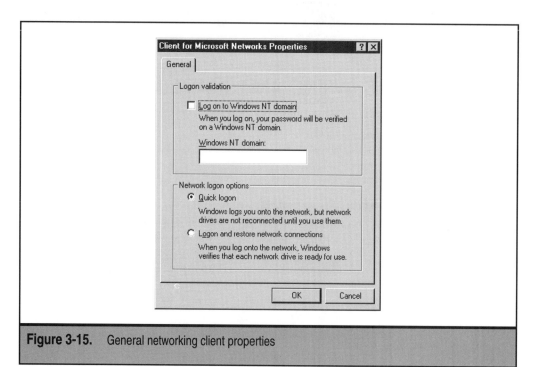

**Figure 3-15.**    General networking client properties

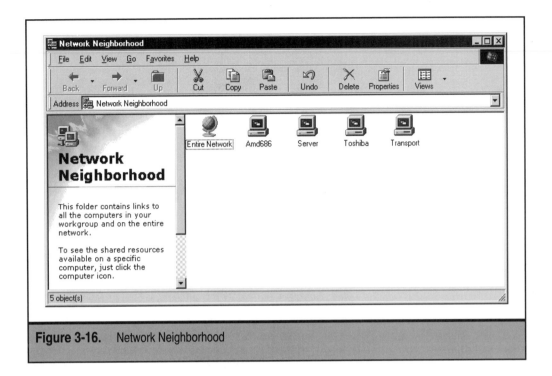

**Figure 3-16.**    Network Neighborhood

Another dialog box opens, displaying all available shared drives on the selected computer (see Figure 3-17). Of course, just like browsing local files on your own computer, you can change the display format between large icons, small icons, details, and list views from either the View menu or by clicking on the Views button on the toolbar.

## Mapping Network Drives

Mapping a drive letter is as simple as right-clicking on the desired drive and choosing Map Network Drive from the pop-up menu to open this dialog box:

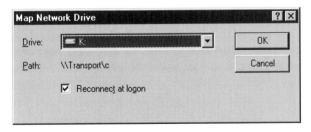

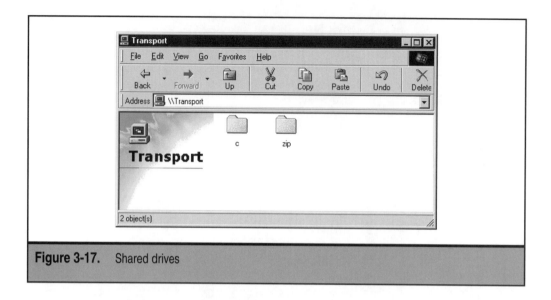

**Figure 3-17.** Shared drives

If the selected drive requires a password, you are prompted to enter it now, as shown here:

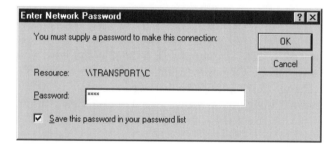

We have been browsing the network and mapping shared drives through the Network Neighborhood. You can also do the same thing from Windows Explorer by expanding the Network Neighborhood and right-clicking on the drive letters that are displayed.

## Configuring Network Printers

Configuring network printers is just as easy as mapping network drives. There are basically two different ways to do it: from the Network Neighborhood or from the Windows Printer dialog box.

## Configuration from Network Neighborhood

You can install and configure any network printer you find in the Network Neighborhood by simply right-clicking on it with your mouse, then choosing Install from the menu. This opens the Add Printer Wizard, which is shown in Figure 3-18.

The wizard walks you through several questions, then gives you the option to print a test page to make sure the printer is installed and working correctly.

## Configuration from Add Printer

The second way to add a printer is from the Printers dialog box. You can open the Printers dialog box by clicking on Start, and selecting Settings then Printers, or by double-clicking on the My Computer icon on your desktop and selecting the Printers icon.

From the Printers dialog box, you can double-click on the Add Printer icon, which launches the Add Printer Wizard. The wizard again prompts you through a series of questions. When prompted to specify whether the printer you are configuring is a Local printer or a Network printer, select Network printer (see Figure 3-19).

The next screen, shown in Figure 3-20, prompts you for the path to the printer. If you know the name of the computer that owns the printer and the share name of the printer itself, you can enter it here. Printer paths use the Universal Naming Convention (UNC)

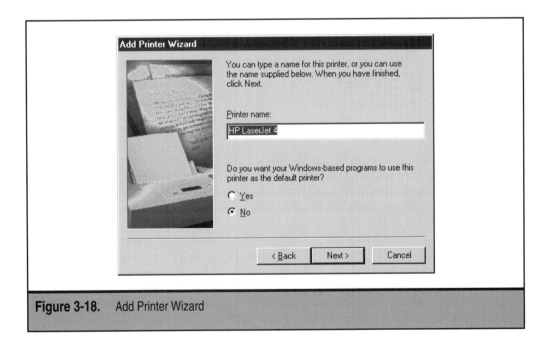

**Figure 3-18.**   Add Printer Wizard

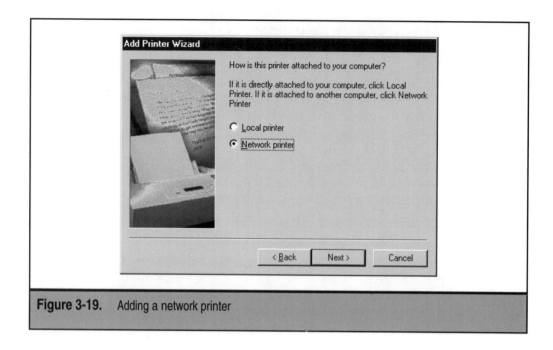

**Figure 3-19.** Adding a network printer

format just like shared drive mappings do. They begin with two backslashes, followed by the name of the hosting computer, another backslash, then the share name. For example, a printer named HPLaser that is owned by the computer named SERVER would be addressed as \\SERVER\HPLaser. If you're not sure of the printer path, click on the Browse button.

The Browse for Printer dialog box, shown in Figure 3-21, looks very similar to the Network Neighborhood, except that it does not show shared drives, only shared Printers.

Explore the Network Neighborhood until you locate the printer you want to install, then simply select it by clicking on the printer then clicking on the OK button. You are returned to the Add Printer Wizard with the proper value already entered in the "Network Path or Queue Name" field. Now, just click on the Next button and complete the rest of the wizard as before.

When you add a network printer, Windows tries to load the necessary printer drivers over the network, from the computer that owns it. If for some reason the drivers on that computer are not compatible with Windows 98, you are prompted to enter your Windows 98 CD-ROM.

Now you can use the network printer the same way you use your own local printers. You can even set it as your default printer or double-click the icon to view the status of your queued print jobs.

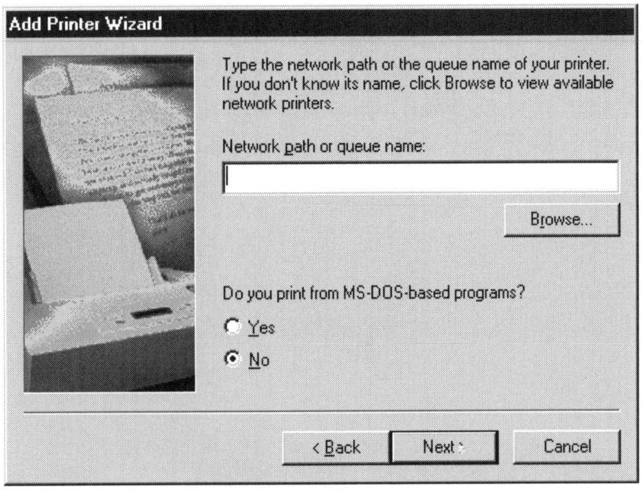

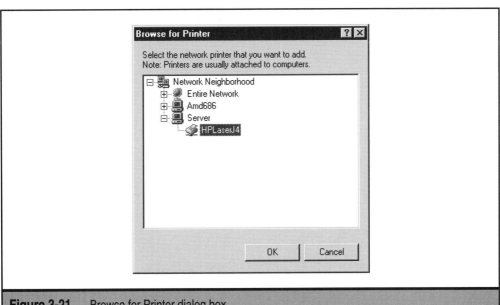

**Figure 3-20.**   Entering the network path or queue name

**Figure 3-21.**   Browse for Printer dialog box

## COMING UP

In Chapter 4, we discuss using Windows 98 in a Windows NT network. The chapter includes another review of networking protocols and step-by-step instructions for Windows 98 network configuration, but this time with a focus toward integrating Windows 98 with Windows NT.

NETWORK
PROFESSIONAL'S
LIBRARY

# CHAPTER 4

# Networking with Windows NT

## What's ahead:

- Why network with Windows NT?
- Connecting with Windows NT
- Working with Windows NT

*"So much depends
upon
a red wheel
barrow."*

— William Carlos Williams

Just three years ago, Windows NT was simply a high-powered alternative to desktop operating systems such as Windows 95. Then, no one would have thought it would ever become an alternative operating system to such powerhouses as Novell NetWare or even UNIX. After all, NetWare and UNIX were both designed to support hundreds, even thousands, of users across entire companies, not just for a person's desktop as with Windows 95. Yet that is just what happened. Windows NT began its rise to power by first becoming a better file and print server than NetWare. It then went on to rival UNIX as a robust, scaleable, and secure platform for executing core business applications.

**SOAPBOX:** Actually, there are two versions of Windows NT. There's Windows NT Server and Windows NT Workstation. Both act and look identical. However, NT Server uses a flat licensing fee to accommodate thousands and millions of users, while NT Workstation uses a per-user licensing structure to accommodate a small number of users.

The best place to see this phenomenal growth is in the Web server industry. Windows NT Server, coupled with Microsoft's Internet Information Server (IIS), has eclipsed what used to be the Internet's primary Web server platform, UNIX. According to Microsoft, over 56 percent of companies planning to deploy Web servers during 1998 are going to do so using Windows NT Server. Compare that with only 8 percent from the same study who plan to deploy Web servers over UNIX.

**RESOURCE:** To find out more about Windows NT Server, point your Web browser toward http://www.microsoft.com/ntserver/default.asp. For Windows NT Workstation, browse instead http://www.microsoft.com/ntworkstation/.

Because Windows NT has been able to mimic and even surpass UNIX and NetWare, chances are you will run into this operating system at some point in your travels. You may need to connect to a Windows NT server in order to print to an office printer. You may need to connect to a Windows NT server to run a shared application. Or you may need to connect to a Windows NT server simply to store files centrally, on a network. Luckily, regardless of your reasons, you will find your experience with Windows NT simple, flexible, even pleasant. This is because Windows NT is almost exactly like Windows 98. It uses the same networking protocols. It connects with the same network resources. It even uses the same interface to browse network services. To connect with a

Windows NT machine from Windows 98, all you need to do is open your Network Neighborhood folder and select the desired machine icon (see Figure 4-1).

Well, it is the same while working from Windows NT. Both Windows 98 and Windows NT machines are treated identically within the Network Neighborhood folder (see Figure 4-2).

As you might expect, despite their similarities, there are some differences between Windows NT and Windows 98 that bear mentioning. For starters, Windows NT uses an entirely different security and authentication system. For example, you cannot access Windows NT data without an authorized user name and password as you can with Windows 98. You must have a user account with proper access rights on a Windows NT server before you can access any of its resources.

During the remainder of this chapter, we explore these similarities and differences as they apply to Windows connectivity. We begin with a quick introduction to Windows NT and then move on to an overview of the requirements for networking with Windows NT. That done, we go through the steps required to set up your Windows 98 networking software. We then connect with Windows NT and end this chapter with some practical advice on how to work with Windows NT resources such as drives, applications, and printers.

# WHY NETWORK WITH WINDOWS NT?

At first glance, Windows NT and Windows 98 appear to be one and the same operating system. As shown previously, they both share similar networking and interface characteristics. But that is where the similarities end. Unlike Windows 98, which was built upon two generations of operating systems (Windows 3.1 and Windows 95), Windows NT in its current incarnation (Windows NT 4.0) is the same operating system now as it was when it was originally built by Microsoft in the early 1990s. From its inception, Windows NT was designed to provide users with a Windows operating environment with four basic important characteristics:

▼   A very high performance kernel

■   A robust application architecture

■   An industry-acknowledged security mechanism

▲   Superior application support

## Performance

Windows NT was built upon an experimental UNIX kernel called the Mach OS, which was multithreaded and preemptive. With these two features, Windows NT is capable of running any Windows NT application built with Microsoft's Win32 Application Programming Interface (API) as though it were multiple applications. That is, it can preemptively assign different threads within such an application to run as though they

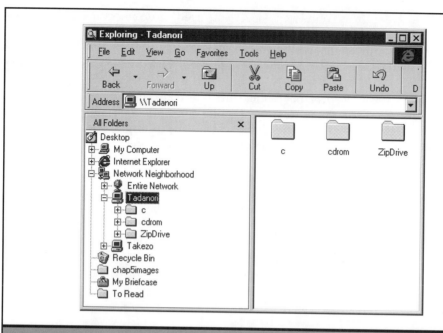

**Figure 4-1.** Connecting to a Windows NT machine from Windows 98

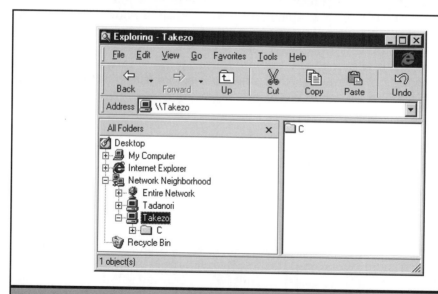

**Figure 4-2.** Connecting to a Windows 98 machine from Windows NT

were unique applications. On a multiprocessor system (a computer with two or more CPUs), these applications can run simultaneously on different processors. The result is, quite simply, blazing speed. To give you an idea of how fast this is, take a look at Microsoft's Web site at http://www.microsoft.com/. Powered by Compaq Pentium Pro servers running Windows NT, Microsoft's Web site (which is comprised of over 35 servers) delivers over 200,000 Web pages and handles over 120 million hits each day!

## Robustness

Speed is not Windows NT's only strong point. Using a technology called protected subsystems, Windows NT can basically isolate these applications and threads from one another in completely separate memory spaces. If one application or thread crashes, the rest of the application or other applications remain unaffected. Moreover, once such an error occurs, that error is trapped and funneled through a service called Dr. Watson. This tool acts a bit like an application debugger in that it can tell you exactly what went wrong.

**SOAPBOX:** The inability to isolate applications from one another has plagued both Windows 3.1 and Windows 95. Though most Win32 applications running on Windows 95 are safely separated from one another, older applications (such as MS-DOS applications) can bring the whole system down. Thankfully, Windows 98 has adopted much of Windows NT's protected subsystem architecture, greatly improving its stability. Also, Windows 98 now sports its own version of Dr. Watson, easing problem resolution efforts.

## Security

Windows NT also scores top marks in security, receiving a C-2 level security rating from the U.S. Government for both the desktop and server. Basically, this means that applications can't steal user names and passwords from one another or from the operating system. It means that Windows NT can be audited to ensure that nothing funny is going on or has gone on in the past. It also means that no one can gain access to a Windows NT machine without a unique user name and password.

**RESOURCE:** We'll get to how these security features affect your ability to connect with a Windows NT machine later in the section entitled "Working with Windows NT," but if you want to read up on C-2 security and Windows NT, you can point your Web browser toward Microsoft's security FAQ at http://www.microsoft.com/ntserver/guide/security_faq.asp?A=2&B=10.

Perhaps the best example of Windows NT's security mechanism is its discretionary access control. This capability lets individual users act as the owners of objects within Windows NT. For example, user A could own a directory such as C:\users\userA. Also, a user could own a service such as a Windows NT backup procedure. Being C-2 compliant means that these two and only these two individuals can manage and control access to their respective services.

## Applications

These features aside, the best reason to network with Windows NT is its application support.

Inarguably, the Windows platform (NT, 95, 98) owns the world application market. There are more developers writing to Windows than to any other operating system. And why not? By writing to one Windows OS via the Win32 API, developers automatically gain application support on the other two Windows OSs. An accounting package that runs on Windows NT, for example, can just as easily run on Windows 98. There are some exceptions, of course. For example, if a developer writes an application as a service and not as a process, that application can only run on Windows NT, which supports both processes and services. This may sound like a mark against Windows 98 and Windows 95, but in reality it is what makes networking with Windows NT worthwhile.

*JARGON:* What's a service and what's a process? Well, a service is basically an application that runs as a part of the operating system and a process is basically an application executed by a user. A service is good for server-only applications, because it does not execute under a user's account, and because it does not have to work totally within the confines of Windows' protected subsystems architecture. This makes it more secure and more powerful. A great example of a service is Windows NT's IIS Web server.

We spend most of this chapter discussing how you can log on to a Windows NT server as a local user, where you can execute applications as processes. However, that is only half of the story. The other half deals with services, where you simply connect with an application running on a Windows NT machine. This is how most network-based applications function. A good example of a process is Microsoft Word. You execute and interact with it directly within the operating system as a specific user. With application services, such as a Web server, however, you can connect to a Windows NT machine without logging on as a user. Your Web client simply talks directly with a Web service running on the server (see Figure 4-3).

## CONNECTING WITH WINDOWS NT

Before you can begin executing applications or storing files on a Windows NT machine, you have to set your Windows 98 client up so that it can talk with Windows NT. Fortunately, if you have already configured Windows 98 to talk to other Windows 98 clients (see Chapter 3), your machine is all ready to connect to Windows NT. This is possible because both Windows NT and Windows 98 can use the same networking protocols. If you've already done so, and you have the network functionality you desire,

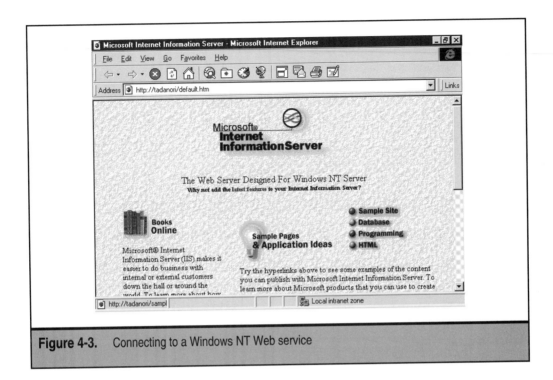

**Figure 4-3.** Connecting to a Windows NT Web service

skip ahead to the last section in this chapter, entitled "Working with Windows NT." However, if you need to install and configure a different protocol than that which you are already using, or if you want to make sure that your existing networking connection is configured properly, do read on.

## What You Need to Know to Network with Windows NT

Before you can begin networking with Windows NT, you need to do a little research. As with any important venture, the more information you have at your fingertips, the smoother the journey will be. Before you begin linking up machines, consider the following two areas:

▼ Protocol Selection

▲ Security and Authentication

In short, you need to know which protocols to use to connect with Windows NT. You need to find out if you have access to your "target" Windows NT machine, gathering the appropriate information. And depending upon the protocol you have selected, you have to find out exactly what you can do once connected.

## Protocol Selection

As stated previously, both Windows NT and Windows 98 have access to the same protocols, which include:

▼ NetBIOS (Network Basic Input/Output System)

■ NetBEUI (NetBIOS Extended User Interface)

■ IPX/SPX (Internetwork Packet Exchange/Sequenced Packet Exchange)

■ ATM (Asynchronous Transfer Mode)

■ DLC (Data Link Control)

▲ TCP/IP (Transmission Control Protocol/Internet Protocol)

If this list looks a bit ponderous, don't worry. Windows 98 really does not need all of these protocols to connect with Windows NT. On the contrary, you can get by with just NetBEUI or just TCP/IP. However, this is not to say that these protocols can be used interchangeably. Each was designed to perform very specific networking tasks with very specific applications and operating systems. For instance, IPX/SPX was built by Novell to give users a client/server connection to their Network Operating System (NOS), NetWare. With IPX/SPX, NetWare users can print to a network printer or open files stored on a NetWare server. TCP/IP was built by the same folks who created UNIX and the Internet to give users peer-to-peer connectivity over Wide Area Networks (WANs). With TCP/IP, users can connect to another machine halfway around the world and work on that machine as though they were sitting right in front of it.

NetBEUI sits between these two protocols in functionality. You can use it to print from or store files on a Windows NT machine. Or you can use it to log on to a Windows NT machine and execute remote applications as though they were local. However, you can't use it to access any IPX/SPX- or TCP/IP-centric applications or services. For example, unless someone built a Web server that used NetBEUI as a transport protocol, you couldn't use NetBEUI to browse Web pages on a Windows NT server. The other protocols listed in this section are not customarily used with Windows NT, although they can be. For this reason, these other protocols are discussed in more appropriate chapters and the current discussion is confined to NetBEUI, TCP/IP, and IPX/SPX.

The magic of networking with Windows NT is that you don't have to really choose between these three protocols. You can simply use them all because Windows 98 can assign more than one protocol to a single Network Interface Card (NIC). However, before you load all of the protocols you've got on your Windows 98 machine, consider carefully your connectivity needs. Each protocol requires processing time. Add protocols indiscriminately, and you'll end up with poor network performance.

**NETBEUI**   NetBEUI, in short, is a quick, lightweight protocol designed for efficient client/server connections within the confines of a Local Area Network (LAN). It was born into the Microsoft Windows family of networking protocols to connect Windows 3.x for Workgroups machines or connect Windows 3.x machines to a Microsoft LAN Manager server. Consequently, it wasn't built to route over WANs, or any network with more than one network segment for that matter. So right up front, be aware that if you intend to connect to a remote Windows NT server (even one in another department in the same company), NetBEUI is not the protocol for you. What NetBEUI can do for you, however, is provide very ubiquitous connections within a predominantly Windows shop. If you've got perhaps 50 or so machines running on a LAN Manager, Windows for Workgroups, or Windows NT single-segment LAN, NetBEUI will get you connected to all parties involved quickly and easily.

**SOAPBOX:**   If NetBEUI sounds a bit low-powered, consider that in all versions of Windows NT, NetBEUI in one form or another has been used as a lightweight communications medium between Windows NT servers. In a Windows NT domain, for example, two or more servers will use NetBEUI to propagate user synchronization information.

**NETBEUI FUNCTIONALITY**   With NetBEUI as your sole network protocol, you are able to connect to Windows NT machines, log into those machines, and manipulate files thereupon. In short, you can perform virtually any Windows NT task. However, NetBEUI is not a complete protocol in the Open Systems Interconnection (OSI) scheme of things. It only covers the Network and Transport layers, hanging the more application-specific Session, Presentation, and Application layers out to dry.

## OSI Protocol Reference Model

The OSI protocol reference model contains the following layers:

| | |
|---|---|
| 7 | Application |
| 6 | Presentation |
| 5 | Session |
| 4 | Transport |
| 3 | Network |
| 2 | Data-Link |
| 1 | Physical |

For this reason, while you are able to connect with a Windows NT machine, that same Windows NT machine isn't able to connect with you. Moreover, you aren't able to connect with yourself (should you wish to do so). What NetBEUI needs is a little help from other more application-savvy protocols such as IPX/SPX or TCP/IP. In essence, what it needs is another protocol to ride over. If you simply add IPX/SPX to NetBEUI, for example, and enable NetBIOS over IPX/SPX, you'll be ready to run NetBEUI applications without having to install the entire protocol stack. For more information about this, see the section entitled "Installing Protocols" later in this chapter. It is suggested, therefore, that you use NetBEUI as a base protocol, to which you add a secondary protocol, depending upon your needs. You'll find it quite useful regardless of what applications you run, as Windows 98, Windows NT, and Windows 95 use it to compile a list of available computers on a network. That is, when you open your Network Neighborhood dialog box, it is NetBEUI that Windows 98 uses to present you with a list of available servers.

**TCP/IP**    By far, of the two choices as secondary protocols for NetBEUI, TCP/IP is the most useful for most networking environments. This robust protocol is as old as the Internet. For the uninitiated, that is right around 30 years. It was developed by a group of college students from the University of California at Berkeley as a networking protocol for a then new operating system called UNIX. It was designed to provide UNIX users with peer-to-peer networking services. For example, an engineering student who needs to log on to another student's UNIX machine to compile or test a program could simply use TCP/IP to establish that connection. The result was that this student's computer became a simple terminal to the other student's.

Because the Internet grew out of the UNIX-based college milieu, today you can use a peer-to-peer TCP/IP application such as FTP to log on to any one of the millions of machines on the Internet to download, upload, or manage files. However, TCP/IP's real fame and usefulness stems from its adoption by Tim Berners Lee in the early 90s as the Web's protocol of choice. If you're browsing the Web in any way, shape, or form, you're doing it via the Hypertext Transport Protocol (HTTP), which rides only across TCP/IP.

**TCP/IP FUNCTIONALITY**    The best part about TCP/IP's success on the Internet is that it has translated to the world of LANs and WANs as well. When you install Windows 98, Windows NT, or virtually any other operating system, your basic, default protocol is TCP/IP. In this way, TCP/IP has become the lingua franca of networking. Everyone understands it. However, that "everyone" still does not include OSs themselves. Windows 98 and Windows NT still must speak NetBEUI or IPX/SPX in order to exchange user name and password information. This is because TCP/IP is still an application's protocol. You will find it most useful for applications like the Web and FTP, but not so for Windows NT. For this reason, we suggest that you use TCP/IP in conjunction with either IPX/SPX or NetBEUI. (We discuss how to do this in the section entitled "Configuring Protocols.")

*RESOURCE:* For more information on network protocols, refer to Appendix B.

**IPX/SPX**  Novell's flagship protocol, IPX/SPX, is a well-rounded, complete protocol designed to provide users with blazingly fast file and print services. It is built into the Novell NetWare NOS as its basic protocol, though recently Novell has expended considerable effort porting IPX/SPX services to TCP/IP. As a matter of fact, Microsoft intends to use TCP/IP as the default protocol on Windows NT. Unlike NetBEUI, IPX/SPX is a complete protocol. It does not need anything more to provide connectivity. It can also function over more than one LAN segment. However, unlike TCP/IP, it cannot provide very good WAN services, placing its optimal-sized network somewhere between what is manageable with TCP/IP and NetBEUI.

**IPX/SPX FUNCTIONALITY**  Because it is a complete protocol, if you choose, you can use just IPX/SPX to connect with your Windows NT machine. All you need to do is ensure that you have the Microsoft Client for Microsoft Networks service installed (more on that in a minute) on the client and IPX/SPX installed on the Windows NT machine (because it is not a typical Windows NT protocol as are NetBEUI and TCP/IP). So why install it? Well, if you are working in an environment that contains NetWare servers, the decision to use IPX/SPX is an easy one. You might, for example, have Novell NetWare Directory Services (NDS) installed on a Windows NT machine, for which IPX/SPX on the client becomes a requirement. Also, you might be migrating to Windows NT from NetWare. Here, you could use IPX/SPX to facilitate that migration because both operating systems support it.

**PROTOCOL RECOMMENDATIONS**  To put all of this protocol talk into perspective, it is recommended that you install a combination of these three protocols based upon the following criteria:

1. For Windows for Workgroups or LAN Manager environments, run NetBEUI.

2. For Internet connectivity or an environment with UNIX workstations, install TCP/IP along with NetBEUI.

3. For a Novell NetWare environment, install IPX/SPX and NetBEUI.

Of course, if you are working in an environment that meets more than one of these criteria, it is suggested that you simply install those protocols required to connect to the machines in use, keeping in mind that NetBEUI requires IPX/SPX or TCP/IP for full functionality. For example, if you have a NetWare environment with LAN Manager servers, install NetBEUI with IPX/SPX. Conversely, if you have a Windows NT environment and Internet connectivity, install both NetBEUI and TCP/IP.

## Security and Authentication

Though not as complicated as protocol selection, researching your security and authentication requirements is no less important. If you don't find out what security requirements you must meet in order to connect to a Windows NT machine, you'll never get your connectivity efforts off the ground.

The first thing to find out is whether or not your target Windows NT machine is a part of a domain. This becomes important later on. If it is not a part of a domain, then it is a part of what Windows NT calls a Workgroup. This is a loose collection of computers that are visible to one another. In either case, you must ensure that you know the name of that domain or Workgroup and that you have a user name and password for it. Here's an example:

▼ Domain or Workgroup: Tadanori

■ User name: bshimmin

▲ Password: mypassword

*JARGON:* What is a Windows NT domain? Quite simply, it is a technology that allows multiple Windows NT machines to act like one machine from a security perspective. Once you log into a domain, you have instant access to all of the servers in that domain to which you are allowed access. This saves you from having to authenticate with each machine one at a time.

To create a user name and password, you must use Windows NT's User Manager for Domains (see Figure 4-4).

Just ensure that this tool is pointing at the right domain or workgroup (e.g., Tadanori), select the User pull-down menu, select New User, and follow the prompts. Figure 4-5 shows the New User dialog box.

If you are not the administrator for the Windows NT domain or workgroup to which you want to connect, you must contact your systems administrator for help with this.

# What You Need to Do to Network with Windows NT

Once you have made up your mind about the protocols you will run and have obtained your domain/Workgroup authentication information, all that's left is to install the protocols and point your Windows 98 client in the right direction.

## Installing Protocols

To begin, click on the Start button from the Windows 98 desktop, select the Settings option, and click on the Control Panel selection. This opens Windows 98's Control Panel, a collection of system configuration utilities. Once there, double-click on the Network icon.

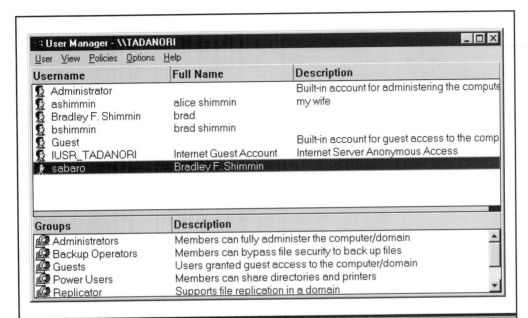

**Figure 4-4.** Windows NT's User Manager for Domains

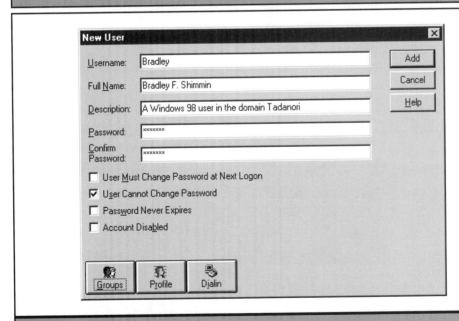

**Figure 4-5.** New User dialog box

▼ *SHORTCUT:* If you don't like double-clicking on icons, select the View pull-down menu from the Control Panel, click on the Folder Options selection at the bottom, and select Web style from the General tab. This enables you to single-click on icons in the Control Panel folder (or all folders, should you choose it) to activate them, just like the Web!

This opens the Network dialog box, from which you perform the rest of the network configuration routine (see Figure 4-6).

Notice in Figure 4-6 that only a dial-up adapter and an NIC (in this case an Intel PCI Ethernet Adapter) are listed as installed network components. Normally, when you install Windows 98, it auto-detects your network adapter and modem and installs a base protocol stack (TCP/IP). Because we are going to install all three protocols (TCP/IP, IPX/SPX, and NetBEUI), we've simply deleted TCP/IP to get a fresh start.

If you already have TCP/IP installed, you can leave it if you wish and simply follow along during the "Configuring TCP/IP" section later in this chapter. If you don't see anything listed in the Network dialog box, then you need to run the Add New Hardware wizard from the Control Panel folder, assuming you have a NIC installed in the first

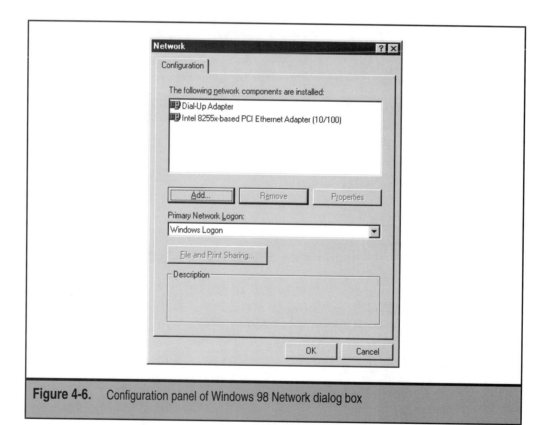

**Figure 4-6.** Configuration panel of Windows 98 Network dialog box

place. If that does not work, you must contact your network administrator or Information Technologies (IT) manager for further hardware assistance before you continue.

To get rolling, click on the Add button from the Network dialog box. This opens a small window from which you can select a number of different networking components. Each of these is further explained a little later, but for now, select the Protocol item and click on the Add button. This opens a dialog box entitled Select Network Protocol. From here, click on the Manufacturer Microsoft, select NetBEUI, and click on the OK button (see Figure 4-7).

This takes you back to the main Network dialog box (see Figure 4-8).

Notice how there are two entries for NetBEUI. One of the nice things about Windows 98 is that if you have more than one NIC or a NIC and a modem, it automatically creates protocol bindings for each device. In Figure 4-8, you can see that each NetBEUI entry points to a different device—one to a modem and one to a NIC. Also notice how there is a new component in the Configuration window, the Client for Microsoft Networks. This is the key to networking with Windows NT. Without it, you won't be able to connect to Windows NT or any Microsoft networking platform. It controls how you access a server, which is further discussed shortly. For now, let's finish adding the other two protocols, TCP/IP and IPX/SPX. Because multiple protocols can use the same client, you can simply configure all of them at the same time. To install TCP/IP and IPX/SPX, just follow the same procedure as when you added NetBEUI, selecting instead TCP/IP from the Select Network Protocol

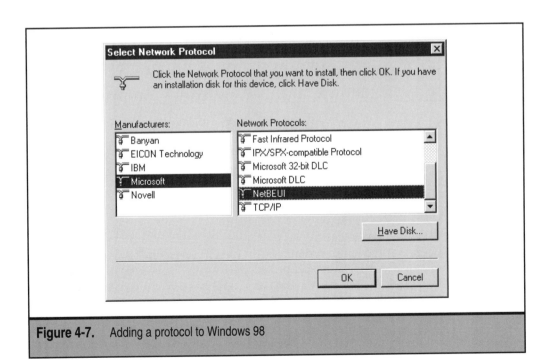

**Figure 4-7.**    Adding a protocol to Windows 98

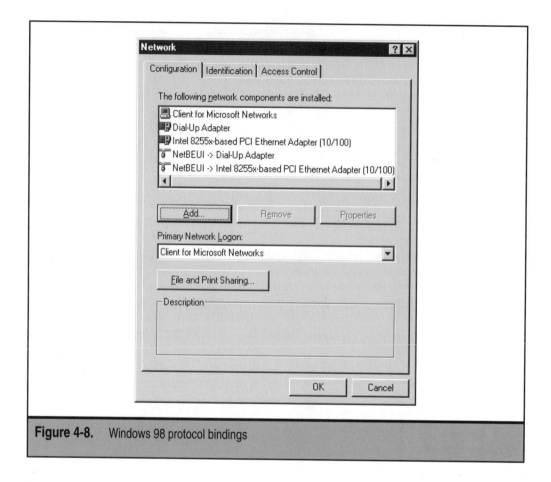

**Figure 4-8.** Windows 98 protocol bindings

dialog box (see Figure 4-9). Now repeat this procedure once again, selecting IPX/SPX instead of TCP/IP, and you'll have installed all of the appropriate protocols based upon our previous recommendations and your network needs.

## Using Your Own Protocols

In this book, we have chosen to use the protocols supplied with Windows 98. However, you are not so bound. You can use protocols provided by any vendor. In Chapter 5, for example, we use Novell's own IPX/SPX protocol stack. Just as you might use Novell's protocol to connect with Novell servers, we've simply chosen to work with Microsoft protocols in connecting with Microsoft servers. But if you prefer or need to use an alternate protocol, all you have to do is follow the same procedure as outlined previously,

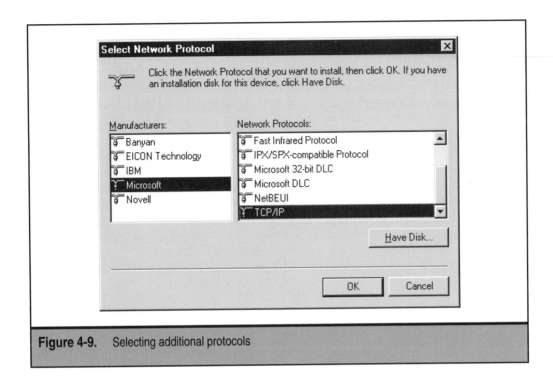

**Figure 4-9.** Selecting additional protocols

but instead of selecting Microsoft, just click on the Have Disk button. This pops up a dialog box like the one that follows.

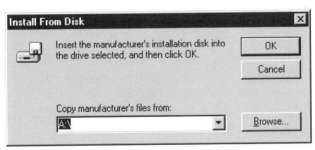

Insert the appropriate vendor-provided floppy or specify the correct file location (such as C:\TMP\), and click OK. That's all there is to it. The *.INF file that comes with vendor-provided protocols such as Novell's IPX/SPX will tell Windows 98 how to install your protocol properly.

**SHORTCUT:**   As you saw in Figure 4-8, when you install a protocol, it is automatically bound to all available devices, including both NICs and modems. This is great because it can save you time reinstalling and reconfiguring duplicate protocols. However, if you aren't going to use protocols such as NetBEUI or IPX/SPX on a dial-up connection via modem, then you might as well remove them. They just slow your computer down. To do this from the Configuration tab in the Network dialog box, click on the protocol you want to get rid of and click the Remove button. That's all there is to it.

## Installing a Service

Now that you've installed your protocols and the Client for Microsoft Networks, you should install a networking service, specifically the File and printer sharing for Microsoft Networks service. This service, though not necessary for basic connectivity, lets you share your printers with other users (see Figure 4-10).

To install File and printer sharing for Microsoft Networks, just click on the Add button from the Configuration tab within the Network dialog box. Then click on the Service component type. This opens a Network Service dialog box (Figure 4-11), from

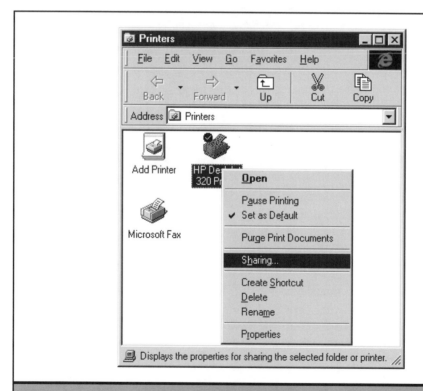

**Figure 4-10.**    Printer sharing with Windows 98

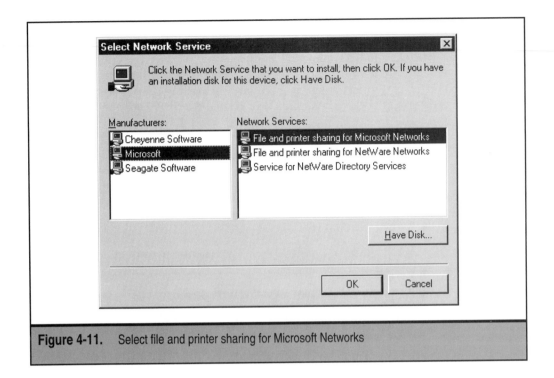

**Figure 4-11.**    Select file and printer sharing for Microsoft Networks

which you should select Microsoft, highlight File and printer sharing for Microsoft Networks, and click OK.

That's all there is to it. There's nothing really to configure with this service. We talk about using it in just a bit. But now, it's time to configure the protocols you recently installed.

## Configuring Protocols

Though it sounds a bit scary, configuring protocols does not require very much effort. You simply have to make a few decisions about such issues as a default protocol, an IP address, NetBIOS, and a few others.

**SETTING A DEFAULT PROTOCOL**    Once you have all of your protocols ready to go, you must tell Windows 98 how to use them in connecting with other computers (especially Windows NT). The first thing to do here depends greatly upon your Windows NT server. Although most modern computers and NICs know how to manage multiple protocols on a single network connection, only one protocol gets to be the primary protocol. In networking with Windows NT using the Client for Microsoft Networks, you are only able to make NetBEUI or TCP/IP your default protocol. IPX/SPX simply cannot be set as such.

Actually, specifying a default protocol is not a do-or-die requirement, but it is a good idea when you connect predominantly to a single server or to a single protocol on many servers. You see, when you boot Windows 98, this primary protocol leaps into action first.

The others simply follow on, which means that if your Windows NT server is running IPX/SPX as its primary protocol, and you're running TCP/IP as your primary protocol, your computer will have to do some extra handshaking in order to connect properly. Once you have determined your default protocol, select the corresponding protocol in the Configuration tab of the Network dialog box and click on the Properties button. Click on the Advanced tab and click on the check box labeled *Set this protocol to be the default protocol* (see Figure 4-12).

**CONFIGURING NETBEUI**    Of the three protocols we installed, NetBEUI is by far the easiest to configure. All you have to do once you've selected either it or one of its partner protocols as a default protocol is ensure that it is bound to the right network component. That is, you must ensure that it is going to talk to both the Client for Microsoft Networks and the File and printer sharing for Microsoft Networks service.

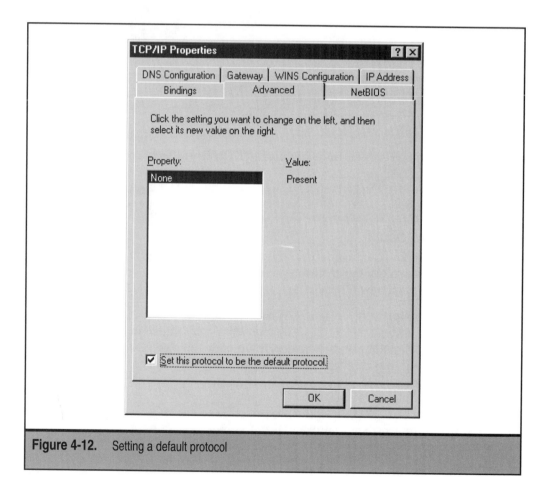

**Figure 4-12.**    Setting a default protocol

**SHORTCUT:**   Actually, you don't need to bind all of your protocols to the File and printer sharing for Microsoft Networks service. You can just bind one of them, perhaps IPX/SPX alone or NetBEUI and TCP/IP together, to this service and remove the bindings from the other protocols using the same procedure as setting up bindings. Again, just as when you removed protocols from unnecessary devices (a modem), this helps your computer run faster.

To ensure that NetBEUI is bound properly, select it from the Configuration tab in the Network dialog box and click on the Properties button. Once there, select the Bindings tab and look to make sure that both the service and the client are selected, as shown in Figure 4-13.

You can leave the Advanced tab alone unless you experience difficulties connecting to Windows NT. For more on such problems, refer to Appendix C.

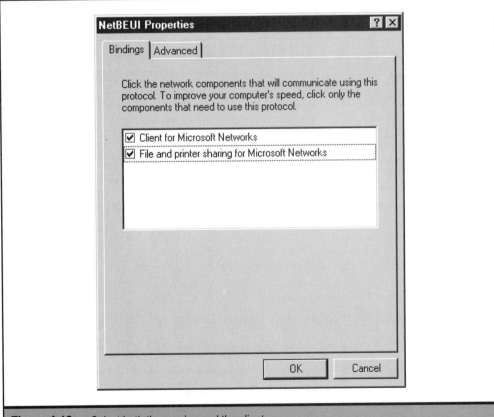

**Figure 4-13.**   Select both the service and the client

*CAUTION:* When you install protocols such as NetBEUI, Windows 98 automatically binds them to all available services (NICs, modems, and so forth). You should take care not to leave NetBEUI bound to all services. Only bind NetBEUI to the services you need. For example, if you won't use it over a modem, ensure that NetBEUI does not bind to that service. The more services a single protocol is bound to, the greater the system load will be and the slower your machine will perform.

**CONFIGURING IPX/SPX**   Going up the scale of difficulty one notch from NetBEUI is IPX/SPX. Here, you of course need to first check to see that it is bound to the appropriate client and service, as stated previously. Second, however, you need to apply your knowledge of the types of applications running on your network to decide whether or not to enable NetBIOS over IPX/SPX. You see, some applications, especially those built to run over Novell, LAN Manager, and IBM OS/2 networks, use NetBIOS as their main session layer protocol. So, if you have one of these networking environments or applications built for these environments running between your computer and a Windows NT machine, you must run NetBIOS over IPX/SPX. To do this, click on the Configuration button as you did with NetBEUI and select the NetBIOS tab. Here, just click the check box, and you're good to go.

*CAUTION:* Like any protocol, NetBIOS requires system resources. Therefore, choose to use it judiciously. If you don't think you need it, don't install it. Your machine will run better.

The last thing you need to do with IPX/SPX is set your Frame Type. Actually, the Microsoft-supplied IPX/SPX protocol does default to an automatic setting that will "supposedly" detect your frame type. But it is better to set it manually, just to be on the safe side.

*JARGON:* A frame type defines the structure of data as it passes over an Ethernet network. As you might imagine, different NOSs use different frame types, which is why you need to select a frame type appropriate to your NOS.

Once you have the IPX/SPX Properties dialog box open, click on the Advanced tab and select Frame Type. Then click on the Value pull-down menu and select the appropriate Frame Type. Just as a reminder, here are the available Frame Types and the type of networks they are associated with.

▼  Ethernet II: Used by DEC systems and AppletTalk Phase I networks

■  Ethernet 802.2: Used by Novell NetWare 4.x networks

■  Ethernet 802.3: Used by Novell NetWare 3.x networks

▲  Ethernet SNAP: Used by AppletTalk Phase II networks and TCP/IP networks

There are also two additional types: the Token Ring and Token Ring SNAP. These are used, as you might suspect, strictly with a Token Ring network infrastructure. If you've got such a network infrastructure, you'll know it.

**CONFIGURING TCP/IP**    The last and absolutely most difficult protocol to configure is TCP/IP. You've got to know a lot of information in order to properly configure this protocol. But before getting to the hard stuff, first open the TCP/IP Properties dialog box just as you did with NetBEUI and IPX/SPX and check your bindings. Once that's done, click on the NetBIOS tab. Notice that if you selected to run NetBIOS over IPX/SPX previously, you won't be able to specify it here, over TCP/IP.

Here's the hard part. Before you can connect to a Windows NT server using TCP/IP, you must first know the following information:

1. Either the IP address of your machine, or the IP address of the machine from which you will receive a dynamically allocated IP address, as with the Dynamic Host Configuration Protocol (DHCP).

2. If you are not using DHCP, and you have no IP address, you must know the IP address of your Windows Internet Naming Service (WINS).

3. If your network connects to a disparate network, such as the Internet or a WAN, you need to know the IP address of that network's gateway.

4. No matter what, you need to know the IP address and domain name for your Domain Name System (DNS) server.

Of these, two are crucial: Your IP address and your DNS server. Without these two, you won't be able to see or be seen by any other TCP/IP-based machines. If you are the administrator of your network, you most likely have all of these at your fingertips, but if you're a power-user, setting up your system all on your own, you definitely have to go to a higher source for this data. There's no room for error here.

**SHORTCUT:**    Actually, if you have an IP address, you can do away with a DNS server, assuming you know the IP addresses of the machines to which you wish to connect. This way, for example, you would simply enter a command such as:

```
Ping 1.1.1.30
```

Instead of

```
Ping myserver.mydomain.com
```

Once you've gotten your TCP/IP data together, the rest is easy. You simply have to plug the numbers into the appropriate fields under the appropriate tabs, including IP Address, Gateway, WINS Configuration, and DNS Configuration (as in Figure 4-14).

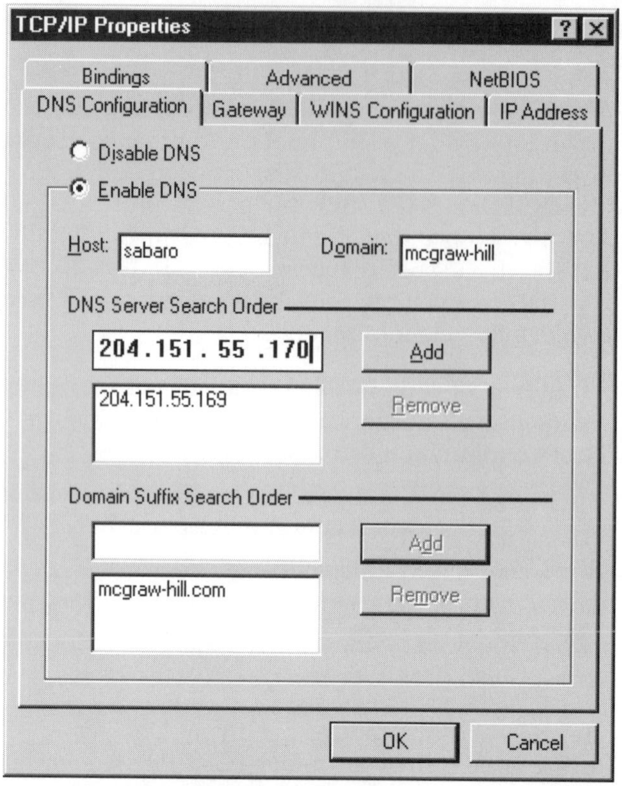

**Figure 4-14.** Inputting TCP/IP information

## Identification

The last step you need to take before you can begin networking with Windows NT is setting up the identification and authentication information on your computer. In essence, you need to tell the world who you are and that you wish to participate in a network. To accomplish this, you must first set up your computer's identity. Click on the Identification tab from the Network dialog box, and enter the name of your computer. The actual name is not important. You could use something like Sabaro. However, it is important that your computer's name be unique to prevent your computer from being mistaken for another computer. Then you must specify a group of computers or a domain to which you will belong under the file entitled Workgroup. You should get this name from your systems administrator, as it must match exactly the Workgroup name used by other members of the immediate network in which you want to work.

*SHORTCUT:* The most typical Workgroup name, believe it or not, is "workgroup."

The last thing to do here is enter a quick description of your computer. A good idea is to enter your full name and department (if applicable). Other computers use this field to get more information about your computer than what might be available from the computer name, Sabaro. When you're done, the Identification tab should look like the example shown in Figure 4-16.

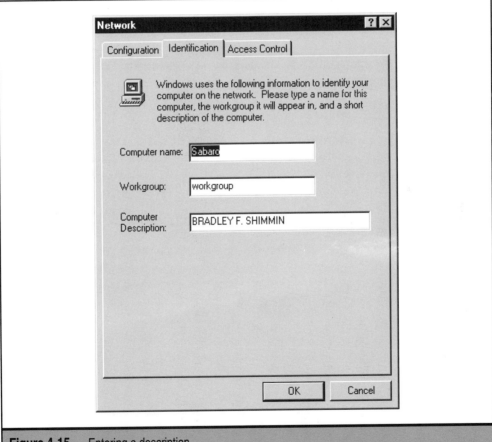

**Figure 4-15.** Entering a description

## Configuring the Client for Microsoft Networks

Now that your machine has a name, you must tell it how to use that name to gain access to a Windows NT machine. To do that, simply select the Client for Microsoft Networks item from the Configuration tab and click on the Properties button. Once there, you can tell your computer how to log on to Windows NT. If you're a member of a Windows NT domain, select the *Logon validation* check box and fill in the Windows NT domain controller's name (see Figure 4-16).

From the same dialog box, if you do not belong to a Windows NT domain, but instead use a Workgroup, you can ignore the *Logon validation* section and choose between two different logon methods:

▼ Quick logon

▲ Logon and restore network connections

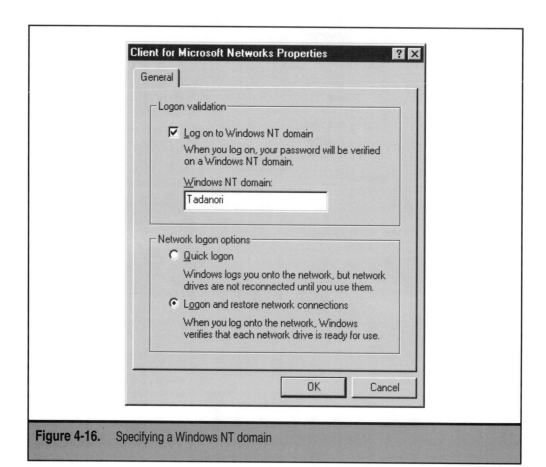

**Figure 4-16.** Specifying a Windows NT domain

Click on the *Quick logon* check box if you only want Windows 98 to restore any existing drive connections to a Windows NT machine that are broken by a reboot or shutdown. This option is the best if you are using a portable computer because it allows you to accidentally set a persistent connection (drive mapping) without reconnecting that drive the next time you boot your machine.

**JARGON:**   What's a persistent connection? With Windows 98, you can create drive letters (D:\, C:\, and the like) that point to remote machines on a network. Once set as persistent, each time you start Windows 98, it looks for those remote machines and reconnects your drive letters.

If you want your connections restored automatically—great for desktop installations—just select the *Logon and restore network connections* radio button, as shown in Figure 4-17.

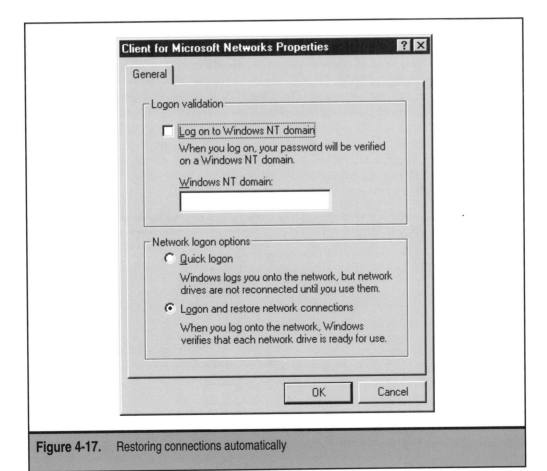

**Figure 4-17.**   Restoring connections automatically

That's it. That's all you need to do in order to connect with a Windows NT machine. However, before you do, it is a good idea to set up some sort of security for your system. We get into that topic in depth in Chapter 16. But for now, let's quickly run through the basic procedure—sans security—you need to perform to allow people to access your machine.

## Access Control

Once you've set up your identification, you must set up a form of access control for your computer. From the Network dialog box, click on the Access Control tab and select one of the two available options. You've basically got to choose between either share-level or user-level access control. With the former, you get to select passwords for each shared item on your computer. With the latter, you get to associate actual user names with each shared item. If you select user-level access control, you must specify the name of a Windows NT machine, on which resides the account names you want to use in securing your Windows 98 machine. We recommend that you go with a shared-level access control as it is the most simple solution, which also affords the most flexibility. And as you see in a moment, it also allows for the most transparent access to your computer. Basically, these two types of security differ in that user-level access requires each remote user to enter a user name and password in order to connect with your machine. User-level access control lets remote users simply connect with a password (or with nothing at all, if you choose to set up your machine that way).

To finish up your access control efforts, go back to the main Network dialog box and use the Primary Network Logon pull-down menu to select Client for Microsoft Networks instead of the Windows Logon default client. This tells Windows 98 to activate these protocols and send out an announcement of your server's availability over the network when you boot up. If you want other computers to have access to your files and printers, click on the File and Print Sharing button on the same Network dialog box and select both check boxes like so:

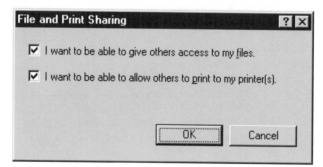

## Shares

To make your computer's files and printers accessible to other computers, you must finish by creating shares for those resources. A share basically identifies resources on your computer that you want to make available to other users on the network. It also identifies which users can access those resources through either user lists or passwords. You learn more about these issues in Chapter 16. So for now, just set up a quick share for your hard drive that allows users to gain access to your hard disk through a simple password. To accomplish this, just go to your Windows 98 Desktop, double-click on the icon labeled My Computer, right-click on the icon for the hard drive (C:), keeping in mind that you can give your hard drive virtually any name you choose. You should see on the resulting pop-up menu an item named Sharing. Click on this to open the Sharing tab on your hard disk's Properties dialog box (see Figure 4-18).

Click on the Shared As radio button to enable sharing on your hard disk, and give your hard disk a name in the next available field. This name appears as the name of your hard disk to other computers. Most people simply use the name, "C." It is also a good idea to enter more about your hard drive in the Comment field (such as your

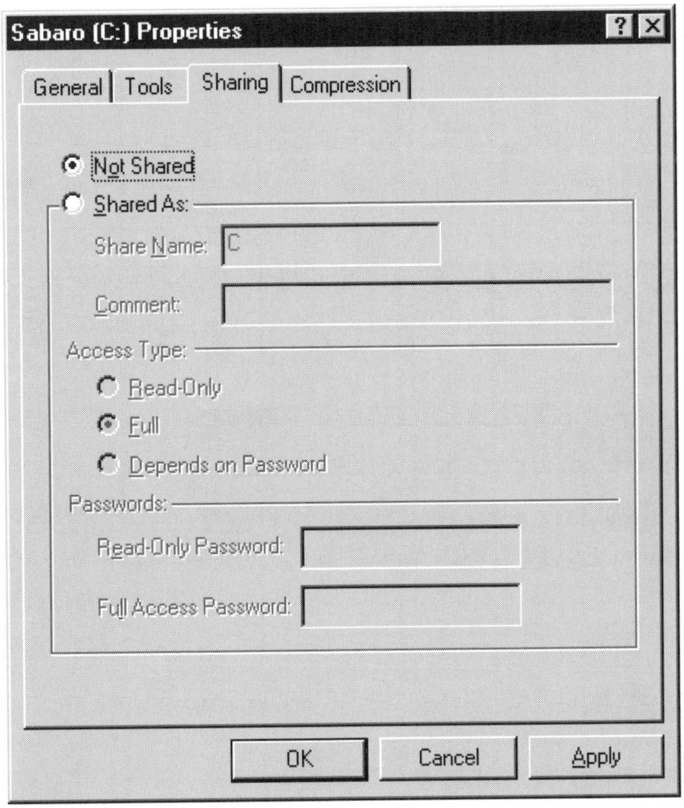

**Figure 4-18.** Setting up a share for your hard disk

department name, or job function) to further assist network users in identifying your computer's resource.

Next, you must set up the Access Type of your computer. For the current purposes, select Full. That gives users the ability to see and execute local files. Next, set a password that network users must enter in order to access your machine.

> **CAUTION:** Be aware that the password you set here must be shared with all of the network users to whom you want to give access. This means that your password will most likely end up taped to a monitor somewhere in your office—not the most secure solution. To better secure access to your machine, set your Access Type to Read Only or Depends on Password. For more information on that, refer to Chapter 16.

When you're done, click on the OK button. You should then see a little hand cradling your hard drive in your My Computer folder (see Figure 4-19).

That's all there is to it. Your machine is now able to connect to Windows NT via TCP/IP, IPX/SPX, and NetBEUI. It is also ready to accept connections from other machines via the same protocols.

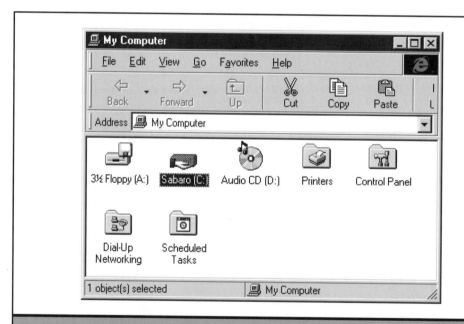

**Figure 4-19.**    Shared hard drive icon in the My Computer folder

# WORKING WITH WINDOWS NT

That was the hard part. Now comes the easy part of networking with Windows NT. We say easy for one simple reason: Working with a remote Windows NT server is just like working with your local Windows 98 machine. Folders, MS-DOS sessions, applications—all aspects of Windows 98 translate to Windows NT.

## Accessing Files

The first thing you probably want to do in connecting with Windows NT is access some files or applications. This requires you to establish a connection with Windows NT. To do that, just go to your desktop and double-click the Network Neighborhood icon. This opens a folder that looks something like the one shown in Figure 4-20.

Notice how there are two types of icons in this folder. One represents your computer and the other represents the Windows NT machine. Naturally, your network will most likely contain many different icons. As a test network, ours only contains the two. But we mention it because it illustrates an important point. That is, if you can see your computer in the Network Neighborhood folder, then others can see it too. If you don't see your own computer, then there is something wrong with your network configuration.

**RESOURCE:** To find out more about errors like this, refer to Chapter 17.

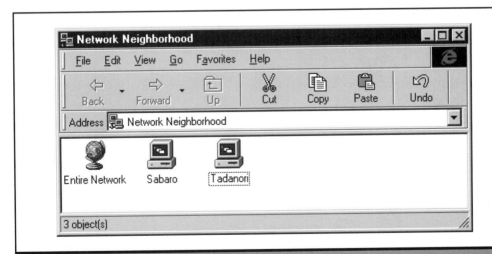

**Figure 4-20.** Network Neighborhood folder

If you're not sure which computer is which in this folder, just right-click one of the icons and select the Properties item. This opens a dialog box containing the computer name and any description of that computer (see Figure 4-21). When you're done, just click on the OK button.

To begin working with the remote Windows NT server, double-click on the desired machine icon. This opens up another folder containing the available resources for that machine (drives, printers, and so forth). Remember, you must have previously set up a user account for yourself on the Windows NT server. From this point on, you can do two things: double-click on the desired resource and begin working through the Windows 98 interface, or right-click on the desired icon and create a drive mapping (see Figure 4-22).

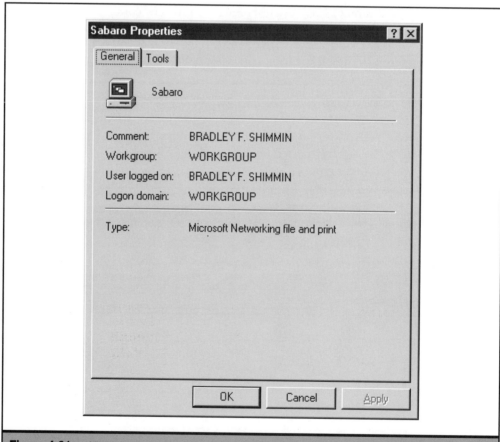

**Figure 4-21.** Viewing a computer's properties via the Network Neighborhood folder

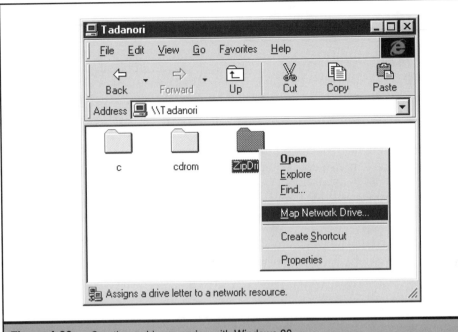

**Figure 4-22.**   Creating a drive mapping with Windows 98

**SHORTCUT:**   If you don't want to continually open your Network Neighborhood folder, you can just drag the icon for a remote machine from the folder to your desktop using the right mouse button. This lets you create a shortcut for that machine right on your desktop. Like magic, you can do the same thing to any folder or resource on a remote machine.

The former method of simply browsing folders works for most of your needs. Once you have begun browsing the remote server, you can open files just as you do locally, by double-clicking on them. You can do the same for applications—assuming, of course, that the application you execute does not require any registry access on the remote machine. That is, the type of access in this discussion is not made for the remote execution of applications such as Microsoft Office. Of course, you can do that if your systems administrator has installed the data files for Office on the server and provided you with a client installation program. Rather, it is designed for the execution of simple applications. For example, you might want to run an installation routine for an application such as Netscape Navigator from the Windows NT machine.

For more control, we suggest that you go with the latter method of connecting in which you set up a drive mapping to Windows NT. To do this, just continue from the example given in Figure 4-22 by clicking on the Map Network Drive item and you'll see a dialog box like this:

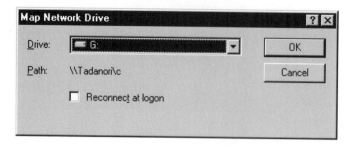

As you can see, you have the option to pick any available drive letter from the Drive pull-down menu. You can also specify that you want to reconnect this drive mapping whenever you first boot your machine. Unless you are using Windows 98 on a desktop computer, it is recommended that you don't reconnect at logon because it presents you with an error every time you boot up, should you not be connected to the same network. When you're ready, just click on the OK button. This opens a new folder with a label corresponding to the drive letter you have chosen. You can do what you like with that folder. The most important thing is that you can now open an MS-DOS box from your Start menu and change drive letters to the newly mapped drive (see Figure 4-23).

*CAUTION:* Mind you, Windows 98 is smart enough to know when you are connected to a LAN. If you boot your laptop without any sort of network connection, Windows 98 won't try to reconnect your network drive mappings. It simply treats you as though you're in stand-alone mode.

You will find drive mappings most useful with older programs that do not know how to interpret Microsoft's UNC notation. For example, a program such as Lotus cc:Mail 2.0 won't know what to make of something like

```
\\Tadanori\c\ccmail
```

But it will know how to deal with something like

```
G:\ccmail
```

*JARGON:* What's a UNC? It stands for Universal Naming Convention (UNC), a standardized method (or should we say syntax) for representing networked resources. You'll recognize one whenever you see the two beginning backslashes (\\).

Using drive mappings are also good because they let you do all sorts of things important to the execution of many server-side applications, such as setting environmental variables. For example, if you have Sun Microsystems' Java Development Kit (JDK) installed on your Windows NT server, you must have CLASSPATH and PATH variables set in order to use the JDK (whether locally or remotely). Well, if you have set up a drive mapping, you can open an MS-DOS session on your local machine, change

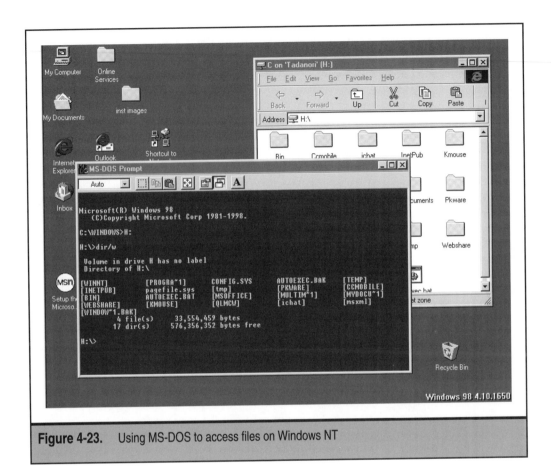

**Figure 4-23.** Using MS-DOS to access files on Windows NT

drives to the drive upon which the JDK resides, set your CLASSPATH and PATH statements as need be, and start coding away, just as though you were working locally.

## Using Logon Scripts

As you saw a bit earlier, you can have Windows 98 automatically restore your network connections when you boot your operating system. This can certainly save lots of time. But that is only going half way. To fully automate your connections and reconnections, you need something that can set up your environment—such as your CLASSPATH and PATH statements. Thankfully, Windows NT provides just such a capability through logon scripts. Once configured correctly, a logon script does just about anything you need, every time you log on to your Windows NT server. That's because the Windows NT logon script feature simply runs the executable of your choice when you first log on to the Windows NT machine.

*CAUTION:* Logon scripts only work with a Windows NT machine that is either a primary domain controller or a member of a domain. This is because you must log on to a Windows NT machine using a user name and password, a feature not directly supported by a stand-alone server using just a workgroup.

You could have the logon script start an MS-DOS batch file (*.BAT), an OS/2 command file (*.CMD), or any executable (*.EXE). For example, you could instruct Windows NT to run a batch file that sets your environmental variables. Or you might instruct it to execute a batch file that backs up your local files to the Windows NT server.

To create a backup logon script, the first thing you need to do is ensure that you are set up to log on to a Windows NT domain when you boot your system. To do this, go to your Network dialog box from the Settings folder. Select the Client for Microsoft Networks, and click Properties. From the resulting Properties dialog box, select the check box labeled Log on to Windows NT Domain and enter the name of your domain in the following field. In the area below this, select the radio button labeled *Logon and restore network connections.* This tells Windows 98 to automatically log on to Windows NT and set up your existing drive mappings. The dialog box should look like the one in Figure 4-24 when you're done.

The next step is to create the batch file that does the required work. Assuming that you've created a drive mapping for the C: drive on your Windows NT server labeled G:, an appropriate batch file (let's call it BACKUP.BAT) might look something like this:

```
echo off
cls
xcopy c:\usr\personal\html g:\bak\usr\personal\html /v/s/e
```

You should place this file on the remote Windows NT server in the root directory. Now, to set up the server side of the equation, go to your Windows NT server and open the User Manager for Domains application. It's located under the Administrative Tools folder from your Start menu. Find your name in the list of Usernames. If you can't find it, you'll have to make your own. To do that, just click on the User pull-down menu, click on New User, and follow the prompts. With a valid user account at your fingertips, double-click on it from the main User Manager for Domains window. This opens a User Properties dialog box. From here, click on the button at the bottom of the dialog box labeled Profile. This opens the User Environment Profile dialog box (see Figure 4-25).

All that remains is to simply enter the name of the program you want to run upon logging on to Windows NT in the field labeled Logon Script Name. In our example, that name would be BACKUP.BAT. When you're done, click on the OK button, close the User Properties dialog box, and restart your Windows 98 computer. After logging on, you should see a screen similar to the one in Figure 4-26.

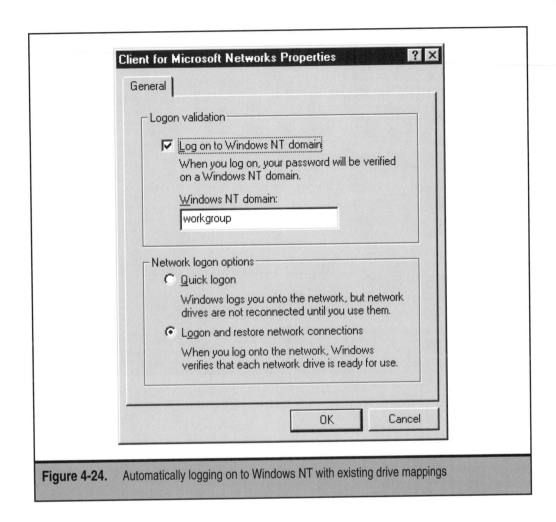

**Figure 4-24.**   Automatically logging on to Windows NT with existing drive mappings

    With this example in mind, you can go on to perform any sort of task upon logging into Windows NT. It's that easy.

## Accessing Printers

One more important feature of networking with Windows NT is the ability to print from the Windows NT server as though you were printing from a local printer. This is by far the easiest feature to use. Basically, all you need to do is connect to a Windows NT printer just as you would a Windows NT drive, in essence creating a printer mapping. Of course, before you can do anything with a Windows NT printer, you must ensure that the target

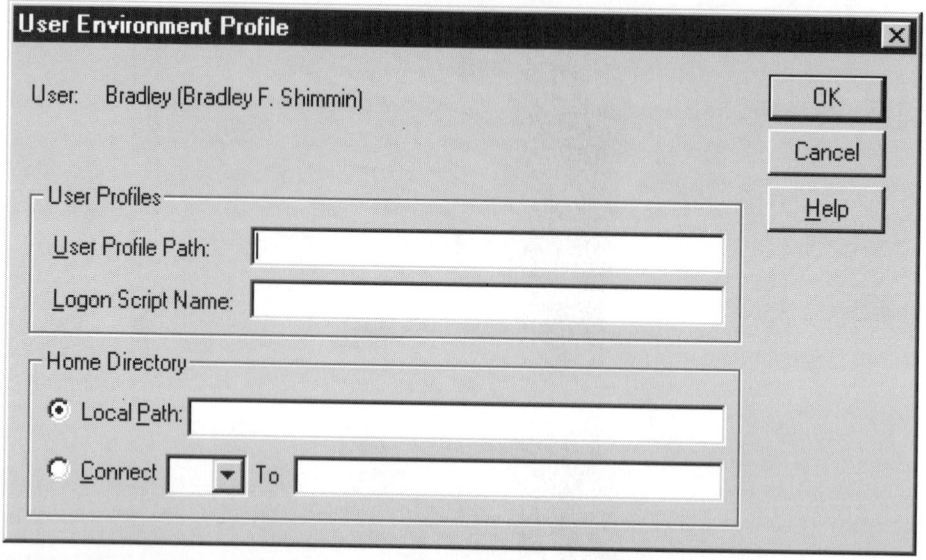

**Figure 4-25.** Entering the Logon Script Name

printer is set as a shared device on Windows NT. To verify this, just open your Printers folder from the Start menu on Windows NT and look for the hand icon underneath your printer (see Figure 4-27).

As you can see in Figure 4-27, the printer on the left is shared, and the printer on the right is not—no hand. If your printer is not shared, you can enable a share for it just as you did with your hard disk by right-clicking on it and selecting the item called Sharing. Click on the radio button entitled Shared and enter a unique name for the shared printer.

Now you're ready to begin working with this printer from Windows 98. There are basically two ways to go about printing with a Windows NT printer from Windows 98:

▼ Open a printer on Windows NT directly.

▲ Install a local pointer to a Windows NT printer.

## Open a Printer on Windows NT Directly

To open a printer directly on Windows NT, just open your Network Neighborhood folder and double-click on the icon for the Windows NT machine. There you'll see the shared drives and printer as shown in Figure 4-28.

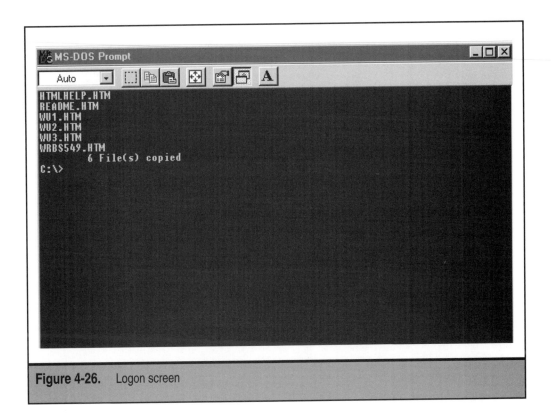

**Figure 4-26.**   Logon screen

Just double-click on the printer and a pop-up box appears asking you if you want to install local software for the printer. Click on the Yes button, follow the Add Printer wizard, selecting the appropriate printer driver. And that's all there is to it. If you open your Printers folder, you'll notice that now you have a printer icon with network piping attached, like so:

HP DeskJet
320 Printer
(Copy 2)

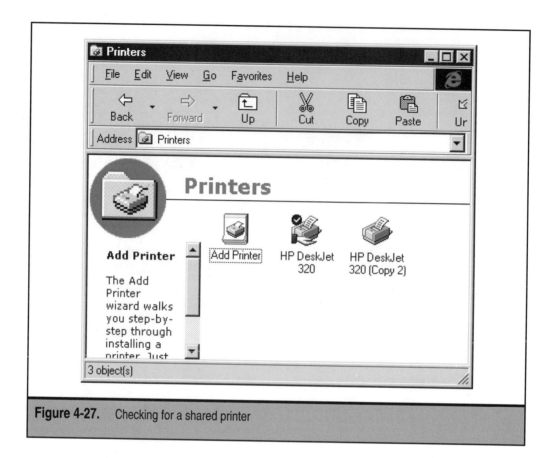

**Figure 4-27.** Checking for a shared printer

This printer will act just like your local printers. You can drag and drop files on it to print them, and you can set it to be your default printer. The only difference is that this printer is really a pointer to software running on the Windows NT server.

## Install a Local Pointer to a Windows NT Printer

The second way to install a network printer is to simply create a new printer that points to the server's printer. To do this, just open your Printer folder from the Settings item within the Start menu. Double-click on the Add Printer icon and follow the Add Printer wizard. Select Network printer instead of local printer, click on the Next button, and then click on the Browse button. This opens a tree view of the available network resources that looks something like the one shown in Figure 4-29.

Just expand the tree as necessary until you find the right printer, highlight it, and click on the OK button. Select the appropriate printer driver, and you're in business. Now from any Windows application, you will be able to print to this printer just as though you were working with an attached printer.

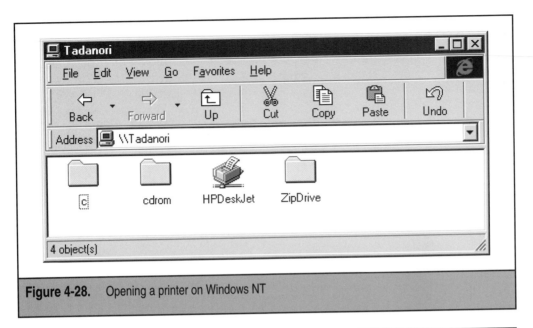

**Figure 4-28.**    Opening a printer on Windows NT

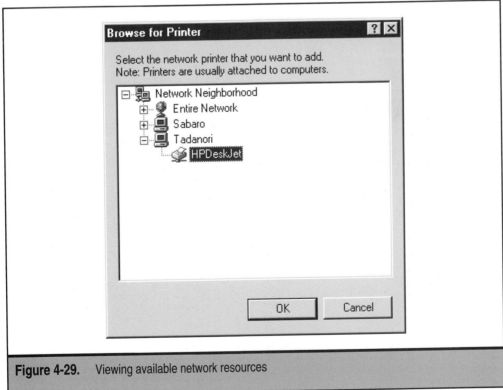

**Figure 4-29.**    Viewing available network resources

## COMING UP

We've certainly covered a lot of territory in this chapter, discovering the benefits of Windows NT, choosing the appropriate protocols to network with Windows NT, installing and configuring those protocols, and lastly learning how to work with Windows NT resources across a network. In the next chapter, we give Novell IntranetWare the same treatment, discussing its benefits, protocols, and the like.

# CHAPTER 5

# Networking with Novell NetWare

## What's ahead:

- NetWare networking features
- Installing the NetWare client
- Getting started with NetWare
- Advanced NetWare services

*"Machinery is the greatest
Earth-medium."*

—Wyndham Lewis, *The Vorticist Manifesto*

You will find that working with Windows 98 in a Novell NetWare environment is quite similar to working in a Microsoft environment. You can log in to a NetWare server much like you log in to a Windows NT server. You can access file and print services on a Novell server in much the same way as you can on a Windows NT server. And you can share the files and printer on your workstation with others, just as you can on a Windows NT machine. Before Windows 98, however, this last statement would not be possible without the addition of a NETBEUI-based Microsoft network, such as Windows for Workgroups 3.11. Novell NetWare has traditionally been a client/server network in which isolated workstations access one or more file and print servers. Workstations could see the NetWare server, but they could not see each other. If these clients wanted to communicate in a NetWare-centric network, they had to adopt a peer-to-peer service such as DR DOS 7, which was formally known as NetWare Lite. With Microsoft Windows 98, NetWare-centric networks contain not just client/server networks, but a combination of client/server and peer-to-peer networks.

This primary benefit of being able to share data across servers and workstations is an integral element in the Windows 98 networking arsenal. However, there are many other benefits built into Windows 98 in a NetWare environment that outweigh traditional MS-DOS and older Windows client capabilities. With Windows 98 on a Novell NetWare network, you can use a single login for all network services; you can share your printer with anyone on the network, or use other's printers in the same manner; you can even gain substantial performance advantages over older network clients; and of course, you can gain access to any NetWare service such as Novell's NetWare Directory Services (NDS), or application such as an Oracle database.

This chapter outlines these advantages, but more importantly, it discusses the best methods to access a Novell network and how to best utilize its services from a Windows 98 workstation. We begin by diving into the complicated matter of configuring the Windows 98 workstation so that it can connect to a Novell network. Here, we talk about installing different protocols and network clients with the ultimate goal of demonstrating the many options available for communicating over a Novell network. If your workstation is already correctly connected to a Novell network, feel free to skip this section and begin reading the section entitled "Getting Started with NetWare." We continue by discussing the basic methods available for using a Novell network. This section shows you how to view your Novell network, execute programs, and print files through Windows 98's user-friendly graphical user interface (GUI). Once you feel comfortable in navigating the network, you can move on to the next section, in which we discuss the more advanced features of the Windows 98 and Novell network. This section includes information about the command line interface, including mapping drives, logging in, and logging out. Finally, we conclude the chapter with a discussion of the security and manageability of your Windows 98 workstation on a Novell network.

# FEATURES OF NETWARE AND WINDOWS 98 INTEGRATION

Windows 98 supports many different third-party networks, such as Banyan VINES and SunSoft, in addition to Novell NetWare. All of these networks can potentially share the benefits of Microsoft's 32-bit virtual device drivers (VxDs), depending on the level of support provided by each third-party vendor; all networks share the benefits of multiple protocol stack support. But Novell NetWare integration has many capabilities that go beyond these other networks. The two main reasons for this is the inclusion of a Microsoft client for NetWare with Windows 98 and the native NetWare client provided by Novell. Although you can use your standard Open Data-Link Interface (ODI) Novell network client drivers—NETX.EXE for 3.$x$ or 4.$x$ networks (with bindery emulation) and VLM.EXE for 4.$x$ networks (with NDS support)—and obtain the same level of performance and capability as you would on a Windows 3.1 or MS-DOS workstation, by utilizing the Microsoft or Novell client, you can gain access to a superset of those capabilities. As mentioned in Chapter 2, these benefits include higher performance, zero conventional memory usage, packet burst protocol support, and auto-reconnect capabilities. Beyond those are more general features within the Windows client for NetWare that will not only enhance your ability to work faster and more efficiently, but also to work more effectively with others.

## Peer-to-Peer

To take advantage of the ability to share your computer's data with others, you will need to utilize both the client for NetWare and a Novell file server (either 3.$x$, 4.$x$, or 5). With two or more Windows 98 workstations and a NetWare server, you can immediately and easily share your system's files and printer through an interesting concept called "pass-through security." If you institute user-level security within the security section of the Network Configuration panel , and you enter the name of a NetWare file server, you can allow users to access your computer based on their security rights as instituted on the NetWare server (see Figure 5-1).

Once you obtain a list of users from the server, you can allow each individual differing levels of security on your workstation.

For example, once you have created a user profile based on the user information obtained from the NetWare server, when that user attempts to access your workstation, his/her user name is first validated against NetWare security information. If his/her user name exists upon that server, the Microsoft peer-to-peer client software on your workstation then checks the corresponding security file for any access rights you have given him/her regarding your hard drive and peripherals. If there are any rights, he/she

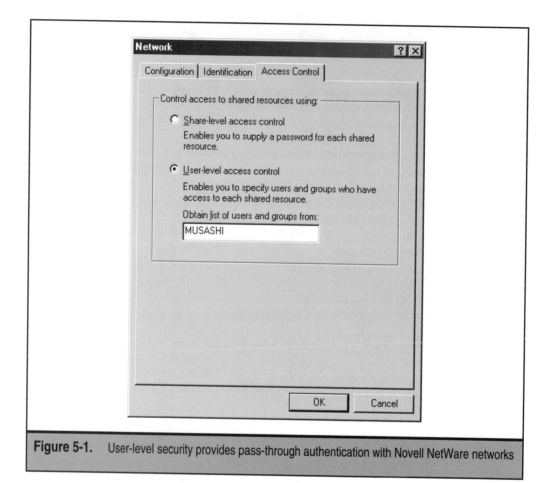

**Figure 5-1.**    User-level security provides pass-through authentication with Novell NetWare networks

is granted access to your system. This peer-to-peer security scheme works for individual users and for groups as well. For example, if you have a group of NetWare users called "accounting," you could give any user belonging to that group access to your directory entitled "ACCT_INFO."

Using groups more frequently than individual users will save you a lot of extra time and work in setting up user accounts on your Windows 98 workstation.

## Access Control

Access Control security features are carried over into the normal client/server aspects of NetWare networking under Windows 98. One such feature, which also works with the standard ODI NetWare client, is the ability to log in to your Windows 98 workstation and any associated NetWare services with only one password upon booting Windows 98. This is called a Network Password (see Figure 5-2).

This allows you to use the initial Windows 98 login screen to access NetWare information on a service-by-service, or application-by-application basis. This service provides an excellent solution to the problem of overabundant password requirements. If you are using NetWare 4.x or 5 with NDS support, this sort of feature will already be familiar to you, albeit in a different, command line format. However, if you are running any version of NetWare with bindery emulation, this feature can save a great deal of time and effort by logging you in to all of your servers at once, with one password.

## Graphical Interface

Through the Windows 98 user interface, you can easily access and use your NetWare file and print servers. You can browse the files contained on your file server as if they were local files on your hard disk; you can find out who you are logged in as; you can logout from or login to any server you wish; you can map drives to particular servers, volumes, or even directories; and you can use Windows Explorer to view and manipulate services on your NetWare server. All of these tasks can be performed from within Windows 98. This is a great improvement over earlier Microsoft Windows versions, which required you to exit from the Windows program before you executed any NetWare commands, such as LOGIN.EXE or MAP.EXE. If you entered one of these commands accidentally from an MS-DOS box within Windows, there was a very great chance that your workstation would lock up shortly after you closed the MS-DOS box.

Also, from the Windows 98 interface, you can directly manipulate your NetWare servers, files, and directories. For example, by highlighting a NetWare server and

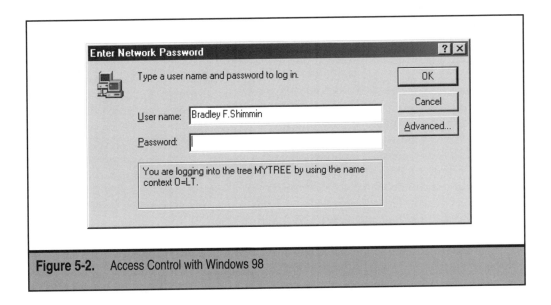

**Figure 5-2.**    Access Control with Windows 98

activating a pop-up activity menu (see the following illustration) with the right mouse button, you can open, explore, attach, detach, and map a network drive, or create a shortcut on the NetWare server.

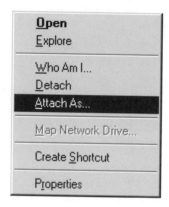

While you access the pop-up menu in the same way for most objects, its contents will differ from object to object. Initiating a menu for a text file lets you print that file, change its attributes, and quickly view its contents. You can also execute any programs (files that end in EXE, COM, or BAT).

This object-oriented approach to server, directory, and file management will make your interaction with NetWare very productive because you will not have to learn any new commands or command syntax in order to deal with different file directories, drives, volumes, or even file servers.

## Command Line Interface

If you prefer to utilize a command line interface when connecting to your NetWare network, Windows 98 can oblige with a full range of Microsoft networking tools as well as a complete access to NetWare's utilities. The nice thing about the Windows 98 network utilities is that they will work for both Microsoft and NetWare networks. You can access a NetWare server as easily as a Windows NT server. For example, to view your currently attached Network services, you need only type **net view**. This gives you a listing of the network resources available to your Windows 98 workstation.

The command line does not, however, allow you to use the NET START command from an MS-DOS window as you could in previous versions of MS Windows. Windows 95 and Windows 98 both start this command with all of your configured parameters before loading the main Windows desktop. If you have installed the Microsoft client for NetWare, for example, Windows 98 executes a command similar to NET START NWREDIR (*NWREDIR* stands for NetWare redirector).

Thus, you will be somewhat shielded from the lower-level functionality of your NetWare network on the Windows 98 side of the command line interface. On the NetWare side, however, you can have full reign. If you want to log out from within an MS-DOS box, you can—although it would not be advisable because all other applications depending upon your NetWare connection would find themselves without network support.

# NDS Support

Windows 98, because it directly utilizes NetWare NDS through VLMs provided separately by both Novell and Microsoft, can give you some additional options when working with NetWare. For example, you can actually log in to the NDS tree (the repository for all network items) and browse the various container and leaf objects. If you want to use one of the objects in the tree, you can simply highlight it and activate the pop-up menu. To utilize one of these items, however, you must have the proper object rights to access, just as with a printer or server object.

# Enhanced Printing

An excellent part of integrating your Windows 98 workstation with a Novell network is the extended printing features available through both the Microsoft and Novell clients for NetWare. You can install a protected-mode 32-bit print server application on your workstation that will allow other peer workstations to access your printer as if it were a part of a NetWare print server configuration. Because this program reads information directly from NetWare print queues, multiple Windows 98 workstations can dispatch print jobs from a central print queue. For network administrators, this will come as a boon because it means that the overall printing capacity of the Novell network can be increased.

# NETWARE INSTALLATION

Although connecting your Windows 98 workstation to a NetWare network can give you some immediate benefits, there are many steps and decisions for you to make along the way. Again, if you already have your Windows 98 client satisfactorily attached to a NetWare network, you can skip this section and move on to the section entitled "Getting Started with NetWare." An administrator has already made the first decision that needs to be made before you connect to a NetWare network. When they created the network, they standardized upon three items: packet drivers, protocols, and network clients. They did this for reasons of manageability and interoperability. If each workstation used a different network client, network administrators could not easily maintain all of the workstations. Similarly, if each network client were to use a different protocol to connect to a file server, most likely only a few would be able to do so. For example, with NetWare 5, Novell has at last standardized upon TCP/IP as its default protocol. If you want to successfully connect with that server, you will have to use TCP/IP instead of the more traditional NetWare protocol, IPX/SPX.

Therefore, if you are connecting to an existing network, you should check with the administrator concerning the appropriate protocols, network client, and packet drivers you should use on your Windows 98 workstation. Once you have obtained this list, you should (if you have not done so already) install the network interface card you will be using to communicate with the NetWare network.

## Installing Hardware

To install a network interface card, you must turn off your computer, remove the outside cover, and insert the card into an available expansion slot. You should, at this point, take note of the hardware configuration of your card: its input/output (I/O) address, Direct Memory Access (DMA) channel, slot number (if applicable), and interrupt number. If you're not comfortable with this or any other part of the installation, check with the system administrator to avoid any problems. After you have installed your card, boot the Windows 98 workstation. After you enter the desktop environment, you are presented with a New Device installation picture. This appears automatically whenever Windows 98 detects a change in your system's hardware configuration. If you do not see such a screen, go to your Control Panel and select the icon named Add New Hardware. Follow the Hardware Installation Wizard. This wizard automatically scans your system, detecting your hardware (and hopefully your new card) and presenting you with its findings (see Figure 5-3).

Select the appropriate manufacturer and model of your network adapter card. You then need to reboot Windows 98. The next step is complicated in that you have to configure the Windows 98 client software so that it can communicate with your network correctly.

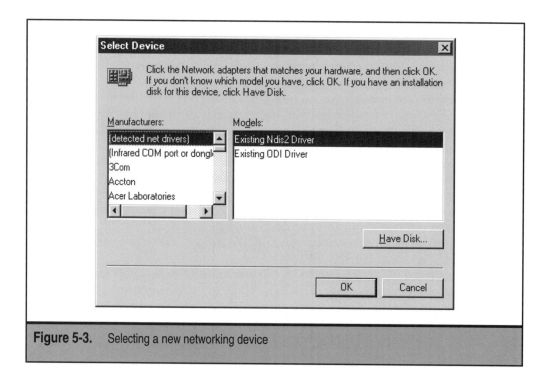

**Figure 5-3.**   Selecting a new networking device

# Installing Software

After you reboot your workstation, you must install the software that enables your new NIC hardware to communicate with a NetWare server. With Windows 98, you can choose between two NetWare clients: the Microsoft Client for NetWare Networks and the Novell Client for Windows 95/98. Both clients give you native access to NetWare's NDS directory. Both allow you to use pass-through security. And both provide you with all of the features mentioned previously. However, there is one major difference: the Novell client can run solely over TCP/IP. The Microsoft client must still utilize IPX/SPX, which could limit its appeal in NetWare 5 shops that have committed to the eradication of IPX/SPX in favor of the more open TCP/IP protocol. So check with your MIS manager before you install either client, to find out what his/her long-term and immediate plans are concerning TCP/IP on NetWare.

*SOAPBOX:* While the NetWare client may support NetWare 5's ability to run only TCP/IP, the Microsoft client provides better stability. It is also easier to maintain, since the networking software is built right into the Windows 98 network application. With the NetWare client, you will have to maintain an external piece of software, which takes control of the Windows 98 client during the boot-up process—always a risky business.

# Installing the Microsoft Client for NetWare Networks

To install the Microsoft Client for NetWare Networks, go immediately to the Control Panel and double-click on the Network icon. This brings you to the main network configuration screen, which contains the following elements: Configuration, Identification, and Access Control (see Figure 5-4).

First, select your new adapter and click on the Properties buttons. Before continuing, you should verify all of the adapter settings, ensuring that you do not have any hardware interrupt or memory address conflicts. If there are no issues, you can check on the packet driver type used by your NIC.

## Packet Driver Types

To connect with your NetWare network, the first software setting you must consider is the driver type settings, which can be found by double-clicking on the Network icon from the Control Panel, highlighting an available adapter, and clicking on the Properties button. Drivers tell Windows 98 how to communicate with your network adapter. There are three different types of network drivers available within Windows 98: enhanced-mode 32-bit and 16-bit Network Driver Interface Specification (NDIS) drivers, real-mode 16-bit NDIS drivers, and real-mode 16-bit ODI drivers. You are free to choose any of these selections, but be aware that unless you possess a 32-bit network adapter card, you will not be able to take full advantage of the 32-bit enhanced-mode client. If you have an Industry Standard Architecture (ISA) computer, do not worry because you can simply select a corresponding, 16-bit enhanced-mode driver.

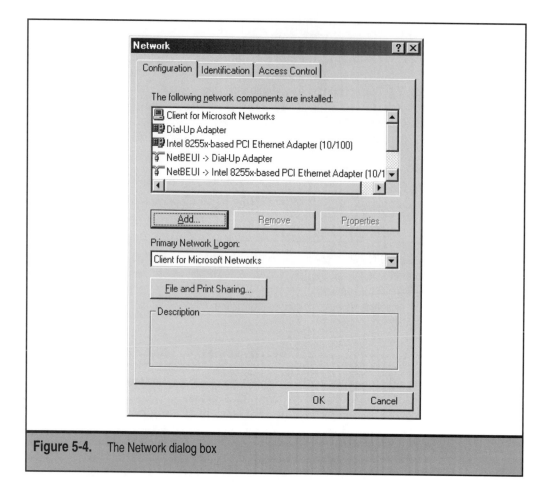

**Figure 5-4.** The Network dialog box

Select the desired driver for your Windows 98 network. Generally, you should initially choose the enhanced-mode driver as it will give you better overall performance.

***CAUTION:*** If you select a real-mode driver, you will have to obtain the packet driver software from the NIC manufacturer. If you choose an enhanced-mode driver, however, Windows 98 will obligingly provide that driver for you. This feature makes the assumption that Windows 98 supports your NIC. But Windows 98 does a great job at supporting all major NIC brands from companies such as Intel, 3Com, Adaptec, and Cogent.

The enhanced-mode driver will be used for purposes of this example. If you experience trouble after installation, you can choose another, more familiar driver such as the real-mode NDIS or the ODI driver. After you have made your selection, click on the OK button to finalize your adapter configuration.

## Protocol

You will not have as many possibilities in choosing your protocol as you did in choosing your driver type. This is because the type of protocol you choose is dictated by the type of NetWare network you use. For each type of network, there is a distinct protocol. Banyan VINES networks use a proprietary protocol, Digital Equipment Corp. networks use DECnet protocols, and SunSoft networks use the Transmission Control Protocol/Internet Protocol (TCP/IP). Although these systems usually make use of one protocol, a NetWare network can basically utilize two different protocols, TCP/IP and Internet Packet Exchange/Sequenced Packet Exchange (IPX/SPX), interchangeably. The majority of NetWare 3.x and 4.x networks still use the IPX/SPX protocols, as it is the default protocol that comes with Novell's network operating system. On the other hand, if you are using a network that utilizes NetWare 5, you will most likely need to select the TCP/IP protocol. As mentioned previously, NetWare 5 is the first version of NetWare to support TCP/IP as a native, default protocol in place of IPX/SPX. However, the Microsoft client does not currently support TCP/IP-only connections to NetWare. Therefore, you should find out which protocol your NetWare 5 server is running before you proceed any further. If your NetWare 5 server is running only TCP/IP, you should skip ahead to the next section, which discusses the installation of the Novell Client for Windows 95/98.

To begin with the Microsoft Client for NetWare Networks, click on the Add button from the Network dialog box, click on the Protocol button, and then click on Add from the Network window. Highlight the Microsoft manufacturer button and then select the IPX/SPX model and click on the OK button. Of course, if you wish to use an additional protocol, either TCP/IP or even NetBIOS Extended User Interface (NetBEUI), select the desired protocol in the same manner.

Now you may have to configure your network protocol to better communicate with the NetWare network. To do this, select the newly created protocol and click on the Properties button. You are presented with a configuration page containing three tabs: NetBIOS, Advanced, and Bindings. The NetBIOS is very important to an IPX/SPX-based NetWare network. In the session layer of the OSI reference model, as discussed in Appendix B, NetBIOS serves an important service for NetWare in that it functions alongside the Named Pipes protocol in providing data transport requests, login and logout services, naming of network nodes, and the broadcasting of server names and locations. In light of these services, you should ensure that the "I want to enable NetBIOS over IPX/SPX" button is checked.

## Client

The next step is to install the NetWare client itself. To do this, click on the Add button from the Configuration panel within the Network dialog box, select Client, and click on the Add button. On the resulting dialog box, select Microsoft from the left pane, click on Client for NetWare Networks from the right pane (see Figure 5-5), and click on the OK button.

This client will enable Windows 98 to talk with NetWare servers in a client/server capacity, but it does not support NDS or peer-to-peer networking.

## Services

To support peer-to-peer networking and access NetWare's NDS directory, you need to install the appropriate client services:

▼   File and printer sharing for NetWare Networks

▲   Service for NetWare Directory Services

These are the heart of Microsoft's Client for NetWare Networks. Without them, others will not be able to access your machine, and you will not be able to access any of the distributed services (printers, servers, or applications), that are housed in NDS. As with the client installation shown previously, click on the Add button from the Configuration panel within the Network dialog box. But this time, select the Service item and click on the Add button. From the resulting dialog box, you should select the File and printer sharing for NetWare Networks item and click on the OK button. Repeat the same steps in

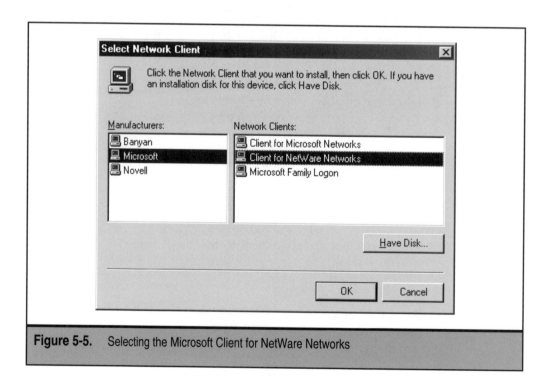

**Figure 5-5.**   Selecting the Microsoft Client for NetWare Networks

order to add the Service for NetWare Directory Services item. Your Configuration panel within the Network dialog box should now contain the following items:

▼ Client for NetWare Networks

■ NIC adapter (such as the Intel 8255x-based PCI Ethernet adapter)

■ IPX/SPX-compatible protocol

■ NetBEUI

■ NetBIOS support for IPX/SPX-compatible protocol

■ TCP/IP

■ File and printer sharing for NetWare Networks

▲ Service for NetWare Directory Services

# Client Configuration Issues

After you have installed the NetWare client and services, all that remains is for you to verify your configuration and enable some last-minute settings. More likely than not, your network connection should be ready to go at this point. But in order to ensure that you and your users don't run into any unforeseen snags at a later date, you should go through the following configuration steps in order to make sure that your protocols, access controls, and clients and services are configured properly.

## Protocol Configuration

First, from the Configuration panel within the Network dialog box, select the IPX/SPX-compatible protocol item and click on the Properties button. From the resulting dialog box, click on the Bindings tab. This is where you set the network services that your packet driver will bind to the selected protocol. You should see two entries:

▼ Client for NetWare Networks

▲ NetBIOS support for IPX/SPX-compatible protocol

You must have a check mark next to the Client for NetWare Networks item. Without this client, you will not be able to connect to any NetWare networks.

**SHORTCUT:** Don't worry if you see other entries in the Bindings tab. If you are going to be communicating with other Windows 98, Windows for Workgroups, or Windows NT machines, you should also see a Windows client item.

Now click on the Advanced tab. From here, you can specify many different settings for your connection with a NetWare server. For example, if you click on the Frame Type item in the left pane, you can then tell your client to connect with the server using a specific frame type, including Ethernet II, 802.2, or 802.3 (see Figure 5-6).

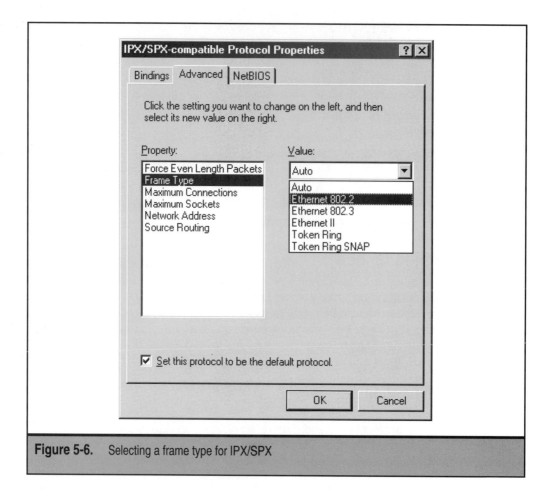

**Figure 5-6.** Selecting a frame type for IPX/SPX

You should only modify the Advanced Settings panel if you experience problems communicating over the network. Of course, as mentioned in Chapter 2, you should verify your network's frame type. For example, if your network administrator has selected the Ethernet 802.2 frame type, you must also select the Ethernet 802.2 frame type. Selecting a frame type different than that used by your NetWare server prevents you from connecting to the network. This, however, only applies to IPX/SPX protocols. If you chose the TCP/IP protocol, you need not worry about this since TCP/IP relies solely upon the Ethernet II frame type.

As a general rule of thumb, NetWare 3.*x* networks will utilize the Ethernet 802.3 frame type, while NetWare 4.*x* and 5 networks will use the Ethernet 802.2 frame type. Novell has migrated to the 802.2 frame type, which is why it appears primarily within NetWare 4.*x* and 5 networks. For more information on these protocols, please refer to Appendix B.

If you have selected more than one protocol, such as both TCP/IP and IPX/SPX, you should ensure that the correct protocol has been selected as the default protocol. For example, if you connect to a NetWare network as your primary service, select IPX/SPX as your default protocol (see Figure 5-6).

When you have finished configuring your protocol settings, click on the OK button. The rest of these selections should be left alone unless, after you have connected to the network, you are unable to either log on to a NetWare server or execute a network program.

## Clients

To ensure that your clients and services are configured correctly, select the Client for NetWare Networks item from the Configuration tab within the Network dialog box and click on the Properties button. Here, you are presented with a number of options, which vary depending on the type of Novell network you are using. If you are attached to a NetWare 4.*x* or 5 network, you should enter the default context in which your workstation resides, the default neighborhood context of your local network, and the preferred tree to which you wish to attach. If you are unsure about any of these entries, you should consult your network administrator. Otherwise, simply enter the two context entries as simple names. For example, a context such as **OU=Accounting.O=Acme_Sales** would be entered as Accounting. You can select your preferred NDS tree from a pull-down list of available NetWare trees.

**SHORTCUT:**   Though not typical, NetWare may ask you to enter your full context instead of a familiar name and user name. Using the preceding example, your complete context should look something like the following:

CN=username.OU=Accounting.O=Acme_Sales.

The CN represents your user name. You can think of this type of X.500-esque notation as a user name that includes your street address (an identity and a location within the NDS directory tree structure). With it, you can access NetWare services from any location. For example, if you traveled to a remote office, which was linked with your central office via NDS, by entering your complete context, you could log in just as though you were sitting at your desk in the central office.

For NetWare 3.*x* networks, you will only be able to modify the Preferred server and First network drive in this window. The Preferred server simply tells Windows 98 the name of the NetWare server you want it to look for first during its boot processes. During this process, if Windows 98 cannot find your Preferred server, it will simply return an error code and attach to the next NetWare server it is able to locate.

## Services

An important service of the Microsoft Client for NetWare Networks is the Service for NetWare Directory Services. This service allows you to work with NDS as a separate entity from NetWare servers. Basically, you can browse the NDS directory tree and look for people and services such as printers, fax machines, and scanners.

To configure this important service, highlight the appropriate entry within the Configuration tab and click on the Properties button. This opens a dialog box that lets you select your preferred NDS tree and set a default workstation context (see Figure 5-7).

As mentioned previously, your context should look something like this:

```
OU=Accounting.O=Acme_Sales
```

The letter "O" stands for organization. The letters "OU" stand for organizational unit. These are the containers to which your workstation and user accounts belong. If you're unsure about your default context, check with your NetWare administrator in order to enter your correct context information.

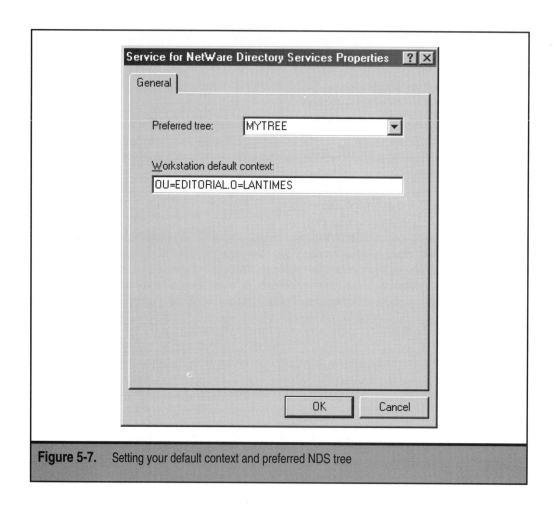

**Figure 5-7.**   Setting your default context and preferred NDS tree

The last service you may need to configure is the File and printer sharing for NetWare Networks. You can access this just as you did with the NDS service earlier. Once you have this service's properties dialog box in view, you can specify whether or not you want your workstation to advertise its file and printer shares as available entities across the network.

You have two options:

▼ Service Advertising Protocol (SAP)

▲ Workgroup Advertising

The first option lets your workstation act and even look like a NetWare server to other clients. The second option uses Windows' traditional advertising method to make your services known through the Network Neighborhood folder, just as though you were an ordinary Windows client. We strongly recommend that you enable Workgroup Advertising, as it will be the least intrusive on the network as a whole. It is also easier for network administrators to control and manage.

**CAUTION:** If you're familiar with the manner in which NetWare advertises its file and print services, you'll think twice about enabling SAP advertising. If your network uses a wide-area link, each workstation that uses SAP advertising will send an enormous, semi-continuous ping across that wide-area link, causing performance headaches throughout your entire organization. Check with your MIS shop regarding their policy on SAP advertising.

## Access Control and Identification

The last pieces in the puzzle include Access Control and Identification. With Access Control, you tell the network how you want to be authenticated as you connect to different services such as NetWare servers. Identification really deals with how your machine appears to other peer-to-peer machines on the network. These peer-to-peer machines will typically be other Windows 98 or Windows 95 machines.

To set your authentication options, from the Network dialog box, select the Access Control tab. This reveals a menu that allows you to set your local hard disk security system as either a share-level access control, or a user-level access control system. If you are running a NetWare-only client configuration, you will only be able to select user-level access control from the available options. If so, in the space provided, enter the name of the server from which your machine can gather user security information.

Next, click on the Identification tab. The last pieces of information you need to provide include a name for your computer, the name of the workgroup to which your computer belongs, and a brief description of your computer. The computer name can be anything you want unless your network administrator has chosen a naming standard. The workgroup name must correspond to an existing workgroup, or your computer will belong to a peer-to-peer network comprised of one computer.

When you're done, go back to the Configuration tab and ensure that the Primary Network Logon pull-down menu lists the Client for NetWare Networks as its default entry. Also, click on the File and Print Sharing button to enable or disable the use of your local print and file services by other machines. If you are not sure about whether or not you should allow such activity, check with your MIS manager for your company's policy on such matters.

*CAUTION:* The File and Print Sharing button should be checked if *and only if* you want other network users to access your files and any attached printer that you may have. Aside from the usual security issues surrounding such a feature, you may want to deselect file and printer sharing because the more services riding on top of one protocol, the slower your machine will operate as it interacts with other network devices.

After clicking on the OK button to install your newly created network service, you are asked to either insert a number of installation disks—as shown next in the section "Installing the Novell Client for Windows"—or provide a location from which Windows 98 can obtain the required network client programs. After installing the required files, you can begin utilizing your NetWare network by simply rebooting your machine. Once the machine restarts, you're presented with a NetWare-centric login prompt, where you must enter your NetWare user name and password (see Figure 5-8).

If you have trouble logging in to NetWare 5, click on the Advanced button. This opens a separate dialog box where you can change your default context, select a different NDS tree, or even choose to connect to the NetWare server in bindery mode (see Figure 5-9).

Why select bindery mode? Pre 4.*x* NetWare servers used an authentication process, which utilized a flat-file database of user names and passwords, called a bindery. When you logged in to such a NetWare server, your user name and password were checked

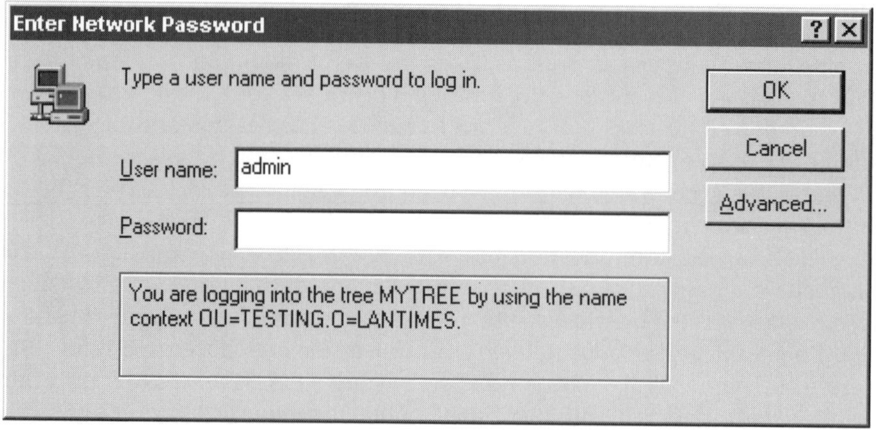

**Enter Network Password**

Type a user name and password to log in.

User name: admin

Password:

You are logging into the tree MYTREE by using the name context OU=TESTING.O=LANTIMES.

OK
Cancel
Advanced...

**Figure 5-8.** Logging in to NetWare 5

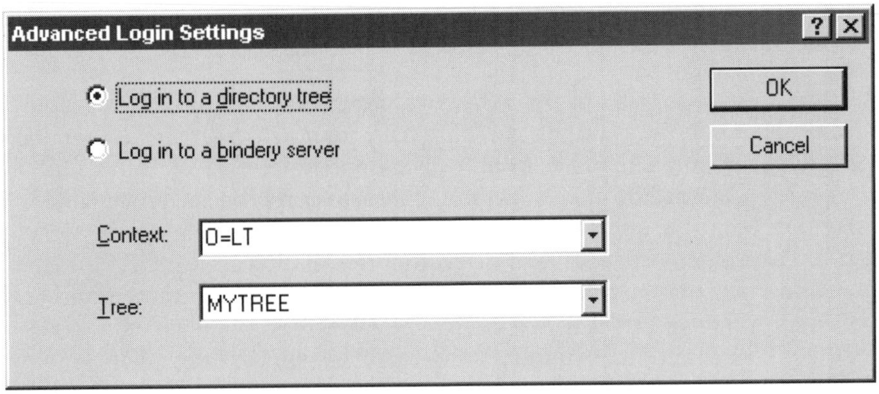

**Figure 5-9.**    Modifying login options

against the appropriate entry in this file. With NetWare 4.*x* and 5, NetWare servers began to look to NDS as the primary authentication mechanism. But these newer servers also maintained a compatibility mode, in which users could authenticate with either NDS or the bindery. Because NDS is very picky about the context used to connect with a server, if you have trouble connecting with NDS, you can use bindery compatibility to simplify things. All you need to know is the name of your server. To use bindery mode, click on the Log in to a bindery server button (as seen in Figure 5-9), enter the name of the NetWare server and click on the OK button. You can then try to log in again, hopefully with greater success.

Once you've logged in to a NetWare server, you can work with it just as you would if it were a Windows 98 or Windows NT server. You can access it from your My Computer folder or Network Neighborhood folder to map drives and access files and services. To find out more about how to work with NetWare, skip ahead to the section entitled "Getting Started with NetWare."

## Installing the Novell Client for Windows

Although Microsoft's NetWare client now supports NDS directly with Windows 98, there are some pretty good reasons to run with the native NetWare client from Novell. For starters, you can take advantage of Novell's NetWare-centric services such as Distributed File and Print Services. And you can choose from a host of options such as a more flexible connection dialog box, robust printer features, and the ability to fine tune your connection settings.

**CAUTION:** At the time this chapter was written, Novell had not yet released a client built just for Windows 98. We used the NetWare 5 beta client for Windows 95. Once Novell ships a Windows 98-specific client, you should expect to see similar features and functionality.

To install the Novell Client for Windows, you must first obtain the appropriate CD-ROM or set of floppies. You can get those from your MIS manager, if you don't have them already. Using the CD-ROM, double-click on the NetWare 5 client CD-ROM icon within your My Computer folder to begin the installation process. When asked, choose the appropriate language and select to install the component for Windows. You will then be asked to choose between a typical or custom installation routine. If you choose the custom routine, you will be asked to specify your connection parameters and to choose whether or not you want to run with both IPX/SPX and TCP/IP. If you choose the typical routine, the installation process immediately removes your existing client software and installs the new client completely without user intervention. It also detects your network settings (server name, default NDS tree, and so on). We recommend that you choose the typical routine, as it lets you change its default setting during the installation process. If you have not already done so, select the typical installation routine and click on the Next button. The new client software is automatically installed, after which, you are asked to reboot your machine, customize your settings, or return to Windows (see Figure 5-10).

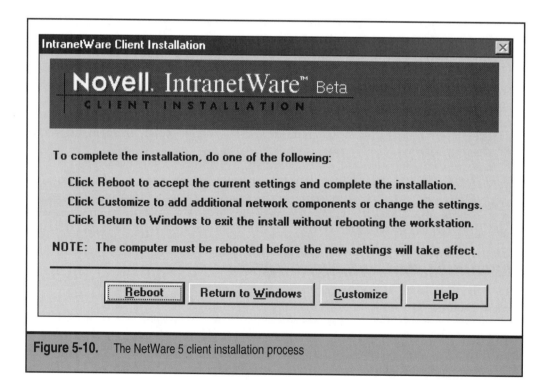

**Figure 5-10.**    The NetWare 5 client installation process

Click on the Customize button to verify the default settings. This opens the Windows 98 Network dialog box. Notice that there are three components in the dialog box:

▼ Novell IntranetWare Client

■ Compatibility Mode Driver

▲ Novell Distributed Print Services

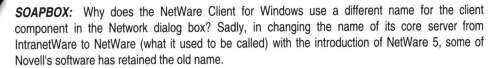

**SOAPBOX:** Why does the NetWare Client for Windows use a different name for the client component in the Network dialog box? Sadly, in changing the name of its core server from IntranetWare to NetWare (what it used to be called) with the introduction of NetWare 5, some of Novell's software has retained the old name.

You can only modify the settings for the first component, the Novell IntranetWare Client. Select this item and then click on the Properties button. This opens a new dialog box, in which you can see what the installation process discovered while installing the client software (see Figure 5-11).

From the IntranetWare Client tab, note any discrepancies between your connection parameters and those discovered by the installation process. If all looks well, click on the Login tab. This dialog box lets you configure the manner in which Windows 98 connects with a NetWare server. You can leave most of these options intact. But we suggest that you at least place a check mark in the first check box, labeled Display connection page (see Figure 5-12).

Doing so lets you modify the manner in which you log in (logging in to an NDS tree, logging directly in to a server, or using a bindery connection). If your MIS manager relies heavily upon NDS, make sure the "Log in to tree" button is selected. You can also tell the client to clear any existing network connections before logging in, which can be useful if you log out of your machine without rebooting.

From here, you can click on the Default Capture tab if you require any specific printing features, such as banners, extra form feed commands, and the like. However, it is very unlikely that you'll need to make any modifications in order to use NetWare's printing facilities.

Lastly, click on the Advanced Settings tab. This opens a dialog box from which you can modify a large number of connection parameters including:

▼ Workstation time

■ Level of security

■ Checksum level

■ Number of connection retries

■ DOS name for the client

■ Log file location

■ Number of printers captured per port

▲ Packet Burst Mode use

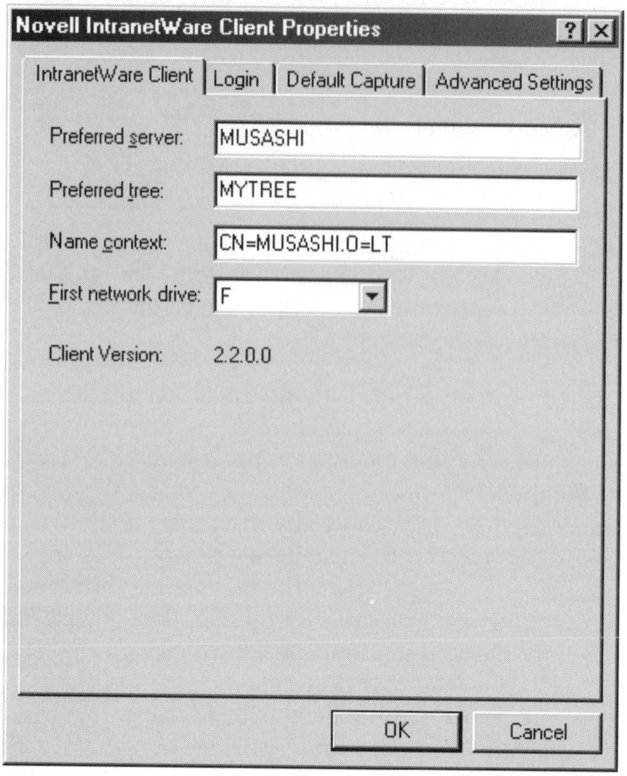

**Figure 5-11.** Viewing NetWare client properties

Unless you're having trouble with your connection, we recommend that you do not modify any of these settings. Of course, if your MIS manager has specified that each workstation under your influence must conform to specific guidelines, such as a higher level of security or increased use of checksums, then these settings will handle just about any configuration requirement imaginable.

Once you've verified your client settings, click on the OK button, which returns you to the Network dialog box. Here, make sure that the Primary Network Logon pull-down menu lists the Novell IntranetWare Client options and click on the OK button. Windows 98 then builds a driver information database and asks you to restart your computer in order to use the new NetWare client. As with the Microsoft Client for NetWare Networks, the Novell client prompts you to log in to your NetWare server via NDS or bindery emulation when your computer restarts.

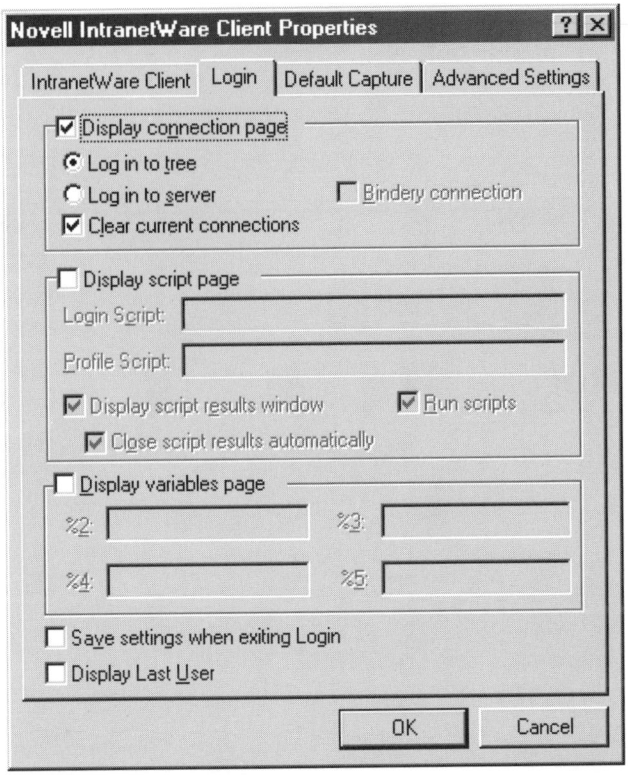

**Figure 5-12.**  NetWare login options

# GETTING STARTED WITH NETWARE

No matter which client type you choose, the best place to start networking with NetWare is to access a NetWare server. Because you already logged on to a NetWare server when you started Windows 98, you will be able to access that server by double-clicking on the My Computer icon on your desktop. This opens a list of all available services, which should include drives that map to NetWare volumes (see Figure 5-13).

As shown in Figure 5-13, NetWare creates a number of default drive mappings (in this case, Z:, Y:, and F:). You can work with these drives as though they were local drives on your machine with one exception. By right-clicking on any of these drives, you can open it in the current window, use Windows 98's Explorer to view its files, and even find files. But unlike traditional drives, you can also disconnect the drive without logging out from the NetWare server.

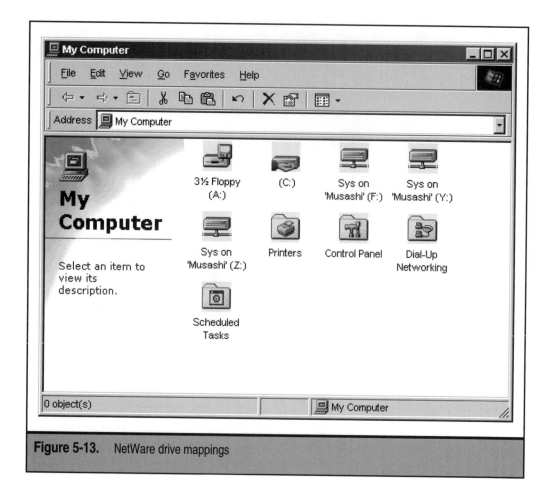

**Figure 5-13.** NetWare drive mappings

If, however, you have not yet logged in to a NetWare server, you can do so by double-clicking on the Network Neighborhood icon from the Windows 98 desktop. This window is your main access point for all NetWare services. Here, you should see at least two computers, one having the name of the NetWare server you logged on to after you rebooted your workstation and the other having the name of your workstation. Although these icons look identical, they allow you to perform very different activities. For example, if you first highlight the NetWare server icon and then right-click, you will notice a small pop-up screen containing a number of options: Open, Explore, Who Am I, Detach, Attach As, Map Network Drive, Create Shortcut, and Properties (see Figure 5-14).

To learn about this server, click on the Properties selection. A window should appear, indicating the name of the server, its make (in this case Novell), its version, revision dates, and copyright information. This window contains read-only information, however; you cannot change any of the information.

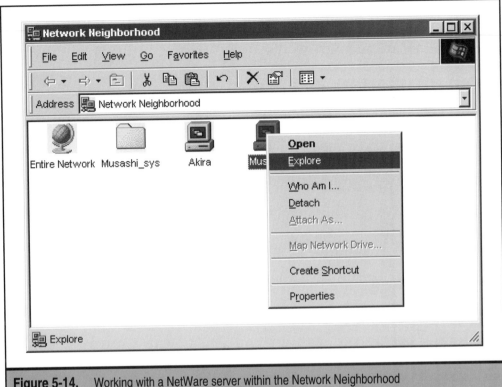

**Figure 5-14.**    Working with a NetWare server within the Network Neighborhood

## Exploring a NetWare Server

To discover more about your NetWare server, open the pop-up menu again and click on the Explore selection. This will launch the Windows 98 Explorer program (Explorer), which is the same program you use to explore the file system of your local machine. Here, it will simply be directed to begin at the selected file server instead of at your workstation (see Figure 5-15).

Explorer provides you with a wealth of information about your file server. For example, if you highlight your NetWare System Volume and select File and then Properties, you will see a window describing real-time information about this volume, such as its size, number of files, number of folders (directories), and the attributes (Hidden, Read Only, System, and so forth). If you would like to explore this volume further, you can activate the pop-up activity menu by placing the mouse pointer on the volume and right-clicking. This menu lets you further explore the volume, open the volume as a window, map a network drive to the volume, create a shortcut to the volume, or view its properties in the same manner as with the pull-down menu.

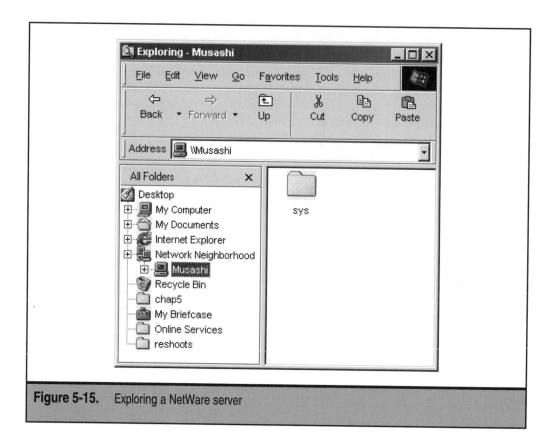

**Figure 5-15.** Exploring a NetWare server

## Executing Network Programs

Explorer is an excellent way to view your NetWare server and its installed volumes, but it is also an excellent way to perform network tasks. For example, you can execute programs and batch files from Explorer. To do this, activate the pop-up menu for the System volume by right-clicking the mouse and then clicking on the Open selection—you can also double-click on the volume folder icon.

Both methods will bring up a folder containing the contents of the System volume. Because Windows 98 is able to directly access NetWare file system information, folders will appear as folders, and files will appear as files. To go a little bit deeper, open the pop-up menu for the folder containing a program such as Microsoft Word for Windows 6.0 and click on the Open selection.

Of course, the Open menu option can be quickly circumvented by double-clicking on the desired object (document, folder, program, and so forth). If the object is an executable program, this starts the program. If the object is a document, double-clicking on it opens it in its associated word processing program. Documents that do not have any detectable associations will appear as white sheets of paper. If you double-click one of these, you are given a dialog box asking you which program you would like to associate with the document. To execute a program, such as the Microsoft Word for Windows installation utility, just double-click on the Setup icon and the program starts directly from the NetWare drive.

## Accessing Additional Servers

These principles can be applied to any file, directory, volume, or server in the NetWare environment. One object is the same as another to Windows 98. However, the server and its attached printers alone must be dealt with a bit differently than the other NetWare objects. This is because Windows 98 considers NetWare servers and NetWare print queues as separate network devices. Under the Universal Naming Convention (UNC) standard, when you view a NetWare server or print to a NetWare print queue, you are accessing completely separate entities. Before you installed Windows 98, you may have only needed to log in once to access all of your NetWare file servers. You can do this with Windows 98 too, but you must first tell Windows 98 which servers you want to connect with and under which names you want to be registered with those servers.

Before you can connect to your other NetWare servers, you must find those servers, and although you can utilize a command line utility to do this, Windows 98 can tell you which servers are attached to your network. As mentioned previously, you can see which NetWare servers are available by double-clicking on the Network Neighborhood icon within the Network Neighborhood window. This opens another window containing icons that correspond to the available network servers, regardless of their type, such as Windows NT, NetWare, or VINES. If you see a server icon to which you want to log in, simply open the pop-up menu with the right mouse button and click on the Login As selection. This opens a standard network login screen like the one shown here, which asks you for a user name and password:

If you are not sure about a user name, click on the Connect as Guest check box and then click on the OK button. If your network administrator has not deleted the guest user account, or if he/she has not placed a password on the guest user account, you will be logged in to the NetWare server. You will not be able to perform the same functions on it as you would on your initial server, however, as a guest account is generally given fewer access privileges.

# Selecting a NetWare Printer

Now that you are able to access NetWare servers and execute network applications, you will most likely want to print from one of these applications. If the printer is attached to your Windows 98 workstation, you can simply select the print option within an application, assuming you installed a printer either during installation or thereafter. But to utilize a printer attached to another workstation or a NetWare file server, you must follow a number of steps. First, from the Start button, select the Settings option, click on the Printers item and then double-click on the Add Printer icon. This opens a printer creation wizard. This is no different than installing a regular printer, except for two things: When you are asked which type of printer to install, select Network printer, and on the following screen, when you are asked to enter the network path to the printer, you must use UNC notation to tell Windows 98 the name of the desired NetWare print queue. If, for example, your print queue is named "Marketing," and the server upon which it is installed is named "Marketing_One," you would enter the following:

```
\\Marketing_One\Marketing
```

If you are unsure about either the server or the print queue's name, you can use the browsing facility to look for the appropriate services as you would use Explorer to search for an appropriate drive and file.

Once you have finished the creation of your NetWare printer object, your next step depends on whether or not the physical printer you wish to utilize is attached to your workstation. If the printer is attached to another workstation or directly to the network, you can immediately use your new printer. On the other hand, a network printer attached to your workstation must be able to communicate with a NetWare print server. This print server, which runs as a NetWare Loadable Module (NLM), resides upon a Novell NetWare server and communicates with the printers attached to its subnetwork. To enable the printer attached to your workstation to communicate with a NetWare print server, select the Properties item from the pop-up menu associated with the new network printer. In case you have created more than one printer (a local printer and a network printer), you can tell the difference between them by the connecting pipe attached to the network printer.

To use your network printer within an application such as Microsoft Word for Windows, you can simply click on the Print button if you have selected the network printer as your default printer. You'll see a dialog box like the one in Figure 5-1. If not, you should select the Print option from the File pull-down menu and then click on the Printer button. This gives you a Print Setup window listing installed printers, which should include your newly created network printer. You can now select the needed printer, and even set it as the default printer.

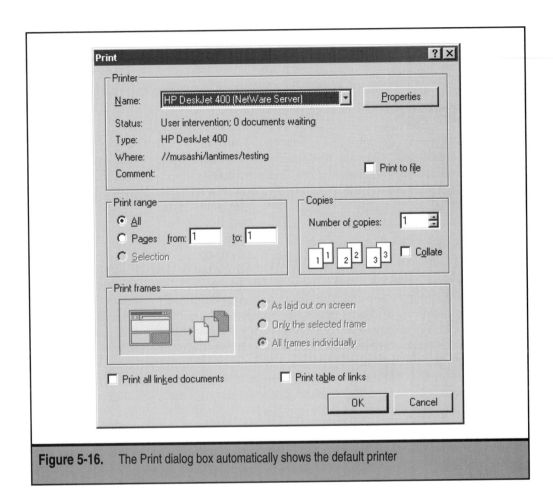

**Figure 5-16.** The Print dialog box automatically shows the default printer

# ADVANCED NETWARE SERVICES

Although the graphical user interface (GUI) of Windows 98 provides thorough network services for Novell NetWare, you may feel more comfortable working from a command line prompt, such as an MS-DOS user interface. You can do this within Windows 98 to perform, for example, a vast number of day-to-day routines such as mapping network drives, changing contexts (with NetWare 4.x and 5), printing files, or viewing directory rights.

This is possible through Windows 98's Virtual DOS Machines (VDMs). These sessions emulate MS-DOS 8086 machines, are capable of supplying over 600K of memory, and have the ability to run both DOS and Windows programs. Once you have established a Novell network connection, you can execute programs from the command line within Windows 98 just as you did with MS-DOS or Microsoft Windows.

There are, however, many other advanced features available within Windows 98. For example, you can map network drives to a NetWare volume or directory from a GUI. You can also ensure that any created drives are re-created the next time you boot Windows 98.

# MAPPING DRIVES

The first task you must accomplish in order to run programs from a NetWare file server involves the creation of a network drive mapping. Drive mappings allow applications to associated drive letters with NetWare resources, such as a volume or directory. There are two ways for you to initially do this: either through a command line or through the Windows 98 GUI.

## Command Line Drive Mappings

When you log in to a NetWare server under Windows 98, three things happen regarding network drives: any network drive mappings specified within your NetWare login script are established, any path statements within your AUTOEXEC.BAT file are instituted as search drive mappings, and any drives previously identified as re-establishable within the Windows 98 GUI are created. Therefore, it is unlikely that you will need to create any drive mappings once you have installed the Windows 98 network client. If need be, however, you can perform any NetWare drive mapping command from an MS-DOS session with the MAP.EXE program. For example, if you want to create a drive mapping for your system volume on a NetWare server, you can enter the following command:

```
MAP G:=MUSASHI/SYS:
```

MUSASHI represents the server name, and SYS represents the volume name. This creates a relationship between the letter G, the file server named MUSASHI and its System volume.

**CAUTION:** Make sure that the MAP command is in your path statement. When you log in to a NetWare server during Windows 98 startup, NetWare will take care of this for you. But if you log in manually from your Network Neighborhood folder, then you won't be able to run the MAP command from any drive location. To remedy the situation, you can either log off using the Start menu and then log back in normally, or you can go to the location of MAP.EXE and execute it directly. Its location is: //SERVERNAME/SYS/ PUBLIC/MAP.EXE

By adding another forward slash and the name of a subdirectory on the System volume, you can map a drive letter to a specific directory. For example, the following creates a new drive letter that starts inside the PUBLIC subdirectory:

```
MAP G:=MUSASHI/SYS/PUBLIC:
```

If you enter the drive letter G: from the command prompt, you'll be taken right to the PUBLIC directory.

Another nice feature about creating drive mappings in this fashion is that any mapping automatically becomes a part of all other processes within Windows 98. In other words, a drive mapping, once established, will work within each MS-DOS session or executed application automatically. However, when you reboot your machine, these command-line-created drive mappings will not be reinstated automatically. You will have to re-create them, as recently discussed.

To see what drive mappings are available to your workstation, just enter the MAP command with no parameters. This gives you a complete path statement, which includes the network drive mappings already in place (see Figure 5-17).

If you make a mistake in mapping a drive letter, you can remove the drive mapping by executing a command similar to this:

```
MAP DEL G:
```

This removes the drive labeled G:. However, if any applications are currently using the drive labeled G:, you will receive an error message indicating an error deleting the specified drive.

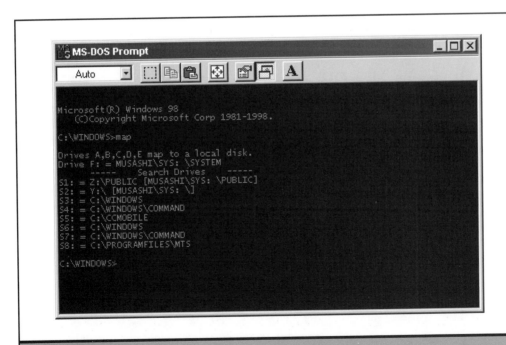

**Figure 5-17.** Checking drive mappings

## Microsoft Command Line Utilities

Microsoft Windows 98 clients come with their own set of network utilities that apply to all supported networks such as Banyan VINES or SunSoft. However, with Novell NetWare, these utilities are really only available at the time you boot your Windows 98 workstation. For example, the NET.EXE command can give you a great deal of information about your NetWare network, such as the number of attached servers and the current mapped drive configurations, but you cannot use it to log on or log off of NetWare servers. That only happens through the initial call to NET.EXE during the boot process. Do not worry, however, because all of the NET.EXE commands are supported through Windows 98's GUI.

But you can use it to gain simple information. For instance, if you type the following, you will see which servers are known to your workstation:

```
NET VIEW
```

As a note, you can use Novell's LOGOUT.EXE to log out from a NetWare server, but be careful because if you log out from the server supporting your last mapped drive, your MS-DOS session will have to be terminated.

**SHORTCUT:** The best way to log out from a NetWare server is to use the Logoff selection from the Windows 98 Start menu. This will disconnect your machine from all network resources and force you to log in again.

## Mapping Drives with the GUI

If you want to create drive mappings that will be reinstated the next time you boot Windows 98, you must either place those drive mappings in your NetWare login script or execute them from the Network Neighborhood window. To create a NetWare drive mapping, simply open the Network Neighborhood. Open a NetWare server icon from the pop-up menu, highlight a NetWare volume, and again open the pop-up menu. This displays a selection entitled Map Network Drive. Click on this selection and you will be given a screen from which you can map a drive (see Figure 5-18).

Select the Drive pull-down menu and choose the drive letter you want to associate with the system volume network. Once you have done this, you need only to ensure that the Reconnect at logon check box has been checked. That is all there is to working with NetWare from Windows 98.

# COMING UP

In this chapter, we addressed the topic of NetWare to Windows 98 connectivity, touching upon client installation issues, configuration tips, and client functionality. In the next chapter, we'll take this knowledge into the realm of the Internet. Historically, Windows

**Figure 5-18.** Mapping a network drive

clients connected with a specific server platform such as NetWare or LAN Manager. However, with the emergence of the Internet, a new, NOS-agnostic platform came into being, which allowed all sorts of server software such as Banyan VINES, Solaris, and the like to function identically. Instead of loading specific protocols for each server, clients could just run TCP/IP alone and connect with all of these servers identically. In the next chapter, we'll set Windows 98 to this task of connecting with a vast array of TCP/IP-savvy servers and services, ranging from Windows servers on your LAN to Web servers on the Internet. Along the way, you'll learn how to install, configure, and utilize a TCP/IP stack on your Windows 98 workstation. So prepare for ubiquitous connectivity. Prepare for the Internet.

NETWORK
PROFESSIONAL'S
LIBRARY

# CHAPTER 6

# Networking with TCP/IP

## What's ahead:

- Types of TCP/IP networks
- Preparing to use TCP/IP
- How to install and configure TCP/IP
- TCP/IP applications
- TCP/IP utilities

*"Let us, then, be up and doing,*
*With a heart for any fate;*
*Still achieving, still pursuing,*
*Learn to labour and to wait."*

—Henry W. Longfellow, *A Psalm of Life*

The Transmission Control Protocol/Internet Protocol (TCP/IP) was created for use as a networking protocol on UNIX computers. It was designed to provide peer-to-peer networking services over Wide Area Networks (WANs), and the early architects of the Internet chose to use TCP/IP. All Internet protocols are based on it, including Hypertext Transport Protocol (HTTP), File Transfer Protocol (FTP), Telnet, Simple Message Transport Protocol (SMTP), Post Office Protocol 3 (POP3), Network News Transfer Protocol (NNTP), and many others.

Installing and using TCP/IP on non-UNIX computers used to be a complicated undertaking that required purchasing protocol stacks and drivers from third-party vendors. Thanks to the popularity of the Internet, TCP/IP is now supported by virtually all shipping operating systems and is the default protocol in most of them, including Windows 98.

As you saw in Chapters 3, 4, and 5, you can use TCP/IP with Windows 98 to network in the traditional sense of using shared files and printers as though they were local resources. In this chapter, our focus is on TCP/IP-specific networking. We review the three common types of TCP/IP networks and discuss preparation to use TCP/IP, as well as installation and configuration of it in Windows 98. Finally, we review the TCP/IP applications and utility programs that ship with Windows 98.

# TYPES OF TCP/IP NETWORKS

When speaking of different *types* of TCP/IP networks, we don't mean to suggest that there are different versions of TCP/IP in use. The distinction has little to do with the physical configuration and workings of the network, and more to do with the applications and access permissions in use on the network. In fact, in many cases, the same physical network infrastructure is used to support all three types of TCP/IP networks simultaneously.

## Internet

Mention TCP/IP and most people immediately think of the Internet. In a nutshell, the Internet is the global network that interconnects all participating computer systems. In practical terms, it is made up of all the public TCP/IP-based Internet servers (Web, FTP, Mail, News, and so forth) and the client machines that access those servers from anywhere on the Internet.

Today, most businesses are connected to the Internet in some way. Many small businesses and companies that are in low-tech industries still use dial-up connections to connect to the Internet through an ISP only as needed (see Figure 6-1). The majority of medium- to large-size businesses are connected to the Internet through dedicated high-speed Internet connections.

Security becomes a big concern when your corporate network is connected to the Internet. For this reason, some sort of firewall or other physical separation must be used to control access to the corporate network from the Internet. The portion of the network that is fully exposed to the Internet becomes known as the *public* network, and the corporate network that is hidden behind the firewall is known as the *private* network.

## Intranet

*Intranet* is a fairly new term that has come to mean the private TCP/IP-based servers and the client machines that access those servers within an organization. Access is restricted and secured by some means, ranging from simple name and password authentication or IP address restriction, to using firewalls and gateways or similar means of isolating the private network from the public network and the Internet.

To many, "intranet" is just a fancy new term for describing the same network that's been called a local area network (LAN) for many years (see Figure 6-2). It's worth noting

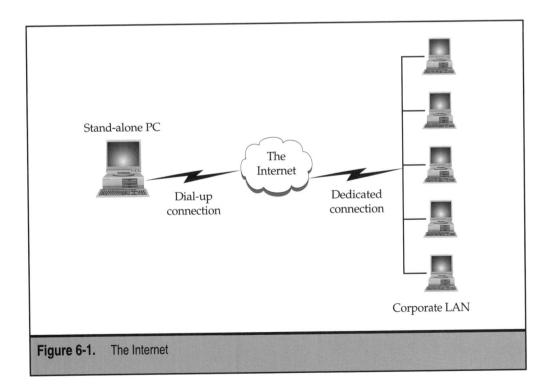

**Figure 6-1.** The Internet

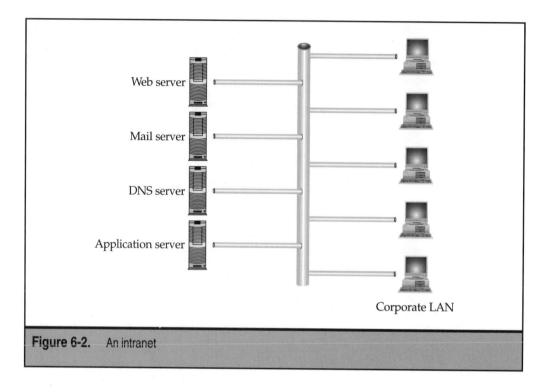

**Figure 6-2.** An intranet

that there are differences. While a LAN may be based on any networking protocol and might allow client workstations to directly access shared resources, an intranet is based on TCP/IP and relies on Internet standard servers to provide services to the client workstations. For example, it is not uncommon for LAN application software to open shared databases and directly manipulate their contents as though they were local files. On the other hand, intranet applications interact with an application server that controls all data access and is responsible for the security and integrity of the data.

At one point, "intranet" meant the private internal network that may or may not be linked to the Internet. But now it's defined by the resident applications and who can use them. It is not uncommon for employees to access intranet applications over the Internet, from home or while traveling.

## Extranet

The term *extranet* is a reference to those network services and TCP/IP-based servers that can be accessed by business partners, suppliers, customers, and others outside a corporate intranet. Like intranets, extranets are also defined by the types of applications available and who can access them.

Depending on your own security needs and network configuration, extranet services are typically provided by servers that reside on the public network with access restricted through password controls. But they may reside on the private network when greater security is needed or when users connect to the private network through Virtual Private Networking (VPN) services.

# PREPARING TO USE TCP/IP

Networking with TCP/IP can be tricky business. When armed with the right information, individual network users don't need a lot of background to configure TCP/IP on their individual workstations. But as a network administrator, you need to understand what each configuration setting actually means and why you are using them.

## Connections

The first thing you need to understand is how your computers are connected to the TCP/IP network. Windows 98 supports traditional local area network (LAN) connections via network interface cards (NICs) and dial-up connections using modems or ISDN adapters.

### LAN

Your corporate LAN is probably either already connected to the Internet or will be in the near future. There are so many different ways to connect a LAN to the Internet that they all couldn't possibly be covered here. The internet service provider (ISP) that you are connecting through and the manufacturer of the connectivity hardware you're using should be able to help you with that task. The current focus is on configuring Windows 98 to use that connection.

You need a valid IP address, a corresponding netmask, and the IP addresses of at least two different DNS servers. If your network is connected to the Internet or another network, you also need to know the IP address of the gateway. If you don't have that information handy, this is a good time to find it so you can follow along as TCP/IP configuration in Windows 98 is discussed. Alternatively, if you have a DHCP server on the network, you don't need to know any of this information because it is configured automatically each time the computer boots up.

If your private network is not and will not ever be connected to the Internet or another TCP/IP network, you can pretty much configure your TCP/IP settings any way you want. Just pick a range of IP addresses to use and identify the appropriate netmask so all workstations know that they reside on the same network segment.

### Dial-Up

Most dial-up connections fall into one of two categories. They are either used to link a single, stand-alone computer with a network via modem or ISDN connection, or they are used as a gateway or bridge to link two networks together.

If you are using a dial-up connection to link a single computer to the Internet or another TCP/IP network, chances are pretty good that you will be using the dial-up networking utilities that are built-in to Windows 98 to dial the host system, establish a Point-to-Point Protocol (PPP) connection, and automatically configure the necessary TCP/IP settings.

If you're using a dial-up connection to link your whole network to the Internet or another TCP/IP network, we'll leave it to you to configure the dial-up equipment by following the manufacturer's instructions. From that point on, for all practical purposes, you have a LAN connection.

# IP Addressing

If you have used other protocols such as IPX/SPX or NetBEUI in the past, but are new to networking with TCP/IP, one of the first things you probably noticed was the amount of work required to configure all the necessary settings before you can use it. Unlike those other protocols, TCP/IP address and routing information has to be specifically assigned to each computer on the network. While this may seem to be a burden at first, you will quickly come to appreciate that it is precisely because of this that the protocol is able to function so well as the basis for the Internet and private Wide Area Networks (WANs).

## IP Addresses

IP addresses can appear complex and intimidating until you realize they are just 32-bit numbers, commonly represented in a human-readable form, called *dotted quad notation*, as four groups of numbers separated by periods (i.e., 208.234.129.50). The IP address is actually made up of two parts—the network number (or subnet), and the host address that identifies the unique device on that network.

## Subnets

In the simplest of terms, there are four classes of subnets:

▼ Class A addresses are for large networks with up to 16,777,214 devices

■ Class B addresses are for medium-size networks with up to 65,534 devices

■ Class C addresses are for small networks with up to 254 devices

▲ Class D addresses are multicast addresses

Most administrators reading this book are probably working with Class C address allocations. But because there are a limited number of Class C allocations available, you might have a fractional Class C address allocation, commonly used when you can't justify the need for all 254 addresses available in a full Class C address block.

**NOTE:** IPv4 is the standard for IP addressing in use on the Internet today. But it's only a matter of time before all available address space will be used up. It is for this reason that IPv6 was created to expand the available address space from 32 bits to 128 bits. Windows 98 uses IPv4 addressing.

# Understanding Subnets and Netmasks

It's easy to determine the class an IP address belongs to by simply examining the first few bits of the address itself. The first bit of a Class A address is always 0. The first two bits of a Class B address are always 1 and 0. The first three bits of a Class C address are 1, 1, and 0. And the first four bits of a Class D address are 1, 1, 1, and 0.

But what about fractional Class C address allocations? When a Class C address block is split into multiple segments, how do you know whether another IP address within the same Class C identifier is in the same network segment? You use a subnet mask, commonly known as the netmask.

The netmask is used to determine whether a packet can be sent directly to the destination address or if it must be sent to the defined gateway address for routing to the appropriate network segment. Netmasks can be tricky to master unless you're good at doing binary number conversions in your head. For the rest of us, the following chart is a valuable reference. Keep in mind that the first three numbers (24 bits) in a Class C address represent the network address. The last number (8 bits) represents the host address. For this reason, the first three numbers (24 bits) in a Class C netmask are always 255.255.255, and the last number (8 bits) is used to identify the number of IP addresses in the network segment. Because the first and last IP addresses in every segment are reserved as the Network Address and Broadcast Address, respectively, the actual number of IP addresses available in each subnet is reduced accordingly.

Figuring out which netmask to use and whether two IP addresses reside in the same subnet can be tricky. The following tables will help you understand which netmask to use, and the range of IP addresses in each subnet.

- **Allocation**   /24
- **Netmask**   255.255.255.0

- **Number of subnets**   1
- **Hosts per subnet**   254

| Network Address | IP Range | Broadcast Address |
| --- | --- | --- |
| .0 | .1–.254 | .255 |

- **Allocation**   /25
- **Netmask**   255.255.255.128

- **Number of subnets**   2
- **Hosts per subnet**   126

| Network Address | IP Range | Broadcast Address |
| --- | --- | --- |
| .0 | .1–.126 | .127 |
| .128 | .129–.254 | .255 |

- **Allocation**   /26
- **Netmask**   255.255.255.192

- **Number of subnets**   4
- **Hosts per subnet**   62

| Network Address | IP Range | Broadcast Address |
|---|---|---|
| .0 | .1–.62 | .63 |
| .64 | .65–.126 | .127 |
| .128 | .129–.190 | .191 |
| .192 | .193–.254 | .255 |

- Allocation /27
- Netmask 255.255.255.224

- Number of subnets 8
- Hosts per subnet 30

| Network Address | IP Range | Broadcast Address |
|---|---|---|
| .0 | .1–.30 | .31 |
| .32 | .33–.62 | .63 |
| .64 | .65–.94 | .95 |
| .96 | .97–.126 | .127 |
| .128 | .129–.158 | .159 |
| .160 | .161–.190 | .191 |
| .192 | .193–.222 | .223 |
| .224 | .225–.254 | .255 |

- Allocation /28
- Netmask 255.255.255.240

- Number of subnets 16
- Hosts per subnet 14

| Network Address | IP Range | Broadcast Address |
|---|---|---|
| .0 | .1–.14 | .15 |
| .16 | .17–.30 | .31 |
| .32 | .33–.46 | .47 |
| .48 | .49–.62 | .63 |
| .64 | .65–.78 | .79 |
| .80 | .81–.94 | .95 |
| .96 | .97–.110 | .111 |
| .112 | .113–.126 | .127 |
| .128 | .129–.142 | .143 |
| .144 | .145–.158 | .159 |
| .160 | .161–.174 | .175 |

| | | |
|---|---|---|
| .176 | .177–.190 | .191 |
| .192 | .193–.206 | .207 |
| .208 | .209–.222 | .223 |
| .224 | .225–.238 | .239 |
| .240 | .241–.254 | .255 |

- **Allocation**  /29
- **Netmask**  255.255.255.248

- **Number of subnets**  32
- **Hosts per subnet**  6

| Network Address | IP Range | Broadcast Address |
|---|---|---|
| .0 | .1–.6 | .9 |
| .8 | .9–.14 | .15 |
| .16 | .17–.22 | .23 |
| .24 | .25–.30 | .31 |

. . . and so on (table abbreviated).

- **Allocation**  /30
- **Netmask**  255.255.255.252

- **Number of subnets**  64
- **Hosts per subnet**  2

| Network Address | IP Range | Broadcast Address |
|---|---|---|
| .0 | .1–.2 | .3 |
| .4 | .5–.6 | .7 |
| .8 | .9–.10 | .11 |
| .12 | .13–.14 | .15 |

. . . and so on (table abbreviated).

As you can see, the further you subdivide your Class C allocation, the more IP addresses you actually lose to the overhead of network and broadcast addresses. The last two tables (Allocation: /29 and Allocation: /30) are abbreviated because it's fairly unlikely that you will ever actually subnet a Class C allocation that far. If you do, the first four entries that are listed should be enough for you to understand the pattern of allocation and complete the table yourself.

## Domain Names

IP addresses are difficult to type and even harder to remember. Fortunately, there is a better way; it's called the Domain Name System (DNS). In a nutshell, the DNS allows you to address other machines with a user-friendly name instead of their IP address. A DNS server is then queried for the corresponding IP address, which is then used to address the TCP/IP packets before they are sent to their destination. For example, you might use www.lantimes.com instead of typing 204.151.55.175 every time you want to visit the *LAN Times* Web site.

Domain names are actually deconstructed from right to left, as delimited by the periods, or *dots* (www.lantimes.com is pronounced "www dot lantimes dot com"). The right-most identifier is known as the top-level domain name. Table 6-1 shows the most common top-level domain names.

Additional top-level domain names have been created for specific countries (such as UK for the United Kingdom and DE for Germany), and several private organizations have proposed the creation of many more.

The next identifier is the registered domain name. Additional identifiers are used to further specify the host in question. For example, www.mydomain.com and ftp.mydomain.com are commonly used to identify the Web and FTP servers for a given domain.

## Routing

Routing is the core feature that makes TCP/IP so well-suited to WAN applications. Packets are successfully routed to their final destination through a combination of both simple and complex routing rules and techniques. The routing rules that client workstations need to understand are actually pretty simple. The complex routing is all handled by sophisticated routing hardware on the Internet Backbone.

| | |
|---|---|
| COM | Commercial Organizations |
| EDU | Educational Institutions |
| GOV | Government Institutions |
| MIL | Military Institutions |
| NET | Major Network Support Centers |
| ORG | Other Organizations (non-profit, for example) |

**Table 6-1.** Top-Level Domain Names

If your organization is large enough to have multiple routers requiring the proper configuration and maintenance of routing tables, you probably have trained personnel on staff to manage them, so that really isn't necessary to discuss here.

As far as a Windows 98 workstation is concerned, there are only three ways to route a TCP/IP packet: direct, through a gateway, or via a proxy server.

## Direct

When the TCP/IP protocol stack needs to send a data packet to another system, it uses the netmask to compare the destination address with the current station address. If the comparison determines that the destination address resides on the same subnet, the packet is sent directly to its destination.

## Gateways

If the comparison determines that the destination is not on the same subnet, the packet is instead sent to the address specified as the network gateway in the TCP/IP configuration. The computer or router at that address is then expected to re-route the packet to the next point closer to its intended destination. This process repeats until the packet reaches the intended recipient. Windows 98 does not have to be concerned with all the details of how the packet is ultimately routed; it only needs to know the address of the designated gateway.

## Proxy Servers

A proxy server is a lot like a gateway, except that all packets are referred to the proxy server without discrimination. This means that even if the destination machine resides on the same subnet, the packet is still referred to the proxy server.

There are a lot of good reasons to use a proxy server, including increased performance and security. When many people on the subnet routinely access the same information, a proxy server that also performs caching can improve performance by reducing the amount of redundant data that has to be sent between your private network and the Internet. Proxy servers can also play a key role in your security plans, providing functionality similar to a firewall by filtering and controlling the packets that are allowed to pass between your private network and the Internet based on criteria such as IP address, port number, and protocol.

# INSTALLING AND CONFIGURING TCP/IP

Before you can begin networking with TCP/IP, you must first make sure that everything is installed and configured correctly. Unlike the IPX/SPX and NetBEUI protocols, TCP/IP requires some manual configuration before it functions correctly.

## Installing

The procedures for installing network adapters and protocols was discussed at length in Chapters 3, 4, and 5. If you are unsure how to do this, you should refer back to those chapters to install the necessary NIC or dial-up network adapter and the TCP/IP protocol before proceeding to the next section, which walks you through configuration of the necessary TCP/IP settings.

## Configuring

If you are connected to a LAN through a NIC, it is important that you configure the TCP/IP Properties correctly. If you are using a dial-up connection to the TCP/IP network, these settings are configured automatically during the Point-to-Point Protocol (PPP) negotiation each time you connect with the remote access server, and it is advised that you do not change any of the default settings in the TCP/IP Properties screens.

To configure the TCP/IP settings, select the TCP/IP entry in the Network dialog box and click on the Properties button. This opens a TCP/IP Properties dialog containing seven tabs. The following sections review each of these tabs and the proper settings you should enter.

**NOTE:** If you use a DHCP server to automatically configure the IP, DNS, WINS, and Gateway addresses, you can skip those configuration tabs, leaving the default settings intact.

### Bindings

On the Bindings tab (see Figure 6-3), you see each of the services that have been installed and you can check and uncheck the selection box next to each item by clicking on the box with your mouse. In most cases, you see at least two entries in this screen: "Client for Microsoft Networks" and "File and printer sharing for Microsoft Networks." If you have installed additional services such as the Microsoft Personal Web Server, you will also see them listed here. If TCP/IP is your primary network protocol, or if you are unsure, you should check all of the boxes on this tab.

### Advanced

With the TCP/IP protocol, there is only one option on the Advanced tab that you need to care about (see Figure 6-4). At the bottom of the window, there is a check box titled "Set this protocol to be the default protocol." Only one protocol can be set as the default protocol at any given time. If this option is grayed-out, it means that another protocol is

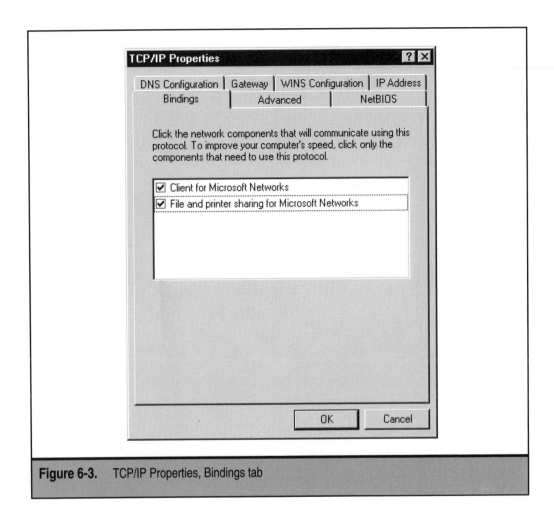

**Figure 6-3.**    TCP/IP Properties, Bindings tab

already configured as the default protocol. You should check this box if TCP/IP is your only protocol or if you are sure that it is the most common protocol on your network.

## NetBIOS

As previously discussed, Windows 98 has the ability to run NetBIOS applications over the TCP/IP protocol. The only configuration setting on the NetBIOS tab is a check box to enable this functionality. You should enable this option if you are using TCP/IP in a

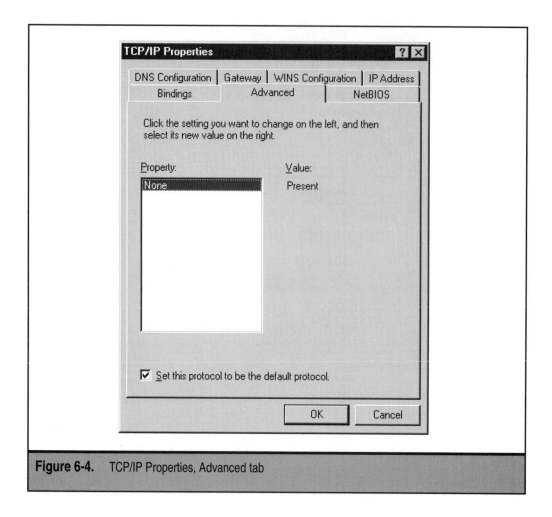

**Figure 6-4.** TCP/IP Properties, Advanced tab

network environment with other Microsoft Windows computers and are not using IPX/SPX or NetBEUI. If you are using the TCP/IP protocol strictly for Internet access, you might as well leave this option disabled.

## DNS Configuration

As discussed earlier in this chapter, the Domain Name System (DNS) is used to convert user-friendly domain names into their respective IP addresses. From the Windows 98 perspective, you need not concern yourself about how to configure or maintain a DNS server, only with how to tell Windows 98 the address of your DNS server.

If you were provided with the address of your DNS servers (it is customary to have at least two—a primary and a secondary), select the option "Enable DNS" and then enter the host and domain names for your computer and the DNS server addresses on the DNS Configuration tab (see Figure 6-5). If you do not have this information, leave the default setting "Disable DNS" alone.

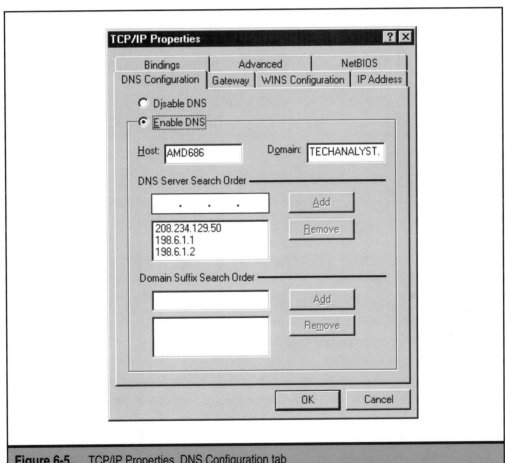

**Figure 6-5.**   TCP/IP Properties, DNS Configuration tab

## Using the HOSTS File to Resolve TCP/IP Host Names

There may be times when you need to access other computers via TCP/IP using their host names, but you either don't have a DNS server or your DNS server may be unable to resolve the desired host name. Windows 98 provides a solution via the use of a special file named HOSTS that resides in the Windows directory. Whenever Windows is unable to resolve a host name via the DNS service, it then checks the contents of this file, looking for a match.

A sample HOSTS file exists in your Windows directory with the file name of HOSTS.SAM, which looks like the following:

```
# Copyright (c) 1998 Microsoft Corp.
#
# This is a sample HOSTS file used by Microsoft TCP/IP stack for Windows 98
#
# This file contains the mappings of IP addresses to host names. Each
# entry should be kept on an individual line. The IP address should
# be placed in the first column followed by the corresponding host name.
# The IP address and the host name should be separated by at least one
# space.
#
# Additionally, comments (such as these) may be inserted on individual
# lines or following the machine name denoted by a '#' symbol.
#
# For example:
#
#      102.54.94.97     rhino.acme.com        # source server
#      38.25.63.10      x.acme.com            # x client host

127.0.0.1       localhost
```

The HOSTS file is particularly useful on small networks that do not have a DNS configured to resolve the host names of each computer on the network. If you need to create a HOSTS file and are unfamiliar with the file format, you can rename or copy the HOSTS.SAM file to HOSTS then edit it, adding your entries at the bottom.

# Gateway

If your LAN is connected to the Internet or another TCP/IP network, you need to tell Windows 98 the address of the gateway, or router, that will route packets between the two networks. All packets destined for IP addresses that are not on the same subnet as your computer are routed to the gateway address for forwarding to their intended destination.

If you know the IP address of the gateway, select the Gateway tab of the TCP/IP Properties dialog box (see Figure 6-6) and enter that information now.

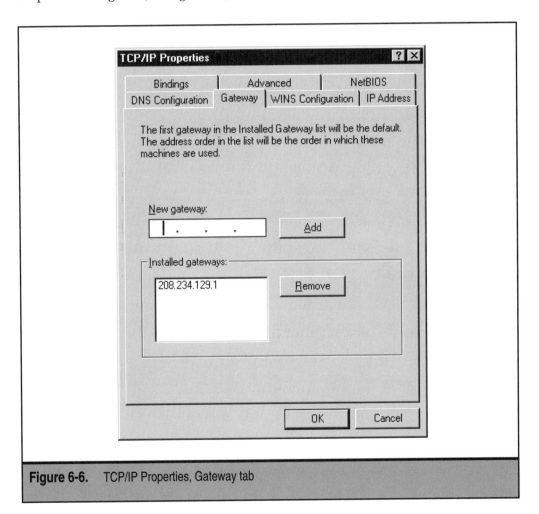

**Figure 6-6.** TCP/IP Properties, Gateway tab

## WINS Configuration

The Windows Internet Naming Service (WINS) is used to resolve the NetBIOS names and IP addresses of other computers on the network. It plays an integral role in Windows 98's ability to browse the Network Neighborhood or locate other computers by name. When a WINS server is not available, or when it does not contain all the station and domain information necessary, a special file named LMHOSTS can be used in its place or as a supplement.

How WINS actually works—and how it interacts with the LMHOSTS file and DNS services—is fairly complicated and completely dependent on whether you have a Windows NT server on the network that is acting as a WINS server.

From the Windows 98 perspective, all that matters is that you enable WINS services and enter the correct WINS server address on the WINS Configuration tab (see Figure 6-7) if you were provided the address of a WINS server by your network administrator. If

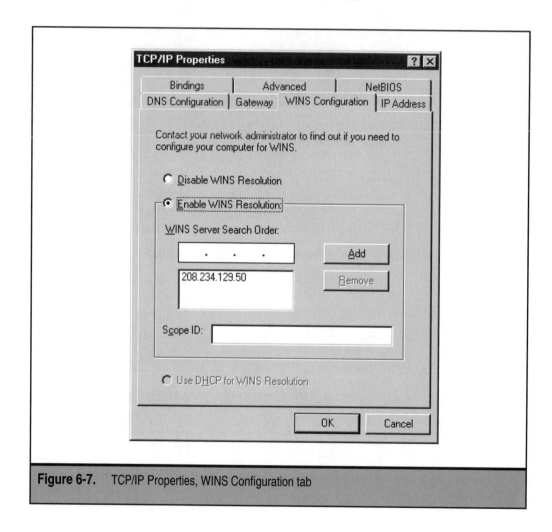

**Figure 6-7.**    TCP/IP Properties, WINS Configuration tab

you do not have this information, you should leave the default setting "Disable WINS Resolution" selected and ignore the rest of that screen.

## Using the LMHOSTS File to Resolve NetBIOS Names

Just as the HOSTS file provides the ability to resolve TCP/IP host names, the LMHOSTS file provides the ability to resolve NetBIOS host names. The sample LMHOSTS file that ships with Windows 98, named LMHOSTS.SAM, looks like the following:

```
# Copyright (c) 1998 Microsoft Corp.
#
# This is a sample LMHOSTS file used by the Microsoft Wins Client (NetBios
# over TCP/IP) stack for Windows 98
#
# This file contains the mappings of IP addresses to NT computernames
# (NetBIOS) names.  Each entry should be kept on an individual line.
# The IP address should be placed in the first column followed by the
# corresponding computername. The address and the computername
# should be separated by at least one space or tab. The "#" character
# is generally used to denote the start of a comment (see the exceptions
# below).
#
# This file is compatible with Microsoft LAN Manager 2.x TCP/IP lmhosts
# files and offers the following extensions:
#
#       #PRE
#       #DOM:<domain>
#       #INCLUDE <filename>
#       #BEGIN_ALTERNATE
#       #END_ALTERNATE
#       \0xnn (non-printing character support)
#
# Following any entry in the file with the characters "#PRE" will cause
# the entry to be preloaded into the name cache. By default, entries are
# not preloaded, but are parsed only after dynamic name resolution fails.
#
# Following an entry with the "#DOM:<domain>" tag will associate the
# entry with the domain specified by <domain>. This affects how the
# browser and logon services behave in TCP/IP environments. To preload
# the host name associated with #DOM entry, it is necessary to also add a
# #PRE to the line. The <domain> is always preloaded although it will not
# be shown when the name is viewed.
```

```
#
# Specifying "#INCLUDE <filename>" will force the RFC NetBIOS (NBT)
# software to seek the specified <filename> and parse it as if it were
# local. <filename> is generally a UNC-based name, allowing a
# centralized lmhosts file to be maintained on a server.
# It is ALWAYS necessary to provide a mapping for the IP address of the
# server prior to the #INCLUDE. This mapping must use the #PRE directive.
# In addition the share "public" in the example below must be in the
# LanManServer list of "NullSessionShares" in order for client machines to
# be able to read the lmhosts file successfully. This key is under \machine\
# system\currentcontrolset\services\lanmanserver\parameters\nullsessionshares
# in the registry. Simply add "public" to the list found there.
#
# The #BEGIN_ and #END_ALTERNATE keywords allow multiple #INCLUDE
# statements to be grouped together. Any single successful include
# will cause the group to succeed.
#
# Finally, non-printing characters can be embedded in mappings by
# first surrounding the NetBIOS name in quotations, then using the
# \0xnn notation to specify a hex value for a non-printing character.
#
# The following example illustrates all of these extensions:
#
# 102.54.94.97     rhino          #PRE #DOM:networking  #net group's DC
# 102.54.94.102    "appname  \0x14"                     #special app server
# 102.54.94.123    popular             #PRE            #source server
# 102.54.94.117    localsrv            #PRE            #needed for the include
#
# #BEGIN_ALTERNATE
# #INCLUDE \\localsrv\\public\\lmhosts
# #INCLUDE \\rhino\\public\\lmhosts
# #END_ALTERNATE
#
# In the above example, the "appname" server contains a special
# character in its name, the "popular" and "localsrv" server names are
# preloaded, and the "rhino" server name is specified so it can be used
# to later #INCLUDE a centrally maintained lmhosts file if the "localsrv"
# system is unavailable.
#
```

```
# Note that the whole file is parsed including comments on each lookup,
# so keeping the number of comments to a minimum will improve performance.
# Therefore it is not advisable to simply add lmhosts file entries onto the
# end of this file.
```

As you can see, the LMHOSTS file has the potential to be more complex than the HOSTS file, but everything you need to know is contained in the LMHOSTS.SAM example file. The file is parsed line-by-line each time Windows is unable to resolve a NetBIOS host name. If the file becomes large, the time required to parse the file can impact performance. You can speed up your system by simply reducing the number of comment lines that exist in the file.

## IP Address

Your IP address is perhaps the most important TCP/IP configuration setting. It can be specified two ways: The computer can obtain a dynamic IP address automatically from a DHCP server every time you boot up, or you can specify a static IP address that never changes (see Figure 6-8).

It is important that no two computers are configured for the same IP address. Doing so results in unpredictable behavior and unreliable communications on both computers. If you were given a specific IP address and subnet mask by your network administrator, select the option "Specify an IP address" and enter this information on the IP Address tab of the TCP/IP Properties dialog box. If you were not provided with an IP address by your network administrator, select the option "Obtain an IP address automatically," which causes your computer to locate the DHCP server and request an unused IP address every time you boot.

# TCP/IP APPLICATIONS

File and printer sharing with Windows 98 was discussed at length in Chapters 3, 4, and 5. As long as you enable NetBIOS over TCP/IP and have either a WINS server or LMHOSTS file, you'll find that it works exactly the same way.

Our focus in this section is on TCP/IP-specific applications such as Web browsing, e-mail, FTP file transfers, and Telnet.

## Web Browsing

Web browsing is certainly one of the most popular TCP/IP applications supported by Windows 98. In fact, full integration of the Internet Explorer Web browser is considered by many to be the most significant enhancement in Windows 98.

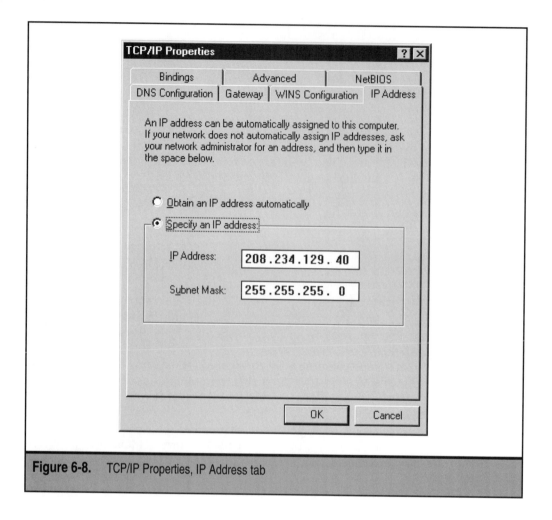

**Figure 6-8.** TCP/IP Properties, IP Address tab

Internet Explorer is discussed at length in Chapter 9, so we won't go into it here.

# E-Mail

Despite the popularity of the Web, e-mail is still the most widely used TCP/IP (Internet) application. Even organizations that do not have full-time Internet connections or that use filtering to restrict employees' use of the Internet almost always maintain the continuous flow of Internet e-mail. Microsoft Exchange and Outlook Express e-mail client software are included in Windows 98.

Messaging, including Exchange and Outlook Express, is discussed in Chapter 10.

# FTP

In the early days of the Internet, before the Web became popular, most files were exchanged using the File Transfer Protocol (FTP). While FTP is still used today, most people never need to use a traditional FTP client. In fact, the version of FTP that ships with Windows 98 is still a DOS text-mode application, controlled by a traditional command-line interface.

FTP is designed to accomplish two things: Upload files from a local computer to a remote host and download files from a remote host to a local computer. The Internet Explorer Web browser actually has built-in support for using FTP to download files from sites that allow anonymous logins. However, if you find it necessary to download a file from a secure FTP server or upload a file to an FTP server, you'll need to use an FTP utility to do it.

The most common use for FTP today is to upload Web pages and graphics files to remote Web site hosting services. But even that is becoming less and less necessary as most Web authoring tools now have built-in support for publishing new and updated content directly to service providers.

One of the trickiest things about using FTP is that the information displayed and the commands necessary to accomplish specific tasks are largely dependent on the FTP server, not on the FTP client software. If you need to use FTP, you should obtain specific instructions explaining how to log on to the server and the commands to use for navigating the site and uploading or downloading files.

**RESOURCE:** If you need to use FTP with any regularity, we recommend that you test-drive a shareware FTP client program called WS_FTP, which can be downloaded from the Shareware.com Web site at http://www.shareware.com. WS_FTP is an FTP client that makes it easy to exchange files with virtually any FTP server through an intuitive GUI user interface.

Installing and configuring Web and FTP services on Windows 98 is discussed in Chapter 13. If you're interested in a more in-depth discussion of FTP, you might want to skip ahead and read that chapter now.

# Telnet

Telnet is a primitive protocol for connecting to host computers and running simple text-mode applications over TCP/IP connections. In a nutshell, it is a text-mode terminal emulation program. As graphical user interfaces (GUIs) and TCP/IP-aware client applications have become the norm, Telnet applications have become almost extinct. Of those that remain, many have been seamlessly integrated into other, more sophisticated, applications that shield the user from the details of using Telnet.

The Telnet client that ships with Windows 98 is a basic but functional implementation, supporting only VT-52 and VT-100/ANSI terminal emulations.

Like FTP, Telnet is a TCP/IP application that most Windows 98 users will never need. Users who do need to use Telnet should obtain detailed instructions from a network administrator.

# TCP/IP UTILITIES

Windows 98 includes several utilities that can be a lot of help when troubleshooting your TCP/IP configuration and functionality. As you might expect, the traditional Ping and Tracert utilities are included with Windows 98, as is Address Resolution Protocol. Three additional Windows-specific TCP/IP utilities—Netstat, Net Diag, and WinIPcfg—are also included.

## ARP

When Windows 98 is ready to send an IP packet to another device on the same TCP/IP segment, as determined by comparing the destination address to the computer's own IP address and netmask, it uses the Address Resolution Protocol (ARP) to determine the physical Ethernet address of the destination. For performance reasons, the operating system maintains a list of recently discovered IP-to-Physical Address translations, which you can view by using the ARP utility.

If you type ARP with no parameters, the system displays a help screen with text like the following:

```
Displays and modifies the IP-to-Physical address translation tables used by
address resolution protocol (ARP).

ARP -s inet_addr eth_addr [if_addr]
ARP -d inet_addr [if_addr]
ARP -a [inet_addr] [-N if_addr]

    -a              Displays current ARP entries by interrogating the current
                    protocol data.  If inet_addr is specified, the IP and Physical
                    addresses for only the specified computer are displayed.  If
                    more than one network interface uses ARP, entries for each ARP
                    table are displayed.
    -g              Same as -a.
    inet_addr       Specifies an internet address.
    -N if_addr      Displays the ARP entries for the network interface specified
                    by if_addr.
    -d              Deletes the host specified by inet_addr.
    -s              Adds the host and associates the Internet address inet_addr
                    with the Physical address eth_addr.  The Physical address is
                    given as 6 hexadecimal bytes separated by hyphens. The entry
                    is permanent.
    eth_addr        Specifies a physical address.
    if_addr         If present, this specifies the Internet address of the
                    interface whose address translation table should be modified.
                    If not present, the first applicable interface will be used.
```

Except for very special circumstances, the only parameter you should ever need to use is the –a parameter, which causes the utility to list all known physical addresses, as shown here:

```
Interface: 208.234.129.40 on Interface 3
   Internet Address      Physical Address      Type
   208.234.129.20        00-00-a0-09-05-3d     dynamic
   208.234.129.30        00-50-4e-00-71-97     dynamic
   208.234.129.35        00-aa-00-21-a6-e7     dynamic
   208.234.129.50        00-00-6e-24-b3-34     dynamic
```

Windows actually uses ARP for every packet it sends, not just those that are destined for the local subnet. This is because all other packets are routed to the designated gateway address, which must always reside on the local subnet.

# Ping

Ping is perhaps the simplest diagnostic tool available for testing TCP/IP connectivity. The Ping utility simply sends out a short message to the specified IP address. Once received at its destination, the message is echoed back to the sending computer. Most Ping utilities, including the version provided with Windows 98, send several ping packets that measure and report the time it takes for each packet to make the round-trip from your computer to the destination and back.

Although you can specify a number of parameters, such as the number of times to ping the destination and the maximum amount of time to wait for a response, the default settings are usually sufficient. The only thing you absolutely have to specify is the destination IP address or host name. For example, to ping www.techanalyst.com, which has an IP address of 208.234.129.50, you can type either of the following two commands:

```
Ping www.techanalyst.com
```

```
Ping 208.234.129.50
```

The response in both cases will look like this:

```
Pinging www.techanalyst.com [208.234.129.50] with 32 bytes of data:
Reply from 208.234.129.50: bytes=32 time=1ms TTL=128
Reply from 208.234.129.50: bytes=32 time=1ms TTL=128
Reply from 208.234.129.50: bytes=32 time=1ms TTL=128
Reply from 208.234.129.50: bytes=32 time=1ms TTL=128

Ping statistics for 208.234.129.50:
    Packets: Sent = 4, Received = 4, Lost = 0 (0% loss),
Approximate round trip times in milliseconds:
    Minimum = 1ms, Maximum =  1ms, Average =  1ms
```

If you ever find it necessary to change any of the other supported parameters, you can access a help screen that lists all available parameters by typing the following command:

```
Ping -help
```

The output from this command will resemble the following:

```
Usage: ping [-t] [-a] [-n count] [-l size] [-f] [-i TTL] [-v TOS]
            [-r count] [-s count] [[-j host-list] | [-k host-list]]
            [-w timeout] destination-list
Options:
    -t              Ping the specified host until stopped.
                    To see statistics and continue - type Control-Break;
                    To stop - type Control-C.
    -a              Resolve addresses to hostnames.
    -n count        Number of echo requests to send.
    -l size         Send buffer size.
    -f              Set Don't Fragment flag in packet.
    -i TTL          Time To Live.
    -v TOS          Type Of Service.
    -r count        Record route for count hops.
    -s count        Timestamp for count hops.
    -j host-list    Loose source route along host-list.
    -k host-list    Strict source route along host-list.
    -w timeout      Timeout in milliseconds to wait for each reply.
```

Ping is supported by all TCP/IP implementations, but for security reasons, some platforms allow you to ignore Ping requests or otherwise turn off Ping responses.

## Tracert

The Tracert utility, which stands for *trace route,* is a handy utility that's not much more sophisticated than Ping, except that it reveals the route taken to get from you to the destination machine. Even the basic usage syntax is identical to Ping—just specify the destination IP address or host name. For example, to ping the *LAN Times* Web site, you could enter either of the following commands:

```
Tracert www.lantimes.com
```

```
Tracert 204.151.55.175
```

The output resulting from either command resembles the following:

```
Tracing route to www.lantimes.com [204.151.55.175]
over a maximum of 30 hops:
  1     5 ms     5 ms     5 ms   x1.TECHANALYST.COM [208.234.129.1]
  2    50 ms    49 ms    50 ms   tnt14.sfo3.da.UU.NET [206.115.155.78]
  3    54 ms    49 ms    50 ms   e1-5.ar2.sfo3.da.UU.NET [207.76.58.162]
  4    49 ms    49 ms    50 ms   452.ATM3-0-0.XR2.SFO4.Alter.NET [137.39.82.78]
  5    50 ms    50 ms    50 ms   190.ATM11-0-0.BR1.SFO1.Alter.NET [146.188.145.217]
  6    52 ms    52 ms    51 ms   h14-1.t12-0.San-Jose.t3.ANS.NET [207.25.133.13]
  7   101 ms   101 ms   100 ms   h13-1.t24-2.Chicago.t3.ANS.NET [140.223.13.18]
  8   124 ms   123 ms   122 ms   f1-1.t60-7.Reston.t3.ANS.NET [140.223.60.208]
  9   122 ms   127 ms   122 ms   f5-0.c60-14.Reston.t3.ANS.NET [140.223.60.210]
 10   129 ms   126 ms   128 ms   www.lantimes.com [204.151.55.175]
```

```
Trace complete.
```

Many of the host names displayed by Tracert have cryptic names that appear meaningless at first glance. But look a little closer and you can actually tell quite a lot about the route your IP packets travel. You can almost always recognize which ISP owns each router by its domain name. In the preceding example, the first hop was to our own router on the TechAnalyst.com domain, the second and third hops were owned by UUNet; the fourth and fifth were AlterNet routers; the sixth through the ninth hops were ANS; and the tenth was to the *LAN Times* Web server.

To view a list of all available Tracert parameters, simply execute the command without any parameters, like this:

```
Tracert
```

The output from this command resembles the following:

```
Usage: tracert [-d] [-h maximum_hops] [-j host-list] [-w timeout] target_name

Options:
    -d                      Do not resolve addresses to host names.
    -h maximum_hops         Maximum number of hops to search for target.
    -j host-list            Loose source route along host-list.
    -w timeout              Wait timeout milliseconds for each reply.
```

Sometimes when you run Tracert, your report contains entries that contain asterisks (*) in place of the response times and the text "Request timed out" in place of the host name. This indicates that the destination is either unreachable, has been configured to ignore ping requests, or that one of the routers/gateways that your request passed through chose not to propagate the request. Because Ping requests are low priority and their delivery is not guaranteed, any router along the path can arbitrarily decide to ignore them. Under normal circumstances, this only happens if the router is experiencing a heavy load or if it has been specifically configured to ignore all such packets.

## Netstat

The Netstat utility displays protocol statistics and current TCP/IP connections. To display the Netstat help screen, simply type the command followed by the question mark, like this:

```
Netstat ?
```

The result from this command resembles the following:

```
Displays protocol statistics and current TCP/IP network connections.

NETSTAT [-a] [-e] [-n] [-s] [-p proto] [-r] [interval]

  -a            Displays all connections and listening ports.
  -e            Displays Ethernet statistics. This may be combined with the -s
                option.
  -n            Displays addresses and port numbers in numerical form.
  -p proto      Shows connections for the protocol specified by proto; proto
                may be TCP or UDP.  If used with the -s option to display
                per-protocol statistics, proto may be TCP, UDP, or IP.
  -r            Displays the routing table.
  -s            Displays per-protocol statistics.  By default, statistics are
                shown for TCP, UDP and IP; the -p option may be used to specify
                a subset of the default.
  interval      Redisplays selected statistics, pausing interval seconds
                between each display.  Press CTRL+C to stop redisplaying
                statistics.  If omitted, netstat will print the current
                configuration information once.
```

By default, Netstat only displays active connections. The -a parameter yields more useful information, including all active ports on the computer that are listening for connection requests. Execute the Netstat program with the –a parameter as shown here:

```
Netstat -a
```

The result is a listing of all known IP addresses as shown here:

```
Active Connections

    Proto   Local Address          Foreign Address                    State
    TCP     AMD686:1026            AMD686:0                           LISTENING
    TCP     AMD686:1075            AMD686:0                           LISTENING
    TCP     AMD686:1075            www.TECHANALYST.COM:nbsession      ESTABLISHED
    TCP     AMD686:137             AMD686:0                           LISTENING
    TCP     AMD686:138             AMD686:0                           LISTENING
    TCP     AMD686:nbsession       AMD686:0                           LISTENING
    UDP     AMD686:1026            *:*
    UDP     AMD686:nbname          *:*
    UDP     AMD686:nbdatagram      *:*
```

If you're connected to a LAN via an Ethernet adapter, Netstat can also display statistics about the number of bytes, packets, discards, and errors sent and received. Execute Netstat now with the following command:

```
Netstat -e
```

The information on your screen should now resemble the following:

```
Interface Statistics

                            Received            Sent

Bytes                       10233263            867465
Unicast packets             16274               9570
Non-unicast packets         1329                100
Discards                    0                   0
Errors                      0                   0
Unknown protocols           832
```

When routing was discussed earlier in this chapter, we said that Windows 98 only uses very simple routing rules on the workstation, based on the destination address compared to the computer's own IP address and netmask. While that was completely true, it only told part of the story. If, for example, your computer contains more than one NIC card, every NIC has to be assigned a unique IP address and Windows has to know which packets to route through which adapter. To see the actual table of routing rules that Windows 98 uses, run Netstat with the -r parameter, as follows:

```
Netstat -r
```

Information like the following output should appear on screen:

```
Route Table

Active Routes:

    Network Address  Netmask           Gateway Address    Interface        Metric
    0.0.0.0          0.0.0.0           208.234.129.1      208.234.129.40     1
    127.0.0.0        255.0.0.0         127.0.0.1          127.0.0.1          1
    208.234.129.0    255.255.255.0     208.234.129.40     208.234.129.40     1
    208.234.129.40   255.255.255.255   127.0.0.1          127.0.0.1          1
    208.234.129.255  255.255.255.255   208.234.129.40     208.234.129.40     1
    224.0.0.0        224.0.0.0         208.234.129.40     208.234.129.40     1
    255.255.255.255  255.255.255.255   208.234.129.40     0.0.0.0            1

Active Connections

    Proto  Local Address          Foreign Address                      State
    TCP    AMD686:1075            www.TECHANALYST.COM:nbsession        ESTABLISHED
```

It's unlikely that you will ever actually need the Netstat utility, but the time you spend playing with it and learning what its output means is sure to be highly educational.

# Net Diag

Windows 98 also includes a more traditional diagnostic program called Net Diag. Net Diag requires that you have control over at least two computers on the network—one to act as the diagnostic server and the other to act as the client.

The first time you run the program, you are asked if the Microsoft Network Diagnostic program is running on any other computers. If you answer No, the program acts as the diagnostic server and begins listening for other computers running the diagnostic program on the network, as shown in the following listing:

```
Microsoft Network Diagnostics will use a NetBIOS provider.
Searching for diagnostic server...

No diagnostic servers were detected on the network.
Is Microsoft Network Diagnostics currently running on any other computers
on the network ? (Y/N)
This computer will now begin acting as a diagnostic server.

Press any key to stop acting as a diagnostic server.
```

You can terminate the diagnostic mode and return to the command line by simply pressing the spacebar.

When you run the program from a second computer while the first computer is acting as the diagnostic server, the computers should detect each other and complete their test sequence without further interference or involvement by the user, as shown in the following output:

```
Microsoft Network Diagnostics will use a NetBIOS provider.
Searching for diagnostic server...

The diagnostic server has been located on the network.
Communicating with diagnostic server. This may take several seconds.
Validating reply from diagnostic server.
The diagnostic server's reply is correct.
This indicates that network information is being sent and received properly.

The command was completed successfully.
```

If no problems are encountered, the program completes its diagnostics without further delay, then returns you to the command line.

## WinIPcfg

The final TCP/IP utility to discuss in this chapter is called WinIPcfg (see Figure 6-9). This utility is the only Windows GUI of the lot and is used to view your current TCP/IP

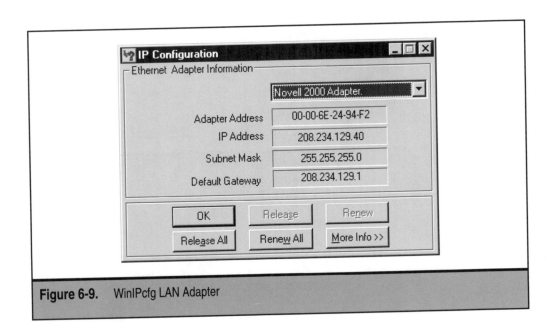

**Figure 6-9.**   WinIPcfg LAN Adapter

settings, including IP address, subnet mask, default gateway, host name, DNS servers, DHCP server, WINS servers, and related information.

If you are using a dial-up connection to connect to the Internet (see Figure 6-10) or a corporate TCP/IP network and you run WinIPcfg when you are not connected, the IP address fields will be all zeroes.

Click on the More Info button to view advanced configuration settings including the address of your DNS, DHCP, and WINS servers (see Figure 6-11).

If you have more than one network adapter installed, which is pretty common on computers that are both connected to the LAN through a NIC and equipped with a modem for dial-up connectivity to the Internet, you can change the display to reflect the current settings for each adapter by clicking on the drop-down control next to the adapter name and selecting the desired entry. You will also find a button next to the DNS Servers field that allows you to cycle through all configured DNS servers in the same order that Windows 98 searches them to resolve domain names.

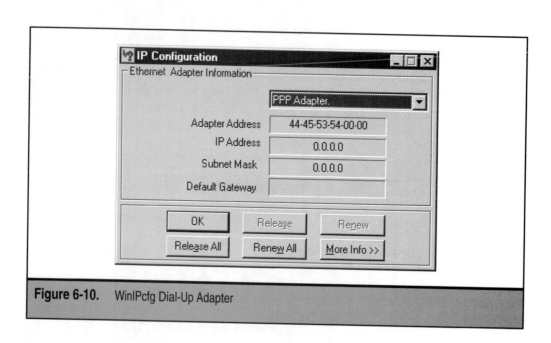

**Figure 6-10.** WinIPcfg Dial-Up Adapter

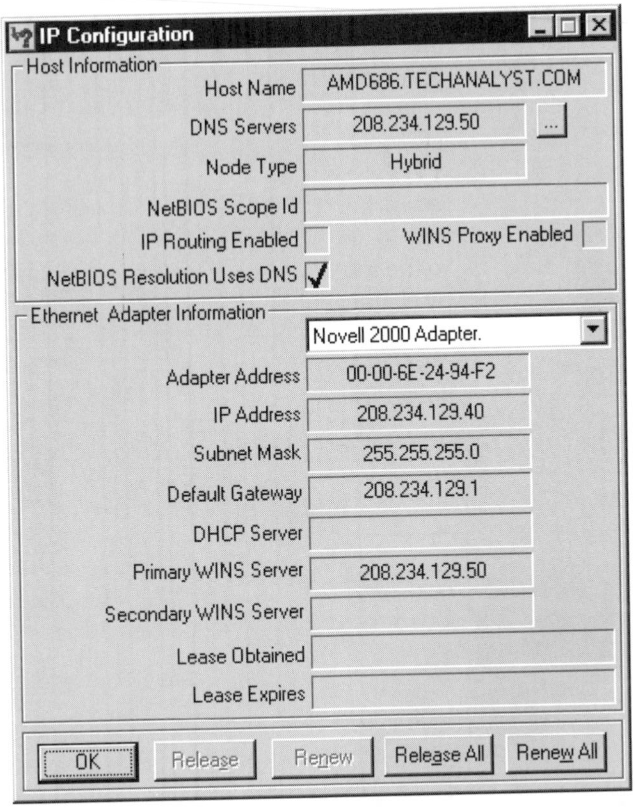

| IP Configuration | | | |
|---|---|---|---|

**Host Information**

| | |
|---|---|
| Host Name | AMD686.TECHANALYST.COM |
| DNS Servers | 208.234.129.50 ... |
| Node Type | Hybrid |
| NetBIOS Scope Id | |
| IP Routing Enabled | WINS Proxy Enabled |
| NetBIOS Resolution Uses DNS | ✓ |

**Ethernet Adapter Information**

Novell 2000 Adapter.

| | |
|---|---|
| Adapter Address | 00-00-6E-24-94-F2 |
| IP Address | 208.234.129.40 |
| Subnet Mask | 255.255.255.0 |
| Default Gateway | 208.234.129.1 |
| DHCP Server | |
| Primary WINS Server | 208.234.129.50 |
| Secondary WINS Server | |
| Lease Obtained | |
| Lease Expires | |

OK    Release    Renew    Release All    Renew All

**Figure 6-11.**   WinIPcfg Details

# COMING UP

In the next chapter, we discuss remote access and telecommuting with Windows 98, including a discussion of configuring the operating system as a Remote Access Server (RAS) and how to telecommute using Windows 98 as your client.

NETWORK
PROFESSIONAL'S
LIBRARY

# CHAPTER 7

# Remote Access and Telecommunications

**What's ahead:**

- Benefits of telecommuting
- Preparing to use Dial-Up Networking
- Remote access with Windows 98
- Using Windows 98 Dial-Up Networking client
- Beyond dial-up: the virtual private networking client

> *"Endurance is the crowning quality,*
> *And patience all the passion of great hearts."*

—Christopher Columbus

The terms "telecommuting" and "remote access" both describe the same general activity—that of using telecommunications technology as a means of accessing computer systems from remote locations. In a practical sense, the difference is that remote access is used to describe any activity in which you communicate with computer systems in a different location, such as accessing the corporate network from home or browsing Web pages in your leisure time. By comparison, telecommuting has come to describe remote access in the context of working from a remote location.

Windows 98 includes powerful yet easy-to-use Dial-Up Networking client and server software that provides remote access and telecommunications functionality. But first it must be installed and configured correctly. In this chapter we'll teach you how to do so.

# BENEFITS OF TELECOMMUTING AND REMOTE ACCESS

The benefits of telecommuting and remote access are fairly obvious but generally fall into two categories: time and money. Time savings can be significant as a result of less time spent commuting to and from the office, and the ability to collaborate with coworkers in different locations or support installations in remote locations without delay. Money is saved for many of the same reasons, and many companies are able to realize substantial savings by reducing the amount of office space and corresponding furniture and equipment required to support their growing number of employees.

Windows 98 is an excellent client platform for telecommuting and remote access because its built-in support for Dial-Up Networking provides connectivity to all popular remote access servers. In addition, the included Dial-Up Server allows you to access your Windows 98 computers or small-office networks from remote locations without investing in expensive remote access equipment or Windows NT Servers.

# PREPARING TO USE DIAL-UP NETWORKING

Whether you are using Windows 98 as a dial-up networking server or as a dial-up networking client, there are certain hardware and software requirements that must be satisfied before you can begin.

## Required Hardware

Dial-up networking is remarkably similar to a local area network (LAN). In both cases, you need to have a physical connection between computers over which they can communicate. But instead of using a network interface card (NIC) and coaxial or unshielded twisted pair (UTP) cabling, dial-up networking uses modems or ISDN adapters (jointly referred to as modems throughout the remainder of this chapter) to communicate over dial-up telephone lines. The most important consideration is that the modems used at the server and at the client must be compatible with each other.

How you physically install your modem depends on whether you have an internal modem or an external modem.

## Internal Modem

By convention, your computer communicates with the modem through a serial port. This is true even when you are using an internal modem. The difference is that with an internal modem, the serial port is built into the modem.

Physically installing your modem is not a difficult task, but due to the wide variety of hardware available, that procedure is beyond the scope of this book. If you are not familiar with this process, you should refer to the documentation that came with your computer and your modem, or consult with your hardware support personnel to complete the physical installation of your internal modem before proceeding.

## External Modem

External modems are all installed in pretty much the same way. The modem typically requires three connections. The first connects the modem to a serial port on your computer using a standard RS-232 serial cable. The second is a power connection. The third connection is for the telephone line.

# Required Software

There are five software components that must be installed and properly configured before you can use Windows 98 for dial-up networking:

▼  Modem driver

■  Dial-up networking component

■  Dial-up adapter

■  Networking protocols

▲  Dial-up server software (only on machines functioning as a dial-up server)

The following sections review each of these components and discuss in general terms how and where they are installed, in preparation for a later discussion of how to use Windows 98 as both a dial-up networking server and as a dial-up networking client. (Note: Throughout this chapter, will assume that you are now familiar with how to perform basic tasks such as opening the Windows Control Panel and other processes that were explained in detail throughout earlier chapters.)

## Modem Driver

Depending on a number of factors, Windows 98 may have auto-detected your modem the first time you started the computer after installing it. If not, you will have to tell Windows to search for it and possibly even install the necessary driver files by manually selecting your modem from a list of supported devices.

To begin, open the Windows Control Panel and double-click on the Modems icon. If no modems are installed, Windows will go directly into the Install New Modem Wizard, as shown here:

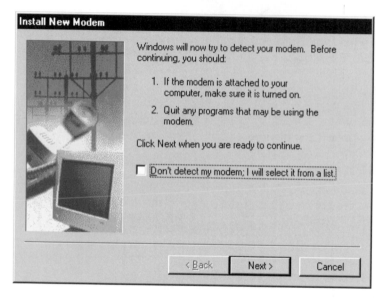

In most cases, it's best to let Windows search for and identify your modem. If the Install New Modem Wizard does not begin automatically and your modem does not appear in the Modem Properties window, you can click on the Add button to launch the wizard at any time. Click on the Next button to continue.

If Windows is able to locate your modem, it displays the Verify Modem dialog box, as shown next. This dialog box identifies the modem that was detected and tells you how it is connected (COM1, COM2, and so forth):

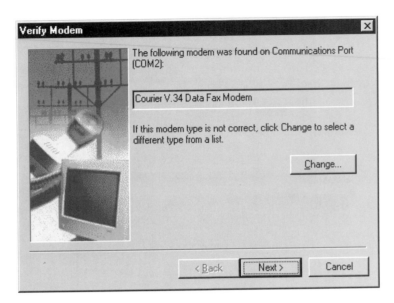

Click on the Next button to complete the wizard.

If no new modems are detected, Windows tells you so and gives you the opportunity to manually select one, as shown here:

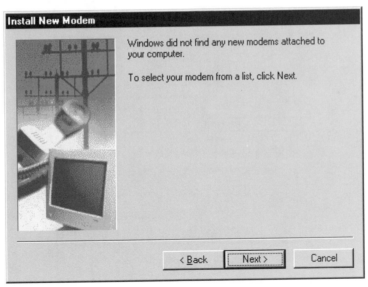

Now your modem should be listed in the Modems Properties dialog box, which should look similar to the following:

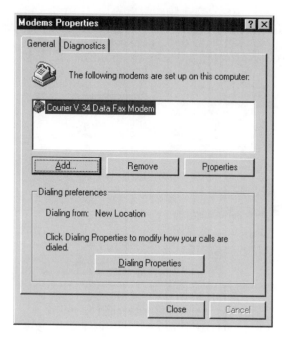

To learn more about the modem configuration and verify that it is working correctly, click on the Diagnostics tab. You'll see a window like this:

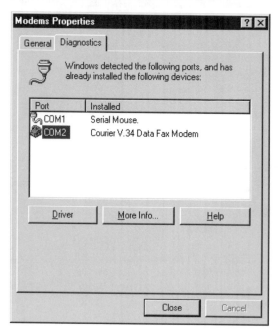

Now click one time on the entry representing your modem to select it, then click on the More Info button. This causes Windows to test its ability to communicate with your modem as it retrieves additional information about the device and displays it on the screen, as shown here:

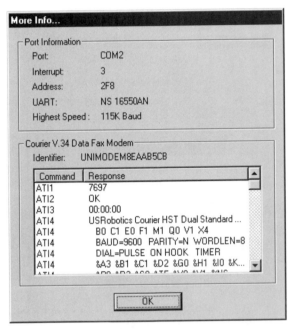

Don't be alarmed if you see entries in the Response window that say "ERROR". This typically means that the particular feature that was queried by the corresponding Command is not supported by your modem. For example, if your modem does not support Fax capabilities, you will always get an error in response to the AT+FCLASS command.

That's it. If you made it this far, your modem is connected to the computer and the necessary software driver files have been installed correctly. If you encountered problems or could not get Windows to recognize your modem, double-check your hardware connections and try again or refer to the documentation that came with your modem in case it requires the installation of special drivers.

**SOAPBOX:** There are many new modems that Windows 98 cannot recognize until you first install special software drivers that are provided by the manufacturer. This is rarely the case with conventional modems, but is not uncommon when working with a "Software Modem" or "Win Modem," because these modems rely on special software to provide some of the functionality that is usually provided by the modem itself.

## Dial-Up Networking Component

The next Windows component you need to install is the Dial-Up Networking component. To install it, or verify that it is already installed, open the Windows Control Panel and double-click on the Add/Remove Programs icon. This opens the Add/Remove Programs Properties window:

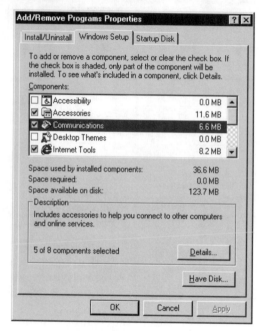

Click on the Windows Setup tab to view installed components and select new components to be installed. The Dial-Up Networking component is contained in the Communications section. Click on that entry once to select it, then click on the Details button to open the Communications dialog box, showing the available communications-related components, as you can see here:

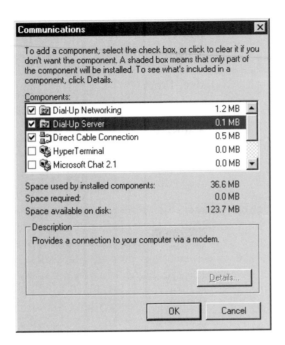

The very first entry in this window should be Dial-Up Networking. If the component is not already installed, as indicated by a check mark in the box on the left, select it now by clicking on that check box. Now close the window by clicking on the OK button, and close the Add/Remove Programs Properties window by clicking on its OK button.

If you selected any components that were not already installed, Windows will now proceed to install the necessary software onto your computer. This process may require your Windows 98 CD-ROM and will likely require you to reboot your computer.

## Dial-Up Adapter

When you installed the Dial-Up Networking component, as was just discussed, the Dial-Up Adapter should have been installed automatically as part of that process. If for some reason it was not, or if you have removed it from the Network dialog box, you need to reinstall it before you can proceed.

Open the Windows Control Panel and double-click on the Network icon. This opens Windows Network dialog box, which was discussed at length in previous chapters and should be familiar to you by now. If you do not see the Dial-Up Adapter in the list of installed components, click on the Add button, specify Adapter, select Microsoft as the manufacturer, then select the Dial-Up Adapter.

Although you can edit the properties of the Dial-Up Adapter just like any other network adapter, you should not do so unless you have a specific reason to do so. Configuration settings for the Dial-Up Adapter are generally determined dynamically when you establish a connection using Windows Dial-Up Networking.

## Networking Protocols

Networking protocols were discussed at length in Chapters 3, 4, and 5, so they are not addressed again here except as they pertain specifically to Dial-Up Networking with Windows 98.

If you are using Dial-Up Networking to connect to your corporate network from a remote location, there are some distinct advantages to using the IPX/SPX protocol, but only if that protocol is used by the other computers on your corporate network. With the IPX/SPX protocol, you are able to see and access other Windows computers on the network just as if you were connected to the network by a traditional LAN connection.

The Dial-Up Networking Server included with Windows 95 is not able to route TCP/IP packets between remotely connected Dial-Up Networking clients and other computers on the corporate network. When you connect to a Windows 98 Dial-Up Networking Server, your visibility is limited to the Dial-Up Networking Server machine only.

*SOAPBOX:* More sophisticated Remote Access Servers such as Microsoft Remote Access Service (RAS) for Windows NT Server do have full support for routing TCP/IP traffic between remotely connected Dial-Up Networking client computers and other computers on the corporate network or the Internet.

If you are only installing Dial-Up Networking for Internet connectivity, TCP/IP is the only protocol you need to install. If you are connecting to a corporate network via a true RAS server, such as Microsoft RAS on Windows NT Server, TCP/IP can be used for full network access.

## Dial-Up Server

Windows 98 ships with an optional component called the Dial-Up Server that allows your computer to act as a single port Remote Access Server. This component must be installed before you can use Windows 98 as a dial-up server.

To install it, or verify that it is already installed, open the Windows Control Panel and double-click on the Add/Remove Programs icon. This opens the Add/Remove Programs Properties dialog box.

Click on the Windows Setup tab to view installed components and select new components to be installed. The Dial-Up Server component is contained in the Communications section. Click on that entry once to select it, then click on the Details button to open the Communications dialog box, which shows the available communications-related components.

The second entry in this window should be Dial-Up Server. If the component is not already installed, as indicated by a check mark in box on the left, select it now by clicking on that checkbox. Close the window by clicking on the OK button, and close the Add/Remove Programs Properties window by clicking on its OK button.

If you selected any components that were not already installed, Windows will now proceed to install the necessary software onto your computer. This process may require your Windows 98 CD-ROM and will likely require you to reboot your computer.

# REMOTE ACCESS WITH WINDOWS 98 DIAL-UP SERVER

With the necessary hardware and software installed, you're ready to configure your computer as a dial-up server. If you're interested in using Dial-Up Networking only as a client, skip ahead to the next section entitled "Using Windows 98 Dial-Up Networking Client."

## Limitations of the Dial-Up Server

The Windows 98 Dial-Up Server has several important limitations. The first limitation you need to be aware of is that it supports only one dial-up connection at a time. Even if you were to connect multiple modems to your computer, you would not be able to service more than one connection at a time. You should consider Microsoft Windows NT Server with Remote Access Service (RAS) if you need to provide remote access for more than one connection at a time.

The second limitation you should be aware of is that Windows 98 does not support IP forwarding, also known as *routing*. This is important if your Windows network is based on TCP/IP because the remote dial-up client will be able to see only the Windows 98 computer that it is connected to. If your Windows network is based on the IPX/SPX protocol, remote dial-up clients will be able to see other computers on the network and access shared files and printers. You should consider Microsoft Windows NT Server with RAS if you need to provide remote access to a TCP/IP-based network or to the Internet.

The third limitation discussed here concerns Virtual Private Networking (VPN). VPN facilitates secure remote access by encrypting all communications between the dial-up server and the remote dial-up client. Windows 98 ships with the VPN Dial-Up Client software adapter, but it does not provide the server component. You should consider Microsoft Windows NT Server with RAS if you need to provide remote VPN connections to your network.

## Configuring the Dial-Up Server

Begin by double-clicking on the My Computer icon on your desktop. This opens the My Computer window, as shown next. Locate and double-click on the Dial-Up Networking icon.

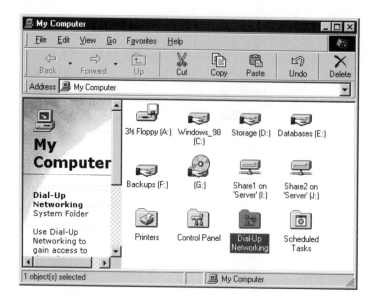

**SHORTCUT:**   You can also access Dial-Up Networking from the Windows Start menu by clicking on Windows Start button, then selecting Programs, Accessories, Communications, and finally Dial-Up Networking.

The Dial-Up Networking dialog box opens as shown next, displaying icons for "Make New Connection" and any dial-up connections that are defined.

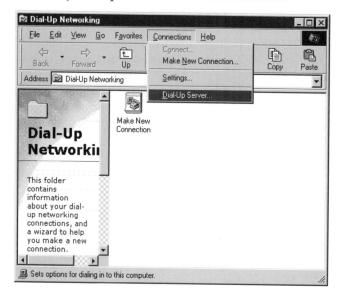

The special thing to notice about this window is the Connections menu item at the top. You can access the Dial-Up Networking configuration settings, including those pertaining to the Dial-Up Server, from this menu.

Go ahead and select the Connections menu, then click on the Dial-Up Server menu item to open the Dial-Up Server configuration dialog box, as shown here:

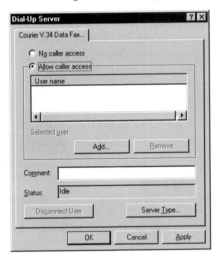

By default, the "No caller access" option is selected. To enable remote access, you must first select the "Allow caller access" option, as shown above. Before clicking on the Apply button, which causes the new setting to take affect and causes Windows 98 to answer incoming phone calls, first make sure that the rest of your Dial-Up Server configuration settings are correct.

Click on the Server Type button to open the Server Types dialog box, as shown in the following illustration:

This dialog box contains three configuration settings. The first allows you to specify the type of dial-up server ("Default"; "PPP: Internet, Windows NT Server, Windows 98"; or "Windows for Workgroups and Windows NT 3.1"). In most cases, you should leave this set to the "Default" setting. If you have trouble logging on to the Dial-Up Server, try changing this setting to the "PPP: Internet, Windows NT Server, Windows 98" option.

The other two options, "Enable software compression" and "Require encrypted password," are both selected by default, and you should leave them that way unless you have a good reason to change them. "Enable software compression" simply tells the computer to enable this functionality if it is supported by the client, resulting in faster throughput and better overall performance. "Require encrypted password" prohibits the exchange of any user authentication information that is not encrypted and should only be used if all computers that connect from remote are running on Windows.

Once you have verified all three settings, click on the OK button to close this dialog box.

The last option you need to select in the Dial-Up Server configuration dialog box is the Change Password option. Click on the Change Password button, then enter the password information you wish to use.

That's all there is to it. Now you're ready to begin accepting remote dial-up connections. Just click on the Apply button to cause your new configuration settings to take effect and you'll be ready to accept incoming calls. As you can see in the following illustration, the Dial-Up Server displays the word "Monitoring" in the Status window while it listens for an incoming phone call.

Once the line rings, it changes the status to "Answering" and instructs the modem to answer the phone. While a user is connected, the status shows the name of the remote user and the time that they connected.

The Disconnect User button is active whenever a remote user is connected to the Dial-Up Server. Clicking on the button disconnects the remote user, even if they are in the process of transferring files, printing, or have shared files open for editing.

# USING WINDOWS 98 DIAL-UP NETWORKING CLIENT

To connect with a remote computer system or network via modem connection, you need to use the Windows 98 Dial-Up Networking Client.

## What Is the Dial-Up Networking Client?

The Dial-Up Networking Client manages everything Windows 98 needs to know about a remote Dial-Up Server in order to connect to it, including the telephone number to dial, name and (optional) password, communications parameters, and appropriate protocol settings. It works hand-in-hand with Windows 98's built-in networking to provide the same functionality whether you are connected via direct-connect LAN or dial-up modem connection.

## Configuring a New Dial-Up Networking Connection

Open the Dial-Up Networking dialog box like you did before—by double-clicking on the My Computer icon on your desktop, then double-clicking on the Dial-Up Networking icon, shown here:

In the Dial-Up Networking dialog box, you will see an icon titled "Make New Connection," as shown next. Double-click on it to begin the Make New Connection Wizard.

The wizard proceeds to prompt you through a series of questions about the connection, beginning with the name you want it to have, as shown in the following illustration. This name is used only for display on your local system and does not need to match the host or computer name of remote dial-up server to which you will be connecting.

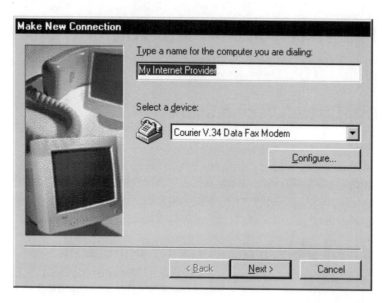

Once you have entered the name, click on the Next button to proceed to the next step.

The next thing you are asked to enter is the phone number that Windows 98 will have to dial to connect to the remote system. Enter it in the space provided, as shown in the following illustration, and click on the Next button to proceed.

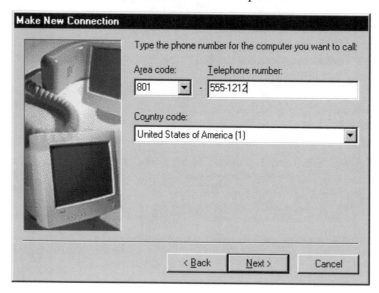

Now click on the Finish button to save your new connection information and create the icon in the Dial-Up Networking dialog box, as shown here:

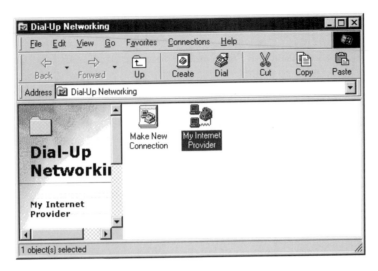

The wizard has finished, but you're not done configuring the dial-up connection yet. Right-click once on the icon representing your new connection, then select Properties from the pop-up menu. This opens the Properties window for your newly created Dial-Up Networking connection, which looks something like this:

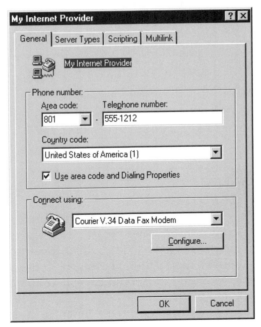

Along the top of the dialog box, you will see four tabs titled "General," "Server Types," "Scripting," and "Multilink." In most cases, you won't need to customize settings on all of these pages, but let's take a look at the available configuration settings so you will be able to find them when you need them.

The General page contains the phone number to dial, includes an option to specify whether to use the area code and dialing properties, and identifies the modem device that will be used to connect when necessary. The Make New Connection wizard should have completed this information based on the answers you gave earlier.

Click on the Server Types tab to select the next page of configuration settings, as shown here:

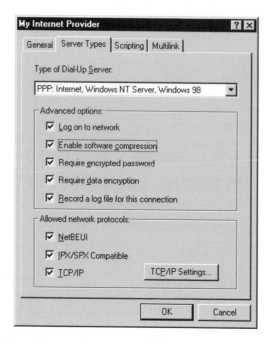

This page of configuration settings controls how you will interact with the dial-up server after the modems have connected.

The "Type of Dial-Up Server" field defaults to the "PPP" option, which is correct if you are connecting to a Windows 98 or Windows NT Dial-Up or RAS server, and for connecting to nearly all Internet service providers (ISPs). Because this is the focus of this book, we recommend you leave this setting unchanged. If you ever have a need to use one of the other available settings, you should consult your system administrator for further instructions before proceeding.

The Advanced options area of this screen contains three options. "Log on to network" is for use when you are connecting to a remote Windows network and you want to log on to that network as though you had a LAN connection. "Enable software compression" determines whether Windows will be permitted to compress data before transmitting it to the server. Compression generally improves throughput and transfer speeds and will be used only if both the client and the server support it. "Require encrypted password" provides a more secure login because your name and password are not sent to the server in human-readable form. If you are not sure whether the server you are calling supports this feature, we recommend first trying the connection with this option selected. If you are unable to connect, disable the setting and try again.

The bottom third of this window is titled "Allowed network protocols" and contains a list of the three network protocols that are supported by Windows 98's Dial-Up Networking: NetBEUI, IPX/SPX, and TCP/IP. By default, all three protocols will be checked, but you should clear the check marks next to any protocol you do not need this dial-up connection to support. You will not be able to connect if you specify a protocol that the dial-up server does not support. Specifying a protocol that the dial-up server does support but that you do not need will only add additional overhead to your connection for no reason.

If you are connecting to a NetBEUI or IPX/SPX network, such as when accessing your corporate LAN via a Windows 98 Dial-Up Server, you can select the appropriate protocol and clear the others. Now you're ready to go—no further configuration is necessary. When connecting to the Internet or to a TCP/IP-based corporate network that supports TCP/IP routing, TCP/IP is the only protocol you need. In rare cases, you may need to specify TCP/IP in addition to one of the other protocols, but it is unlikely.

Unlike the other two protocols, you *do* need to configure the TCP/IP protocol settings, as shown in the next illustration. This is done by clicking on the TCP/IP Settings button.

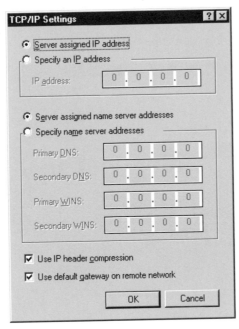

In some cases, all necessary TCP/IP settings will be configured automatically during the PPP handshake and negotiation. More often than not, you have to specify some of the information yourself.

The first choice on this screen is between "Server assigned IP address" and "Specify an IP address." If you are unsure, you should leave this set to "Server assigned IP address" because most dial-up servers dynamically assign IP addresses from a limited pool of available address space as you connect to the system. Once you disconnect, the IP address is released to the pool of available addresses so it can be reused by another connection.

The next choice you have to make is between "Server assigned name server addresses" and "Specify name server addresses." Chances are pretty good that you will have to select the second option and manually enter the primary and secondary DNS and WINS server addresses. As the number of non-technical users using Dial-Up Networking has grown, network administrators have come to rely on increasingly intelligent Dial-Up Networking servers to reduce their support costs by automatically configuring as many settings as possible. Most dial-up servers in use today, however, still require that the user manually specify these addresses.

**SOAPBOX:** If you are able to connect to the dial-up server and use the Ping utility to communicate with other computers by IP Address (such as 204.151.55.175), but are unable to do so using the host name (such as www.lantimes.com), this usually indicates either that you did not enter the required DNS addresses or that you entered them incorrectly.

Click on the OK button to save your changes and return to the prior Server Types configuration screen.

Click on the Scripting tab to select the next page of configuration settings, as shown here:

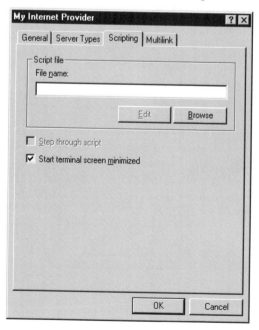

Before the advent of the Point-to-Point Protocol (PPP), which includes all necessary logon and negotiation information in its own handshake, users had to craft special login scripts for each dial-up server they connected to. In general, scripting is cumbersome, imprecise, error-prone, fragile, and completely unnecessary. For this reason, we will not delve into the details of how to create or use dial-up scripts. If you are connecting to a system that requires scripting, ask your system administrator to provide you with the necessary login script for use with Windows 98 Dial-Up Networking.

Click on the Multilink tab to select the next page of configuration settings, which looks like this:

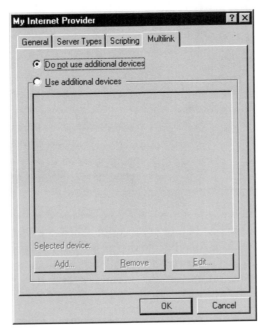

The ability to link two or more dial-up network connections and treat them as a single, faster connection is known as Multilink. Until now, Multilink has been the exclusive territory of ISDN and other, specialized and expensive networking hardware. Windows 98 includes the ability to Multilink even with standard modems, as long as the dial-up server you are connecting to also supports this feature. If the server you are dialing supports this feature, your system administrator will provide you with specific instructions for properly configuring this option.

That's it. Your dial-up connection is ready to use. Click on the OK button to save your settings and return to the Dial-Up Networking dialog box.

# Connecting to a Remote Dial-Up Server

To connect to a dial-up server, simply open the Dial-Up Networking dialog box and double-click on the icon representing the connection you wish. The Connect To dialog box opens, shown here, giving you the opportunity to change certain connection settings before dialing:

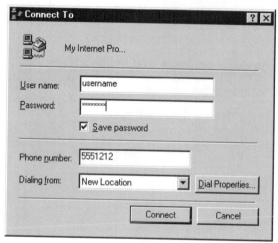

If this is the first time you have used the connection, you will need to specify your login user name and password before continuing. Click the "Save password" option if you would like Windows to remember your password so you do not have to type it in each time you connect. When you're ready to dial the server, click on the Connect button. Windows 98 dialer dials the phone number and attempts to log on using the information you specified.

**SHORTCUT:** You can create a shortcut for any Dial-Up Networking connection you use frequently by simply right-clicking on the desired icon, dragging the icon to your desktop, and releasing the mouse button, then selecting the option to create a shortcut.

Once you are connected, Windows 98 displays the Connection Established dialog box, as shown here:

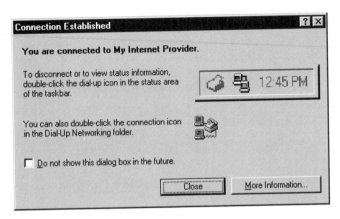

This dialog box contains important information. It confirms the name of the connection that was successfully established and it tells you how to get more information about the connection or disconnect. The most important part is the reference to the dial-up icon in the system tray—on the taskbar, near the time display and volume control. Double-clicking on the dial-up icon in the system tray opens a "Connected to…" dialog box, shown next, with information about your current connection.

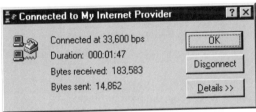

The display contains your connection speed, duration, and the number of bytes sent and received through the connection.

That's all there is to it! You're now connected to the Internet, another Windows 98 computer, or a corporate RAS server using Windows 98's Dial-Up Networking. You can proceed to access the network just as described in prior chapters, with the few limitations discussed earlier in this section.

## Automatically Connecting to the Internet

Windows 98 provides a mechanism to automatically dial a designated Dial-Up Networking connection whenever any application on your computer attempts to use TCP/IP services. This is most helpful for automatically connecting to the Internet when you open your Web browser or e-mail client software.

To enable this feature, open the Windows Control Panel, double-click on the Internet icon to open the Internet Properties dialog box, and then select the Connection tab to see the connection settings, which look like this:

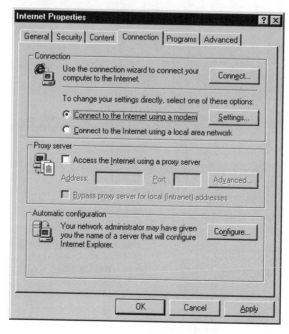

Select the option "Connect to the Internet using a modem," then click on the accompanying Settings button to open the Dial-Up Settings dialog box, shown here:

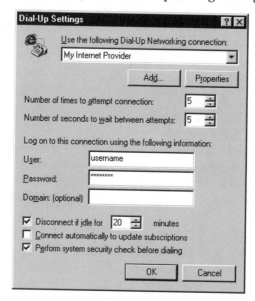

Select your preferred connection from the drop-down list, make sure your correct username and password are entered in the appropriate fields, and click on the OK button to exit the Dial-Up Settings screen and on the OK button again to exit the Internet Properties dialog box.

## Advanced Configuration

From the Dial-Up Networking dialog box, select the Settings option on the Connection menu to open the Dial-Up Networking settings window:

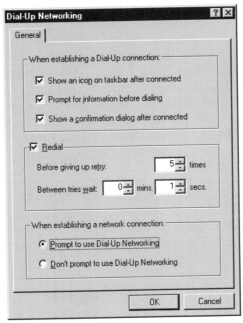

From here, you can control quite a bit of the way that Windows 98 Dial-Up Networking behaves—such as whether to show an icon on the taskbar after connecting, redial settings, and whether or not to prompt before connecting through Dial-Up Networking. The settings on this screen are pretty self-explanatory and help is available by clicking the question mark control on the title bar, then clicking on the option you want help with.

# BEYOND DIAL-UP:
# THE VIRTUAL PRIVATE NETWORK CLIENT

Windows 98 ships with the Microsoft Virtual Private Networking (VPN) Adapter. When used in conjunction with a properly configured Windows NT Server, the VPN Adapter allows you to establish a secure, encrypted connection to your corporate network over the Internet or any other public TCP/IP network. It even provides the ability to tunnel other protocols, such as NetBEUI and IPX/SPX over the connection.

The VPN Adapter works just like the Dial-Up Adapter. The only difference in the way you use it is that when you create a new Dial-Up Networking connection, you specify the VPN Adapter and you use the IP Address of the Windows NT server instead of entering a telephone number.

To use the VPN connection, you first connect to the Internet using your primary Dial-Up Networking connection, then open the Dial-Up Networking connection corresponding to your VPN connection. The VPN Adapter takes care of determining which IP packets should be routed to the private network versus those that should be allowed to pass through your primary Dial-Up connection to the Internet.

It really is just that simple and does not require any new networking components or configuration screens other than those that you have already used in this chapter. Because the specific details of which protocols to enable and which IP Address to use are dependent on the VPN server with which you are connecting, we'll leave those details to your network administrator. If this service is available to you, your network administrator has probably distributed detailed instructions for properly configuring all the necessary settings.

# COMING UP

The Network Neighborhood is a powerful tool for exploring and accessing other computers on the network. In the next chapter, we talk about what you can do with it and how to use it effectively.

NETWORK
PROFESSIONAL'S
LIBRARY

# PART II

# Working with Windows 98

NETWORK
PROFESSIONAL'S
LIBRARY

# CHAPTER 8

# Working with the
# Network Neighborhood

**What's ahead:**

- What is the Network Neighborhood?
- Preparing to use the Network Neighborhood
- Working with the Network Neighborhood

*"We must all hang together,
or assuredly we shall all
hang separately."*

—Benjamin Franklin, at the signing of the
*Declaration of Independence,* July 4, 1776

Windows 98 contains many enhancements and new features, but most of them are unseen and therefore not fully appreciated by the majority of users. One enhancement you can't help but notice is the integration of Internet Explorer (IE) as the universal user interface (UI) throughout Windows. IE has replaced standard Windows components from the Desktop to Windows Explorer, including the Network Neighborhood and My Computer windows.

The benefits of using Internet Explorer in Windows 98 as the common UI for browsing and accessing the Network Neighborhood and My Computer are many. The most obvious benefit is that users require less training and support because all of these components have the same look and feel. Once you know how to use one, you pretty much know how to use them all. On a deeper level, it also signifies a major shift in the way we think about, or don't think about, the location and physical proximity of files, printers, and other resources—in very much the same way that we have all learned to access and download files from Web sites from all over the world, as though they are in the same room with us.

Nowhere is this more apparent than when working in the Network Neighborhood.

# WHAT IS THE NETWORK NEIGHBORHOOD?

When you installed Windows 98, it created an icon on your desktop called Network Neighborhood. This is your window to the network. From here, you can view and access the files and printers that are shared by other computers connected to the network.

As stated previously, in Windows 98 the Network Neighborhood window uses the Internet Explorer engine to display, navigate, and access other computers on your network. Shared files can be browsed, viewed, and manipulated almost as if they are on your own hard drive. Drive letters can be mapped to shared disks on other computers and printer drivers can be installed and configured, enabling you to print to shared network printers as though they are local printers, connected directly to your own computer.

**NOTE:**   The Network Neighborhood is also discussed in Chapters 3, 4, and 5.

# PREPARING TO USE THE NETWORK NEIGHBORHOOD

At the risk of stating the obvious: You must be connected to a network before you can access the Network Neighborhood. If you open the Network Neighborhood window when your network adapter isn't working or without any networking protocols installed, you get an error message and will not be able to browse the Network Neighborhood.

If you are unable to browse the Network Neighborhood, refer to Chapters 3 through 6 of this book for a discussion of how to properly configure Windows 98 for networking.

When you configured your network settings for the first time, you may not have paid much attention to the values you used for the Computer and Workgroup Names on the Identification panel of the Network dialog box. Let's review those settings now to make sure they are set properly, before we go into the specifics of how to work with the Network Neighborhood.

Open the Network dialog box and select the Identification tab (see Figure 8-1).

**SHORTCUT:**   You can quickly access the Network Configuration dialog box by right-clicking on the Network Neighborhood icon on your desktop, then choosing Properties from the pop-up menu.

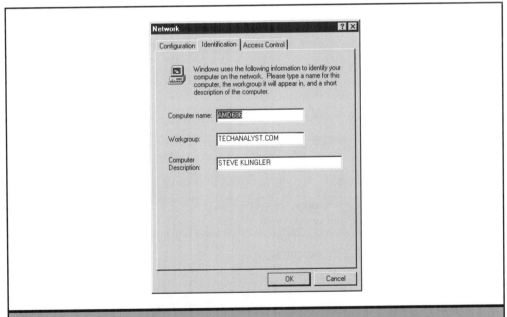

**Figure 8-1.**   Network Identification

Let's start with the Workgroup name. Workgroups are a simple way of identifying and grouping several computers together, usually because they share a common purpose or reside in the same department. These are the computers that you are most likely to share files or printers with. When you open the Network Neighborhood window, the default view displays the names of all available computers that belong to the same workgroup that you do.

The workgroup designation does not limit your ability to communicate with or access shared resources that are owned by computers belonging to a different workgroup from your own. In fact, you'll see how to do just that a little bit later in this chapter in the section titled "Navigating the Network Neighborhood."

# WORKING WITH THE NETWORK NEIGHBORHOOD

The Network Neighborhood window uses the Internet Explorer (IE) engine, which means that it looks and feels a lot like the IE Web browser as well as every other IE-based Windows 98 component. Even so, it's worth discussing how the Network Neighborhood user interface (UI) works and how it differs from the IE Web browser.

Let's take a look at both Internet Explorer and the Network Neighborhood, as shown in Figures 8-2 and 8-3.

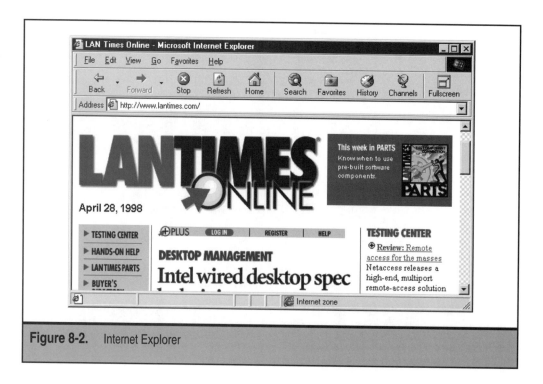

**Figure 8-2.**    Internet Explorer

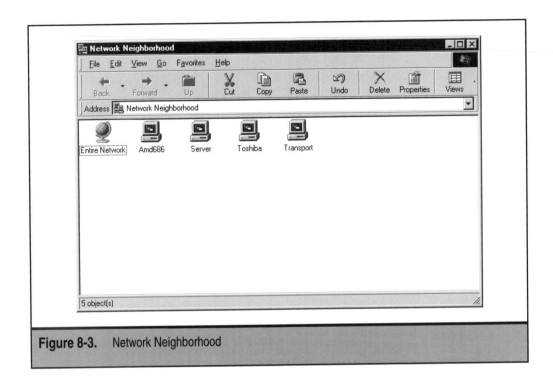

**Figure 8-3.**  Network Neighborhood

Despite seemingly different purposes, these two windows look almost identical. Aside from the window contents, only the toolbars are different. Where IE has icons for Search, Favorites, History, Channels, and Fullscreen, the Network Neighborhood has icons for Cut, Copy, Paste, Undo, Delete, Properties, and Views.

If the computer you are interested in is listed in the window, you can open a view of its shared files and printers (see Figure 8-4) by double-clicking on its icon. If that computer is configured for Share Level (password protected) access, you may be prompted for the correct password before the window opens.

From here, you can continue to explore the available files and printers by double-clicking on the desired selection. This is also the proper place to map a network drive or install and configure a network printer.

# Mapping Drives

When you map a network drive, you are telling windows to assign it a local drive letter so you can then reference and access the shared drive over the network just like you would if it were a local hard drive. Like most actions in Windows 98, there are two ways to map a network drive—either from the Map option on the File menu or from the pop-up menu that you activate by right-clicking on the desired icon.

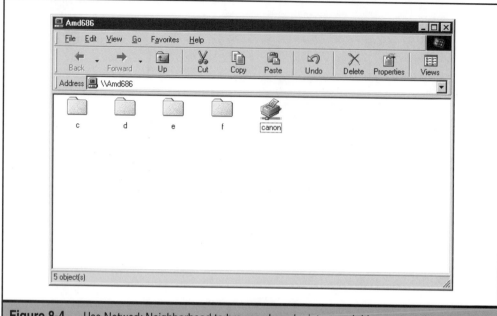

**Figure 8-4.** Use Network Neighborhood to browse shared printers and drives on another computer

This dialog box, shown in Figure 8-5, is pretty simple. All you have to do is select the drive letter you want to use and check the "Reconnect at logon" option if you want Windows 98 to automatically map this drive the next time you reboot and log on to Windows as the same user.

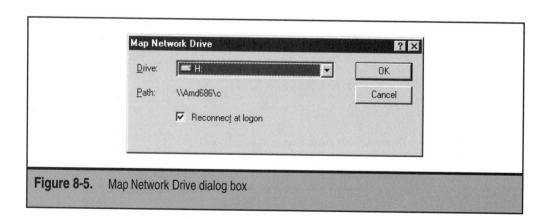

**Figure 8-5.** Map Network Drive dialog box

If you right-click on an icon, you see a pop-up menu with the following options:

▼ **Open**   Open the selected drive in another window

■ **Explore**   Open the selected drive in Windows Explorer

■ **Find**   Locate files on the selected drive

■ **Map Network Drive**   Assign a local drive letter to the shared drive

■ **Create Shortcut**   Create a shortcut to the selected drive

▲ **Properties**   View additional information about the selected drive

# Network Printers

Network printers work a little bit differently than shared drives. Shared drives are typically mapped to a local drive letter either every time you boot, or as needed. However, to use any printer in Windows 98, including network printers, you have to first install the necessary printer drivers and configure your connection to the desired printer.

If you're not already there, browse the Network Neighborhood and open the view of another computer on your network that has a shared printer available for use. Once there, right-click on the printer's icon to activate the pop-up menu (see Figure 8-6).

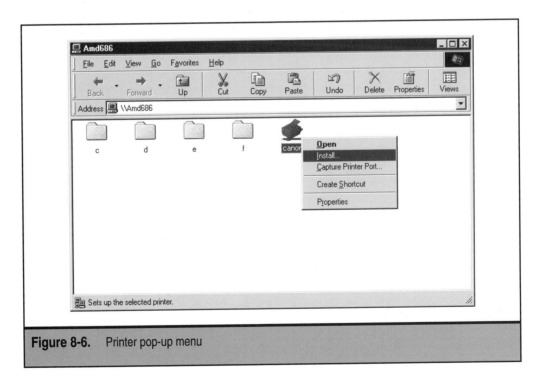

**Figure 8-6.**   Printer pop-up menu

The pop-up menu contains several options:

▼ **Open**   Open the selected printer

■ **Install**   Install the selected printer

■ **Capture Printer Port**   Capture the selected printer to a local printer port

■ **Create Shortcut**   Create a shortcut to the selected printer

▲ **Properties**   Display additional information about the selected printer

The first thing you want to do is install the selected printer. This configures the printer for use on your system, including copying the necessary driver files to your own hard drive and placing an icon for the printer in your Printers folder.

When you click on Install, the Add Printer Wizard opens and prompts you through a series of questions necessary to install and configure the printer for use on your system. If you need additional help with this process, please refer to the step-by-step instructions in Chapter 3.

Use the Capture Printer Port option if you need to print from DOS applications and the Open option to view or cancel active print jobs.

# Navigating the Network Neighborhood

When you first open the Network Neighborhood window, you should see two different kinds of icons. The first resembles a blue Globe on a yellow stand and is titled Entire Network. Following that, you should see a series of icons that looks like computers, one for each active computer on the network that belongs to your workgroup.

If the computer you are looking for is not listed, there are three possible explanations: The computer could belong to a different workgroup, it could be turned off, or it is not configured properly for file or print sharing. There's nothing you can do if the computer is turned off or configured incorrectly, but there are two ways to easily locate the computer if it simply belongs to another workgroup.

## Browsing the Entire Network

The simplest way to locate another computer is to double-click on the Entire Network icon and navigate through the available workgroups until you find the computer you are looking for. (See Figure 8-7.)

Once you select the Entire Network you are presented with a new screen containing one or more icons, each representing a different workgroup on your network, including one for your own workgroup. Double-clicking on any of these icons opens a view of only those computers that belong to the selected workgroup, as shown in Figure 8-8.

This view is very similar to the first Network Neighborhood window you saw, except that it does not contain an icon for the Entire Network and both the Title Bar and Address Toolbar now reflect the name of the selected workgroup.

If you are looking for a particular computer, you could continue to browse through all available workgroups using this same process, but this can get tedious if your network is

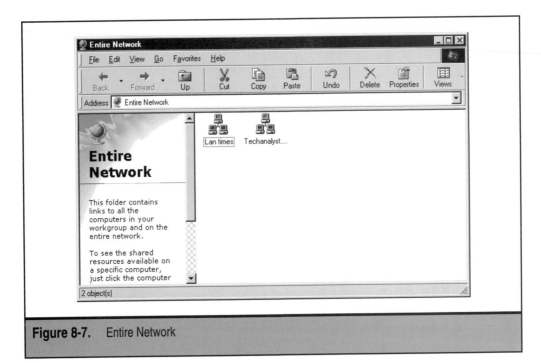

**Figure 8-7.**   Entire Network

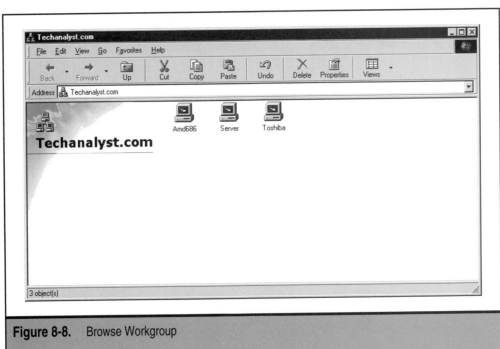

**Figure 8-8.**   Browse Workgroup

large or partitioned into several different workgroups. Fortunately, there is an easier way to find a computer if you already know its name.

## Windows Explorer

For some reason, the Network Neighborhood window does not include a Find or Search option for locating computers by name, but the Windows Explorer does. To access this feature, open Windows Explorer, select the Tools menu, then select Computer from the Find menu option, as shown in Figure 8-9.

From here, you can simply type the name of the computer you wish to locate, then click on the Find Now button. After a short delay, the window expands to display the Name, Location, and Comment values for all matching computers that were found on your network.

From here, you can double-click on the desired computer (see Figure 8-10) to open a view of its shared files and printers just as if you had located the computer by browsing the Network Neighborhood.

## Advanced Options

The Windows 98 Network Neighborhood provides some pretty sophisticated administration tools, accessible only by authorized users. As a Network Administrator,

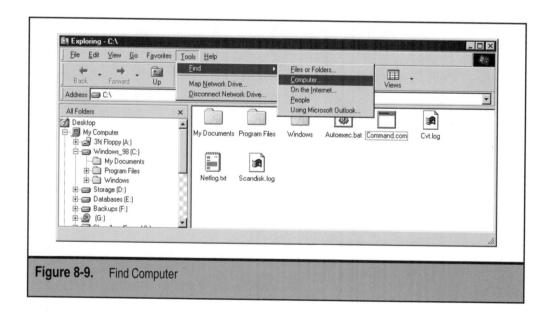

**Figure 8-9.**    Find Computer

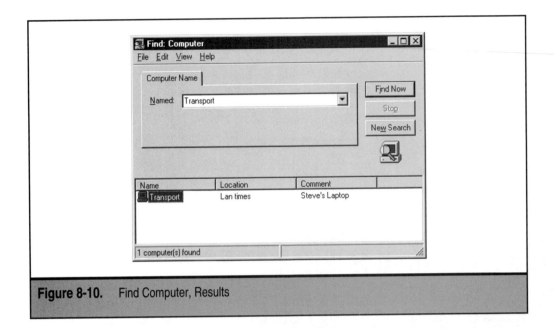

**Figure 8-10.**   Find Computer, Results

you will find the ability to remotely manage shared resources on other workstations particularly useful.

## Configuring Windows 98 for Remote Administration

The first step is to enable Remote Administration on your workstations. To do this, open the Password Properties dialog box from Windows Control Panel, then select the Remote Administration tab, which is shown in Figure 8-11.

Select the option labeled "Enable remote administration of this server" and either enter a password if you are using Share Level access control, or specify the users and user groups that are allowed to remotely manage the system if you are using User Level access control.

## Remotely Administering a Windows 98 Workstation

To access the Remote Administration function, open the Network Neighborhood and right-click on the icon representing the desired computer, then select Properties from the pop-up menu. Select the Tools tab in the Properties dialog box that opens (see Figure 8-12).

This panel contains three buttons for Watch Server, Monitor Computer, and Administer File System. We're interested in the third option. By selecting this option, you can manage the shared resources on the selected computer, such as access control lists and passwords.

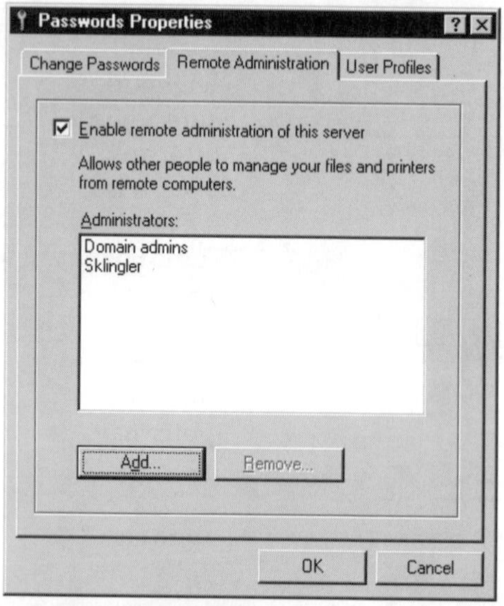

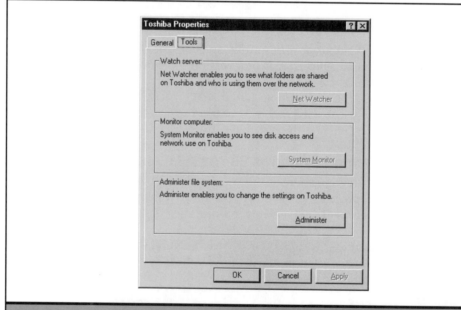

**Figure 8-11.** Remote Administration

**Figure 8-12.** Remote Admin, Tools

# Customize the UI

Like all of the other UI components that are based on IE, you have quite a bit of control over the look and feel of Window's Network Neighborhood. These options are accessed through the View menu, which is shown in Figure 8-13.

The available choices, as shown in Figure 8-14, are pretty self-explanatory. If you're not familiar with these options, the best way to learn is to experiment and just try them all! You really can't hurt anything.

Be sure to review the options available under the Folder Options selection of the View menu. From there, you can choose between Classic or Web style UI or select the Custom option and configure the view settings directly.

The Web style interface, shown in Figure 8-15, is interesting because items are selected by simply moving the mouse over them, and opened with a single-click instead of the usual double-click. Notice how the computer names are all underlined, like links on a Web page.

The View tab in the Folder Options dialog box provides a number of additional options (see Figure 8-16). You will probably want to change some of these options even if you leave all other display settings at their defaults.

Power-users will probably want to change a few of the default settings, so that context-sensitive help is available for all options in this dialog box, by first clicking on the

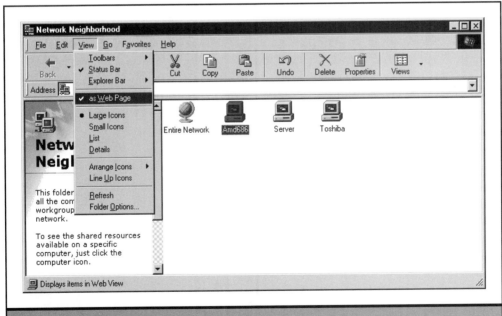

**Figure 8-13.**    Network Neighborhood View menu

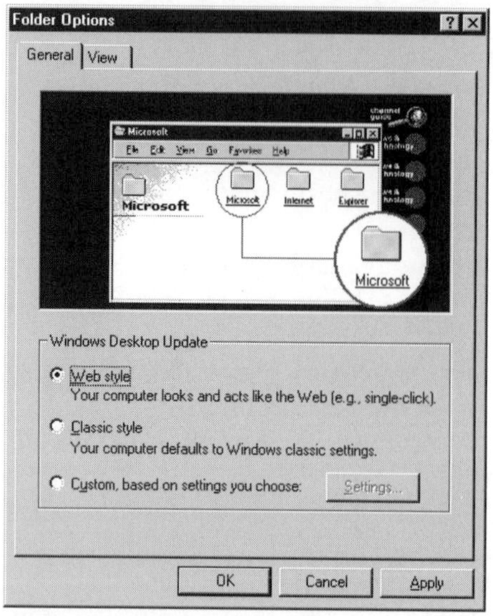

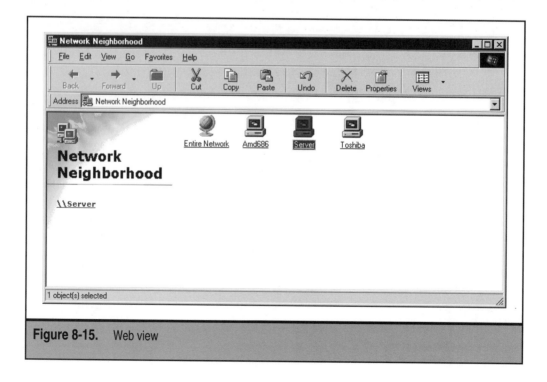

**Figure 8-14.** View options

**Figure 8-15.** Web view

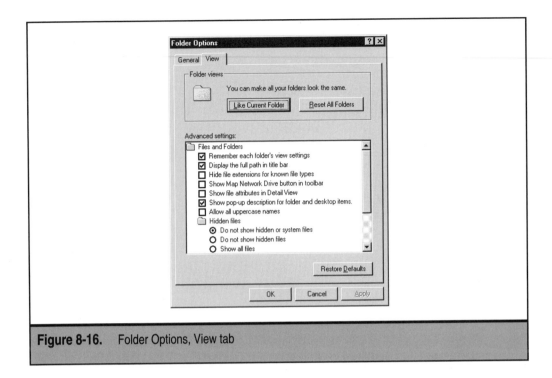

**Figure 8-16.**    Folder Options, View tab

question mark (?) on the right side of the Title Bar, then clicking on the option you are interested in.

# COMING UP

The next chapter is all about browsing the Internet with Internet Explorer. Even if you already know how to surf the Web with Internet Explorer, you're sure to pick up a few tips and tricks as we discuss configuration options, including performance and security issues.

# NETWORK
## PROFESSIONAL'S
# LIBRARY

# CHAPTER 9

# Browsing the Internet with Internet Explorer

**What's ahead:**

■ Your new user interface

■ Connecting with Internet Explorer

■ Working with Internet Explorer

■ Fine-tuning Internet Explorer

*"What we call the beginning is often the end*
*And to make an end is to make a beginning."*

—T.S. Eliot, *Little Gidding*

As you saw in the last chapter, Windows 98's user interface (UI) has changed dramatically from that of Windows 95. Of course, it still has the basics, such as files, folders, a Start menu, and a trash can. But through an integrated Web browser, it looks more like the Web and less like a traditional operating system (OS). Instead of double-clicking on icons, you can single-click on them. Instead of opening a file folder, you can open a Web page. Instead of using a button to go to the previous folder, you can use right and left arrows to navigate forward and backward through folders, all just as you do on the Web.

That is the magic and the heart of Windows 98. With its integrated Web browser, called Internet Explorer, the UI on your desktop and the UI of the Internet become one and the same. For example, if you right-click on your Taskbar, select Toolbars, and click on the Address item, you'll notice that a text field appears where your application icons normally reside, as shown here:

Yes, it is a field for a Uniform Resource Locator (URL), just like the one in your Web browser. Only this one is a part of your Windows 98 OS. If you're connected to the Internet or a TCP/IP network, just enter your favorite URL in this field and press the ENTER key. This action opens Internet Explorer using your URL as a parameter (see Figure 9-1) to open the corresponding Web site.

**CAUTION:**  If your Windows 98 client is not connected to a TCP/IP network such as the Internet, this won't work since Internet Explorer requires TCP/IP in order to connect with any Web site. If you don't have TCP/IP installed, you'll receive an error indicating that the server could not be found. To remedy this right now, just skip ahead to the section entitled "Configuring Internet Explorer."

This integration is important simply because it can help you become more productive as it removes any navigational distinction between the Internet and your PC. By breaking down that barrier, it fosters the use of the Internet's Hypertext Markup Language (HTML) as the prime medium for conveying information both on your PC and on the Internet. Internet Explorer together with its sister products let you work with HTML documents either remotely or locally as though they were regular old documents like Word or Excel files. Chapters 11 and 12 discuss more about such products as Outlook Express, Internet Explorer's sister product that enables you to work entirely within

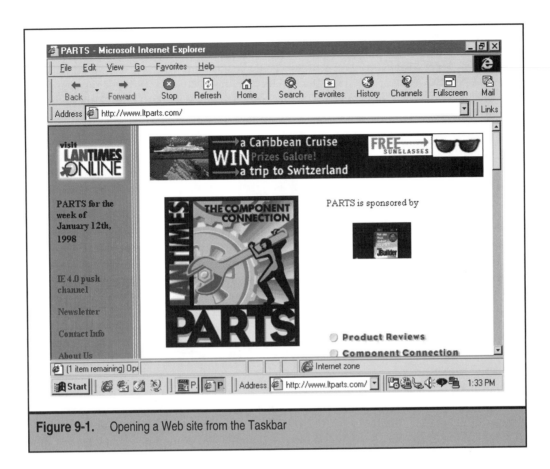

**Figure 9-1.** Opening a Web site from the Taskbar

HTML when sending and receiving messages. That is, you can compose and reply to messages by writing HTML.

**SOAPBOX:** Microsoft is so dedicated to the Web that at the time of this writing, they plan to make HTML the default file format for all Microsoft Office applications, including Word, Excel, and PowerPoint.

Nifty navigation and document features aside, because Internet Explorer and its sister applications ship as a part of Windows 98, you should take the time to acquaint yourself with Internet Explorer. Of course, some of the reasons to do so are readily apparent. For example, you should know intimately the one piece of software that your users will use the most. That way, you can readily answer such questions as, "How do I set my proxy server settings?" or "My security settings won't let me download a Java applet; how do I change them?"

Some of these same concerns were addressed in the last chapter, "Working with the Network Neighborhood" (the PC's perspective on connectivity). In this chapter, we do the same, only from the Internet side of that coin. That is, we take a close look not at the Windows 98 UI, but at Internet Explorer as it relates to the Internet.

**RESOURCE:** If you're already familiar with Internet Explorer but looking for management techniques for Internet Explorer, skip to Chapter 15. There, you learn how to use Microsoft's Internet Explorer Administration Kit (IEAK) to deploy and maintain Internet Explorer across multiple Windows 98 clients.

We show you how to set up, configure, and use Internet Explorer effectively to connect to and utilize the Internet, whether you connect to the Internet from your Local Area Network (LAN) or via a dial-up connection. Along the way, we explore security issues, special features, and customization techniques.

Why spend so much time addressing Internet Explorer? After all, it's just an application. Well, yes, it is just an application. However, your users will use it or another Web browser such as Netscape Communications Corp.'s Communicator to perform probably 60 percent of their daily tasks, including browsing the Internet, exploring local and remote network resources, chatting with other users, and of course sending and receiving e-mail.

But more importantly, your users will use Internet Explorer to run mission-critical, corporate applications. With thin-client technologies such as Java and ActiveX, corporate IS can create applications that perform traditional functions such as Accounts Receivable or Human Resource, which do not reside permanently on your users' PCs. Instead, they live on a centralized server. Users simply point their Web browsers at these networked applications and download them for temporary, local use.

**RESOURCE:** The use and benefits of thin-client technologies such as Java and ActiveX are discussed further in Chapter 12.

Therefore, it is essential that you have a firm understanding of Internet Explorer. You will be the first line of defense in trying to answer user problems as they work within Internet Explorer. You will be the one users first call to complain that a Web site, which was recently available, has suddenly returned an unknown error.

## YOUR NEW USER INTERFACE

Of course, Internet Explorer is not the only Web browser on the market. So, before we dive into the inner workings of Internet Explorer, let's take a moment and discuss some of the benefits it holds over its competitors. As discussed in the preceding section, its primary advantage is its strong integration with the Windows 98 OS. In that regard, it is without equal.

**SOAPBOX:** Netscape Communications Corp.'s Navigator and Communicator both provide OS integration similar to that of Windows 98 and Internet Explorer. However, Internet Explorer's Web integration is far superior to that of Netscape. By the time this book reaches print, Netscape should offer what it calls Constellation, a Web-centric UI that is supposed to function like that of Windows 98 and Internet Explorer. However, at the end of the day, it is just a Web browser, riding on top of the Windows 98 OS. You can shut it down and work only with Windows 98. Internet Explorer, on the other hand, is always available and running because it is your file folder, your Taskbar, your very desktop.

However, it has other benefits including strong security, lightning-quick performance, and support for cutting-edge technologies. Together with OS integration, these benefits make Internet Explorer the perfect platform for your users to carry out many of their daily tasks.

## Technologically Adept

The best reason for sticking with Internet Explorer on Windows 98 is its support for emerging and established technologies. With Internet Explorer, you can take advantage of some of the best capabilities the Internet has to offer. For example, it comes with multilingual support, audio support via RealAudio, and Virtual Reality Modeling Language (VRML) support. It also comes with cutting-edge technologies such as Dynamic HTML, Extensible Markup Language (XML), ECMA Script (that's standardized JavaScript), and Hypertext Transport Protocol (HTTP) version 1.1. With these technologies, your users—and your boss—can rest assured that Windows 98 is up to the challenge whenever new applications become available. With its XML-based Webcasting technology, for example, Internet Explorer is able to bring the Web directly to your users' desktops. Users can simply point Internet Explorer at a Web site, indicating that they want to be made aware of any changes to that site, and Internet Explorer will take care of the rest, either downloading the changes for off-line viewing or sending the user an e-mail message explaining the changes.

## Fast

The speed at which a Web browser can download content is of the utmost importance. However, most browsers have the ability to download HTML documents with equal speed using cache technologies. But that is where the similarities end. By using an advanced Just-In-Time (JIT) compiler for Java, Microsoft has been able to beat the competition when it comes to Java execution. For example, as of November 1997, Internet Explorer (version 4.0) held the current high score for downloading and executing Java applications using Pendragon Software Corp.'s CaffeineMark Java benchmark tool. The only other browser to come close to Microsoft's Internet Explorer 4.0 score was Microsoft's own Internet Explorer 3.02.

## Secure

If for no other reason, you will appreciate Internet Explorer for its security. With Internet Explorer and its sister products (Outlook Express and NetMeeting), you can establish secure connections with others across the wilds of the Internet with impunity. That is because these products rely upon an emerging technology called digital signatures (also called certificates). Pioneered by Microsoft, RSA Data Security Inc., Sun Microsystems Inc., and other cryptography-conscious companies, digital signatures let applications authenticate directly one with another, without human intervention. Normally, you enter a password to access secure content on a server. Well, digital signatures allow applications to perform the same sort of procedure with Internet Explorer. For example, a Java-based stock ticker application, which resides on a server, can use digital signatures to ask Internet Explorer if it is okay to download and execute its code.

**RESOURCE:**  If you're interested in digital signatures, you can jump ahead to Chapter 10.

While most browsers support digital signatures, Internet Explorer is the only one to provide advanced security features such as Security Zones and a Content Advisor. These technologies sidestep the entire digital signature issue, enabling you to protect your users from potentially dangerous downloadable applications by disallowing some or all functionality between Internet Explorer and suspect servers. For example, you can tell Internet Explorer that it cannot download Java applets (applications) from a particular Internet domain. This is an important feature, which we'll explore in more detail in the section entitled "Security Zones," because it can protect your users from the potential threat involved in downloading Java applications. For example, a rogue Java applet could be used to gain access to your system files.

You can also tell it not to download content that contains particular ratings as determined by the Recreational Software Advisory Council.

# CONNECTING WITH INTERNET EXPLORER

Now that you know a little about Internet Explorer and its many benefits, it's time to take it out for a test drive. Luckily, you don't have to do anything in order to install Internet Explorer. As an integral part of the Windows 98 OS, Internet Explorer comes pre-installed.

## Accessing Internet Explorer

There are a number of ways your users can access Internet Explorer that bear mentioning. Basically, you can start Internet Explorer from

▼   The desktop

■   The Start menu

- ■ The Taskbar
- ▲ A file folder

Starting Internet Explorer from the desktop is quite simple. Just double-click on the Internet Explorer icon. The same applies to starting Internet Explorer from the Start menu. Just click on the Start button and select the Programs item. Then select the Internet Explorer item and click on Internet Explorer. You've already seen how to start Internet Explorer from the Taskbar (refer to Figure 9-1). The neat trick is accessing Internet Explorer from a file folder. Because it is a part of the Windows 98 OS, every time you open a file folder, you're really starting Internet Explorer, and it is an easy step to get from one to the other.

To see how this works, just open a file folder such as the My Computer folder. It's on your desktop. Double-click on it, and a window opens, similar to the one shown in Figure 9-2.

Notice how familiar this interface is to Internet Explorer. The only difference is that the toolbar icons correspond to file tasks, such as copying, cutting, and pasting. Of

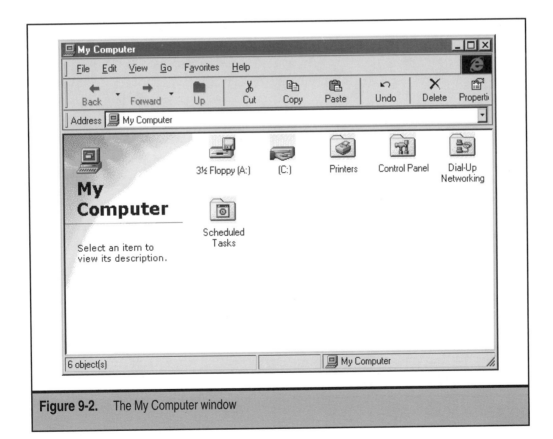

**Figure 9-2.** The My Computer window

course, instead of a Web page, the main folder area contains icons for your hard drive, printers, and so forth.

*JARGON:*   Actually, a file folder in Windows 98 is a Web browser. You're really not looking at icons within a file folder, you're looking at an HTML document containing pictures and hypertext links for those icons.

Now notice that the Address bar contains the name of the current folder, My Computer. To turn this file folder into Internet Explorer, just highlight this name and type the URL of your favorite Web site. Press ENTER, and watch as the toolbar icons change to accommodate Web-centric tasks such as searching, page refreshing, stopping, and navigating. Figure 9-3 shows what the folder looks like if you enter the URL for LAN Times Online. In essence, Internet Explorer changes to match the context in which you are operating. Whether you're looking at a local directory or at a Web site, it automatically accommodates its surroundings by changing its interface.

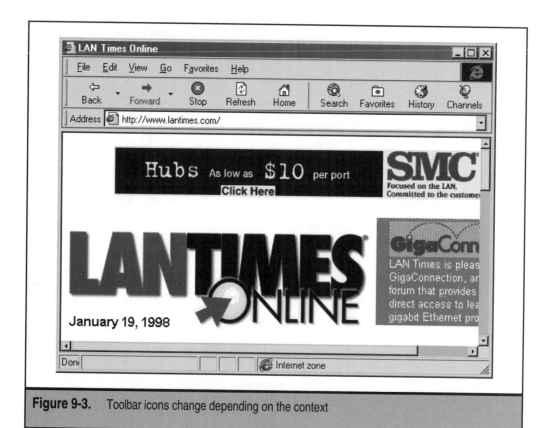

**Figure 9-3.**   Toolbar icons change depending on the context

# Configuring Internet Explorer

Once you have Internet Explorer running, the next thing you need to do is configure it. This is a fairly simple task, requiring you to tell Internet Explorer who you are, how it should connect to a network, and what sort of security to use.

## Automatic Configuration

Of course, if you're using IEAK to configure and install Internet Explorer, all you need to do here is point Internet Explorer at the appropriate server. This can set the settings for Internet Explorer's identification, security, features, and even its appearance. You can read more about IEAK in Chapter 15. To use Automatic Configuration, just click on the View pull-down menu from the main Internet Explorer screen and select Internet Options. This opens the Internet Options dialog box, from which you manage all aspects of Internet Explorer (see Figure 9-4).

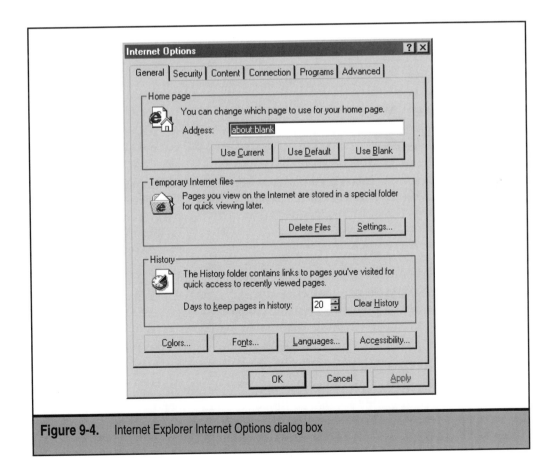

**Figure 9-4.**   Internet Explorer Internet Options dialog box

Click on the Connection tab and click on the Configure button at the bottom of the page under the Automatic Configuration heading. This opens the Automatic Configuration dialog box, which looks something like this:

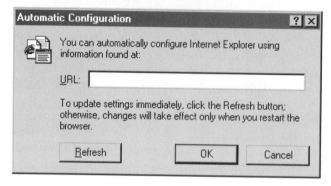

Just enter the full URL for the configuration file in the URL field and click on the OK button. The URL might look something like

```
http://server.corp.com/ie/config/
```

Once you've got the URL in place, you can use this same dialog box later on to update Internet Explorer's configuration by clicking on the Refresh button.

## Setting Your Identity

Once you've pointed your users at an automatic configuration file, you should encourage (or even require) your users to set up a personal profile for use with Internet Explorer. It helps them work more effectively with Internet Explorer's sister applications (Outlook Express and NetMeeting). This is because all three applications share the same address book. For example, once you have created a profile in Internet Explorer containing your name, e-mail address, and so forth, Outlook Express automatically sends the appropriate subset of that information as a file attachment in the form of a Business Card file (called a vCard) to the intended recipient. When the recipient opens this message, the vCard can be imported into a personal address book for later use.

To create an identity for Internet Explorer, open the Internet Options dialog box (shown in Figure 9-4) and click on the Content tab. Click on the Edit Profile button in the Personal Identification section. This opens a Properties dialog box, similar to the one shown in Figure 9-5.

Here you can specify a user name, e-mail address, home address, work address, digital ID, and NetMeeting servers. Notice how the first name is already filled in under the Personal tab. Windows 98 uses your user ID name to give you a starting place. But you can set it to anything you want. Regarding the rest of the information on this page, you can pick and choose which parts you fill in. Nothing is mandatory. However, you should enter as much information as possible, unless corporate privacy policies dictate otherwise. The more information you provide about yourself (or a user) here, the more

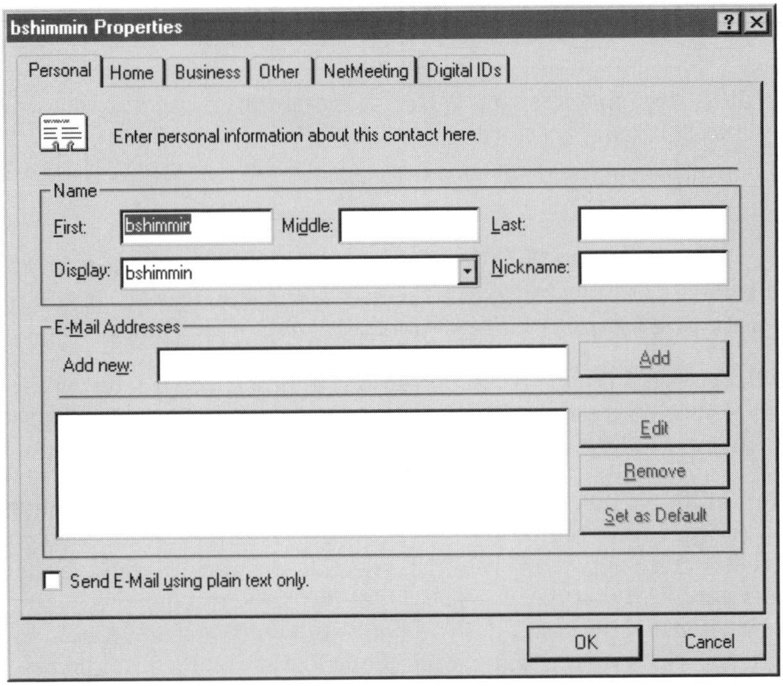

**Figure 9-5.**   Personal panel of a user's Properties dialog box

information other users have access to when you send them an e-mail message or log on to a Web service. The only drawback to this approach is that any information entered here becomes available to the outside world. For example, when you connect to a Web site, an application on that Web site could ask to see the contents of your profile. Therefore, it is strongly recommended that you consider very carefully this feature within the framework of your company's privacy guidelines.

## Setting a Connection

Once you've created an identity, you should tell Internet Explorer how you wish it to connect with the available TCP/IP networks. Luckily, Internet Explorer, by default, can use the TCP/IP stack attached to your Network Interface Card (NIC). This means that if your LAN is using TCP/IP, and if it contains any Web servers, you're already in business. You can open Internet Explorer and browse Web sites right away.

The Internet is another matter. Even if you have access to a TCP/IP network, you may not have access to the Internet. If you're not sure, ask your IT manager. If you have such a connection, he or she will most likely give you a proxy server URL, which we use in just a moment.

**SHORTCUT:**  If you're not sure if your LAN connects directly to the Internet, open an MS-DOS dialog box and enter the following command:

```
Ping 204.151.55.175
```

This is the IP address for LAN Times Online, which is available only on the Internet. If you get an error message stating that the request timed out, then you don't have direct access to the Internet. You might want to have them ping http://www.lantimes.com, which will test DNS as well.

If you don't have a direct connection to the Internet, you'll have to use a dial-up connection via your modem. But in either case, you must tell Internet Explorer what it needs to do in order to reach the Internet.

**USING A DIRECT CONNECTION**  To use a direct connection, from the Internet Options dialog box, click on the Connection tab. Here, you've got basically two connectivity options. To connect directly to the Internet, select the appropriate radio button from the Connection section. All that remains is to enter the name of your proxy server, should you have one. As stated previously, if you don't know this, just ask your IT manager for the appropriate URL. From the same Connection tab, click on the Proxy Server check box under the Proxy server section. This brings the Address and Port fields into focus, in which you should enter the appropriate URL. For example, you might have a proxy server URL that looks like this:

```
http://mhc-pac:33333
```

**JARGON:**  What are those 3s? Most Web servers use TCP/IP port 80 to communicate. However, most, if not all, proxy servers use an alternate port, such as 33333 or 81. This just tells the Web browser over which port it should try to make a connection with the proxy server, so don't forget it when entering your proxy server URL.

If your company does not use a proxy server for internal Web sites, just put a check in the Bypass check box. This tells Internet Explorer to use the proxy server settings only for Web sites that exist on the Internet.

**USING A MODEM CONNECTION**  To use a modem instead of a direct connection, from the same Connection tab in the Internet Options dialog box, select the *Connect to the Internet using a modem* radio button. You should then click on the Settings button in the same area to verify which modem Internet Explorer will try to use. You should see at least one modem in the resulting Dial-Up Settings dialog box (see Figure 9-6).

Should you not see any modem settings, click on the Cancel button and use the Internet Connection wizard to set up a new connection. Just click on the Connect button

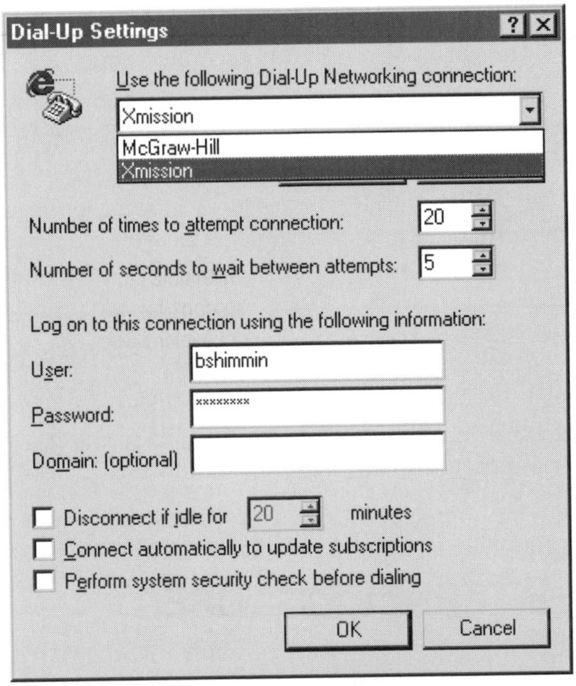

**Figure 9-6.**    Internet Explorer's Dial-Up Settings dialog box

at the top of the Connection tab to launch the Wizard. This leads you step-by-step through the process of installing and configuring modem software. This is the software your computer will use to access your modem in making a connection to the Internet. To find out more about this, go back and read Chapter 7.

If you do see a modem as in Figure 9-6, select the appropriate modem and enter any necessary configuration information on the same dialog box. You should not need to re-enter a user name and password. You should have set those when you created your modem settings. As far as the rest of the options go, our recommendations are as follows:

▼ Set the number of dial attempts to a number between 10 and 20. This frees you from manually re-dialing in the case of a busy signal.

■ Set the number of seconds to wait before re-dialing to a number over 5. Anything shorter might not be enough time for your modem to recycle from a failed dialing attempt.

■ If you go back and forth between Internet Explorer and other applications a lot, do not tell Internet Explorer to disconnect after a certain number of idle minutes. If, however, you want to download something large, and you don't want to wait around to disconnect, select the check box named *Disconnect if idle for 00 minutes,* and set an appropriate Disconnect time.

■ If you want your computer to dial the Internet automatically to retrieve subscription content (more about that in Chapter 12), check the *Connect automatically to update subscriptions* box.

▲ If you are using Web and FTP services locally, you should select the last check box, which performs a system security check each time you dial. This alerts you to any potential sharing security issues, such as an unsecured FTP account.

**RESOURCE:**  For more information on setting up remote connectivity for Internet Explorer, see Chapter 7.

That's all there is to getting Internet Explorer up and running. From here on out, the only questions you should get from your users should include content navigation and customization questions.

# WORKING WITH INTERNET EXPLORER

Working with Internet Explorer is fairly easy, requiring only that new users do a little investigating in order to get the hang of things. All of the product's features are readily available either from Internet Explorer's menus or from its toolbar. However, there are some tricks and traps you may want to set to memory as you go about answering user questions.

## Getting Help

The best thing you can do to help users get acquainted with Internet Explorer is to point them toward its built-in help system. In the long run, it will save you time and them aggravation, as it will grant them self-sufficiency. As a general rule, should users get lost at any point, tell them to simply click on the Help pull-down menu and follow their nose (so to speak). This contains menu items for both local and online (Internet-based) help programs, including:

▼ Contents and Index

■ Product Updates

■ Web Tutorial

■ Online Support

▲ Microsoft on the Web

***CAUTION:*** Make sure your mobile users know that all but the Contents and Index programs reside on the Internet and not locally. If they are not connected when they click on Internet-based help programs, they'll either get an error message, or Internet Explorer will try to automatically dial their modem connection.

## Content and Index

Naturally, the best place to start seeking help is locally with the Contents and Index program (see Figure 9-7).

New to Windows 98 and Internet Explorer is that their help systems use HTML as their default medium. This lets users quickly navigate through the available data—and there's a lot of data to go through. Notice in Figure 9-7 how traditional Web toolbar buttons such as Back and Forward let users work the way they are used to working on the Web. With Internet Explorer's Contents and Index help program, there are a number of usability-centric topics such as exploring the Web, printing and saving information, and using security features. If they don't see what they're looking for under the Contents tab, they can either browse keywords under the Index tab or search for any words under the Search tab.

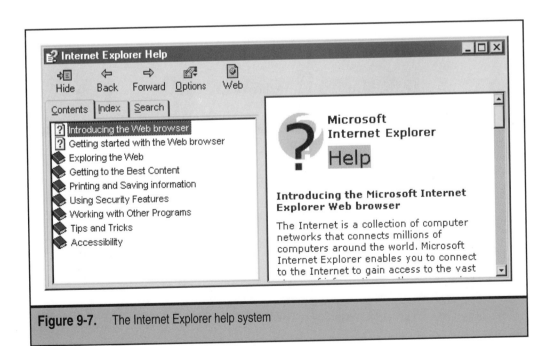

**Figure 9-7.** The Internet Explorer help system

## Product Updates

Regarding the other help programs available with Internet Explorer, you should admonish users not to use the Product Updates program, unless you plan on giving them free reign over what software they download and run on their machines.

**RESOURCE:**   Actually, if you don't want users updating Internet Explorer themselves, you can use the IEAK to lock down this option from the Help pull-down menu. For more on this, see Chapter 15.

This may sound a bit autocratic, but there are many application components for Internet Explorer available. And you may not wish to support them all. If, however, you choose to allow such behavior, the Product Updates program will connect to Microsoft's Web site and quickly determine which components have already been installed, which are upgradable, and which have not been installed (see Figure 9-8).

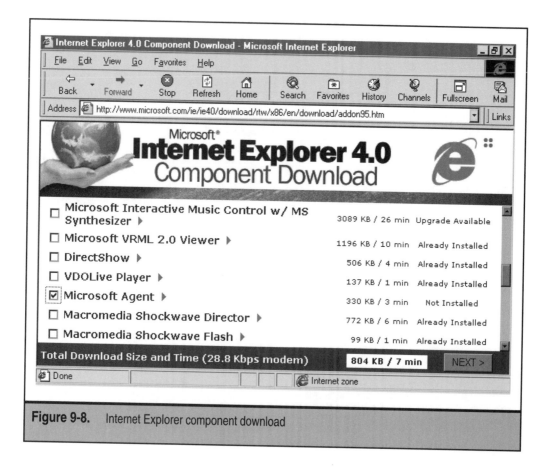

**Figure 9-8.**   Internet Explorer component download

Using this service, users can place check marks next to components they wish to download. The application tells them how many Kilobytes they are scheduled to download and how long it will take to download those Kilobytes. Clicking on the Next button at the bottom of the page opens another page from which users can select a download site closest to them geographically and download the components by pressing the Download Now button. (As a general rule, the closer the site, the quicker the download.) That's all there is to it. The new components are automatically downloaded and installed.

## Web Tutorial and Online Support

The remaining two avenues of help come direct from Microsoft's Web site. We highly recommend the Web Tutorial as a mandatory training course for new Internet Explorer users, though those used to working with previous versions of Internet Explorer may find this tutorial either redundant or too advanced. You see, for new users, there's an Internet Basics course; it takes them step-by-step through an introduction to the Internet. But the rest of the online tutorial is really geared for systems administrators who wish to build and manage their own Web service.

The last help application, Online Support, requires users to register their software with Microsoft. Although you may have purchased a site-wide license for Windows 98 and Internet Explorer, we suggest that you instruct your users to start this application and fill out the registration form. It's quite simple, asking only for an e-mail address, user name, password, and some simple demographics. Once your users have filled this out, they'll have access to a slew of online resources, including troubleshooting Wizards, Microsoft's entire knowledge base, and downloadable applications. For example, with the online, natural-language-based search engine, users are able to ask real-world questions in the form of "How do I subscribe to an Internet Channel?" or "How do I clear my disk and memory cache?"

# Navigating Content

Really, very little has changed from previous versions of Internet Explorer as far as general navigation goes. You've got Forward, Back, Stop, Refresh, and Home buttons just as before. However, there are some new tricks up Internet Explorer's sleeve, which bear mentioning.

## The Toolbar

The first thing you may notice about Internet Explorer's new toolbars is that they contain more icons than those of previous versions.

**FULLSCREEN MODE**   Now you've got icons for new items called Fullscreen and Channels. We'll get to Channels in a moment. Click on the Fullscreen icon, and you'll find Internet Explorer magically transformed into a kiosk-looking application. This mode is very effective in creating a more immersive Web experience by removing many of the traditional distractions. For example, Windows 98's Taskbar disappears, as do Internet Explorer's pull-down menus, leaving only minimized toolbar icons (see Figure 9-9).

Not surprisingly, this mode also conserves valuable screen real estate, which is a real plus for laptop users who may have only 640 × 480 screen resolutions.

**TOOLBAR NAVIGATION** Not only are there new toolbar icons, but some of those icons function differently. Notice that if you click on the Favorites icon, the usual pull-down menu does not appear. Instead you see a separate page open up on the left-hand side of the screen, as shown in Figure 9-10.

Panes like the one on the left side of Figure 9-10 are called Explorer Bars. You can access them from the Search, Favorites, History, and Channel toolbar icons. Their primary purpose is to help you navigate through content with much greater speed and accuracy. They achieve this goal by allowing you to use the left side of the screen to

**Figure 9-9.** Internet Explorer in Kiosk mode

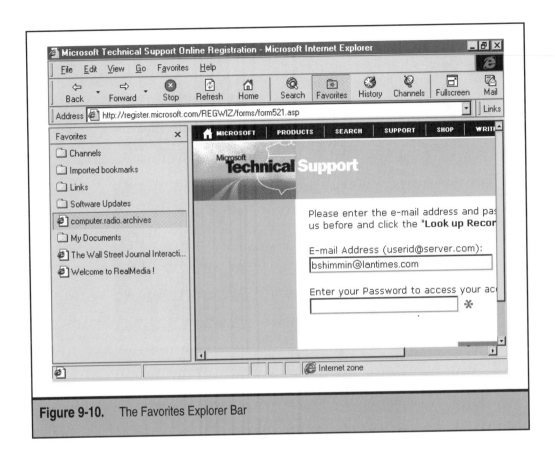

**Figure 9-10.**   The Favorites Explorer Bar

navigate between Web pages, leaving the right side available to display those pages. Instead of selecting a Web page from a pull-down menu, which disappears after the selection, the Explorer Bars remain visible, allowing you to see the hierarchy for a selected Web page. The History Explorer Bar, for instance, is organized by date and then by Web site, grouping pages by the time you accessed them and by the Web site from which you accessed them. If one page is a home page for a particular site, you can then get a sense of which of the following pages are part of that Web site (see Figure 9-11).

**SHORTCUT:**   Look at the pop-up window in Figure 9-11. By hovering your pointer over a particular Web page link, a pop-up window will open, displaying the complete title and URL for the highlighted Web page link.

The same principle holds true for the Favorites and Channels Explorer Bars. Each contains a hierarchy of folders and Web pages. However, the Search Explorer Bar

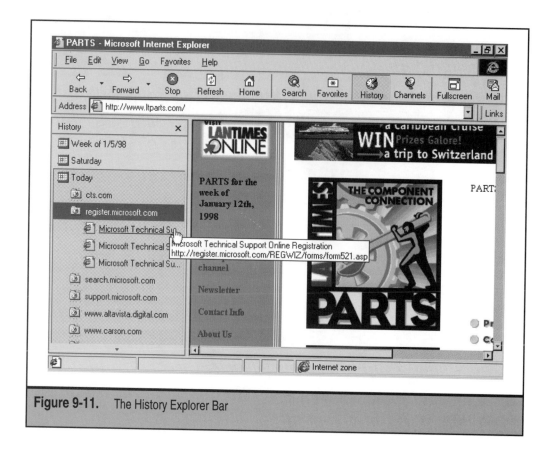

**Figure 9-11.**   The History Explorer Bar

contains something a little different. While you can access the other Explorer Bars while your computer is not connected to the Internet, the Search Explorer Bar uses live content on the Internet to give you access to one of the Internet's many search engines, including Yahoo, Excite, AOL NetFind, Infoseek, and Lycos. It defaults to a different engine each day, but you can select your favorites from a pull-down menu (see Figure 9-12).

Just enter your search criteria in the available field, click on the submit button (which is typically labeled "Submit"), and you'll see a brief list of your search results appear in the same window as the Search Explorer Bar, as shown in Figure 9-13. Just click on the desired search results entry, and the corresponding Web page will appear in the regular portion of the Internet Explorer interface to the right.

## The Address Field

The last navigation tool at your disposal is the Address field itself, where you traditionally enter URLs by hand. As usual, you can click on the down arrow within the Address field and get a list of the most recently typed URLs similar to the following.

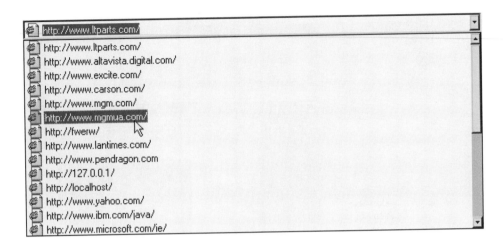

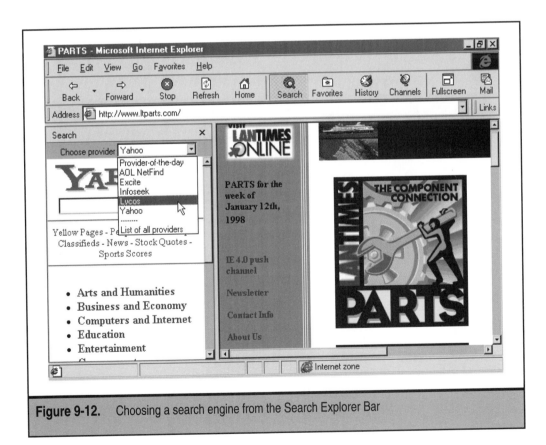

**Figure 9-12.**   Choosing a search engine from the Search Explorer Bar

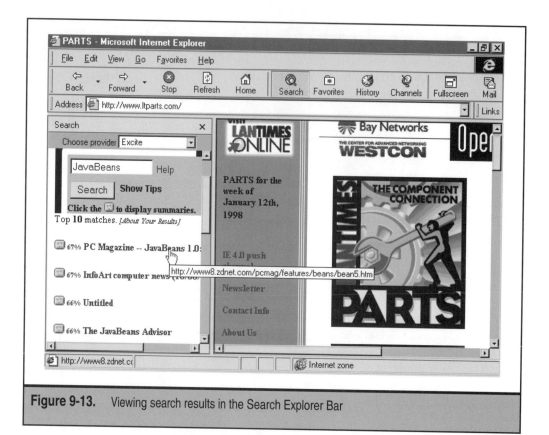

**Figure 9-13.** Viewing search results in the Search Explorer Bar

However, with Windows 98 (and more specifically Internet Explorer version 4.0), the Address field is a bit more useful than this. For instance, it now sports auto-completion. When you begin to type a URL, this feature actually finishes that URL for you. For instance, if you begin to type:

```
http://www.lan
```

it finishes the URL by adding the matching suffix (as highlighted text)

```
http://www.lantimes.com/
```

Moreover, if you've entered a number of URLs relative to the URL currently being entered, Internet Explorer simply brings up the first in the series. You can then use the up and down keys to cycle through the available, matching URLs. It's quite a time saver.

# FINE-TUNING INTERNET EXPLORER

Now that you've seen the basic help and navigational features of Internet Explorer, let's finish up this chapter with a discussion of the many customization, performance, and security issues you may encounter in deploying Internet Explorer as a part of Windows 98.

## Appearance

Windows 98's Internet Explorer is unique among many applications in that it is without barriers to human interactivity. Most applications support only one language; most supply only a few fonts and colors; and most do not make allowances for handicapped persons. Internet Explorer, on the other hand, can accommodate your personal tastes, your linguistic background, and even your special needs, all with very little effort. Let's say, for example, that you have a business unit operating in Hong Kong, China. With Internet Explorer, you can use the Product Updates application from the Help menu to download complete support for Chinese characters.

### Handicapped Access and Personalization

Before spending much time on languages, let's begin with accessibility solutions for the handicapped. If you have users who cannot use a mouse, all features in Internet Explorer are available from the keyboard. For example, by pressing the TAB and SHIFT-TAB keys, you can navigate forward and backward between Web pages. Another great feature is for those with sight impairment—automatic focus highlighting. That is, when you move a mouse over a hypertext link (either in text or within a graphic), Internet Explorer can draw a box around graphics and underline text. You can also instruct Internet Explorer to always display the alternate text for figures.

**RESOURCE:** For more information on Microsoft accessibility resources, point your Web browser at http://www.microsoft.com/enable/ or call (800) 426-9400.

**SETTING ADVANCED ACCESSIBILITY FEATURES**   To set these particular accessibility features, just open the Internet Options dialog box from the View pull-down menu and click on the Advanced tab. A very complex-looking set of options appears, as shown in Figure 9-14.

Take a close look at this panel. A great deal of time is spent here during the remainder of this chapter. At the very top of this tab, you'll find two Accessibility options. The first, which talks of moving the system caret with the focus and selection changes, is for people using a text-only Web browser such as Lynx. Enabling that selection simply helps their reader make the appropriate transitions from one page element to another as they browse

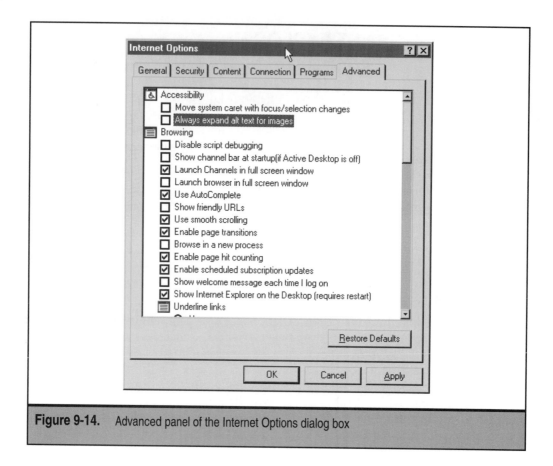

**Figure 9-14.**    Advanced panel of the Internet Options dialog box

the Web. The second element tells Internet Explorer to display the alternate text (denoted with ALT="sometext" in HTML), even if the size of the related image is not large enough to display the text. One last item to change within the Advanced tab for accessibility relates to underlining links. Just scroll down until you see the heading Underline links. There, choose the Hover radio button. As mentioned previously, this tells Internet Explorer to underline hypertext links and highlight hypertext images whenever you bring the pointer over one or the other.

**SETTING GENERAL ACCESSIBILITY OPTIONS**    If you go to the main General tab within the Internet Options dialog box (available from the View pull-down menu), you'll notice three buttons across the bottom of the panel: Colors, Fonts, and Accessibility. Actually, it also contains a button for Languages, but we'll get to that in the "Language Support" section a little later.

**SHORTCUT:** Although the following material really relates to those with a visual impairment, you can apply it to your particular tastes. For example, in setting a User style sheet, you can set up your own Cascading Style Sheet (CSS) to use your favorite fonts and colors.

If you have users with visual impairments, you can help them set up default colors and fonts for Internet Explorer. Of course, you can set a Windows color scheme for Windows 98, but that will not change the way online content looks within Internet Explorer. If you click on the Colors button at the bottom of the General tab, you'll see a Colors dialog box that looks like this:

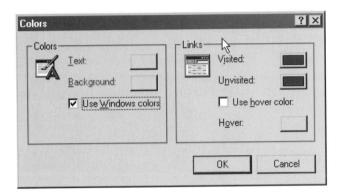

To set your own colors for the content within Internet Explorer, deselect the *Use Windows colors* check box. This allows you to then change the text and background colors, using the two pop-up buttons directly above. Of course, the colors you choose are entirely up to you, but for the highest possible contrast, select black for the background and white for the text color. On the right side of this same dialog box, you can tell Internet Explorer which colors to use for hypertext links and hover colors (for when you hover the pointer over hypertext links). Again, the choice is up to your personal tastes; however, for the utmost readability, you should leave the colors as is and use the hover selection highlighting described previously.

**SETTING FONTS**    The last items you can set to affect the appearance (either for personal taste or for accessibility) of Web-based content are the type and size of fonts you use. To do so, click on the Fonts button from the General panel of the Internet Options dialog box. This opens a Fonts dialog box similar to the one in Figure 9-15.

Here you can select the character set you use, which will, of course, depend upon which language you speak (more on that in the next section). You can also set default fonts and a font size. The proportional font is that which Internet Explorer uses for regular text. Internet Explorer uses the Fixed-width font to display such items as addresses, code samples, and the like.

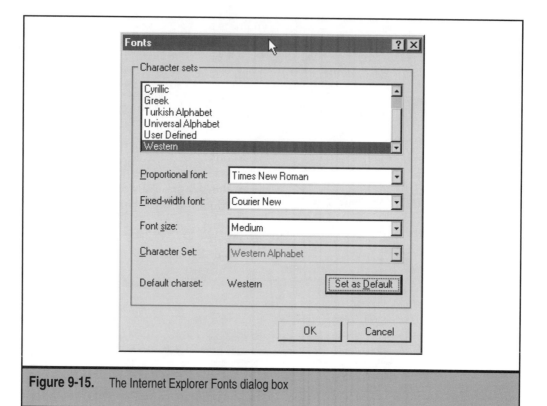

**Figure 9-15.** The Internet Explorer Fonts dialog box

**SHORTCUT:** Normally, for regular text, a serif-based font such as Times New Roman is the best. However, Windows 98 ships with two fonts that were designed specifically to enhance readability on computer screens. They are Trebuchet and Verdana. They are sans-serif fonts, which are proportional (meaning you can make them as big as you like). Give them a try; you might find them better suited to your tastes as well as needs.

Select the font you think will look the best or provide the best readability. You may need to experiment here, but that's okay. Your eyes are precious and deserve the help. Then all you need to do is select your desired font size. Your choices range from Smallest to Largest, of course. If you have a high-resolution monitor, you may want to choose a larger font, just to speed up reading chores. Likewise, for visual impairments, the larger the font the better.

**SHORTCUT:** Setting a default font from the Internet Options dialog box forces Internet Explorer to use those fonts at all times. However, you can revert to a different font size on-the-fly from the View pull-down menu.

Once you have set font options, all that remains is to click on the Accessibility button at the bottom of the General panel within the Internet Options dialog box, select all of the check boxes under the Formatting heading, and click on the OK button. This tells Internet Explorer to use your font selections. In doing so, you in effect override all of the font settings specified within the Web pages you view.

## Language Support

Often, you or one of your users may need to access content that is in a language other than your or their mother tongue. To remedy this situation, you can use the Internet Explorer Component Download facility. It's available from the Help pull-down menu under the Product Updates item. Once you click on the Product Updates item, you connect to Microsoft's Web site, where an application will evaluate which software components have already been installed on your system (see Figure 9-16).

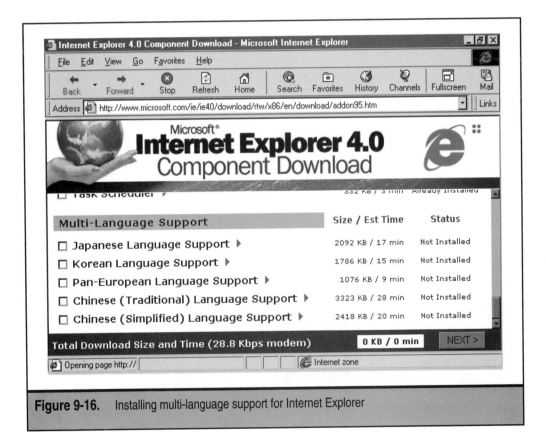

**Figure 9-16.**    Installing multi-language support for Internet Explorer

Scroll to the bottom of the resulting Web page. There, you'll see the available languages, which include:

▼ Japanese

■ Korean

■ Pan-European (covers most Romance and Germanic languages)

■ Chinese (traditional)

▲ Chinese (simplified)

Select the language you require by clicking on the appropriate check box and click on the Next button. This opens another Web page from which you can select a download site. As noted previously, choose one that is closest to you geographically. Click on the Install Now button, and Internet Explorer takes care of the rest.

> **CAUTION:** Don't download these language components willy-nilly. They are quite large, ranging in size from 1076 Kilobytes to 3323 Kilobytes. 2092 Kilobytes, for example, takes about 17 minutes to download over a 28.8Kbps connection.

The next time you reboot your machine, open the Internet Options dialog box and click on the Languages button from the General panel. This opens a Language Preference dialog box, where you should click on the Add button. Select the language that falls under the language component you downloaded earlier and then close all of the dialog boxes. Now you can simply browse a Web page containing the appropriate language, such as Japanese (see Figure 9-17).

If you don't see your language displayed properly, just click on the View pull-down menu, select Fonts, and click on the appropriate language.

## Performance

Although customizing the way Internet Explorer displays content is important (or just fun), the ability to manage the way it handles performance issues can mean the difference between productivity and frustration. In other words, if Internet Explorer can't present content and applications in a timely manner, you can't do your job—and neither can your users. Fortunately, you can customize Internet Explorer to better accommodate your available bandwidth.

To overcome a slow connection, the best thing you should do is click the Advanced tab in the Internet Options dialog box (accessed under the View pull-down menu). Once there, scroll down to the Multimedia selection and deselect the following items:

▼ Show pictures

■ Play animations

■ Play videos

- Play sounds
▲ Smart image dithering

When you're done, click on the OK button. From here on out, whenever you access a Web page, Internet Explorer will only show you the HTML text for that page, leaving off all of the bandwidth-intensive multimedia content. The first four are pretty straight-forward. They all require a great deal of bandwidth to download. The last item, Smart image dithering, forces Internet Explorer to draw images not all at once, but smoothly, a bit at a time. It does not require any more download time, but it takes longer for Internet Explorer to render.

**SHORTCUT:** Many power users, even users with a lot of bandwidth, choose to only display text. Doing so helps them navigate faster.

Another way to speed up a slow connection is to use Hypertext Transport Protocol (HTTP) version 1.1. This version of HTTP is just getting established on the Internet, so

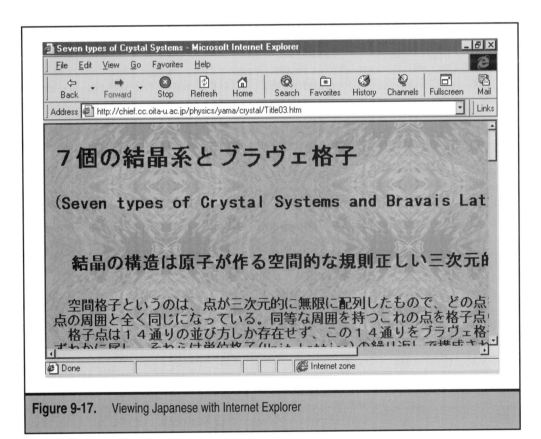

**Figure 9-17.** Viewing Japanese with Internet Explorer

not a lot of servers support it. But it can provide great performance gains. If you select to use HTTP 1.1 from the HTTP 1.1 settings section at the bottom of the Advanced panel of the Internet Options dialog box, Internet Explorer will try to use it as its default protocol. Of course, if a server does not support HTTP 1.1, Internet Explorer will simply drop back to HTTP 1.0. Be aware, however, that dropping back to HTTP 1.0 will incur a slight drop in performance.

> **CAUTION:** Don't select to use HTTP 1.1 through a proxy server in the same section of the Advanced panel. If your proxy server does not support HTTP 1.1, Internet Explorer will not be able to fall back properly.

Though not directly related to connection speeds, there is one performance feature you may want to set. If you want to download and run Java applications, and you have a slow connection, you should make sure that Internet Explorer uses the Java JIT Compiler. The JIT compiles Java code into machine code on-the-fly, removing redundancies and optimizing memory usage—all of which adds up to a substantial performance increase. To make sure this is set, click on the Advanced tab of the Internet Options dialog box, scroll down to the Java VM (Virtual Machine) section, and click on the Java JIT compiler-enabled check box.

> **CAUTION:** The only downside to the JIT compiler is that some Java applications may not work well with Internet Explorer's JIT. So if you receive any sort of error message while executing Java applets, you may want to consider deselecting JIT support before reloading the applet.

# Security

The most important customization of Internet Explorer you can make has nothing to do with how it looks or how it performs. It has everything to do with security. After all, the Internet can be a very, very scary place. To give you an example of the dangers that lie in wait for you and Internet Explorer, consider that between Microsoft and Netscape, both companies have issued over six security patches for their 4.0 and above Web browsers. All of these patches were designed to counter specific attacks that affect users. For example, one attack allowed attackers to use Internet Explorer as a gateway to the popular personal finance program, Quicken. It then tried to force Quicken to make a deposit in the attacker's bank account over the Internet.

Despite this seemingly poor track record, Internet Explorer has a number of security features you can exploit in order to protect yourself and your users from the wiles of the Internet. With features such as Secure Sockets Layer (SSL), Security Zones, and certificates, you can take control of your security risks.

## Secure Sockets Layer

The first place to start in securing Internet Explorer is to enable SSL for both versions 2.0 and 3.0. This lets Internet Explorer set up a secure connection with SSL-enabled servers and content. Once a connection over SSL is established with such a server, whatever data your users post or receive will be secured using the nearly unbreakable Public Key encryption algorithm. To make sure these two versions of SSL are enabled, click the Advanced tab of the Internet Options dialog box and scroll to the security section. There, select both versions using the appropriate check boxes.

The only problem with SSL is that the Web pages Internet Explorer (and other browsers) save to disk as cache are not secured. Anyone who gains access to a Windows 98 machine can read these files as regular Web pages. To get around this problem, you've got two choices. You can have Internet Explorer delete those Web pages before it has a chance to write them to disk, or you can ask Internet Explorer to delete those saved pages when it is closed. It is safer to choose not to write encrypted SSL pages to disk. But if you need to access those files more than once while working in Internet Explorer, you may want to simply delete those pages at the end of each browser section. To set either of these, from the same Security section, select the appropriate check box.

**SHORTCUT:**  While you're there, make sure that you select the first check box named "Enable Profile Assistant." This sends the personal information you entered previously when Web servers request cookie information from Internet Explorer.

## General Security Options

Our recommendations regarding the other check-box items under the Advanced tab are as follows:

▼ **Warn if form's submit is being redirected**   If you are concerned about the content you submit in an HTML form being sent across the Internet from the current host to another server, you should definitely enable this feature. It at least gives you a heads-up if this is the case.

■ **Warn if changing between secure and not secure mode**   If you work with a lot of secure content via SSL, you may want to enable this feature as it reminds you when you leave or enter secure mode. Just watch the lower portion of the Internet Explorer window. It displays a lock whenever you access an SSL document.

■ **Check for certificate revocation**   If you work with a lot of ActiveX controls or Java applets, make sure this is enabled. It does a reverse lookup for each certificate you intend to download, asking the certificate authority if that certificate is still valid. This is important simply because it takes the job of choosing whether or not to trust a certificate out of the user's hands.

■ **Warn about invalid site certificates**   This feature does the same thing except on a much more limited scale. It just checks to make sure that the URL for a certificate is valid. If the certificate owner's Web site is not available, then that person's certificate should not be trusted.

▲ **Cookies** Here you've got a couple of options. You can have Internet Explorer always accept cookies, prompt you before it accepts a cookie, or disable all cookie usage. We recommend that unless you are terribly paranoid about others being able to write data to your hard disk, you use the first option. There are simply too many reputable sites using cookies to disable them. If you ask to be warned about them, you'll spend all of your time choosing to allow a cookie to be sent.

## Security Zones

To finish off your security settings, click the Security tab of the Internet Options dialog box. Here, you'll find an interesting feature called "zones" (see Figure 9-18).

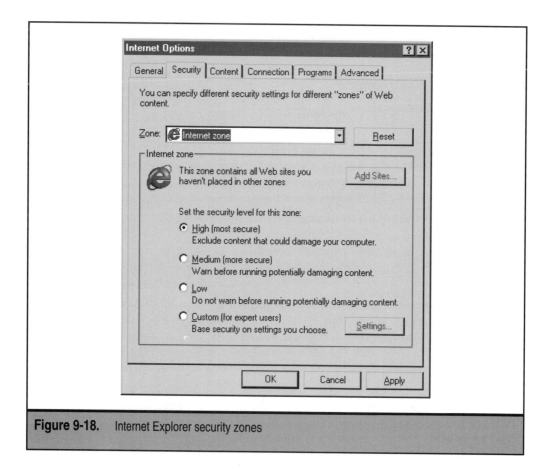

**Figure 9-18.** Internet Explorer security zones

These zones represent different levels of security for Internet Explorer. They represent collections of Web sites, or more specifically, individual URLs. There are four of them:

▼ **Internet zone**   This contains all URLs, except those specified within other zones, or those contained in your intranet.

■ **Local intranet zone**   This contains all URLs that are a part of your local intranet. As the systems administrator, you need to specify these.

■ **Trusted site zone**   This holds Internet URLs that you trust implicitly.

▲ **Restricted site zone**   This contains URLs that you occasionally visit but do not trust.

**ZONE SECURITY LEVELS**   Within each zone, you can choose from four different security levels:

▼ **High**   This setting is supposed to protect your computer from damage caused by potentially rogue software, such as Java applets, JavaScript applications, or ActiveX controls.

■ **Medium**   This setting does the same as the High setting, but allows you to decide whether or not to download the potentially dangerous software.

■ **Low**   This setting just runs the potentially dangerous software without notification.

▲ **Custom**   You can use this setting to customize the level of security for a given zone.

Actually, you can consider these zones and security levels a sort of security shortcut. You need only select the level you think most appropriate, and Internet Explorer makes all of the dependent settings for you. There are over 16 different security settings that Internet Explorer can automatically set for each level. For example, a zone marked with a high level of security does not download both signed and unsigned ActiveX controls. It forces Java to use its highest security settings. And it disables file downloads. In comparison, a zone marked with low security enables both signed and unsigned ActiveX controls and allows Java to function with fewer security constraints.

You are free to choose the level of security you think most appropriate for each zone, but you should, for all but the intranet zone, use either the high or medium security levels. In this way, at the very least, you force your users to make a conscious decision as to the safety of downloadable software. If, however, you do not like any of the available settings for high, medium, or low security levels, click on the Custom radio button and then click on the Settings button to the right. This opens a lengthy dialog box (see Figure 9-19) in which you can pick and choose individual security features mentioned previously.

**ADDING URLS TO EACH ZONE**   Security zones certainly have the potential to make Internet Explorer a very secure platform. However, they are relatively worthless, unless they contain the appropriate URLs. For each zone—except the Internet zone—you can

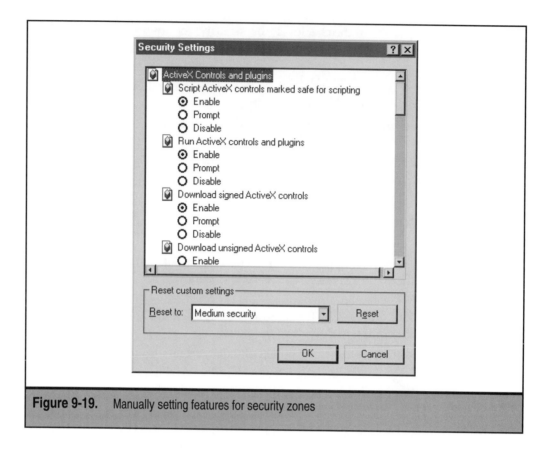

**Figure 9-19.** Manually setting features for security zones

add the URLs to which you wish to apply a given level of security. With the local intranet zone, for example, just select it in the Zone drop-down menu and click on the Add Sites button. This opens the Local intranet zone dialog box that looks like this:

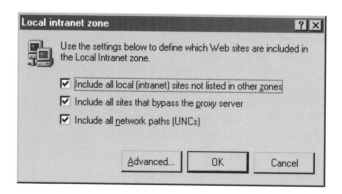

Here, make sure that all of the check-box items are selected, as this catches almost all of your local servers automatically. This saves you from having to manually enter them. If you discover, however, that some intranet servers are not being assigned to the local intranet zone, you can add them manually by clicking on the Advanced button from this dialog box. Here, you can enter the URLs for inclusion by hand. Don't worry if you have a lot of sites. Internet Explorer lets you enter them using wildcard characters. This lets you account for multiple URLs with a single zone. For example, you could enter the following URLs:

▼   *.//*.somesite.com (grabs all protocols for all servers at the domain called *somesite*)

▲   http://*.somesite.com (grabs all HTTP servers for the domain called *somesite*)

By the way, this same technique and dialog box applies when entering URLs for the other zones.

That's all there is to it. Once you've got your servers portioned in the appropriate zones, you can rest easy knowing that your users won't download unwanted or unsafe content.

# COMING UP

In the next chapter, the exploration of Windows 98's networking tools continues by diving into Outlook Express, its Internet-savvy e-mail client. Light years ahead of the old guard client called Exchange, Outlook Express allows you and your users to take advantage of many Internet technologies such as the Lightweight Directory Access Protocol (LDAP), HTML, and digital certificates. So grab your Rolodex and get ready to set up, configure, and use Outlook Express to communicate as you've never communicated before.

# CHAPTER 10

# Messaging with Windows 98

## What's ahead:
- Introduction to Outlook Express
- Installing and configuring Outlook Express
- Using Outlook Express
- Working offline

*"They never taste who always drink;*
*They always talk who never think."*

—Mathew Prior, *Upon a Passage in the Scaligerana*

Electronic messaging, and Internet e-mail in particular, is a powerful communications technology that has revolutionized the way business is done today. Instead of printing every document so it can be faxed or mailed to other people, we now send electronic messages with file attachments that are delivered almost instantly to any e-mail address, anywhere in the world.

E-mail found its way onto the Internet long before the World Wide Web became popular. Even today, more people use the Internet to send and receive e-mail than for browsing Web sites. If this seems surprising to you, consider that every commercial e-mail program on the market today either natively supports Internet mail or can exchange Internet mail by using a specialized mail gateway.

Just as the World Wide Web has become more graphical, interactive, and sophisticated, so has e-mail. Outlook Express, which ships with Windows 98, now supports embedded HTML, active content, file attachments, and personalized stationery.

# INTRODUCTION TO OUTLOOK EXPRESS

Over the past few years, Internet e-mail as defined by the Simple Mail Transport Protocol (SMTP) and the Post Office Protocol v3 (POP3) has become the de facto messaging standard. Even legacy systems that were built on proprietary protocols, like Microsoft Exchange and Lotus Notes, now support SMTP and POP3. This is a welcome consolidation because it now means that you only need to have one e-mail client installed on your computer to access all of your e-mail accounts and exchange messages with practically anyone.

Unlike Windows 95, which included two different e-mail programs, Windows 98 ships with only one messaging solution. Microsoft chose to standardize their messaging client software on Outlook Express. The Microsoft Exchange client software, which was distributed with Windows 95, is not included on the Windows 98 CD-ROM.

Outlook Express is an easy-to-use and very capable messaging solution. In addition to traditional e-mail, it also supports newsgroups, multiple accounts, a built-in Address Book, digital signatures, stationery, spell checking, and simple folder management.

## Internet E-Mail

At one point, Internet e-mail messages were limited to plain text. Today, most e-mail client software, including Outlook Express, also support messages formatted with HTML, including embedded graphics, sounds, background images, and JavaScript.

Internet e-mail refers to messages that are exchanged using the SMTP, POP3, and IMAP protocols. SMTP is used for sending messages either directly to recipients or to their mail servers for holding until they are able to retrieve it. POP3 is used by most e-mail client software to retrieve messages from a mail server on demand. IMAP is similar to POP3 in that it is used by e-mail client software to access e-mail messages stored on a mail server.

The primary difference between POP3 and IMAP is that with IMAP you can read, store, and organize your messages into folders on the mail server itself without first downloading the messages to your local system. Mobile users will probably want to download their messages so they can work offline. If you use e-mail from multiple locations and always have a connection to the mail server, IMAP has the advantage that you always have access to all of your new and archived messages without storing multiple copies on your local system. POP3 is still the standard for ISP-based Internet e-mail accounts because ISPs want you to pick up your e-mail and get it off their server quickly. IMAP is becoming increasingly popular on corporate mail systems.

# Newsgroups

Newsgroups are group discussion message bases. Messages are not addressed to anyone because they are readable by everyone. Newsgroups are a great way to solicit or offer feedback and commentary on a wide variety of topics.

When we speak of newsgroups, we often speak of Usenet news. This is because Usenet is one of the oldest and certainly the largest collection of newsgroups on the Internet. Nearly all ISPs operate news servers that carry the full assortment of Usenet newsgroups. But you can also create your own private newsgroups for the purpose of controlled communication with your employees and customers, and ISPs often create local newsgroups for the purpose of communicating with their own customer base.

# Multiple Accounts

Today, it's not uncommon to have an e-mail account for work and another for personal use. You might also find it useful or necessary to access the Usenet newsgroups on your ISP's news server, customer support newsgroups on a vendor's news server, and internal company newsgroups on a corporate news server.

Managing multiple e-mail accounts or access to multiple news servers used to be a complicated undertaking, but Outlook Express makes it easy with built-in support for multiple accounts. Incoming e-mail from all accounts is accessed through the unified inbox, and you can control which account is used when sending new messages.

# Address Book

The Address Book is a great place to keep track of names, addresses, phone numbers, e-mail addresses, and other information about the people you communicate with. You can use the Address Book to quickly address new messages to the intended recipients, or type their names in one of the address fields and let Outlook Express automatically locate them in the Address Book to get their e-mail address when you send the message.

# Digital Signatures

Few would argue the usefulness of Internet e-mail. But it does have a serious weakness that prevents many people from using it when conducting serious business: It's not secure. You can't rely on a message's integrity or authenticity unless you know for sure that it has not been tampered with and that it was actually sent by the person named in the From address field.

Message integrity is of concern because Internet e-mail is seldom sent directly from the sender's computer to the recipient's. Instead, it typically flows from the sender's e-mail software to the mail server then relayed to the recipient's mail server where it waits to be picked up by the recipient. Sometimes messages are relayed through one or more additional mail servers along the way. Every time a message is stored on or passed through a mail server that you don't control, it is susceptible to being tampered with. It's worth pointing out that it is highly unlikely and very difficult, although not impossible, to do this due to the large volumes of e-mail passing through commercial mail servers every day.

Authenticity is a greater concern because it's so easy to pretend that you are someone you aren't when sending e-mail messages through the Internet. Nearly all Internet e-mail client software allows the user to directly modify their account settings, including their display name and return e-mail address. You probably know someone who has received e-mail bearing the return address of the President of the United States, Bill Gates, or some other celebrity. To compound the problem, few Internet e-mail servers require users to log on when relaying messages through them, and there is nothing in the SMTP specification that would allow a compliant e-mail server to authenticate the source of a message destined for a user on their system.

Several e-mail products, including Outlook Express, have addressed this problem by using digital IDs to encrypt and electronically sign all, or selected, messages before they are sent. When a signed message is received, the e-mail software is able to verify the integrity of the message contents and verify the sender's authenticity.

# Signatures and Stationery

When communicating via written correspondence, it is common to print on business letterhead or personal stationery. Doing so typically tells the recipient something about you. Your letterhead probably has the company name, address, phone and fax numbers, and a logo. Your personal stationery may be colored with your name at the top and some sort of pattern or image that portrays your personality in the background or along the borders. Unfortunately, this personalization is often lost when communicating via e-mail because most e-mail is authored using simple text and typically signed with a first name, if signed at all.

Outlook Express provides some tools to help you regain some of the personal touch that has been lost. It is capable of automatically inserting a preformatted signature block at the end of each message you send, and it can add stationery patterns and backgrounds to your messages.

## Spell Checker

Few mistakes stand out so glaringly or leave such a lasting impression as misspelled words in your business correspondence. When you talk to someone on the telephone, they can't tell whether you know how to spell the words you're speaking or not, and most of us are accustomed to spell checking typed letters and memos before they are printed and mailed. So why don't we spell check our e-mail messages before sending them?

Outlook Express not only has a built-in spell checker, there is also a configuration option that causes the software to automatically spell check each message before it is sent.

## Folder Management

Some people immediately delete each message after they read and respond to it. Others like to keep a copy around for future reference. For those of us who like to keep an archive of important messages, it quickly becomes apparent that letting all those old messages stack up in our inboxes doesn't make for a very well-organized or functional message archive.

Outlook Express addresses this need by providing a very simple and easy-to-use system for creating, managing, and using folder archives. Additionally, folders can be organized into a hierarchy, or tree structure, that allows you to quickly locate and reference old messages.

# INSTALLING AND CONFIGURING OUTLOOK EXPRESS

Two things are necessary before you can use Outlook Express to communicate with others. You need to have a properly configured account on the appropriate mail or news server, and you need to install the software. If you have an account with an ISP, all the information you need to configure Outlook Express for e-mail and news should have been provided to you either at the time you signed up or shortly thereafter. If you are using Outlook Express to access a corporate e-mail server, check with your IS or IT department for the necessary information.

## Installing the Software

Outlook Express is included on the Windows 98 CD-ROM. Depending on how you installed the software, it may have been installed along with the operating system. You can check by looking on the Start menu under Program | Internet Explorer. You will need to install the software if you do not have an Internet Explorer folder on the Programs menu, or if Outlook Express is not listed in that folder.

To install the software, open the Windows Control Panel and select the Add/Remove Programs icon. When the Add/Remove Programs Properties dialog box opens, select the Windows Setup tab and locate the entry for Microsoft Outlook Express. Place a check mark in the box next to the entry, then click on the OK button at the bottom of the window. Windows 98 then proceeds to install the software. If you installed Windows 98 from a CD-ROM, you should have the disk handy and be prepared to insert it in the drive when you are prompted to do so.

That's all there is to it. The software is now installed on your computer, and you're ready to configure it with the proper settings for your e-mail and news server accounts.

## Launching Outlook Express

In the typical Windows 98 installation, there are at least four ways to launch Outlook Express:

▼ **From the Desktop**   When Outlook Express is installed, Windows typically places an icon for it on your desktop. To launch Outlook Express from the desktop, simply click on its icon.

■ **From the Start Menu**   To launch Outlook Express from the Start menu, select the Outlook Express entry under Programs | Internet Explorer.

■ **From Internet Explorer**   While in Internet Explorer, select Mail from the Go menu or click the Mail icon on the toolbar and select Read Mail from the pop-up menu.

▲ **From the Taskbar**   If the Quick Launch Toolbar is enabled, you will see four small icons on the taskbar representing Internet Explorer, Outlook Express, Show Desktop, and Channels. You can launch Outlook Express by clicking on its icon.

The first time you launch Outlook Express, it automatically executes the Internet Connection Wizard and prompts you for your account information. More information on configuring e-mail accounts is found later in the section titled "Configuring an E-mail Account."

## Customizing the User Interface

When Outlook Express is launched, the screen should look something like the one shown in Figure 10-1.

The first thing to do is to customize the user interface. Begin by selecting the View menu and ensuring that both the Toolbar and Status Bar items are checked, then click the menu item titled Layout to open the Window Layout Properties dialog box, shown here:

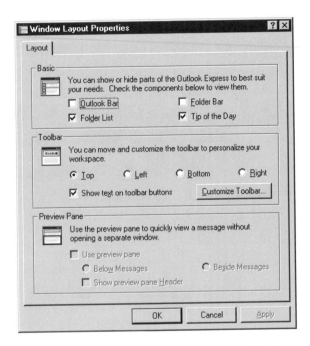

This dialog box is divided into three sections titled Basic, Toolbar, and Preview Pane. Each controls a different aspect of the user interface.

## Basic

Under the Basic heading, you can control which components (Outlook Bar, Folder List, Folder Bar, and Tip of the Day) are displayed on the screen and which are hidden. Refer to Figure 10-1 to see where each of these components is located.

**SOAPBOX:**   Our preference is to enable the Folder List and disable the other three options. This frees up precious screen space and leaves a very clean desktop while preserving quick access to the archive folders we have created.

## Toolbar

The Toolbar section allows you to control placement of the toolbar within the Outlook Express window. By clicking on the Customize Toolbar button, you can specify which items will appear on the toolbar.

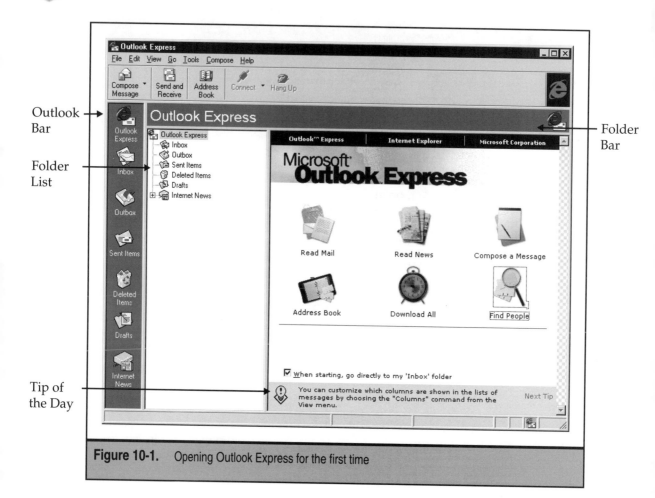

Outlook
Bar

Folder
List

Tip of
the Day

Folder
Bar

**Figure 10-1.** Opening Outlook Express for the first time

**SOAPBOX:** Our preference is to position the toolbar at the top of the window and disable the text descriptions to preserve screen space. If you are new to Outlook Express, you will probably want to enable the text descriptions until you become familiar with each of the icons.

## Preview Pane

The final section, titled Preview Pane, allows you to control whether or not you can read your messages without opening them in a separate window, commonly known as previewing the message. If the preview pane is enabled, you can also control where the pane is displayed and whether or not message headers are included in the preview pane.

**SOAPBOX:**   We recommend enabling the preview pane and selecting the option to display it below the messages. Unless you have a very high-resolution screen, you probably don't have enough screen space to use the option for placing the preview pane beside the messages. The decision whether or not to display message headers in the preview pane is a matter of personal preference; some people like to see them, others don't. For us, it depends on the amount of screen space we have. We turn it off when running in 800 × 600 on a laptop, but turn it on for use at the desktop with a screen resolution of 1024 × 768.

## Configuring an E-Mail Account

To configure an e-mail account, open the Internet Accounts dialog box by selecting the Accounts item on the Tools menu. You'll see a dialog box like the one shown here:

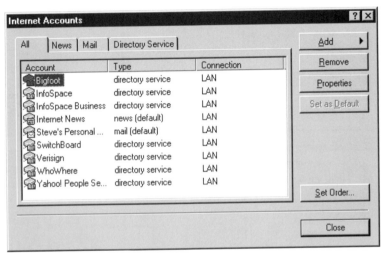

Click on the Add button and choose Mail from the pop-up menu. This opens the Internet Connection Wizard, which prompts you through a series of questions beginning with your name as it will appear when others view the messages you send them. On page two, you are prompted to enter your e-mail address, which will be shown to the recipient and will be used whenever someone replies to a message you sent them. On page three, you need to tell Outlook Express whether your mail server uses POP3 or IMAP and the address of the Incoming and Outgoing mail servers. The fourth page prompts you for your account information. You can leave the password field blank if you do not want to store your password on the computer. The fifth page simply asks for a "friendly name," which will be used on the screen display. Page six allows you to specify how you connect to the network, and page seven does nothing more than congratulate you for completing the process.

If you have more than one e-mail account, you can add each one using the same procedure, then highlight the account that you want to be the default when sending new messages and click the "Set As Default" button.

If you answered all of the questions, your e-mail account should be ready to go. Even so, you should take a minute to familiarize yourself with some of the other settings that you can control on an account-by-account basis. For example, if you access the same POP3 e-mail account from two locations, such as if you check your business e-mail account from home or your personal e-mail account from the office, you will want to configure the second location to leave messages on the server. This way, you will be assured of having a complete archive of all messages at the primary location even if you read some of those messages at another location. This setting is found on the Advanced tab, about halfway down the panel under the Delivery heading.

## Configuring a News Account

Configuring a news account is very similar to configuring an e-mail account. Start by clicking on the Add button, then select News from the pop-up menu to activate the Internet Connection Wizard. The Wizard prompts you for your name, e-mail address, news server address, and a friendly name.

**SOAPBOX:** Many organizations compile mailing lists from the return e-mail addresses found in newsgroup postings, then they send unsolicited bulk e-mail, commonly known as "spam," to everyone on their list. If you want to be anonymous or just want to protect yourself from a bunch of unsolicited e-mail, you can enter bogus information for your name and e-mail address.

## Options

Outlook Express is highly customizable. In addition to the user interface options already discussed, you can exercise a great deal of control over how the software behaves by changing the available configuration options. The configuration options are accessible by clicking on the Options item on the Tools menu.

This window is organized into seven tabs: General, Send, Read, Spelling, Security, Dial Up, and Advanced, as shown here:

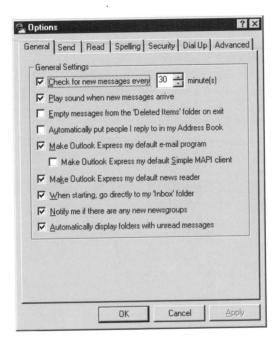

Not all of these options are described here because most are pretty self-explanatory and context-sensitive help is available everywhere by first clicking on the question mark (?) button, found in the upper-right corner of the window, then clicking on the item you want to learn about.

## General

We recommend paying special attention to certain options on the General panel, as explained in this section.

**CHECK FOR NEW MESSAGES EVERY X MINUTE(S)**    This is an important option to enable. It tells Outlook Express to automatically check for new messages each time you launch it, and again every so many minutes while it is still open. If this option is not enabled, you will have to manually command Outlook Express to check for new messages.

**SOAPBOX:**  If you connect to your mail server over a dial-up Internet connection and have configured your system to connect to the Internet as needed, Windows 98 will automatically trigger the dialer whenever Outlook Express tries to contact the mail server if a connection does not already exist. If desired, you can suspend this feature by selecting the Work Offline option from the File menu in Outlook Express.

**WHEN STARTING, GO DIRECTLY TO MY 'INBOX' FOLDER**    This option causes the software to default to the message window, with focus set to the Inbox folder, each time you start the program. The full version of Outlook has other functionality beyond that found in Outlook Express, but with Outlook Express, it's a pretty safe bet that you intend to check for new messages each time you launch the software.

## Send

On the Send panel, shown here, you can control a number of options that come into play when composing a reply or sending a message:

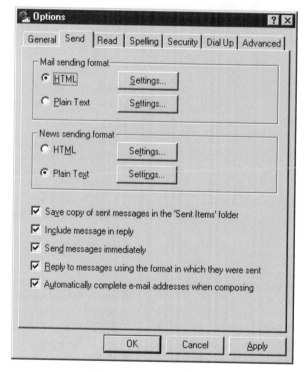

The first option here is the file format to use for Mail and for News. If you know that the people you communicate with have Outlook Express, you can take advantage of Outlook's support for rich message content by specifying use of the HTML format. However, if you mostly communicate with users of other e-mail programs, you may want to specify the Plain Text option.

If you want to keep a record of your own correspondence, be sure to enable the option titled "Save copy of sent messages in the 'Sent Items' folder."

## Read

Here is what the options on the Read panel look like:

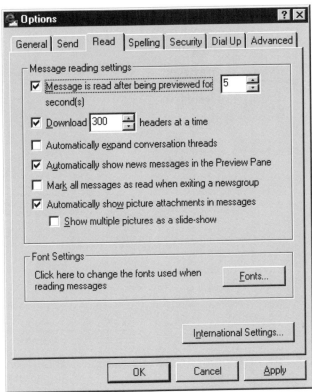

The only option we recommend changing on this screen is the very first one, titled "Message is read after being previewed for x second(s)." Most messages can be read in the preview pane without opening them in a separate window. With this option enabled, you don't need to open a separate window for Outlook Express to mark the message as read. Setting the time to a small value, like two or three seconds, allows you to move quickly through your messages while still leaving enough time for you to pass over those messages that you don't want marked as read just yet.

## Spelling

The options on the Spelling panel look like this:

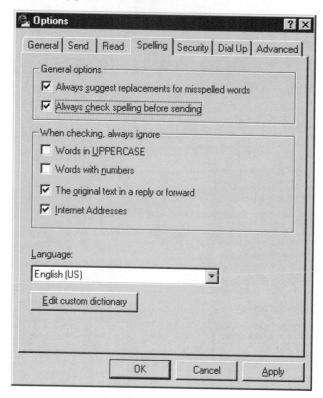

When conducting business through electronic communications, even simple spelling errors can leave a lasting impression. It's always a good idea to spell check your correspondence before sending it. We recommend enabling the first two options on the Spelling panel titled "Always suggest replacements for misspelled words" and "Always check spelling before sending." This ensures that every message you create is spell checked before it's sent.

## Security

The Security panel, shown next, is divided into three sections: Security Zones, Secure Mail, and Digital IDs.

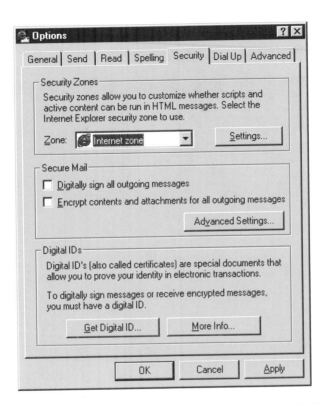

The only option most users will ever use on the Security page is the Security Zone, which works just like it does in Internet Explorer. More advanced users, including anyone concerned about protecting the security and authenticity of the messages they send, will want to pay close attention to the remaining configuration options. Under the Secure Mail heading, you can specify whether Outlook Express should automatically digitally sign or encrypt messages and file attachments of all outgoing messages. The Advanced button leads to another configuration screen where you can specify your preferred encryption algorithm and control whether your public key is included with outgoing messages. But before you can send encrypted or digitally signed messages, you must first get a digital ID. Clicking on the "Get Digital ID" button launches Internet Explorer and walks you through the process.

## Dial Up

The options on the Dial Up panel are shown here:

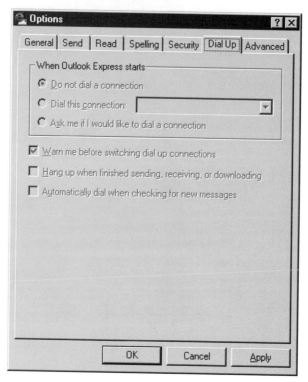

If at least one of the Mail or News accounts configured in Outlook Express is set up to use a dial-up connection, you will be able to control how and when a connection is dialed, whether you will be warned before switching to another dial-up connection, whether it will automatically dial when checking for new messages, and whether to hang up when finished sending and receiving messages. Users that access the Internet through the corporate network should not need to use dial-up connections for any of their Mail or News accounts. If no accounts are configured for dial-up access, the options on this page will be grayed-out and inaccessible.

## Advanced

The last panel, which contains the Advanced options, looks like this:

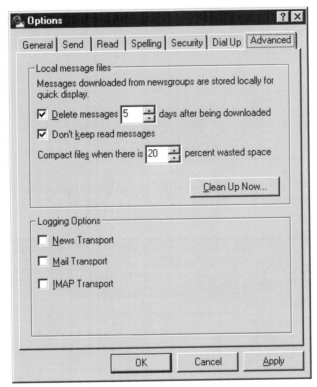

The Advanced page contains options that control how long newsgroup messages remain on your system and contains options for logging News, Mail, and IMAP Transport activity. You probably won't need to change any of these settings.

# Inbox Assistant

The Inbox Assistant automatically sorts through your incoming mail, then moves or copies each message to the appropriate folder, forwards them to someone else, replies with a predetermined message, or deletes the message from the server without downloading it.

The Inbox Assistant can be accessed from the Tools menu. When you select Inbox Assistant from the Tools menu, the following dialog box appears:

The first time you open the Inbox Assistant, the list of Inbox rules is empty. Click on the Add button to create a new rule for the Assistant to follow. The following dialog box appears:

The top half of the window contains the rules that are used to determine whether this rule applies to any given message. You can specify values for the To, CC, and From address fields, the Subject, which account the rule applies to, and the minimum message size that the rule applies to.

The lower half of the window describes the action that should be taken on each matching message. Choices are to move the message to a specified folder, copy the message to a specified folder, forward the message to a specified e-mail address, reply to the message with a canned response, do not download the message, and delete the message from the server.

Once you finish adding a rule, you are returned to the Inbox Assistant with the new rule listed in the window. When new messages are retrieved from the server, each rule is checked in order. To rearrange the order of the rules in the window, simply select a rule by clicking on it once then click on the Move Up or Move Down buttons until the rule moves into the desired position.

The remainder of the controls in this window are pretty self-explanatory. The Remove button deletes the currently selected rule, the Properties button opens the rules definition window so you can edit it, and the OK and Cancel buttons close the window, returning you to Outlook Express.

## Stationery

With Outlook Express, you can control how new messages are formatted, including the font, stationery, and signature block. To do so, select the Stationery option from the Tools menu. You'll see the following dialog box:

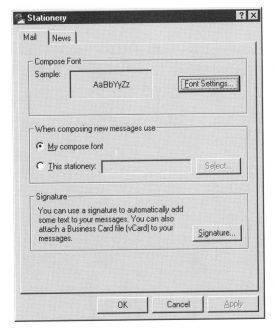

The Mail panel of the Stationery dialog box is divided into three sections. The first describes the default font that will be used when composing a new message. The second section allows you to specify whether to use the default font or a selected stationery. The final section is for specifying the Signature block that will be automatically appended to the end of each message. Each of these settings can be controlled independently for Mail and News messages by clicking on the appropriate tab at the top of the window.

Click on the Select button to browse the available stationery formats in the Select Stationery dialog box, shown here:

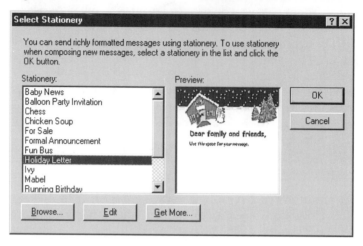

Select the one you wish to use. From here, you can also load new designs and edit existing ones.

To customize the signature block, return to the Stationery window and click on the Signature button to open the Signature properties window, which looks like this:

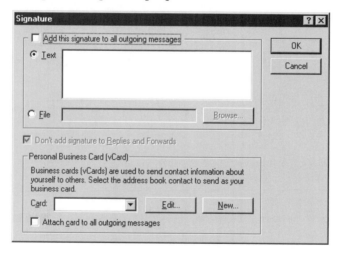

In this window, you can specify a signature that will be appended to the end of each outgoing message by either typing it into the text window or specifying the file on disk that contains the desired text. In addition to the signature block, you can also attach a Personal Business Card to each message. Business cards are actually Address Book entries. If you have not yet created an entry for yourself in the Address Book, click on the New button to do so now.

# USING OUTLOOK EXPRESS

Now that you have installed and configured Outlook Express, you're ready to begin using it. When you launch Outlook Express, the screen should resemble the one shown at the beginning of this chapter in Figure 10-1.

If you are looking at the Outlook Express start page, click the option near the bottom of the screen titled "When starting, go directly to my 'Inbox' folder," then click on the Inbox folder that appears in the Folder List on the left side of the window. When you click the Inbox folder, the messages in your Inbox will appear, as shown in the following illustration:

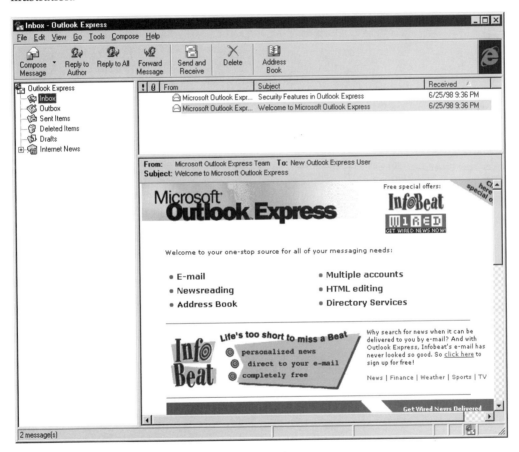

***SOAPBOX:***   When Outlook Express was started for the first time, it automatically created two messages and placed them in your Inbox. You should take a few minutes to review these messages as they contain helpful information about security and using Outlook Express.

# E-Mail

All e-mail activity in Outlook Express is centered around the Inbox. This is where most users will spend the majority of their time. Unless you have configured the Inbox Assistant to automatically move incoming messages to another folder as they are received, they will all appear in the Inbox and will remain there until you move or delete them.

You will notice that the number of unread messages in each folder is displayed inside parentheses next to the folder name in the Folder List, which occupies the left frame of the Outlook Express window if you configured the Layout according to the instructions earlier in this chapter. Unread messages are easily recognizable in the message frame because they are listed in bold. Once a message has been read, or previewed for the specified amount of time, its status changes as indicated by returning the message header to the normal font style.

The order in which messages are displayed can be controlled by simply clicking on the desired column heading. Clicking the heading more than once toggles the display between ascending and descending order. This is particularly helpful if you want to view messages by sender's name, or with the most recent messages listed first in the window.

## Reading Messages

If you have configured your copy of Outlook Express to use the Preview Pane, most messages can be read in that pane without explicitly opening it in another window. If the Preview Pane is not enabled, you need to open each message individually in order to read them. Even with the Preview Pane, you will still need to open messages that contain file attachments or formatted contents that don't fit well within the Preview Pane.

There are several ways to open the currently selected message: press ENTER, select Open from the File menu, press CTRL-O, or simply double-click on it. This causes Outlook Express to open another window that contains the selected message. If there are any file attachments, they are displayed in a frame at the bottom of the window.

File attachments, can be saved to disk by selecting the Save Attachments option on the File menu or by right-clicking on the desired file attachment. The right-click method opens a pop-up menu with options to Open, Print, Save As, or QuickView the file.

## The Toolbar

Most of the actions you will need to perform are accessible from the toolbar. The buttons on the standard toolbar, from left to right, perform the following functions:

▼ **Compose Message** Used to create a new text message. You can also click on the down arrow next to this button to select from the available Stationery.

■ **Reply to Author** Used to compose a new message as a response to the currently selected message. The message will be addressed to the address specified in the reply-to address, the subject will be the same but with "Re:" prefixed to it, and depending on your configuration settings, the body of the message may be quoted and included in the new message body so you can refer to it in your response.

- **Reply to All**   The same as Reply to Author except that it also includes in the Cc address field all other message recipients specified in the current message's To and Cc address fields.

- **Forward Message**   Like Reply to Author except the To address field is left blank and the Subject line is prefixed with "Fw:" instead of "Re:".

- **Send and Receive**   Forces Outlook Express to immediately send any messages waiting in the Outbox and retrieve any new messages found on the mail server.

- **Delete**   Moves the selected message to the Deleted Items folder. Depending on your configuration settings, the Deleted Items folder may be purged each time you exit the program.

▲  **Address Book**   Opens the Address Book.

Additionally, each of these actions, plus others, can be accessed through the pull-down menus. If you have not done so, you should take a few minutes to become familiar with the items available on each pull-down menu.

## Sending a Message

When you compose a message, whether it is a new message, reply, or forwarded message, you work from a window similar to the following:

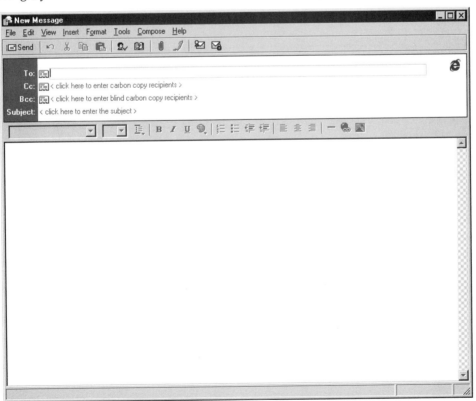

This window is simply divided into two main areas. The top contains all necessary addressing, or "header," information. The lower area contains the message body.

When addressing a message, you can directly type in the recipient's e-mail address, select it from the Address Book by clicking on the index card icon next to any address field, or type the user's name and allow Outlook Express to match it with the appropriate e-mail address as found in the Address Book.

While entering text into the body of the message, another toolbar, located between the message header and body, becomes activated and available for use. These buttons generally affect the visual formatting of the selected text within the window. You can learn the functionality of any icon by hovering over it with your mouse pointer, which causes a short description to appear in a pop-up window.

When you're ready to send the message, either click on the Send button on the toolbar, select the Send option from the File menu, or press ALT+S. The message is placed in your Outbox folder and either sent immediately, if you have an Internet connection, or held until you do connect manually.

## Finding a Message

Sometimes you need to find and review an old message that has been archived in one of your folders. To locate a message that has been filed in one of your folders, first select the folder you want to search then select Find Message from the Edit menu. The following dialog box appears:

You can search by address, subject, or message body text and can optionally constrain the search to a specified date range by completing the corresponding fields then clicking on the Find Now button. All matching messages are listed in the lower portion of the window, where you can browse the list of matching messages or double-click on one to open it.

# News

Using Outlook Express to read news is a lot like reading e-mail. The main difference is that there are typically a lot more messages, none of them are addressed to you, and when you compose a message, you don't address it to anyone.

After you configure your news account, Outlook Express gives you the opportunity to select the newsgroups you wish to subscribe to. You can select additional newsgroups at any time by choosing the Newsgroups option from the Tools menu. The Newsgroups dialog box appears:

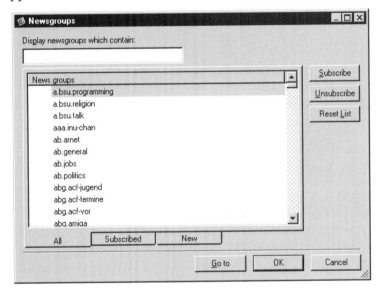

You can access the newsgroups that you have subscribed to in much the same way that you access any other folder from the Folders List. Click on the plus sign next to the name of your news server to reveal the list of subscribed newsgroups.

Sometimes it is useful to access a newsgroup without subscribing to it. You can do so by opening the same window you used to select newsgroups, but click on the Go To button instead of the Subscribe button after you highlight the desired newsgroup in the list.

# Address Book

The Address Book is also very simple to use and pretty self-explanatory. To access the Address Book, either click on the Address Book button on the toolbar, select Address Book from the Tools menu, or press CTRL+SHIFT+B on your keyboard. The Address Book window, shown here, appears:

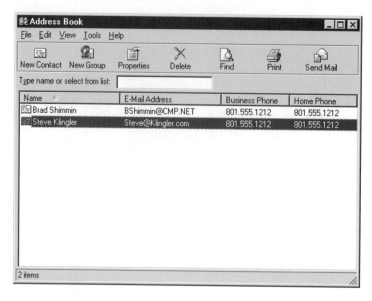

The Address Book allows you to enter individual contacts and to create mailing groups, which are simply a collection of individual contacts that can be address by a single name. To send a message to everyone in a mailing group, simply addressed the message to the group name and Outlook Express replaces the group name with the list of individual addresses as the message is sent.

New contacts can be entered by clicking on the New Contact button on the toolbar, selecting New Contact from the File menu, or pressing CTRL+N on your keyboard. A new contact window appears:

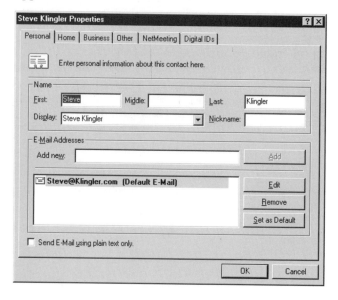

While viewing the Address Book, you can control the order in which entries are listed in much the same way that you do when working with messages. Click on any column header to sort the display by the data found in that column.

You can also quickly search for any entry by selecting Find from the Edit menu to open the Find People dialog box, shown here:

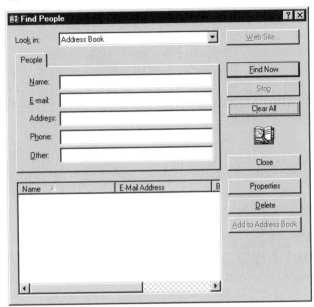

From here, you can search the Address Book by name, e-mail address, address, phone, or other. Simply enter the data you want to search by then click on the Find Now button to initiate the search. All matching entries are displayed in the lower portion of the window.

## Finding People

In addition to searching the Address Book, the Find People dialog box is also capable of searching public directory services such as Yahoo People Search, Bigfoot, Infospace, Infospace Business, Switchboard, Verisign, and WhoWhere. To do so, simply select the desired search engine from the pull-down menu labeled "Look in:".

# WORKING OFFLINE

Mobile users and those who connect to the Internet through dial-up connections often find it necessary to read and compose messages when they are not presently connected to the Internet. This is known as *working offline*.

Outlook Express provides built-in support for working offline. If the TCP/IP protocol stack is not active or if the software cannot connect with your e-mail server for any reason, a small yellow triangle appears on the status line and it automatically functions in a forced offline mode. In this state, the software continues trying to connect with your mail server according to the polling frequency you have configured.

If you know that you are disconnected and don't want Outlook Express to repeatedly attempt to reach your mail server, you can force it into a true offline mode by selecting Work Offline from the File menu. This disables all attempted communications between Outlook Express and any configured mail server.

You might be wondering why you would ever want to force offline mode when the software can put itself into a forced offline state anyway. Consider this: If you have configured Windows 98 to automatically dial and connect to your Internet Service Provider (ISP) on demand, it will attempt to do so every time Outlook Express attempts to connect to the mail server. However, if you force the software to work offline, it will never cause Windows to dial your ISP.

# COMING UP

Chapter 11 is all about using Windows 98 to communicate with other people via the Internet using Microsoft Network, NetMeeting, and Microsoft Chat.

# NETWORK
## PROFESSIONAL'S
# LIBRARY

# CHAPTER 11

# Communicating with
# Windows 98

## What's ahead:

- Communication tools at your service with MSN
- Collaborating with NetMeeting
- Chatting with Windows 98

*"Only by the form, the pattern
Can words or music reach
The stillness, as a Chinese jar still
Moves perpetually in its stillness."*

—T.S. Eliot, *Burnt Norton*

As you saw in the last chapter, Microsoft Exchange and Outlook Express are great tools for sending and receiving e-mail. Outlook Express' simple idea of using HTML as an e-mail file format, for example, just blows the doors off conventional ideas of how people communicate by stepping beyond plain old textual e-mail. But did you know that Windows 98 and Internet Explorer come with even more tools that not only help you communicate, but collaborate, convey, and discover? Actually, you've got everything you need to use Windows 98 as a communications platform, all the way from basic Internet connectivity to advanced collaboration tools. For example, there's one tool for chatting via the keyboard, one for sharing applications, and one for accessing the Internet. When you install Windows 98 and Internet Explorer you automatically gain access to these capabilities within the following Microsoft communication tools:

▼ The Microsoft Network
■ NetMeeting
▲ Chat

At first glance, you may think that the Microsoft Network differs greatly from NetMeeting and Chat, both of which provide very focused communication services. However, The Microsoft Network is much more than a simple avenue to Internet connectivity. Put simply, the Microsoft Network gives you instant Internet connectivity as well as access to a host of communications tools such as an application for finding a friend online and various communication forums. Actually, you don't even need the Microsoft Network to get to the Internet. You can simply use your existing Internet Service Provider to access the Microsoft Network's many communication tools.

No matter how you get to the Internet, with NetMeeting and the right hardware, you can create a truly virtual meeting room in which members can see each other, hear each other speak, exchange files, and even draw on a white board. And Microsoft Chat lets you easily and quickly talk with others via a combination of text and emotive graphics.

In this chapter, we take a close look at these tools one at a time, showing you how to install, configure, and use them. From a user's perspective, we talk about how these tools can dramatically improve your productivity through effective communications. And from an administrator's perspective, we teach you how to best manage these products, discussing security, performance, and support issues as we go.

# COMMUNICATION TOOLS AT YOUR SERVICE

These tools are free-of-charge to Windows 98 and Internet Explorer users. Of course, using those tools will cost you. As with any communication tool that relies upon the Internet, you've got to have an Internet connection, which costs money. With the Microsoft Network (MSN), for example, you can get the software free of charge, but you must sign up for MSN's Internet connectivity. Some of the software comes pre-installed with Internet Explorer, while some must be downloaded from Microsoft's Web site. As with Outlook Express, when you install Windows 98 and Internet Explorer, you automatically install NetMeeting. However, Microsoft Chat may not come pre-installed. Installing Microsoft Chat is discussed a bit later in the section entitled "Chatting with Windows 98." But overall, to install and use all of these tools, you need an Internet connection. MSN, which is a suite of online communications services, can provide you with an Internet connection. However, if you have already set up your connection to the Internet via dial-up networking (as you saw in Chapter 7), or if you already have a direct connection to the Internet via your Local Area Network (LAN), then skip to the section entitled "Collaborating with NetMeeting."

If you don't have access to the Internet, you can take advantage of one of the Internet Service Providers (ISPs) included with Windows 98. You've got your choice from among the following.

▼   AOL

■   AT&T WorldNet Services

■   CompuServe

■   Prodigy Internet

▲   The Microsoft Network

Any of these will provide you with Internet connectivity, though some are further along than others when it comes to supporting Internet protocols such as the Post Office Protocol (POP) for e-mail or Network News Transfer Protocol (NNTP) for Newsgroups. For example, CompuServe is still struggling to provide POP access to its users. The result is that these users must use CompuServe's built-in e-mail client, which does not support such emerging technologies as HTML and even outbound file attachments. Both CompuServe and AOL use proprietary newsgroup technologies, eschewing the more open, Internet-savvy NNTP standard.

However, all provide useful and unique online services adjacent to the Internet, and each has its special charm and worth. AOL, for instance, draws together millions of users each week in public forums and intimate chat rooms. AT&T WorldNet Services draws together the world of telephone and Internet connectivity under one, easy-to-manage provider. CompuServe, long the domain of technologists, still provides excellent technical content not available anywhere else. Prodigy is said to be the easiest of all online services to use and navigate. And MSN, of course, will appeal to Windows 98 users as an excellent place to share Windows applications and information and access the Internet.

## The Microsoft Network

MSN is very much like the other online services mentioned in the preceding section. It provides worldwide e-mail, Internet connectivity, as well as its own private services such as special interest forums, software downloads, and original entertainment. However, MSN holds a special place in the hearts of many Windows 95, Windows NT, and now Windows 98 users as it provides a number of Windows-centric services such as Microsoft technical support documents, software patches, and the like—perfect content for Windows administrators and users.

### Online Services

For the purposes of this chapter, we'll talk just about MSN as a communications tool for Windows 98, not as an ISP. For help using these other connectivity tools, refer to Chapter 7. However, if you want to get started quickly with any of these online services, just click on the Start button, select Programs, and click on the Online Services folder shown here.

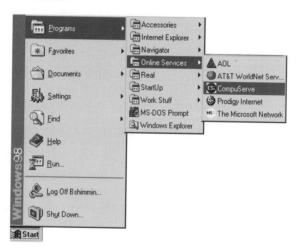

Click on the service you prefer and Windows 98 begins installing its software. From here on out, you need only follow the prompts, providing the appropriate information where needed, and then you're on your way to Internet connectivity and global collaboration. One word of caution: These services are not free. If you sign up for more than one, you will pay for more than one.

## Configuring the Microsoft Network

As with the other online services, MSN can be installed from the Start button. After clicking on the Microsoft Network button within the Online Services folder, you should see a dialog box much like the one shown in Figure 11-1.

Figure 11-1 shows the Installation Wizard. By following its prompts, you can easily install and configure the client software required to connect with MSN's online service. It begins by asking you to name your country and telling you to read the MSN Member Agreement. Take the time to read and agree to this document, as it contains MSN's acceptable usage guidelines—basically, the do's and don'ts for using MSN. The Installation Wizard creates a dial-up connection for MSN, asking you to select your modem. It then restarts your computer, if needed.

**CAUTION:**   If you've set up file sharing via TCP/IP, as with a local FTP or Web service, you may see a security warning window asking you to disable file and printer sharing. We suggest that you take Windows 98's advice and do so. Leaving your system open to TCP/IP file sharing, even with password protection, is simply an invitation to disaster. If someone were to obtain your IP address, for example, that person might be able to connect to your local machine from the Internet and steal or damage your data.

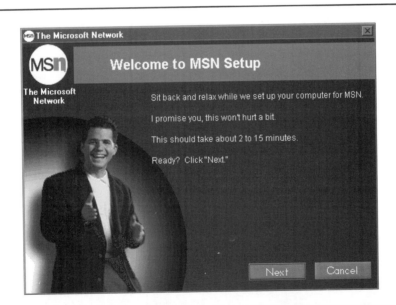

**Figure 11-1.**    MSN Installation Wizard

Once the initial setup is complete, you need to tell Windows 98 how you want to connect to MSN. You can tell it to create a direct dial-up connection, or you can tell it that you will use an existing Internet connection to access MSN. Also, if you are already a member of MSN, you can tell Windows 98 such, bypassing much of the remaining configuration process. Windows 98 then automatically dials a toll-free number to finish configuring MSN. This process is carried out online, where MSN asks you some personal information such as your name, address, and phone number. It then asks for your payment method and other relevant financial information. The last piece of information you need to deliver is a new user name and password. Once that's done, you can exit the Wizard and double-click on the desktop icon labeled The Microsoft Network to connect to MSN. This opens the MSN Sign-In dialog box shown in Figure 11-2.

**SOAPBOX:** If you have an existing Internet account, you may be asking why you should sign up for two, incurring twice the cost, especially when much of MSN's content is available from the Internet. As you'll see in just a moment, while much of MSN's content is freely available, none of its services are available to non-MSN members. For example, only MSN members can use many of its newsgroups (especially those dedicated to Windows 98) and all of its applications, including an instant messaging service called Friends Online.

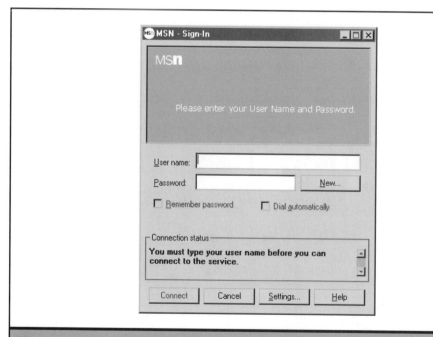

**Figure 11-2.** MSN Sign-In dialog box

Here, you must enter the user name and password you just created. But before you can connect, you must set a local telephone number through which you can access MSN. To do this, click on the Settings button. This opens a dialog box entitled Connection Settings. From the Dialing tab in this dialog box, click on the Phone Book button, and in the Phone Book dialog box (Figure 11-3), select the phone number nearest your town.

You can select a backup number in the same way. When you're done, click on the OK button. Then click on the Connect button in the next screen to dial MSN.

**SHORTCUT:** If you are the only one using your computer, you may want to click on the check box entitled *Remember password from the MSN Sign-In dialog box*. This allows you to automatically dial MSN without your intervention. Otherwise, you'll have to re-enter your password each time you connect.

Once you're connected, MSN asks you to set up a few features such as Content protection (for children) and e-mail, and that's all there is to it. Interestingly, the MSN interface does not appear as a new application as in the past. In line with Microsoft's conception of an integrated Web and desktop, you access MSN through Internet Explorer (see Figure 11-4).

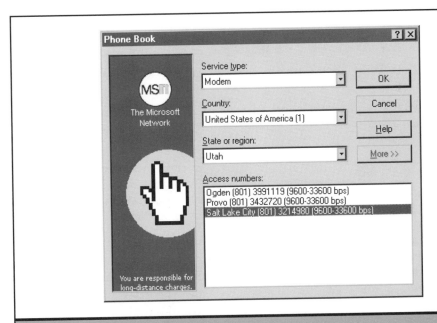

**Figure 11-3.**   Select an access number

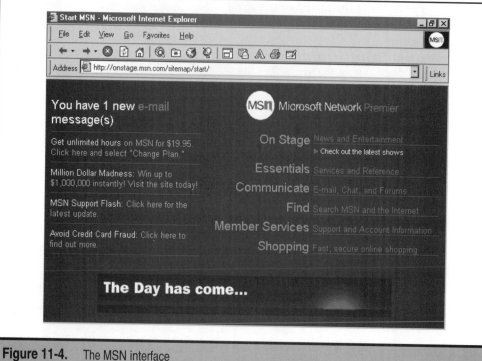

**Figure 11-4.**   The MSN interface

From this interface, you can perform all sorts of useful tasks. You can send and receive e-mail, chat, enter MSN forums, search for other MSN members, find things on the Internet, and even shop online.

**SHORTCUT:**   Notice in the upper-left corner of this interface some text indicating that the user has 1 new e-mail message. If you click on that text, Windows 98 launches Outlook Express. From there, you can send and receive e-mail over MSN and the Internet just as you learned in the last chapter.

Feel free to wander about the MSN service. You'll find a host of great information and services. And best of all, you'll never get lost. Because it uses Internet Explorer as its interface, you can navigate forward and backward through content using the Forward and Backward buttons from the toolbar. If you find a page you like, you can just click on the Add to Favorites button to add it to your bookmark list. If you do get lost, from virtually every page on MSN, there is a hypertext link that will take you back to the MSN Member Services page.

Moreover, you don't need to have Internet Explorer open in order to find your way around. MSN actually becomes a part of your Windows 98 operating system. It is always available from your desktop and within your Microsoft applications. To access any of the MSN services from the desktop, just right-click on the MSN icon (it looks like a pointing finger) that is in the status bar tray. This opens a pop-up menu containing all of the navigational elements you need in order to connect to and interact with MSN online (see Figure 11-5).

## Communicating with MSN

The most important part of MSN is its community. Using its many special-interest forums and chat rooms, you can exchange information with MSN members, talk with friends, or listen in on public meetings. To access these services, click on the Communicate heading from the MSN start page. This opens a new Web page in Internet Explorer from which you can enter these services (see Figure 11-6).

MSN Forums are great because they go far beyond the capabilities of traditional Internet newsgroups, which only allow users to post and view messages. Within each MSN forum, you can chat with other Forum members, post to bulletin boards, check out file libraries, see related sites, and read through transcripts from recent Forum

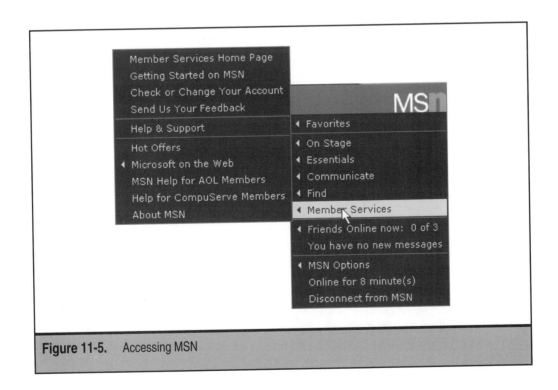

**Figure 11-5.** Accessing MSN

**Figure 11-6.** The MSN Communicate home page

discussions. The best and most relevant example of this concerns the Windows forums, which include Windows NT, Windows 95/98, and even Windows CE. To get to these forums from MSN, just open the MSN pop-up menu from the status bar tray, click on the Essentials selection, select Computers & Software, and click on Computing Central. This opens Internet Explorer with the Computing Central page. Here, click on the Forums tab at the top of the page. Scroll down the All Forums box and click on Windows 95/98 under the Operating Systems heading. A new Web page opens in Internet Explorer that looks like the one in Figure 11-7.

Here, you're able to read through a nice Windows 95/98 glossary, participate in a chat room, or browse the available Windows 95/98 newsgroups.

On a more personal note, one of the best of these is the Friends Online service. It's a private communication system just for you and your friends (or colleagues). Of course, those friends must be members of MSN. To get started with this, just click on the Communicate text from the Friends Online text on the left-hand side of the Communicate Home page. Click on the Add Friends button and enter either a user's last name or e-mail address when prompted. When you're done adding members, you'll see a screen

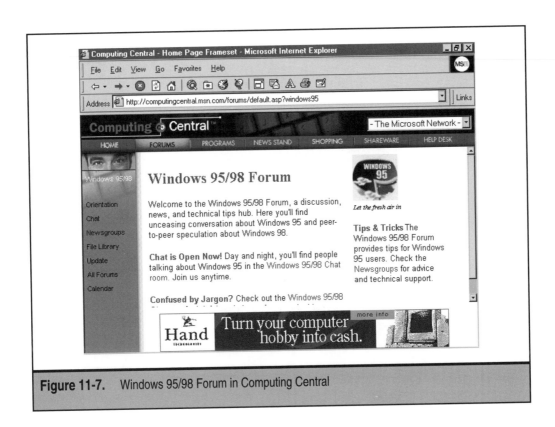

**Figure 11-7.** Windows 95/98 Forum in Computing Central

indicating whether or not those friends are currently connected to MSN, as shown in Figure 11-8.

If you see that a friend is online, click on his or her name, type a private message in the field at the bottom of the page, and click on the Say it text. The beauty of this feature is that it is integrated with Microsoft's NetMeeting application. NetMeeting as a stand-alone application is discussed in the next section. But while you're in MSN, you can access it from the Friends Online service. If a friend is online, you can click on his or her name and select the Start NetMeeting Session text. This opens a NetMeeting session with your friend. If your friends are not online, however, you can always send them a quick e-mail message with MSN by clicking on their names.

# COLLABORATING WITH NETMEETING

Certainly MSN and other online services are useful communications platforms, but they really appeal to the consumer of broadly available information, not those who need to exchange and collaborate on information with a limited number of people. Windows 98

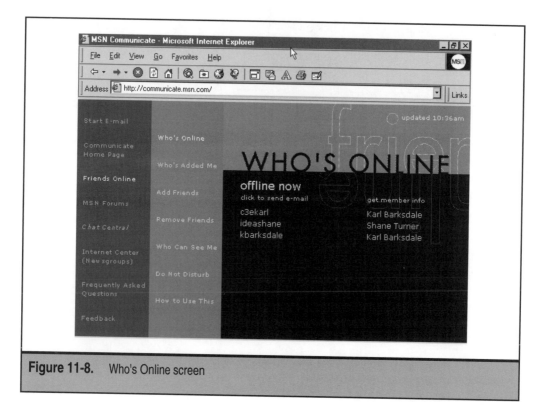

**Figure 11-8.** Who's Online screen

and Internet Explorer include a tool capable of providing this sort of communication. It's called NetMeeting, and it's a complete collaboration package. As mentioned previously, it lets you talk to others over the Internet using your voice or text. It lets you see and be seen by others over the Internet. It lets you share applications, send and receive files, and even draw on a white board.

## Configuring NetMeeting

Using NetMeeting is quite easy. You just connect to a NetMeeting server, select the user or users with whom you want to communicate, and begin. However, setting NetMeeting up is a bit complicated. You have to not only enter personal information but also configure your hardware to use NetMeeting. To run all of NetMeeting's features, you need to have an audio card with speakers and a microphone as well as a videoconference camera such as the Intel ProShare and the network to support it. If you don't have all of these pieces of hardware, you can still use the non-multimedia features of NetMeeting, such as chatting, file sharing, and white-board collaboration.

To get started with NetMeeting, just click on the Start menu, select Programs, click on the Internet Explorer item, and select Microsoft NetMeeting. This opens a Wizard that takes you though the rest of the configuration process. The first dialog box of this Wizard contains some explanatory text. Click on the Next button to continue. On the next dialog box, you are asked to indicate whether or not you want to log on to a NetMeeting directory server whenever you start NetMeeting.

**JARGON:**  What's a directory server? A directory server is a central repository for a great amount of user information such as names, phone numbers, and e-mail addresses. These servers support the Lightweight Directory Access Protocol (LDAP), a search protocol used by most Web browsers as well as NetMeeting. NetMeeting uses LDAP to search for and connect with other users.

First, unless you have a permanent connection to the Internet via a LAN, we suggest that you do not instruct NetMeeting to automatically connect to a directory server at start up. Doing so will preempt all functionality each time you start NetMeeting. Think of it as an e-mail server. You don't want to connect to the server until it is time to send and receive messages. It is the same with NetMeeting. Until you are ready to communicate with someone, you should not connect to the NetMeeting servers. After all, you may not use the same server each time you communicate with NetMeeting, so why wait for it to force a sometimes-lengthy connection with no reason.

The next decision you need to make regards which directory server you want NetMeeting to use as its default directory. Microsoft provides a number of duplicate servers. They are the ones with names like

```
Ils.microsoft.com
```

```
Ils2.microsoft.com
```

```
Ils3.microsoft.com
```

Why so many? Because NetMeeting ships with Windows 98 and Internet Explorer, there are literally millions of NetMeeting users out there, looking for other users with which to connect. This means that at any given time, a single directory server might process thousands of simultaneous requests. The other directories that don't have duplicate entries belong to Four11, a third-party directory service provider. Initially, the directory you choose really doesn't matter. However, if later on you have trouble finding users, or you run into performance problems, you can always change to a different default server. When you're done, click on the Next button and fill out your personal information. This is the information that is posted on these directory servers for others to see.

The Comments field is a handy place to put a quick description of your reasons for using NetMeeting. For example, you could say that you are working on a particular project, such as "Environmental Impact Statement" to let others with similar interests know why you're online. You can also use this field to let other NetMeeting members know what you're interested in. For example, you could say, "I'm in Utah, looking to talk with other Utahans." Or you can leave this field blank if you don't want to give others any information beyond your basic connectivity information (name, e-mail address, and so forth). When you've finished this, click on the next button. There is quite a bit of personal information you can make available with NetMeeting (all of which is designed not to violate your privacy, but to help others single you out from the crowd). For example, you can share your first name, last name, e-mail address, your city, state, and country.

The next dialog box asks you to describe your purpose for using NetMeeting. You've got three options:

▼ **Personal use** This selection contains the most people and the broadest content.

■ **Business use** Choose this if you want to connect with business professionals.

▲ **Adult use** Select this only if you don't mind content that is adult in nature.

Not surprisingly, we suggest that you select the *Business use* option, as it contains people that are quite simply there to do business. Don't worry if you don't know which category to select. You can change it later as you work with NetMeeting. Click on the Next button, and you're asked to enter the speed of your Internet connection. Just choose the one that matches your modem speed. Conversely, if you have a direct connection to the Internet, select the LAN radio button.

**SHORTCUT:** If you don't have a sound card or video adapter installed on your machine, do not fear. NetMeeting just skips over these configuration steps, allowing you to get started right away with chatting and file/application sharing.

The next dialog box enables you to test your system for a sound card, assuming it is compatible with NetMeeting, and to set the appropriate sound level. Click on the Test button to find out how your sound card and speakers stack up. If you hear the test pattern, click on the Next button to test your microphone. Here, just read the text given to you and watch the simulated LEDs to make sure that they reach into the right side of the dialog box. Lastly, you're asked to perform similar configuration steps with your video hardware. And that's all there is to setting up and configuring NetMeeting. Now you're ready to start collaborating.

**SHORTCUT:** If you are concerned about posting personal information on the NetMeeting server, remember, your personal settings (name, e-mail address, and the like) are not required, nor is their validity. That is, you can declare yourself to be anyone you want. For example, you could use just your first name as your first name and your company name as your last name. As you'll see in a moment, there's also a way to bypass the NetMeeting server altogether for private, one-on-one communications.

## Using NetMeeting

When you finish configuring NetMeeting, you see an Internet Explorer-like interface open up that contains your audio speaker and microphone levels, your category (business, personal, adult), and the NetMeeting server to which you want to connect (see Figure 11-9).

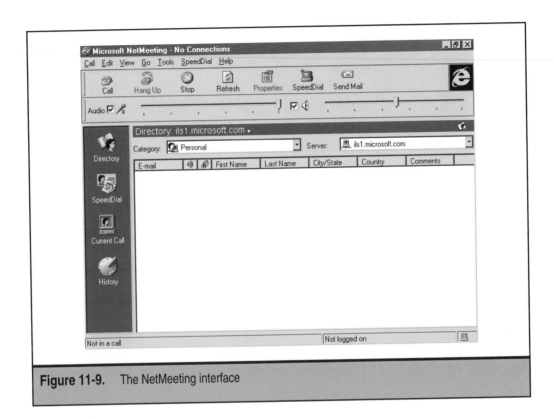

**Figure 11-9.**   The NetMeeting interface

## Connecting NetMeeting

To begin working with NetMeeting, all you have to do is click on the Refresh button. If applicable, NetMeeting automatically dials your online service to establish a connection to the Internet. Once it connects with the default server, it populates the white space on the screen shown in Figure 11-9 with users with whom you can communicate, as shown in Figure 11-10.

**CAUTION:**   If you receive an error message indicating that there is a problem connecting with the selected directory server, use the Server pull-down menu in the upper-right portion of the screen, choose an alternate server, and then try to log on to the new server.

Notice that you can see whether or not each individual in the NetMeeting directory has audio, video, or both. Don't worry if you only have audio or just text. When you connect with one of these individuals, both systems fall back to the lowest common denominator. But before you connect with someone, you need to make yourself available to others online by clicking on the Call pull-down menu and selecting *Log On to* [*servername*]. Notice how it contains the servername you selected earlier.

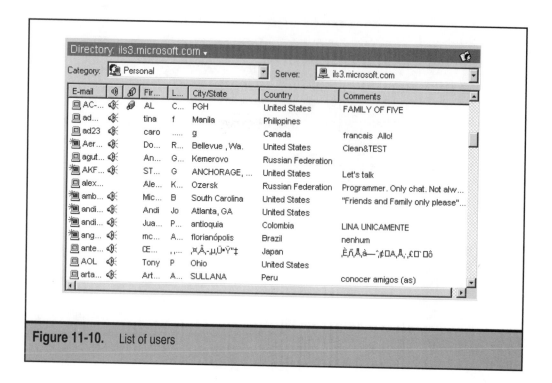

**Figure 11-10.** List of users

**SHORTCUT:** If you're having trouble locating someone, just click on the sorting buttons across the top of the directory listing window. You can sort the listing by any of the listing fields, including e-mail address, audio access, video access, first name, last name, city/state, and so forth.

**MAKING CALLS** When you find someone with whom you want to communicate, just highlight that person's name and click on the Call button. This opens a dialog box where you can enter the person's address. Because you have highlighted someone, however, the address has been filled in for you. In this dialog box, there's a pull-down menu called Call Using. It defaults to Directory Server, but you can and perhaps should change it to automatic or TCP/IP. Because there are so many people using Microsoft's NetMeeting servers, they are occasionally unable to place your calls. When you're ready, click on the Call button. NetMeeting then attempts to establish a connection with the selected user. If the person you have selected is not accepting calls at this time, you are prompted to send him or her a message instead. Otherwise, NetMeeting opens a window called Current Call (see Figure 11-11).

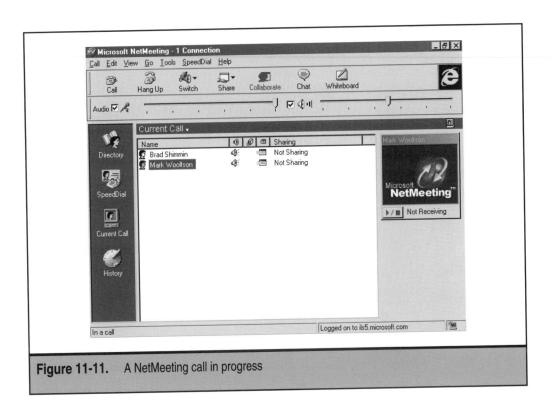

**Figure 11-11.**   A NetMeeting call in progress

For organizations, a very useful feature of NetMeeting is its ability to link together more than two people. Unlike most conference software packages, it does not just establish a one-on-one connection. You can join existing conferences, and you can invite many people to join a single conference. In order to create a meeting in which many people can join, click on the Call pull-down menu and select Host Meeting. This marks your listing with a starburst in the main directory window, as shown in Figure 11-12. The starburst indicates you can accept many calls.

***CAUTION:***   Sadly, though NetMeeting can simultaneously connect multiple parties within a single conference, it cannot provide voice and video support to all parties at once. Only two, point-to-point connections can exchange video and audio simultaneously.

This means that you don't have to call others. They can simply call you directly without intervention on your part. To join an existing conference, just do as you did earlier when connecting with an individual. The person on the other end will simply accept or reject your call. (We'll talk about this in the next section.)

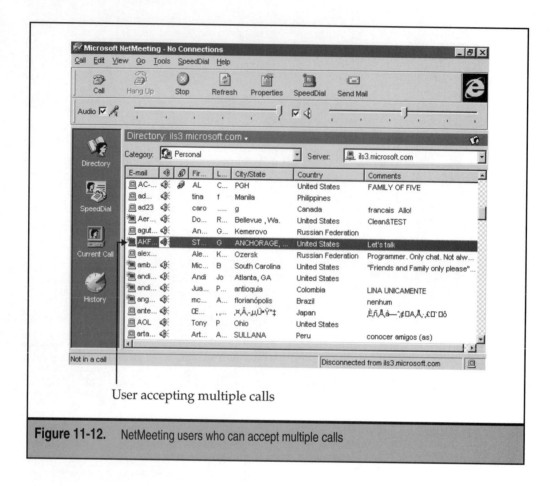

User accepting multiple calls

**Figure 11-12.** NetMeeting users who can accept multiple calls

**RECEIVING CALLS** Receiving calls is quite easy. You can instruct NetMeeting to either accept or screen all incoming calls automatically. For example, when you're in a call, NetMeeting can pop up a box asking you if you want to accept an incoming call, like so:

Conversely, NetMeeting can simply allow others to connect to you automatically. We suggest that you first screen all incoming calls. As a worldwide service, NetMeeting can attract people from all walks of life and all interest areas—some of which you may not want joining your important project meeting unannounced. To let others connect automatically, click on the Tools pull-down menu, select Options, and click on the resulting dialog box's General tab. Here, click on the check box marked *Automatically accept incoming calls*. If you do not wish this, just make sure that same check box is deselected. For even more privacy, you can log into a server without displaying your personal information. This way, only those who know your e-mail address can connect with you. To do this, click on the Calling tab from the same dialog box and put a check mark in the box indicating that you don't want to list your name in the directory.

## Using NetMeeting Tools

The main NetMeeting window shows you which capabilities (audio, video, and file sharing) the other person has available to him or her. Also, notice that on the left side of the screen there is a small box. If you and your connected party have video hardware, you will see his or her picture in this box. The audio is automatic. Just begin speaking, and your party is able to respond to you just the same. If you would like to do more than videoconference, choose one of the four available tools: Chat, Whiteboard, File Transfer, and application sharing. If you have both audio and video, they will always be available to you no matter which of these four applications you are using.

*CAUTION:* The only drawbacks to all of these features concern performance and capacity. For example, the more features you open, the slower your connection becomes. Also, not all of NetMeeting's features work for two or more people at once. Chatting and sharing an application works with many people at once, but video and audio only work between two people simultaneously.

To start chatting with the connected user, for example, just click on the Tools pull-down menu and select Chat. This opens a small dialog box in which you can exchange text messages. Click in the field entitled Message, and type a few words in greeting. When you're ready to send a message to a remote user, click on the button to the left of the dialog box (it looks like a piece of moving paper) and watch your message move to the large window (see Figure 11-13).

The great part about NetMeeting's Chat program is that in large meetings with two or more people, it allows you to talk privately with specific meeting members. To do so, click on the Send To pull-down menu from the same window and select the target user. You can also use the Options pull-down menu to specify how data appears in the Chat program. For example, you can instruct Chat to display the date and time in addition to the user's name for individual entries. This can be very useful as you can save ongoing

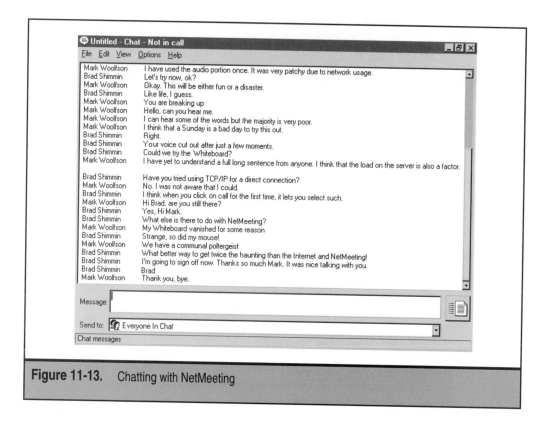

**Figure 11-13.**    Chatting with NetMeeting

chat sessions. Say you've got a weekly project meeting. You can use the ongoing chat sessions as a sort of meeting minutes. To save a session's data, when you exit chat, tell the program to save the session when prompted, and the next time you open Chat that data will appear. If you want to save data from your recent chat session, you can simply use the Save As selection from the File pull-down menu. This allows you to save your chat session as a text file.

**WORKING WITH THE WHITEBOARD**    You can access the Whiteboard in the same manner as the other NetMeeting tools. Click on the Tools pull-down menu and select Whiteboard. This tool is great for online brainstorming, as it lets you be creative with both text and images. Whatever you write or draw locally can be seen remotely. Likewise, whatever a remote person writes or draws is seen locally (see Figure 11-14).

With the Whiteboard, you can draw or write just as though you were working in Windows' Paint program. You can draw shapes, type text, change colors, and the like, just as with Paint, but with one exception—its net-centricity. You see, Whiteboard comes with a number of tools that let you point to items remotely, lock contents to prevent others from changing those contents, and synchronize local and remote positions on the Whiteboard. For instance, you can tell the Whiteboard to keep anyone else from

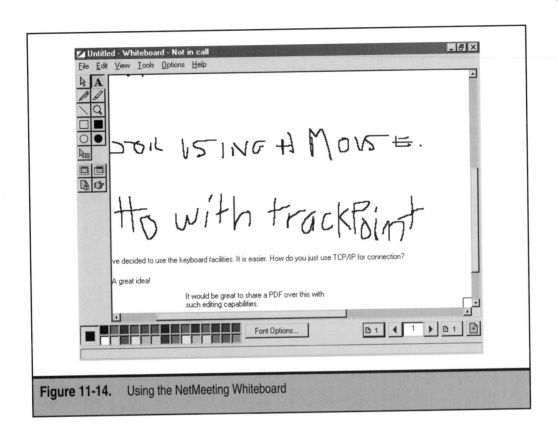

**Figure 11-14.**  Using the NetMeeting Whiteboard

modifying your work. And you can move the screen around on the remote users'
machines to point them at a specific item.

**FILE TRANSFER**    One other useful tool you have at your disposal in communicating with
NetMeeting is file transfer. Basically, you can instruct NetMeeting to post a file directly to
a remote user's hard drive. The default local file location is

```
C:\Program Files\NetMeeting\Received Files\
```

While connected with a remote user, you can ask him or her if it is okay to send a file.
If he or she agrees, click on the Tools pull-down menu, select File Transfer, and click on
Send File. This opens a regular Windows File Open dialog box, from which you can select
the file to be sent. When you've got it, click on the Send button, and the file is sent to the
remote user's default NetMeeting local file location. If the thought of receiving unwanted
files scares you, don't worry. The nice thing about this feature is that if another user starts
sending you a file, and you decide that you don't want that file, you can use the Cancel
Receive selection from the File Transfer pull-down menu. Likewise, you can cancel a send
in the same way.

This is a great feature of NetMeeting; however, we suggest that you enforce restrictions that disallow users from employing it with those outside of the company. That is, because NetMeeting does not contain any built-in virus protection software, if you allow users to exchange files with those outside of your company, you greatly increase the chances that a virus will hit your company. For example, a user could download a Microsoft Word macro virus and send it off to others in the company without your knowledge.

**SHARING APPLICATIONS** While chatting, drawing on a Whiteboard, and sending and receiving files is nice, the one feature of NetMeeting that surpasses all others is its ability to share active applications. If you have Microsoft Excel open, for example, you and a remote user can actually work together within the same application with the same data, as though the application were local to both parties. To do this, first make sure that you have the desired application and document open, then establish a connection with a remote user, click on the Tools pull-down menu, and select Share Application. You can also open this application after making a connection. The important thing is that you must have the application running before you can share it. This reveals a pull-down menu listing the available applications. Pick the application (or applications) you want to share by clicking on them (see Figure 11-15).

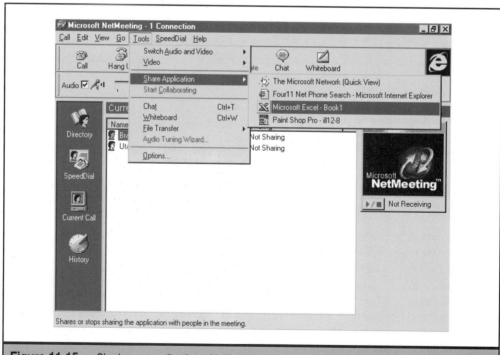

**Figure 11-15.** Sharing an application with NetMeeting

This enables you to let others see what's going on in your applications. But they won't be able to do any work with your applications. To make this possible, click on the Tools pull-down menu and select Start Collaborating. From now on until you reverse this process, other conference users are able to make changes to your data, so be careful.

When you're done collaborating, click on the Hang Up button. By default, NetMeeting automatically creates a SpeedDial account for each person with which you connect. You can then use that account to connect with those people directly, without first connecting with a NetMeeting server. The next time you start NetMeeting, you can then click on the SpeedDial button on the left-hand pane of the main NetMeeting window. This opens a window containing a list of your SpeedDial entries, which shows whether or not those users are logged in (see Figure 11-16).

If an entry is logged in, highlight his or her name and click on the Call button, and NetMeeting automatically places a call to that person.

**BYPASSING THE NETMEETING DIRECTORY SERVER**    The great part about NetMeeting is that once you have created a SpeedDial account with another person, you don't need NetMeeting's directory servers anymore. That is, you can use SpeedDial to place a call

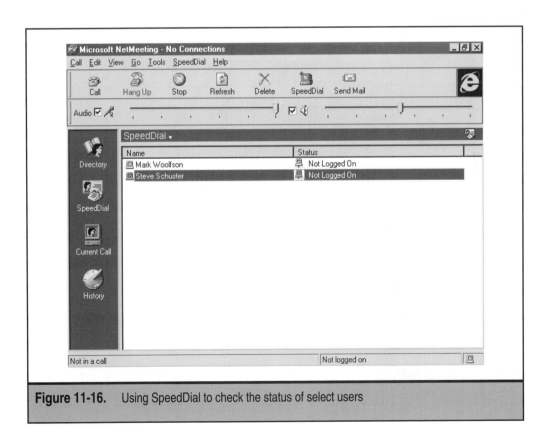

**Figure 11-16.**    Using SpeedDial to check the status of select users

directly to a remote user's machine. Of course, the only way this works is if that remote user has a static IP address, which is not very common on the Internet at this point in time. If a user with whom you want to connect has a static IP address, then when you use that person's SpeedDial account, your machine automatically establishes a direct connection with that person. Otherwise, the SpeedDial account uses one of NetMeeting's directory servers to locate that person's dynamic IP address. Either way, you won't have to think about it. NetMeeting does the leg-work for you.

However, if you don't want to use NetMeeting's directory servers at all, and you know the static IP address of a remote user, you can simply add a SpeedDial account for that person, which establishes a direct connection. To do this, click on the SpeedDial pull-down menu from the main NetMeeting window and click on the Add SpeedDial selection. This opens an Add SpeedDial dialog box that looks like the one in Figure 11-17.

Here, in the Address field, add the IP address of the remote user to whom you want to connect. That address should look like this:

```
204.151.55.163
```

Once you've created an IP address entry, click on the following pull-down list entitled Call using. Here, select Network (TCP/IP) instead of Directory Server. This tells NetMeeting to bypass the servers and force a direct connection. Make sure the *Add to SpeedDial list* check box item is checked and click on the OK button. This creates a new

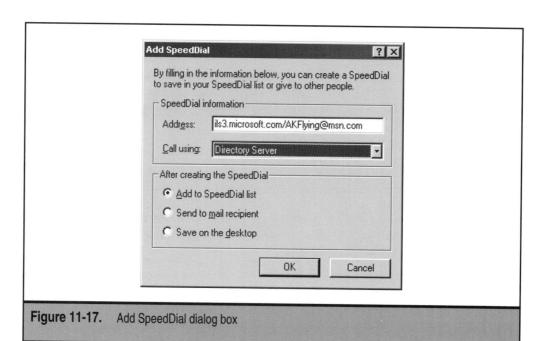

**Figure 11-17.**   Add SpeedDial dialog box

SpeedDial entry that looks just like the ones you created previously. But with this entry, when you right-click on it and select Call, it attempts to make a direct connection with the remote user.

*JARGON:* What's the difference between a static IP address and a dynamic IP address? If you have a static IP address, each time you connect with the Internet, your machine will use that IP address as its unique identifier. If you have a dynamic IP address, each time you connect to the Internet, your ISP will assign a unique (usually different) IP address to your machine.

# CHATTING WITH WINDOWS 98

If you don't need all of NetMeeting's capabilities, there is an alternative program called Microsoft Chat. Formerly called Comic Chat, this simple, text-based chat program can get you up and running quickly and easily. Unlike NetMeeting, chat does not require any special hardware to take full advantage of the product. All you need is an Internet connection and Microsoft Chat. Also, it does not require as much from the server-side of the street. In other words, you won't run into as many errors while connecting to a Microsoft Chat server.

## Installing Microsoft Chat

Microsoft Chat does not come as a pre-installed component with Windows 98 and Internet Explorer. So, in order to use it, you must first connect to Microsoft's component download center for Internet Explorer. To do that, open Internet Explorer, click on the Help pull-down menu, and select Product Updates. This connects you with the Component Download center. Internet Explorer asks you if it is okay to check the status of your installed components. Say yes to this, and Internet Explorer returns the Web page shown in Figure 11-18.

Click on the Microsoft Chat check box and click on the Next button at the bottom of the page. This opens a new page, from which you must choose the closest download server. The closer a server is to you geographically, the faster the download time will be. Once you have selected a server, click on the Download button and Internet Explorer will download and install Microsoft Chat. Once it has been downloaded, reboot your machine and you'll be ready to use Chat. To get started with Chat, click on the Start menu, select Programs and then Internet Explorer, and click on Microsoft Chat. If you're already connected to the Internet, this opens a Connect dialog box asking you to enter a server and chat room name (see Figure 11-19).

## Using Microsoft Chat

A good place to start is with the chat.msn.com address. It contains a vast number of general chat rooms. Likewise, you should select the radio button that shows all available chat rooms to get a good idea of what's in store with Microsoft Chat. Doing so opens

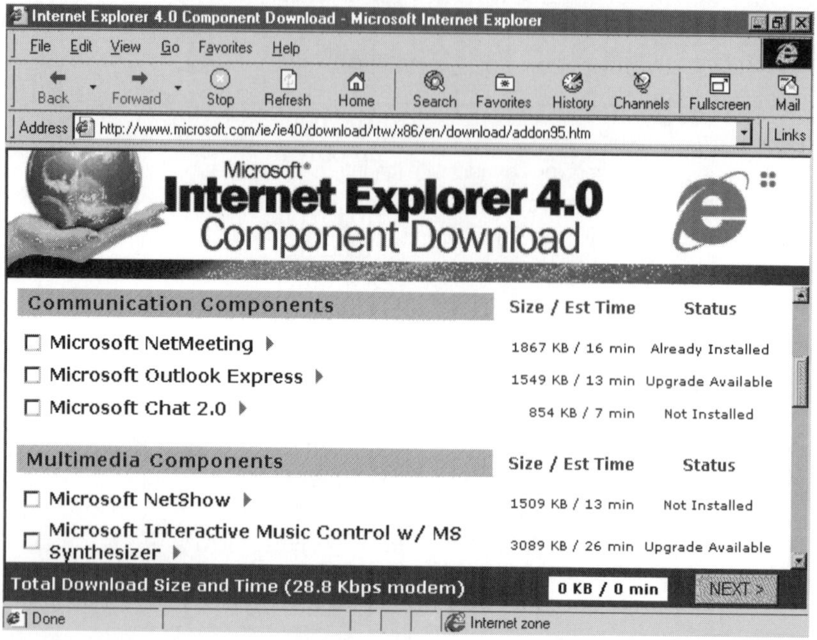

**Figure 11-18.** Component Download Web page

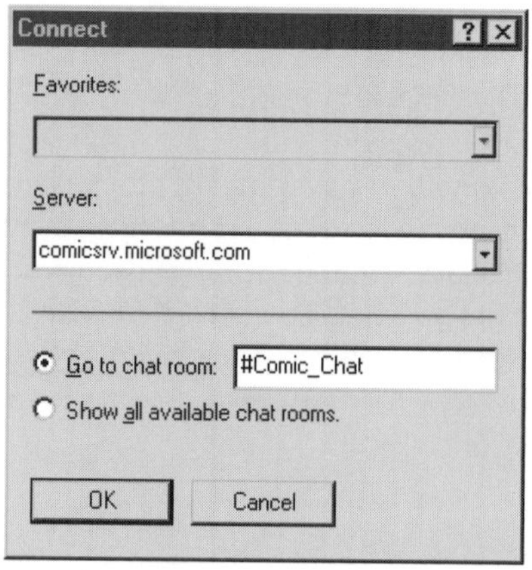

**Figure 11-19.** Connecting to a chat room with Microsoft Chat

the Chat Room List dialog box containing all of the available chat rooms on chat.microsoft.com as, shown in Figure 11-20.

As you can see, there is a vast array of available chat rooms. Notice how each room lists the number of currently active members. To enter a room, just pick a chat room, highlight it, and click on the Go To button at the bottom of the window. This opens a very interesting window that contains what can only be described as a comic strip (see Figure 11-21).

It's a bit strange to think of using a comic strip to communicate, but actually, once you get used to it, the comic strip interface makes reading and responding very fast. That's because each member of a chat room receives a different identity. That way, you can associate different conversational threads with unique individuals, clearing away much of the confusion that usually accompanies chat rooms. If you look in the upper-right window pane, you'll see which identity you've been assigned. When you type a message in the lower window pane, your message appears in a comic strip entry, spoken by your personality. With the lower-right window pane, you can select a particular mood (facial gesture) that accompanies your message, which can be a pretty slow process. Luckily, Chat shapes your mood according to your message. Questions get a questioning look. Exclamations get a forceful look. Of course, if you don't like the comic interface, you can

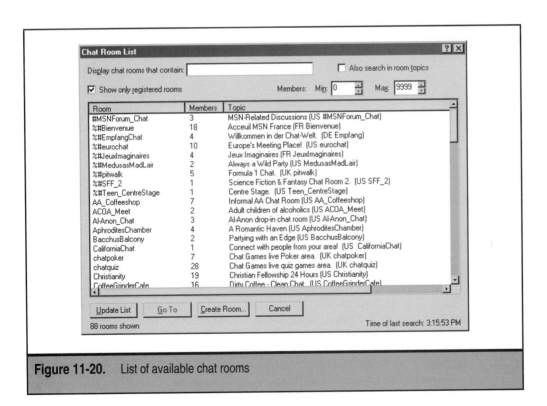

**Figure 11-20.**   List of available chat rooms

**Figure 11-21.** Microsoft Chat in action

click on the View pull-down menu and select Plain Text. This changes the comic interface into a traditional chat client, displaying only text.

## Creating a Chat Room

Once you get used to working with Chat, you can create your own chat room. You can then invite others to join your room or simply wait to see who shows up. To create a chat room, click on the Room pull-down menu and select Create Room. This opens the Create Chat Room dialog box in which you can specify a name for your room and set some parameters (see Figure 11-22).

**SHORTCUT:** The next time you start Microsoft Chat, the introductory dialog box will show your new chat room as the default chat room. Just click on the OK button when the dialog box appears, and you'll automatically enter your custom chat room!

Make sure you enter a full description within the Topic field. This is what your guests will rely upon in looking for your chat room. As you can see in Figure 11-22, there are a

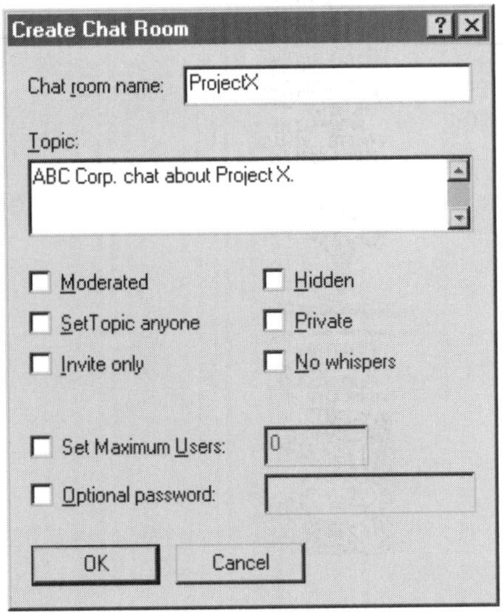

**Figure 11-22.**    Creating a chat room with Microsoft Chat

number of security options. This is an important facet of Chat. Because Chat is available as a public service on the Internet, you can expect a number of unwanted visitors. You can set a password for the chat room (recommended for any sort of business-oriented meeting). When users log into your chat room, they'll have to enter this password. You can then send this password via e-mail to those you wish to allow access to the room. Alternatively, you can select the Invite only check box. But this requires you to manually invite people who are logged into the chat server. Feel free to play around with these settings. But be aware that Microsoft Chat is not the most secure platform in the world for online communications. You may think you know the identity of a user in your chat room, but really there's no way to verify such. Someone may intercept your e-mail message with the password. Or someone may log on to the Chat server with the same nickname you are expecting someone else to use.

# COMING UP

In the next chapter, we dive headlong into a very exciting and new arena of Windows 98 connectivity called Active Content and Webcasting. Bringing together the ubiquity of the Internet, downloadable applications, and the power of push technology, Active Content and Webcasting lets you access information and applications on the Internet or your private LAN without leaving your desktop. Basically, Active Content describes down-loadable applications such as ActiveX controls and Java applets. Webcasting describes a set of technologies used by Windows 98 and Internet Explorer to subscribe to these downloadable applications as well as any online content. For example, you can subscribe to a news channel, a stock ticker, or even a corporate application. Once you've subscribed, these elements come down to your machine automatically. And once you have them locally, you can work with them even if you're not connected to the Internet or your LAN.

# CHAPTER 12

# Working with Active Content

## What's ahead:

- Basic, managed, and true Webcasting
- Working with Active Content
- Webcasting management
- Working with downloadable applications

*"Alas, how is't with you,*
*That you do bend your eye on vacancy,*
*And with th' incorporal air do hold discourse?"*

—Shakespeare, *Hamlet,* Act III, Scene IV

As you saw in the last three chapters, Windows 98 is a powerful communications platform, providing powerful Web, messaging, and collaboration tools. With Internet Explorer, you can provide your users with state-of-the-art access to the best the Web has to offer. With Outlook Express, your users can easily access both internal and Internet messaging servers. And with collaboration tools like NetMeeting and the Microsoft Network, your users can use the Internet as their personal conference room. In all, these technologies are designed to help Windows 98 users reach out from their PCs to global resources and individuals. But what if the opposite where true? What if global resources and individuals could in essence reach into your user's PC and convey important information?

Windows 98 hopes to make this idea possible with what Microsoft calls Active Content. Actually, this moniker applies to a broad range of subscription services and applications, all of which work to bring content and applications right to the users, without their intervention. Active Content is entirely Web-centric and includes some of the following applications and technologies:

▼ **Webcasting sites**   The art of automatically downloading Web sites

■ **Active Channels**   Web sites built just for Webcasting

■ **Active Desktop**   Your desktop acting as an off-line Web browser

■ **Internet Explorer**   The vehicle through which you can work with Webcasting

▲ **Java applets, ActiveX controls, and scripts**   The stuff of Active Content, downloadable content and applications

Active Content, through these capabilities, is designed to improve user productivity. With an Active Content technology called Managed Webcasting, for example, users can automatically receive changes to a Web site, which they can then view on- or off-line. A sales force could take the latest content from your Web site along with them on a remote sales call. They wouldn't have to borrow a client computer; they wouldn't have to rush to print prices before heading out the door. All they would have to do is pull the off-line Web site up on their laptop and guide the client through the latest prices.

Active Content is not just supposed to benefit users. And as you might imagine, with technologies like Java applets, your company can reduce application deployment and management costs along the way. With Java applets, users could receive the latest application updates automatically. For example, your MIS department could build an accounts receivable (AR) application as a downloadable Java applet. Doing so can put to an end the monotonous task of manually updating each PC, one at a time. Any time the MIS department makes a change to this AR applet, they can just update one central Java applet. All users will automatically download this up-to-date applet for local use.

At first blush, this may sound terrifying, especially from a corporate perspective. But if used in the right context with the right controls, Active Content can be as safe as any other Internet technology. For instance, as you saw in Chapter 9, Internet Explorer can safeguard your users' workstations from errant or mischievous Java applets. And with Security Zones, you can restrict your users from using Active Content from inappropriate sources.

Of course, your company may choose not to allow this type of interactivity. Because many downloadable applications such as ActiveX controls and Java applets can do harm to a user's PC, many companies choose to disallow their use. So before you enable Active Content, check with your MIS manager.

**RESOURCE:**   For more information on Windows 98 security, see Chapter 9.

With these security issues firmly in mind, we begin with a quick introduction to this nebulous term, Active Content. Along the way, we show you how to work with Active Content from a user's and a manager's perspective.

# WHAT IS ACTIVE CONTENT?

What exactly is Active Content? Well, it's really an umbrella term, covering a number of applications, technologies, and procedures. Adding to the previous description, Active Content can be broken down into the following main categories:

- ▼ Downloadable content (Web sites, subscriptions, and channels)
- ▲ Downloadable applications (such as ActiveX controls and Java applets)

These technologies, applications, and techniques all come with Windows 98 and Internet Explorer (IE). Both fall under the concept of subscriptions, meaning users subscribe to them just as they would to a magazine. And they all work together in concert to provide you and your users with an interactive, automated, and flexible content delivery mechanism for Web content. With them, you can build corporate applications and content that are tailor-made for your users. But before we get to working with and developing such information sources, let's take a look at each to see how they all fit together under the umbrella of Active Content.

## Downloadable Content

As you might guess, the active dissemination of content is at the heart of Active Content. That includes Web pages, entire Web sites, and customized content called *channels*.

Windows 98 and IE accomplish the dissemination of this content through Webcasting, which works to get remote content onto the user's desktop without the user's intervention. The user can then work with that content whether or not he or she is connected to the source of that content. Overall, this concept is called *push*. In essence, it connotes the act of pushing information from a server to a number of users.

The concept of push is quite popular at present. Many companies such as Netscape Communications Corp. and Verity Corp. have used it to automate the delivery of everything from Web sites to corporate applications. Netscape, for example, has released a product called Netcaster. It comes with Navigator and Communicator 4.*x* products and enables users to subscribe to Web content. For Windows 98 and IE, push falls under two different technologies underneath the larger umbrella of Active Content:

▼   Basic Webcasting

▲   Managed Webcasting

**SOAPBOX:**   Push has become an over-hyped concept as of late. Seemingly innumerable vendors have released push products designed to automatically download everything but the kitchen sink. However, the truth of push is that most products (including Windows 98 and IE) do not really use push in its most literal sense. Nearly every push application requires the user to initiate the contact with the server upon which the push content resides and manually ask for the push content. These sorts of applications are more accurately labeled *smart pull* products.

## Basic Webcasting

This push feature of Windows 98 and IE enables users to download content from any Web server for later use, off-line. Users can automate this process by setting a download schedule, so the process can happen while users are away from their PCs. Once a Web site has been downloaded (see Figure 12-1), users can interact with it as though it was still on the remote server.

Alternatively, users can choose to receive notification of changes made to that content as it resides on the Web server. A user, for example, can set an update schedule that Windows 98 and IE uses to determine if any changes have occurred since the last update. If there have been any changes to the content, an e-mail message is sent to that user indicating such. In essence, Webcasting acts like a user-initiated subscription service. The Web server need not know anything about Basic Webcasting users. They simply instruct Windows 98 and IE that they want to either download the content or notify the users of any changes to that content.

## Managed Webcasting

Managed Webcasting takes this a step further by empowering the Web server. Instead of allowing users to either check for changes or download content on a regular schedule, Managed Webcasting enables Webmasters to choose which content is available for subscription and at what schedule. The result is what Microsoft calls an Active Channel.

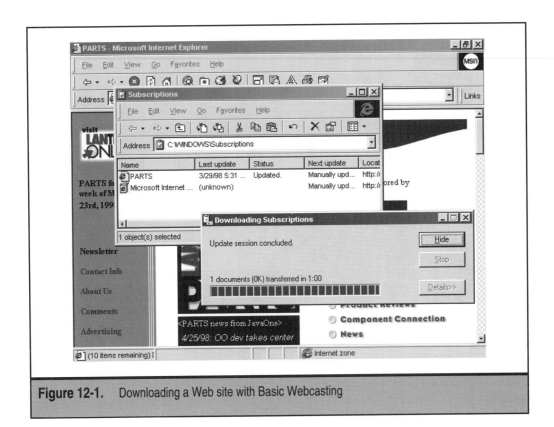

**Figure 12-1.** Downloading a Web site with Basic Webcasting

*JARGON:* What's an Active Channel? Think of it as you would a TV channel. Like TV channels, when you access an Active Channel, you see whatever it is the Active Channel owner has scheduled for your viewing pleasure. For instance, a news source could publish coverage of the NCAA Final Four games as an Active Channel. During the game, you could then visit the Active Channel to find out the score, statistics, and the like.

With an Active Channel, a Webmaster could tell Windows 98 and IE users that their Web site should only be downloaded on every other Tuesday, and that only certain Web pages from that site should be downloaded. Webmasters can also choose how their Web sites appear to subscribers. For example, they can instruct Windows 98 and IE to display their Active Channel as a screen saver, as a part of the Windows 98 desktop, or as an Active Channel within IE (see Figure 12-2).

Managed Webcasting relies upon a very interesting technology, the Channel Definition Format (CDF). CDF allows developers to define how their Active Channels appear to users. Basically, developers create a CDF file, which contains the Web pages, schedule, and appearance for the Active Channel. Users simply point IE at this file, and it tells IE exactly how to interact with the data referenced in that file.

**Figure 12-2.** An Active Channel

**RESOURCE:** Though building CDF-enabled Web sites is beyond the scope of this book, you may want to read up on CDF technologies. The best place to start is with Microsoft's Site Builder Network. Browse to http://www.microsoft.com/workshop/prog/ie4/channels/cdf1-f.htm. There, you can find out how to build your own Managed Webcasting subscriptions with CDF.

## Downloadable Applications

What makes Basic and Managed Webcasting worthwhile is quite simply downloadable applications. You see, when you subscribe to a Web site, if it contains applications, those programs simply tag along for the ride when the Web site is downloaded for local use. Once downloaded, such an application can either function autonomously or in concert with on-line data. For example, if you subscribe to a Web page containing Microsoft's

Investor stock ticker, it can provide you with ongoing stock prices and news items whether or not you are connected to the Internet like so:

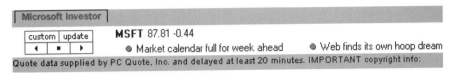

When you see a news item or stock price that interests you, you can simply click on it within the stock ticker to link directly to the corresponding news story or corporate stock information, respectively.

These downloadable applications are usually built with Internet-savvy technologies such as Java applets, ActiveX controls, and scripting languages. An ActiveX control such as the Microsoft Investor stock ticker, for example, lives within a Web page. So when you download it as an Active Content subscription, it basically installs itself within IE or on your Windows 98 Desktop, where it runs as though it were a part of your operating system (OS). If Microsoft were to modify this application on the server, your subscription would automatically download and install any changes, providing you with constantly up-to-date code.

# WORKING WITH ACTIVE CONTENT

Now that you know what Active Content is all about, let's put it to work, subscribing to various Web sites and Active Channels through Basic and Managed Webcasting. Along the way, you will work with downloadable applications where appropriate. All you need to get started with Active Content is IE and an interesting Web site.

***CAUTION:*** Webcasting with Windows 98 and IE may present you with some networking issues. For instance, if you use dial-up networking for your network connectivity, Webcasting will attempt to dial the Internet to update your subscriptions. If you do not wish your computer to automatically dial the Internet, this can be troublesome. For this reason, make sure you read the management sections for both Basic and Managed Webcasting. They tell you how to overcome this issue through manual and interactive updates.

## Working with Basic Webcasting

Basic Webcasting is all about convenience and performance. It comes with IE as a basic Webcrawling service. That is, it can automatically scan a selected Web site at predetermined intervals and download the site's content. For example, the first time you run Basic Webcasting on a Web site, it downloads the entire Web site (or as much of the site as you specify). You tell it how often to repeat this action. And the next time Basic Webcasting returns to this same Web site, it only downloads the changes that have occurred since the last time. Specifically, Basic Webcasting automatically:

▼ Downloads all or part of a Web site for off-line viewing

■ Notifies you via e-mail of any changes to a Web site

▲ Notifies you via a visual flash of any changes to a Web site

The first two of these actions have already been described. The third simply places a Flash on the Web page icon on your Favorites menu next to changed Web pages. You can use all of these features together, or you can use one feature at a time. But no matter how you use Basic Webcasting, it can save you the trouble of having to repeatedly check your favorite Web sites for any changes. It lets you know of any changes to that site via e-mail. In the same way, Basic Webcasting can save you precious time. Because it can download a Web site (or a subset thereof) to your hard disk, when you access that site, it appears instantly—no more waiting for GIFs, Java applets, and the like to download and render in your Web browser.

To get started with Basic Webcasting, open IE and browse to your favorite Web site. Once you've got a Web page (the home page or any page of your choosing) active in IE, click on the Favorites pull-down menu and click on Add to Favorites. This opens a dialog box that looks something like this:

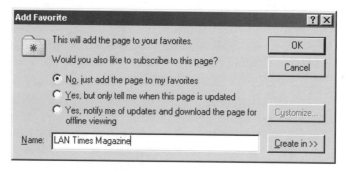

If you were to click on the OK button with the default radio button checked (which reads, "No, just add the page to my favorites"), IE would simply place the URL for the active Web page in your Favorites list. However, if you click one of the two alternative radio buttons, you'll add the URL for the active Web page to your Basic Webcasting service. Those two buttons are labeled:

▼ Yes, but only tell me when this page is updated

▲ Yes, notify me of updates and download the page for off-line viewing

Both options add the URL for the active Web page to your Favorites list. Both options also allow you to receive an e-mail message or view the flash on the Favorites pull-down menu indicating changes to the URL's Web page. The second option simply adds the option of downloading the URL's Web page to these features.

## Basic Webcasting with a Flash

To take advantage of the Flash notification option alone, click on the second radio button, labeled "Yes, but only tell me when this page is updated." At this point, click on the OK button, and IE returns you to the newly added Web page. This instructs IE to use the default settings for Basic Webcasting. That is, it automatically checks the URL's Web page for changes each day and shows you a Flash icon if the Web page has changed.

**SOAPBOX:** If you don't use a desktop computer with a permanent connection, or if you use a desktop with a low-bandwidth network connection such as a modem, you will find this option most useful. Although it requires you to manually check your Favorites list to see if your subscription Web pages have changed, it does not require much bandwidth. It merely pings the Web site to see if the Web page in question has changed since it was last updated. More specifically, it scans the Web site's home page and compares its content with the content that was cached locally the last time you added this Web site to your Webcasting services.

To see whether or not your Web page has changed, click on the Favorites pull-down menu and highlight the item corresponding to the Web page you just added to your Favorites. If it has changed since you added it, you'll see a red Flash on the Web page icon to the left of the item. Now, rest your pointer on this item, and you'll also see a pop-up window displaying the dates and times you last visited and updated the page (see Figure 12-3).

If you want to access that Web page, just click its Flash icon. IE takes you to that Web page just as it would with any Favorites Web page. But after loading this page, if you click on Favorites again, you'll notice that now the Web page's corresponding item no longer has the Flash icon (see Figure 12-4). Furthermore, if you click on that item, you'll notice a pop-up window that only displays the name and URL for the Web page.

The Flash won't return until IE scans the Web site to see if it has changed. In our example, IE connects with the Web site 24 hours from the time you last accessed it.

## Basic Webcasting with E-Mail

Using the Flash feature with Basic Webcasting is useful. But it still requires you to manually check your Favorites list to see which Web sites have changed. However, you can tell IE to tell you when sites change via e-mail. To take advantage of this feature, just do as you did with the Flash feature: Browse to your favorite Web site, click on the Add to Favorites item from the Favorites pull-down menu, and click on the second radio button labeled "Yes, but only tell me when this page is updated." This time, however, do not click

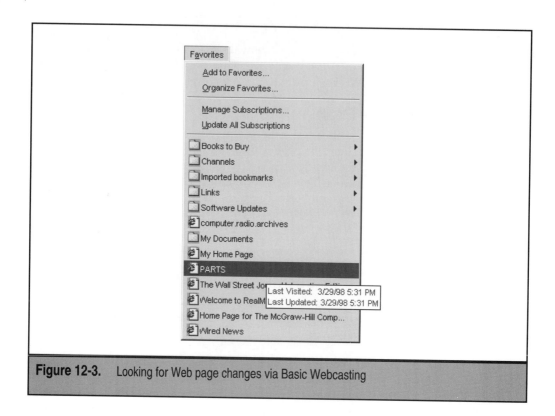

**Figure 12-3.** Looking for Web page changes via Basic Webcasting

on the OK button. Instead, click on the Customize button. This starts the Subscription Wizard, which leads you step-by-step through all of the available Webcasting options (see Figure 12-5).

On the first page of the wizard, click on the second radio button, labeled "Yes, send an e-mail message to the following address." If you see an e-mail address directly below this radio button, then your computer is ready to use Basic Webcasting with e-mail. If there's no address, or if the address is incorrect, you'll need to click on the Change Address button. This opens a quick dialog box in which you can enter your e-mail address and the address of your e-mail server.

**CAUTION:** Don't worry if you don't see your e-mail address. Basic Webcasting uses your personal information profile to ascertain the e-mail address to which it will send changed content notifications. So if you haven't filled out your personal information profile in IE, Basic Webcasting will not know where to send your messages. You can access this profile in the Internet Options dialog box under the View pull-down menu. For more information, refer to Chapter 9.

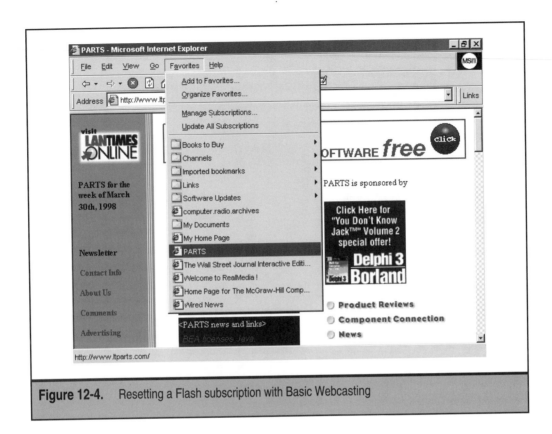

**Figure 12-4.**   Resetting a Flash subscription with Basic Webcasting

Click on the Next button, which takes you to a dialog box that asks for a user name and password. If your mail server requires such, you should click on the radio button labeled "Yes, my user name and password are:" and enter the appropriate information in the available fields. When you're finished, click on the Finish button, and when you return to the original Add Favorite dialog box, click on the OK button, and your new subscription is ready to go.

***SHORTCUT:***   For Internet users: Don't worry if you're not sure what your user name and password are. Unless you specifically set a user name and password for your mail server when you signed up for your account, just enter the user name and password for your account. That should do the trick.

As with the Flash feature of Basic Webcasting, the e-mail feature checks your Web page each day for changes. If it finds any, it displays the Flash icon on your Favorites

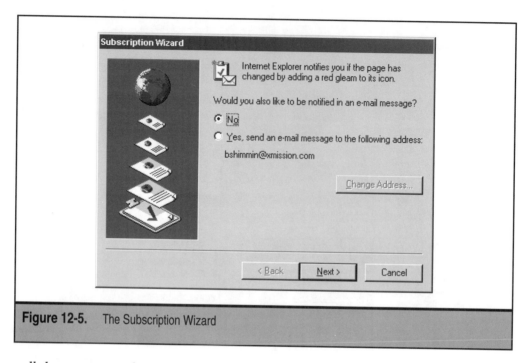

**Figure 12-5.** The Subscription Wizard

pull-down menu and sends you an e-mail message telling of the changes, from which you can connect directly to the Web page (see Figure 12-6).

## Basic Webcasting with Downloaded Content

While the Flash and e-mail features of Basic Webcasting can save you from having to manually check for changed data, you can add to that service the ability to download a Web page or an entire Web site for off-line viewing. For laptop users or desktop users that rely upon dial-up connections to the Internet, this feature should prove quite useful. For example, a sales representative could take his or her Web site's product catalog to a client's office for off-line viewing. Instead of relying upon an Internet connection or borrowing an employee's computer, the sales representative could simply bring up the Web site locally and interact with it as though it were remote. Yet, desktop-bound employees with permanent Internet connections will find this feature useful as well. By downloading an entire Web site during the night, an employee could immediately bring up the downloaded Web site in the morning without having to wait for the content to download over the company's Internet connection.

While this capability is useful for mobile workers and desktop users alike, it should be used with caution, not abandon. If every user on a corporate network chose to download the Wall Street Journal Web site each morning at 10:00 A.M., for example, the corporate Internet connection would be brought to its knees in short order. If performance is that important, your company may want to invest in a proxy server, which does the same thing as Basic Webcasting by downloading Web sites and storing them locally for quicker

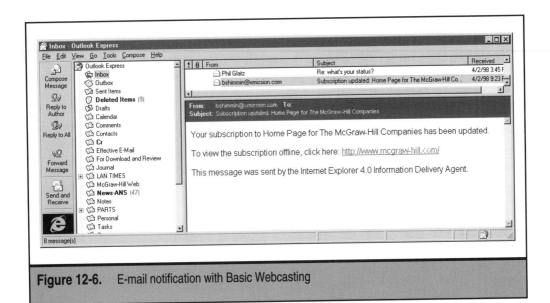

**Figure 12-6.**    E-mail notification with Basic Webcasting

access. Therefore, you should set carefully crafted parameters for your users. A good policy is to allow users to only download the home page for each Web site (we'll get to this in just a moment).

**SHORTCUT:**  As you might imagine, this problem extends beyond the corporate boundaries. If every Windows 98 user were to download the Wall Street Journal at 10:00 A.M., the Web server itself would be brought down under the strain. For that reason, Microsoft built into IE a randomization routine designed to stagger such requests.

To use Basic Webcasting to download a Web site, just do as before: Browse to your favorite Web site, click on the Favorites pull-down menu, and select Add to Favorites. From the ensuing Add Favorite dialog box, click on the last radio button, entitled "Yes, notify me of updates and download the page for off-line viewing." At this point, you can simply click on the OK button, and you'll be returned to the Web page. This establishes a Basic Webcasting subscription for this Web page with the following parameters:

▼ Only the active Web page will be downloaded, excluding all the pages linked to this page.

■ The Web page will be downloaded each day at or around 12:00 P.M. (remember, Microsoft randomizes the exact time).

■ The Web page's images and Active Content (ActiveX controls and Java applets) will be downloaded.

▲ Your computer will not download the Web page unless it is sitting idle.

If you don't like these settings, don't worry. In the next section, you'll see how to modify them to suit your needs.

So how do you work with Web pages once they've been downloaded through Basic Webcasting? It's really quite easy. If you're connected to the Internet, and you enter the URL for such a Web page, IE opens that page just as it normally does. But if you tell IE that you're not connected to the Internet, and you open the same URL, it opens the local copy just as though it were still remote. To test this out, just select the File pull-down menu and click on the Work Offline item. Now, enter the URL for a Web page to which you've subscribed. The same Web page appears as before, only this time with some subtle differences (see Figure 12-7).

First, notice how IE thinks you are not connected to the Internet. You can tell by the crossed out network icon at the bottom center of the browser window. You can also tell because on the status bar at the top of the browser window, IE displays the words "Working Offline." But this is only half of it. If you drag your pointer over a hypertext

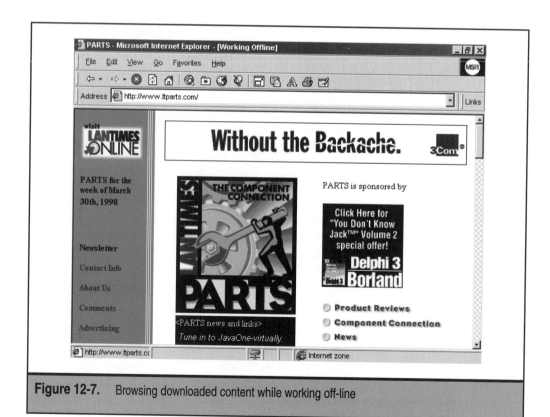

**Figure 12-7.** Browsing downloaded content while working off-line

link, you'll notice that the traditional pointer has been replaced with a finger and a universal no sign like this:

If you click on the hypertext mode of your subscription Web page while off-line, IE simply asks you whether or not you want to go on-line to retrieve the linked item. If you say yes, IE returns to on-line mode. If you say no, it stays in off-line mode. If you want to return to on-line mode without following a hypertext link, you can repeat the steps you took to make IE run in off-line mode. In this way, you'll always switch back and forth between downloaded content and live content on the Internet and always know in which mode you are working.

## Working with Managed Webcasting

Managed Webcasting is much like Basic Webcasting in that it lets your users download Web sites for off-line reading. But instead of relying on the user to set a schedule and determine how much of a Web site they download, Managed Webcasting leaves all of that to the content providers (or Webmasters). Using what Microsoft calls the Channel Definition Format (CDF), content providers can indicate which Web pages to include in a subscription, on which day, and at what time of day, your Web browser should download the subscription. Why is this useful? Well, by turning control of the subscription over to content providers, you won't have to figure out when a Web site's content is scheduled to change. Also, you won't have to manually select which Web pages to download as subscriptions (these are called Active Channels). A content provider simply creates a CDF file that describes these parameters and posts that file to the Web site. Then, when users come to a CDF-enabled Web site, they open this file, which in turn tells the user's IE how to manage the Active Channel. But the real beauty of this feature is that you can still call all the shots. When you sign up for an Active Channel, you have the option of sticking with the scenario established by the content provider or modifying that scenario to suit your needs. Depending on how the CDF file was set up, you'll see your Active Channel in one of three ways:

▼   An Active Channel as a part of IE

■   A Windows 98 Active Desktop item (Web page)

▲   A Windows 98 screen saver

By and large, most Managed subscriptions show up as Active Channels. Users interact with these subscriptions through Windows 98 as though they were regular Web sites. Less likely, but no less interesting is a Managed subscription that uses Windows 98's own Desktop as a Web browser. The last option, which is also not as usual, tells Windows 98 to display a subscription as a screen saver. For example, a news service such as Pointcast could use the screen saver to display stock quotes and news items in place of your regular screen saver. Because your users will work with all three in the same manner, and because Active Channels are the most prevalent, those are used as our example. How to work with Active Content that can function as an Active Desktop item or a screen saver is discussed in the last section of this chapter, entitled "Working with Downloadable Applications."

So how do you know when a Web site uses Microsoft's CDF to allow Managed Webcasting? It's quite simple. Look for a channel icon that looks something like either of the following:

 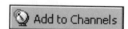

When you find one of these icons, click on it and you'll see a dialog box that tells you how the Active Channel is set up (see Figure 12-8).

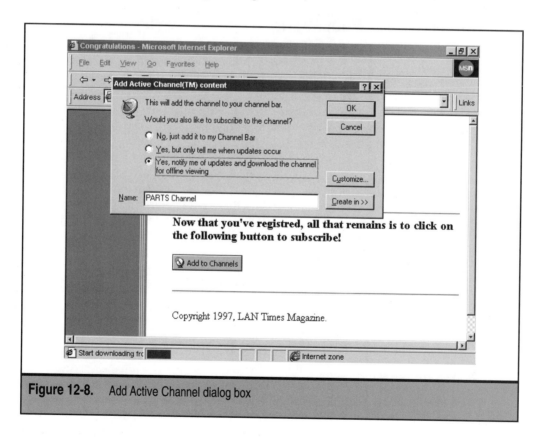

**Figure 12-8.**   Add Active Channel dialog box

Here, you've got the option of going with the default settings of the Active Channel or selecting your own settings. If you want to just go with the default settings, click on the OK button. This returns you to the original Web page and sets up your Active Channel. If you want to change or at least view the Active Channel's settings, click on the Customize button.

**SOAPBOX:** We recommend that you at least take a look at the Active Channel's settings to make sure that you feel comfortable with the amount of content that will be downloaded to your machine and at what schedule that content will be downloaded.

This opens a Subscription Wizard that is similar to the one you used with Basic Webcasting. The first option you can view or change is the amount of content that the Active Channel downloads. You can either go with the default setting (which could be any number of Web pages) or download just the channel's home page. When you're ready, click on the Next button, and you'll be able to choose whether or not you want to receive an e-mail message when the Active Channel is updated (this option works just as it does in Basic Webcasting). To continue, click on the Next button, and you'll be able to accept or reject the content provider's schedule (see Figure 12-9).

In Figure 12-9, you can see the default download schedule. In this case, the Active Channel downloads content every seven days. If you select to manually download the content, you have to update the Active Channel by hand (you'll see how in the next

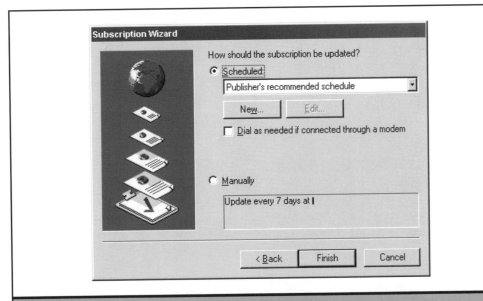

**Figure 12-9.** Accepting or rejecting an Active Channel schedule

section). Notice also that you can have IE dial your Internet connection without your intervention. If you feel confident that your machine disconnects successfully, go ahead and tell the Subscription Wizard to do so. However, you may want to experiment with this feature, allowing it to dial automatically while you're sitting at the computer. If all goes well, you can leave the setting as is. If not, you can change the setting (again, as you'll see in the next section). When you're ready, click on the Finish button and then click on the OK button from the Add Active Channel dialog box. You will see a new pane open on the left side of the screen with a number of new items. This pane is called the Channel bar. It contains links to the Web pages that are included in your newly created Active Channel (see Figure 12-10).

You can now interact with the new items as you would with links on your Favorites list. If you click on one of the new items, IE opens the corresponding page locally. The next time you open IE, you can access this Active Channel by clicking on the View pull-down menu, selecting the Explorer Bar item, and clicking on Channels. This opens the same pane as in Figure 12-10. Just click on the appropriate item, and IE opens content that is stored locally and up-to-date.

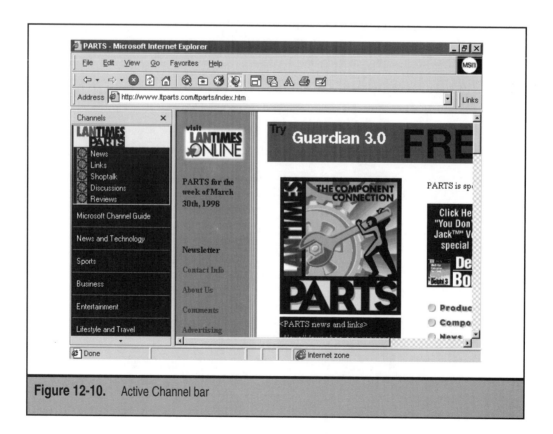

**Figure 12-10.**    Active Channel bar

# Webcasting Management

Basic and Managed Subscriptions are certainly easy to use. Your users should be able to get along without any user intervention. However, you and your users can take the initiative in maintaining these subscriptions. For example, you can manually update your subscriptions. Notice back in Figure 12-3 on the Favorites pull-down menu the following two items:

▼   Manage Subscriptions

▲   Update All Subscriptions

Clicking on Update All Subscriptions will forcefully update all of your subscriptions, regardless of their schedules. It downloads content, sends off e-mail messages, or simply displays Flashes for changed Web sites. You may want to do this if you're not sure of the schedule you've set for a subscription. Or, if you are getting ready to disconnect from the network (intranet or Internet) as with a laptop, you may want to perform this operation. But beware—updating all of your subscriptions can take some time. Think of it this way. Each Web page to which you subscribe can contain anywhere from 30K to 500K worth of content (on average). So, if you subscribe to 20 large Web pages, you could end up downloading 10MB of data, which could take anywhere from five minutes to two hours, depending upon the speed of your connection. Of course, this is a worst-case scenario because IE only downloads changed content. Unless each Web site changed out its entire content, your download time will be dramatically less.

Fortunately, Microsoft understands the difficulties in committing to an action, which you have very little control over. When you click on the Update All Subscriptions item, a Downloading Subscriptions dialog box opens (see Figure 12-11).

This dialog box tells you how large each subscription is and how much content you've downloaded in what period of time. If at any time you choose to bypass one of the subscriptions because it will take too much time to download, you can just highlight it in the lower window and click on the Skip button. And of course, you can stop the entire operation by clicking on the Stop button. Either way, your subscriptions won't be hurt. They simply continue on with their existing update schedule.

While this is useful to ensure that you've got up-to-the-minute content, it doesn't let you determine how your subscriptions will function. To take a much more active role in the management of your Basic and Managed Webcasting subscriptions, click on the Manage Subscriptions item. This opens a Windows folder called Subscriptions, which contains your current subscriptions (see Figure 12-12).

You can use this folder to manage any of your Basic Webcasting subscriptions. It tells you when Internet Explorer last updated your subscription, its current status, its absolute location (URL), schedule, size (local disk space used), and its priority. Because this folder works just like any other Windows folder, you can work with your subscriptions as though they were just files. For example, to delete a subscription, you can just highlight it and press the DELETE button (denoted by an "X").

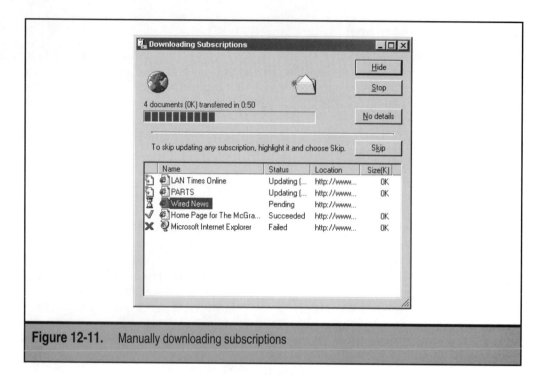

**Figure 12-11.**    Manually downloading subscriptions

Notice how some of the items in Figure 12-12 have Flash icons. Those contain new content that you have not yet seen. To manage any of these subscriptions, right-click on its name in the main Window and select the properties item. This opens a Properties

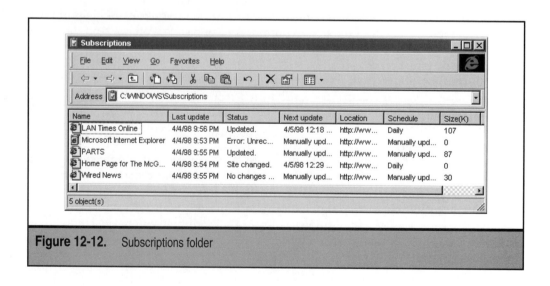

**Figure 12-12.**    Subscriptions folder

dialog box for the highlighted subscription. From here, you can see a summary of the subscription's settings. You can also unsubscribe from the subscription, or choose how you are notified of changes. For example, if you are running into performance issues with subscriptions that download changed content, you can instruct your users to change the subscription type to a notification-only subscription, which only sends out an e-mail message and/or displays a Flash for changed content. You can also change the e-mail address to which updates are sent. But most importantly, you can use the Properties dialog box to change the subscription's schedule. To do this, click on the Schedule tab (see Figure 12-13).

If you would like to control the schedule, but maintain as much automation as possible, click on the Scheduled radio button. This puts into action the publisher's schedule, if the subscription is a Managed Webcasting subscription. If it is just a regular Webcasting subscription, it shows you that the Web site will be updated daily at 12:00 P.M. If you want to easily change that schedule, click on the Scheduled pull-down menu, where you can click on either daily, weekly, or monthly updates.

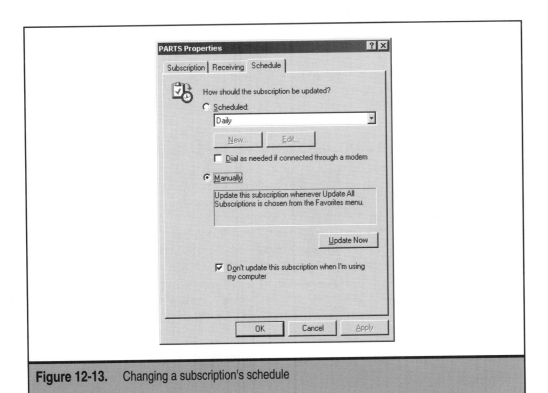

**Figure 12-13.** Changing a subscription's schedule

> **SHORTCUT:** For telecommuters and mobile users, IE can completely automate the subscription process. If you leave your computer on at night, just click on the check box labeled "Dial as needed if connected through a modem." Your computer then connects to the Internet and updates your subscriptions automatically. If, however, you don't want to be disturbed by this process (if a subscription comes due while you're working), just click on the check box labeled "Don't update this subscription when I'm using my computer."

If you need to set a more specific schedule, click on the Edit button. This opens a dialog box in which you can tell Internet Explorer the exact day, time, and interval for updates. That's all there is to managing your subscriptions. But that's not all there is to Active Content.

# WORKING WITH DOWNLOADABLE APPLICATIONS

As mentioned earlier, Basic and Managed Webcasting can do much more than download Web pages. If those Web pages contain applications (Java applets or ActiveX controls), those applications are downloaded as well. In a nutshell, this means that you can store and interact with these applications locally. You don't have to connect to the Internet in order to run them. Usually, when you close Internet Explorer (IE), any downloaded applications become unavailable. That is, unless they are a part of Web pages to which you subscribe. Notice the small black box with the heading "<PARTS news and links>" in Figure 12-10? That is a Java applet that scrolls the latest news items. When you subscribe to the Active Channel containing that application, it resides locally. When you click on a news item, the applet launches IE, connects to a news server and displays the appropriate news item.

## Adding Downloadable Applications to Your Desktop

Downloadable applications can also reside outside of IE. Using what Windows 98 calls the Active Desktop, you can add downloadable applications to your Windows desktop that remain ever available whether or not you are connected to a network. There are many applications built just for the Active Desktop. And they act much like traditional subscriptions in that you subscribe to them, and they automatically download up-to-date content and services. For example, there are news and stock tickers, sports score tickers, weather displays, clocks, and even satellite tracking systems, all built to run on your desktop. As with Managed Webcasting content, you'll know when you see one of these applications on the Internet because it will be denoted with an Add to Active Desktop icon like this:

**RESOURCE:** Don't know where to find Active Desktop components? Try Microsoft's Active Desktop Gallery. You can find it on-line at http://www.microsoft.com/ie40/gallery/. There, you can download various applications from Microsoft, CNET, ESPN SportsZone, and MSNBC.

Before you download one of these applications, consider a few words of caution. As with Basic and Managed Webcasting, whenever you download and maintain an application locally on your desktop, be aware that the application may require a certain amount of bandwidth. For example, a news service Java applet might need to connect to a server every hour. For this reason, make sure that you and your users understand and agree with the requirements of downloaded applications. Of course, as with Webcasting, you can control (to an extent) the behavior of these applications. That is discussed in just a moment. Also, consider that these applications may not be what they claim to be. That is, some downloadable applications might be malicious. Fortunately, IE comes with some security measures. For Java applets, IE can disallow any deviant activities such as writing to the hard disk. And for ActiveX controls, IE can require a valid digital certificate.

**RESOURCE:** For more information on these security measures, read through Chapter 9. There, you'll learn how to disable Java applets and ActiveX controls, work with digital certificates, and secure sites via IE's Security Zones.

## Adding an Active Desktop Item

Once you've found a desirable application, click on its Add to Active Desktop icon. IE asks you whether or not you want to add the item to your desktop. Click on the Yes button. If you have not already made your Active Desktop active (which is done during the installation process), you are given the chance to do so by clicking on the Yes button when asked if you want to enable your Active Desktop. Once that's done, IE will pop up a dialog box that looks something like this:

As with other types of Webcasting, you can choose to accept the default settings for the application subscription by clicking on the OK button. Or you can customize that subscription by clicking on the Customize Subscription button. For now, click on the OK button. You'll see how to change these settings in just a moment. IE then downloads the application. Note that this can take some time depending upon the application's size. When the application is downloaded, you are returned to your Windows 98 Desktop, where you will see the new application embedded in the background image (see Figure 12-14).

## Managing Downloaded Applications

You can interact with the application by moving your mouse over it. This pops up a gray border as shown in Figure 12-14. Just click and drag on the gray border to move the application around the screen. If you click on the "X" in the upper-right corner, Windows 98 removes the application from your desktop, but it does not delete it. You can reapply it by customizing your desktop. To do that, right-click anywhere on the desktop and select Active Desktop. Notice the menu item labeled Update Now. This performs the same function as updating your subscriptions from IE. It forces your applications to gather the most recent information on-line. Also notice how there's a check mark next to the item labeled View as Web Page. If you click on that item, your desktop returns to its normal

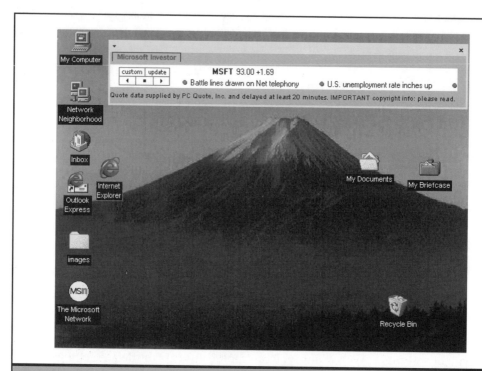

**Figure 12-14.**    An Active Desktop application

appearance, hiding any downloaded applications from view. From this same pop-up menu, click on Customize my Desktop. This opens the Display Properties dialog box from which you can modify your existing application subscriptions (see Figure 12-15).

Notice the check mark next to the item labeled Microsoft Investor Ticker? It indicates that the application is active on your desktop. To remove it, leaving other applications in an active state, click on the check box. You can disable all applications in the same way by clicking on the check mark next to the text stating that you want to view your Active Desktop as a Web page. When you click on the OK button at the bottom of the window, the item no longer appears. To modify the properties of an Active Desktop application, highlight it and click on the Properties button. This opens a dialog box like the one shown in Figure 12-9. As you might guess, you can also get to this same dialog box in the same manner from the Subscriptions folder as shown in Figure 12-12. From this dialog box, you can work with Active Desktop applications just as you would with any subscription, adjusting their update schedules, setting an e-mail address, and the like.

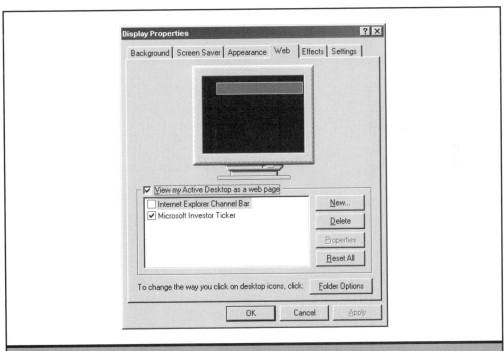

**Figure 12-15.**   Managing your downloaded applications

# COMING UP

Now that you've seen how Windows 98 and Internet Explorer can help you and your users make better use of Web sites and downloadable applications, we'll spend the next chapter discussing how you can build your own Web server, from which you can host Webcasting services. We'll show you how to install, configure, and maintain Microsoft's Personal Web Server (PWS), a light-weight and easy to use Web server capable of housing workgroup-sized Web sites right out of the box.

ETWORK
ROFESSIONAL'S
IBRARY

# CHAPTER 13

# Creating Web Services

## What's ahead:

- Introducing the Microsoft Personal Web Server (PWS)
- Web security considerations
- Configuring PWS
- Creating and publishing Web content with PWS

*"From one basin*
*to another—*
*stuff and nonsense."*

—Issa

The Web. It pervades our lives. While at home, we see Uniform Resource Locators (URLs) advertised on television. At work, we spend over 90 percent of our time on the Internet working within the Web. Web servers are popping up everywhere, on the Internet, at the office, and in the home. We use them to gather information. We use them to disseminate information. Even in the face of e-mail, which still reigns as the killer application, the Web is fast becoming the platform of choice for electronic communication. Likewise, we look to the Web's Hypertext Markup Language (HTML) as the medium for this communication. Our e-mail messages arrive as HTML documents. Our word processors speak HTML as their native tongue. Together, this medium and platform are driving and promise to continue to drive the way we do business, the way we play, and the way we define ourselves.

How often have we heard coworkers refer others to their "home pages" for downloading an application or reading a proposal? How often have you heard friends or relatives suggest that you check out their Web sites for absolutely no reason whatsoever? In terms of cultural impact, you could look at the Web as the next generation fax machine. Faxes are global, and fax machines are ubiquitous. Anyone with a phone line can own and operate a fax machine. And over these telephone lines, faxes can bring two complete strangers together. Likewise, when someone publishes a document on the Web in Singapore, that document may appear in someone's Web browser in Cincinnati.

The difference between fax machines and the Web is that fax machines can act as both a sending and receiving device. The problem, unfortunately, is that the Web requires very different sending and receiving devices. While it seems that everyone has a Web browser, not everyone has a Web server. Luckily, as the economic usefulness and cultural importance of allowing more and more people to act as senders of information became increasingly apparent, vendors rushed in, providing affordable products and services. The result: Web servers have quickly found their way into our daily lives. What once belonged solely to the domain of $30,000 UNIX workstations and network engineers can now be had by anyone with a phone line and a PC. The best example of this trend is Windows 98. Anyone who buys Windows 98 automatically has the ability to act as a Web server.

**RESOURCE:** Because Web services work over TCP/IP, it will pay to have a good understanding of how TCP/IP works with Windows 98. In this chapter, a fundamental knowledge of TCP/IP is assumed, so if at any point you feel lost, just refer back to Chapter 6.

# INTRODUCING THE MICROSOFT PERSONAL WEB SERVER

To provide Web server capabilities, Windows 98 comes with the Personal Web Server (PWS). It ships with Windows 98, free of charge. However, it does not install automatically along with Windows 98—more on that later. In this chapter, from both a user's and manager's perspective, Microsoft's PWS is put to work in Windows 98. You'll see how you can use these services personally or within a workgroup to enhance productivity and communication. For example, you can install PWS on a Windows 98 machine within each department in your company. From these servers, your departments can easily and quickly share valuable information. Accounting can post contact information for payroll check questions. Human Resources can post the company vacation calendar, health care information, and policy manuals. Along the way, you'll see how to set up Windows 98 to act as a Web server using shares or user accounts. You'll see how to install and configure your Web server, outlining performance, management, and security issues.

Microsoft's PWS is not a new feature on the Windows landscape. Windows 95 users have had access to a personal Web server almost since the operating system's introduction in August of 1995. With it, users have been able to publish Web documents right from their own machine. And conversely, they've been able to use their machine as a staging or testing server. Once they've verified that their Web pages are functioning correctly, they simply move them from the personal Web server to an Internet Service Provider (ISP) Web server or corporate Web server. The latter of the two strategies, however, was by far the norm. This was due in part to PWS's limited manageability and functionality. For instance, it did not have any sort of monitoring system. Its logging utility was bare bones, to say the least. And it could not take advantage of new technologies such as Active Server Pages (ASP).

Fortunately, with the version of PWS that ships with Windows 98, that has all changed. Though it is still only able to handle ten simultaneous connections, PWS now comes equipped with an arsenal of management utilities and new features. Here's a sample of those features and functionality:

▼ **Traffic monitoring**  PWS comes with real-time graphs, displaying site traffic statistics such as requests per day, visitors per day, requests per hour, and visits per hour.

■ **Home Page wizard**  With the new wizard, which guides you through the creation of a home page, you won't need to know any HTML or scripting languages.

■ **Guest Book and Drop Box options**  These two interactive features automatically allow visitors to your Web page to sign a guest book or leave you a private message.

- ■ **New management interface**  PWS now comes with the Personal Management Interface application, which helps you manage, configure, and monitor your Web site.

- ▲ **Enterprise application support**  PWS comes equipped with full support for ASP as well as Microsoft's Transaction Server, giving you the opportunity to create enterprise-class, interactive Web applications.

**SOAPBOX:**  The only downside to the new PWS is that it no longer provides File Transfer Protocol (FTP) services. With previous versions, Windows 95 users could set up an FTP server from which other users could download or upload files. Actually, the new PWS does support FTP services, but only on Windows NT 4.0. You see, as a Win 32 application, it can run on Windows 95, Windows 98, and Windows NT. Because Windows NT has been deemed Microsoft's strategic platform for high-end services, Microsoft thought it best to only allow FTP services on Windows NT. Frankly, considering FTP's reputed security failings, restricting it to a professionally managed server may be the safest option.

Of course, to use PWS and take advantage of these new features, you must meet the minimum system requirements in order to install and use it. According to Microsoft, those requirements are:

| Hardware Component | Minimum | Recommendation |
| --- | --- | --- |
| Processor | 33 MHz 486 | 90 MHz Pentium |
| RAM | 16MB | 32 to 64MB |
| Free hard disk space | 20MB (for minimum install) | 100MB |
| Monitor | VGA | Super VGA |

That's all you need to install and run PWS on your Windows 98 machine.

## Before You Install Web Services

Before you jump headlong into Web services, you must first consider the impact they will have on your Windows 98 machine. It is no trivial matter to act as a server, nor is it trivial to allow your users to function as servers if you're an administrator. When you make a Windows 98 machine a Web server, you automatically create the following issues:

- ▼ Server and network performance
- ■ Content responsibility
- ▲ Server maintenance and security

## Server and Network Performance

From the user's perspective, the addition of a Web service will exact some degree of machine performance. Consider an Internet-based Web site such as http://www.microsoft.com. This site garners millions of hits each day and hundreds of simultaneous connections each second.

*JARGON:* What's a hit? Well, every time a Web browser connects with a Web server and requests a part of a Web page, such as an image, a piece of text, a table, and the like, the Web server registers that single request as a hit. Conversely, a single page view is the collection of all of the hits that go into requesting a single Web page.

In order to accommodate such a high load, Microsoft uses an Alpha cluster (group of interconnected, duplicate servers), running Microsoft's own Windows NT and Internet Information Server (IIS). While all of these products are built to accommodate huge system loads, Windows 98 is not. It does not support the high-performance Alpha chip (running on X-86 chips alone), and its Web server does not support hundreds of simultaneous connections, like IIS does. Windows 98's Web server, PWS, only supports upwards of ten simultaneous connections. The actual number of simultaneous users will vary depending upon the speed of the processor upon which PWS is running.

## Content Responsibility

While performance can limit Windows 98's ability to deliver large amounts of data via the Web, a far more serious limitation rests in your own ability to control content. If you intend to use Windows 98 for personal use, you can use its Web server to publish whatever you want. Of course, you are subject to the laws of your state and nation regarding regulated content and copyright/trademark ownership. For instance, you can't publish your copy of Microsoft Word 97 or make available a controlled munition like Pretty Good Privacy (PGP). Users must pay Microsoft for Word 97, and PGP contains encryption software that is not exportable by order of the United States Government.

The same rules apply to your place of business. If you as a user choose to publish something that breaks a state or national law, your company may be responsible for that act. Therefore, if you choose to allow users to publish on the Web, you must first get the okay from management. The answer most likely depends upon whether or not your network is exposed to the Internet (people on the Internet can access your local machines). If your machines are exposed to the Internet, your manager may allow users to publish content only after signing a terms-of-use contract. This document is basically a disclaimer—a waiver of responsibility—indicating that the user is legally responsible for the content he or she publishes. For networks that do not have Internet exposure, a similar agreement may still be in order, simply to protect the company and users by providing a set of ground rules for the publication of online content.

## Server Maintenance

The last two issues in setting up Web services on your users' machines concerns the physical maintenance and security of those machines. Again, someone has to take responsibility for Web publishers, answering technical questions and resolving technical issues such as broken links, TCP/IP port failures, and directory access problems. Fortunately, Windows 98 makes things pretty foolproof when it comes to Web services. Once you've installed and configured both services, the only thing that will interrupt their services is the user. For example, PWS runs in the System Tray and is available from the Control Panel, which means that each time a user reboots his or her machine, PWS restarts the machine, restoring services without user input.

**JARGON:** What is the System Tray? It is the space within your Taskbar that displays the current time and any resident applications. These applications usually include system applications such as sound, power management, and virus software. PWS, by the way, is one of these applications. They don't run as full programs, but they do remain active within Windows 98. In other words, when you start Windows 98, those applications become automatically available.

However, if a user changes directory access rights, directory privileges, and the like, the resulting issues can suddenly become your problem. The bottom line is: Be prepared. If you make these services available, you should be prepared to become accountable for any situation that may arise.

One last note concerning maintenance: Software woes are by far the least of the Web's problems. The most trouble your users will have concerns the maintenance of the published content itself. The problem harks back to issues of responsibility. You are responsible for any content made available by your users. Imagine if a marketing department decided to publish its quarterly sales results for the rest of the company's perusal. Such a situation is optimal because it could cut down on the usual paper flow throughout the office. However, should the content be in error, or should it suddenly become inaccessible (for whatever reason), the phone calls will naturally come your way.

**SHORTCUT:** To facilitate a quicker problem-resolution cycle, you may want to post your e-mail address at the bottom of each page on your user's machines. You could simply instruct your users to append an HTML snippet like the following to the bottom of each Web page:

```
"If there are any problems,
please contact
<ahref="mailto:your_address@your_company.com">
your_address@your_company.com</a>.".
```

## System Security

Whether you do it for your users or yourself, in order to set up and run Web services, you must create a secure environment in which those services can run. That is, you must secure your machine from attack. Up until this point, we've discussed the ramifications of publishing information freely from your Windows 98 Web server. Now, we must tackle the even greater problem of keeping certain pieces of information from being published openly. As with e-mail, some pieces of data are simply meant for one pair of eyes, not all of those on the Internet. Of course, it is easy to imagine such issues for a service like FTP, in which users actually log on to your machine.

But did you know that the Web itself is an avenue through which perpetrators can gain unauthorized access to your machine? By overrunning a URL (adding extra text after the normal URL), some perpetrators have been able to execute applications on the server. All they need to know is the location of the application they want to run. You must ensure that those users can only access the directories you deem safe. Otherwise, a miscreant could steal your private documents. Or worse, that person could destroy sensitive system files such as SYSTEM.INI or PROGMAN.INI. Luckily, PWS, now in its fourth incarnation, has withstood such attacks—or if it has not, Microsoft has provided an appropriate security patch, removing the problem. Still, you should do all you can to ensure that the weak link in the security chain is not you.

**WINDOWS 98 SECURITY SETTINGS**    The first thing you should know about securing your Web server is that PWS uses an entirely different security mechanism than Windows 98. Windows 98 can use a number of different security mechanisms, including:

▼　Anonymous

■　Basic

▲　Windows NT/Challenge and Response

With *anonymous* access, people can view any folder they want, even in restricted directories. The beauty of anonymous access is that it runs alongside the other two security mechanisms, augmenting their services. And yes, this sounds like the same problem we've been talking about overcoming. Yet, it is important because you can use it to fill in the gaps you leave behind in creating user name and password access restrictions. You see, unless you secure the entire root directory for your Windows 98 system, you have to specify user and group access rights for all sub-directories in order to provide complete access to those sub-directories. If you miss a folder, no one will be able to access it. However, if you enable anonymous access, those missed directories become accessible.

The primary type of access used by Windows 98 is *basic*, which simply provides user name and password access to your Windows 98 directories. It employs Windows' base64 encoding to encrypt user names and passwords as they cross the wire. Base64 is basically an e-mail format that encodes information in an immediately unreadable format. This is a very fast mechanism, but it is not very secure, as the base64 encoding scheme can be easily captured and read by anyone with a packet capturing and decoding device. However, for LANs and workgroups that are not exposed to the Internet, this mechanism should do fine.

For those companies with some exposure to larger enterprise networks or the Internet, the *Windows NT/Challenge and Response* mechanism is the best security mechanism. It uses a Windows NT Domain Controller to provide highly secured user name and password encryption. This service is only available on networks running Windows NT. It won't work if you only have a Windows 98 or Novell NetWare network.

**THE PWS SECURITY MECHANISM**   Microsoft's PWS, on the other hand, uses its own security mechanism, which is completely separate from those used by Windows 98 (see Figure 13-1).

It uses a share-level mechanism that is similar to the anonymous share system used by Windows 98.

**SOAPBOX:**  Strangely, previous versions of PWS supported these three levels of security. In accordance with Microsoft's strategy to make Windows 98 a workgroup-level server, leaving Windows NT as an enterprise-class server, these services are only available on PWS installation in Windows NT.

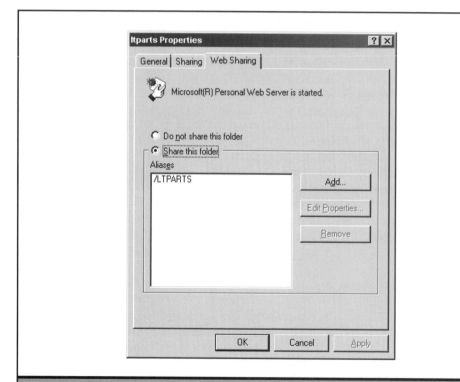

**Figure 13-1.**   Web sharing is separate from file sharing in Windows 98

There are only two differences. First, when you create a Web directory, PWS simply makes that directory available to all anonymous users. For example, if you happen to have set up a user name and password for a particular shared directory (which is also specified as a Web directory), PWS overrides that security, allowing users without names or passwords to view the contents of that directory. You then have the ability to set a limited number of Web-specific security settings for that directory. Second, only those directories specified as a part of your PWS Web site are accessible to the outside world through anonymous authentication.

In essence, PWS overrides the security system of Windows 98. This means anyone can gain access to your Web server's directories with PWS, no matter what security settings are in place within Windows 98. But it also means that unlike Windows 98's traditional share-level security, you don't have to account for each and every directory on your machine. In other words, only directories that fall below your Web site's root directory are available to the outside world.

*JARGON:*   What's a root directory? Just as your PC has a root directory (C:\), so does your Web server, only its root directory is actually a sub-directory of your PC's root directory. With PWS, for example, the Web server's root directory is C:\WEBSHARE\WWWROOT\. This means that users cannot access any files above the WWWROOT directory—a very nice security mechanism.

Is this mechanism safe? For the Web, yes. You see, aside from security threats mentioned in this section (such as the overrun attack), the Web provides a fairly innocuous level of access to your machine. Based upon the Hypertext Transport Protocol (HTTP), the Web can only view documents, retrieve documents, and submit a limited amount of information to the server. These levels of interaction can be summed up under the following three services:

▼  **Read**   This is the ability for a Web browser to view HTML files. The only security threat here is one of privacy. If you don't want outsiders viewing particular directories, you can simply exclude those directories from your Web server.

■  **Execute**   This is the ability for a Web browser to start a server-side application such as a guest book. The only security threat here is that posed by the application itself. If an application is built poorly, or it is malicious, it could cause harm. However, because you as the administrator of your own machine must choose which applications to run, the responsibility is uniquely yours.

▲  **Run Scripts**   This is the ability for a Web browser to run applications embedded within Web pages. These applications are called scripts, and they're built with such languages as JScript, VBScript, and JavaScript. The security threats posed by these applications depend upon the level of security within the user's Web browser.

Not surprisingly, these are the three Web-specific security settings available to you with PWS. For each directory you add to PWS, you have the option of allowing or disallowing any of these features. But before getting to the specifics of setting up these security settings, it's time to install and configure your Web server.

# WORKING WITH PWS

Security issues aside, PWS is very easy to work with. It just takes a few moments to install the software and publish your Web content. Throughout the remainder of this chapter, you'll go through the steps required to get your server up and running. You'll start with its installation, and then take a quick tour through its many features and configuration options. You'll end by quickly setting up some sample content, specifying its location, and setting its security parameters.

## Installing PWS

As you might expect, with all of the unique security capabilities involved with Web services, Microsoft has chosen not to install PWS automatically with Windows 98. Instead, a pointer to PWS is installed. To get to that, click on the Start menu, select Programs and then Internet Explorer, and finally click on the Personal Web Server icon. This opens a Web page (see Figure 13-2), which basically contains instructions on finding

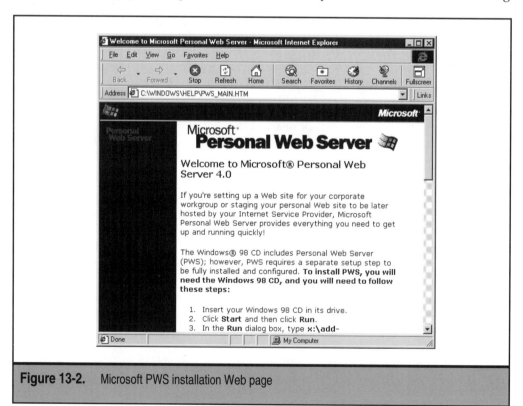

**Figure 13-2.** Microsoft PWS installation Web page

the PWS installation program. You can follow along, if you like. But the shortcut to starting the PWS installation routine is to first make sure your Windows 98 CD-ROM is available (let's say as drive E:). Click on the Start button and select Run.

**CAUTION:**  This information is based upon a pre-release version of Windows 98. While the overall content won't change, the directory structure of the Windows 98 CD-ROM may shift in the actual shipping product. To make sure you've got PWS available on the Windows 98 CD-ROM, just open an MS-DOS box, go to the drive assigned to the CD-ROM and type: **dir pws/s**. This tells you exactly where the PWS sub-directory is, should it change from what is mentioned here.

In the resulting dialog box, enter the following string:

```
E:\add-ons\pws\setup.exe
```

Click on the OK button, and Windows 98 begins installing PWS, revealing the wizard shown in Figure 13-3.

From here on out, it's straightforward. You can just follow the Setup wizard. To continue with the installation, click on the Next button and read through the following licensing agreement carefully. If there are no problems, click on the Accept button. The next screen (see Figure 13-4) allows you to choose the type of installation you want (minimum, typical, or custom).

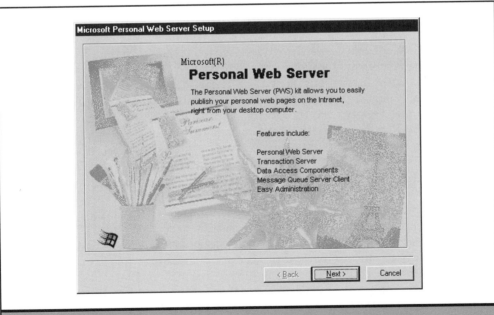

**Figure 13-3.**   PWS Setup wizard

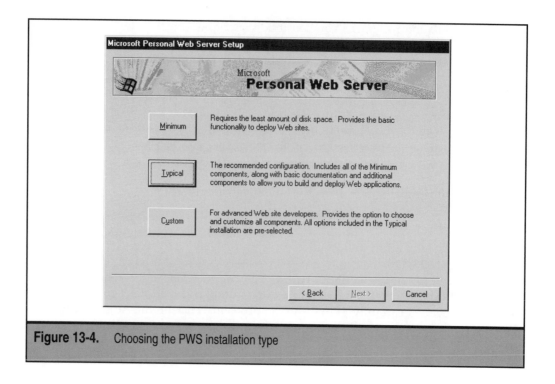

**Figure 13-4.** Choosing the PWS installation type

If you're installing PWS on a user's machine on which you will retain control over the server and its content, we suggest that you choose the minimum option. This installs only those components necessary for the Web server. It does not install any documentation, and it takes the least amount of disk space. Otherwise, we suggest that you choose the custom option. It installs all of the available components, plus electronic documentation. It also allows you to specify many features such as Web directory locations, security options, and the like. To proceed with the custom option, click on its button.

This opens a component selection dialog box, from which you can select which PWS services you want to install. By default, it installs Microsoft FrontPage 98 Server Extensions, Microsoft data access components, the PWS service itself, and Microsoft Transaction Server. Unless you plan on using the Transaction Sever for enterprise Web development, deselect it. When you're ready, click on the Next button. This opens a series of dialog boxes that list the default directory structure for Web services. Unless you need to modify these directories, it is strongly suggested that you leave them as is. You see, some third-party products look for these directory structures while installing software. One missed directory could spell disaster during installation. That's all there is to it. At this point, PWS simply finishes installing the Web services, prompting you only to click on the Finish button and then choose to restart Windows 98.

Once Windows 98 restarts, the setup process finishes, updating your shortcuts. Your new Web server is all set. To take it out for its maiden voyage, open Internet Explorer from your Start menu and type the following URL in the Address field:

```
http://localhost/
```

This tells your Web browser to open the default page from the root directory of your Web server. The word "localhost" is a TCP/IP convention that uses a static IP address of 127.0.0.1 to basically send a round trip TCP/IP connection from your Web browser to the Web server running on the same machine. If you have given your computer a name, you can replace localhost with that name, bypassing the round trip IP address. Actually, you can use either localhost or the name of your computer. The URL for your machine would then look like this:

```
http://musashi/
```

Either way, you will be able to access your Web server right from your Windows 98 machine. If all goes well, you should see a Welcome screen describing PWS (see Figure 13-5).

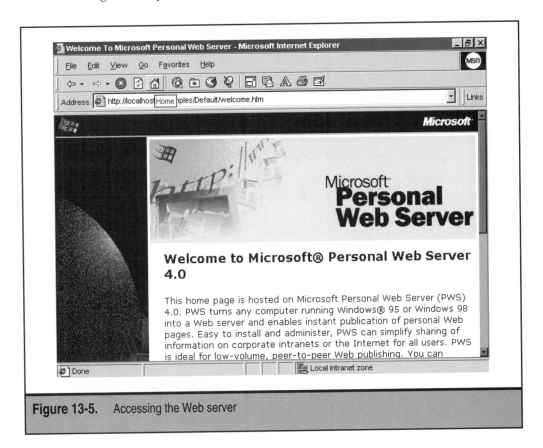

**Figure 13-5.** Accessing the Web server

# Configuring PWS

Go ahead and minimize Internet Explorer. Notice in the desktop's System Tray that you've got a new icon that looks a lot like a hand holding a flashing page. If you right-click on that icon, you'll see a quick pop-up menu from which you can start, stop, and pause, or continue Web services:

**SHORTCUT:** If you can't wait to read through the rest of this section, PWS comes with a visual tour that leads you through PWS's many features. Click on the Tour view icon and follow the instructions.

You can also select the Web server's properties from this same pop-up menu. Click on the Properties button to get acquainted with PWS. Doing so opens a dialog box called the Personal Web Manager, which contains all you need to create, maintain, and use Web content (see Figure 13-6).

Like Outlook Express, the Personal Web Manager uses a left-hand pane to display icons for all possible views. These include:

▼ **Main**   Monitor the status of your Web server.

■ **Publish**   Move your Web pages to the PWS file system.

■ **Web Site**   Set up a home page through a quick and easy wizard.

■ **Tour**   Take a guided tour through PWS's many features and uses.

▲ **Advanced**   Manage directories for your Web server and specify various settings.

This is the interface through which you will manage all aspects of your Web server and your Web content. In the remainder of this chapter, you'll spend most of your time in the Main and Advanced views, where you'll set up and manage PWS. The publishing views are covered in the next chapter.

## Publishing Information

Let's begin with some housekeeping information. In the Main view, notice the information under the heading of Publishing at the top of the window. Here, you can see where your home page is located, stop your Web service, and view the contents of your Web server's root directory. If you click on the home page link (in our case,

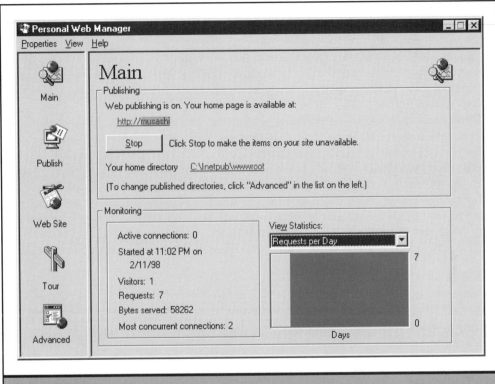

**Figure 13-6.** Personal Web Manager

"http://musashi"), a window similar to Figure 13-5 opens. This is the home page for PWS. We'll leave this page as is, so go ahead and close Internet Explorer and return to the Personal Web Manager.

*CAUTION:* Normally, you would make this the default page for Internet Explorer in order to gain quick access to personal Web information such as your favorite links, e-mail addresses, and phone numbers. However, because PWS uses a Web page containing no HTML, just VBScript code, you may have a hard time modifying this page to suit your own needs. Therefore, wait until Chapter 14, where you will create a new home page that is created strictly with HTML.

Notice the large button that says Stop. As you might expect, that button terminates your Web server process on Windows 98. Normally, you have no reason to stop your Web service. However, there are some instances that might require such measures. For example, on a slower machine, you may need to shut down the Web service in order to conserve system resources for other work. Also, when installing some software packages, especially those that are dependent upon TCP/IP services, you may need to shut down the server before installation to avoid any sort of software failure. Lastly, you may need to shut down the server in order to perform server or content maintenance. To shut down your server, click on the Stop button. Notice how the Stop button is then replaced with a Start button. Also, notice how the lower portion of the Personal Web Manager has been grayed out (see Figure 13-7).

If you or other users on your network were to try connecting to your Web server now, you'd receive a server error indicating that the server is not responding. To restart your Web server, just click on the Start button, and everything will return to normal.

Once the server has restarted, notice how your home page and home directory links have reappeared under the Publishing heading. The home page link was explored earlier in this section. Now let's take a look at the home directory link. You will find this hypertext link quite useful as it quickly takes you to your Web server's root directory, using Windows 98's Explorer tool (see Figure 13-8).

Take note of the Address field's entry. In our example, it contains:

```
C:\WEBSHARE\WWWROOT
```

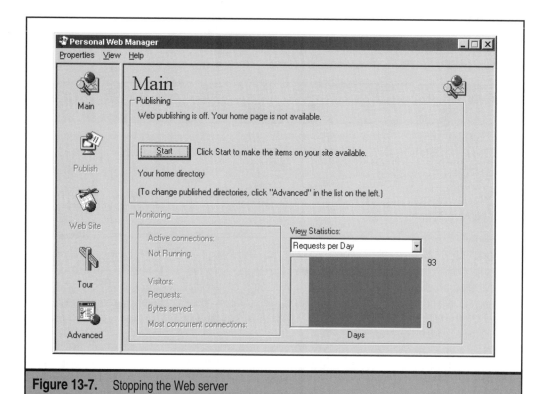

**Figure 13-7.** Stopping the Web server

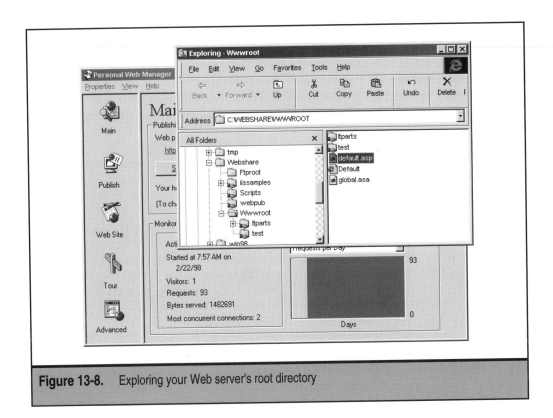

**Figure 13-8.**    Exploring your Web server's root directory

With this information at your fingertips, you can gain access to the root directory through any of your applications, such as a Web page editor like FrontPage Express. You can also browse directly to this directory without first going through the Personal Web Manager. It is simply there as a convenience.

## Monitoring Information

Close Explorer and return to the Personal Web Manager. Notice in the lower portion of the Main view the information housed under the Monitoring heading. This area contains information about how often people access your Web server. It contains a number of metrics including:

▼  Requests per Day

■  Requests per Hour

■  Visitors per Day

▲  Visitors per Hour

What's the difference between visitors and requests? Well, each time a user connects to your Web server and browses around through a number of pages, that connection is called a visit. Each time a user connects to your Web server and downloads a Web page and its constituent elements, each individual element is called a request. For example, if you were to open a Web page with some text, a table, and one image, your Web browser would basically make three different requests, one for each item. These requests are really the same as hits. To access these different statistics, just click on the View Statistics pull-down menu from the Monitoring section (see Figure 13-9).

The information at the left, which includes Active connections, visitors, and requests, remains static, no matter which statistic you view under the View Statistics pull-down menu. These statistics are meant to give you a visual representation of the traffic and usage patterns found on your server. So why should you care about such metrics? They help you understand how often people are accessing your server, which in turn can help you understand how well your server is performing its tasks. For instance, if you notice that your visitors per hour is growing rapidly to the point where you might exceed PWS's ten concurrent user limit, you may want to upgrade to a larger server, such as Microsoft's Internet Information Server (IIS). Actually, there's a quick way to tell the maximum number of concurrent connections your Web server has experienced. Just look to the

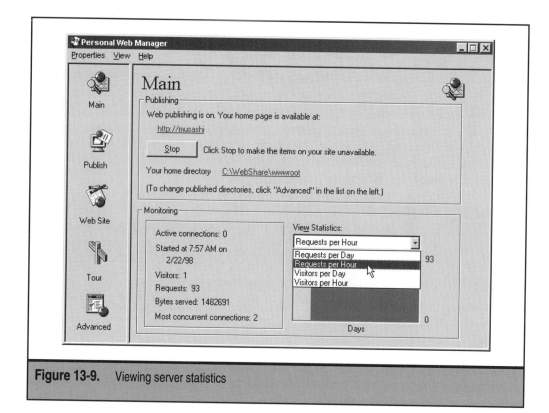

**Figure 13-9.**    Viewing server statistics

bottom of the Monitoring section (refer to Figure 13-9). There, you should see an item called *Most concurrent connections*. Just keep your eye on that number. If it hovers around eight, nine, or ten, then you're in need of an upgrade.

## Advanced Options Information

The last stop in the tour of PWS is the Advanced Options view. To open this view, click on the last icon in the lower left-hand corner of the Personal Web Manager. This opens a window that contains a virtual directory listing and a few miscellaneous settings (see Figure 13-10).

Within the top window, entitled Virtual Directories, you are able to add content (directories containing Web pages) to your Web site. You are also able to set security options for those directories, and even delete those directories no longer in use. Notice how there are a number of virtual directories already present. These include IISADMIN, IISHELP, IISSAMPLES, SCRIPTS, and WEBPUB. The first three directories, which are pretty self-explanatory, contain documents and applications that help you manage PWS and create great Web content. Of these three, you can access the IISHELP and IISSAMPLES directories, if you have directory browsing enabled. But, it is suggested that

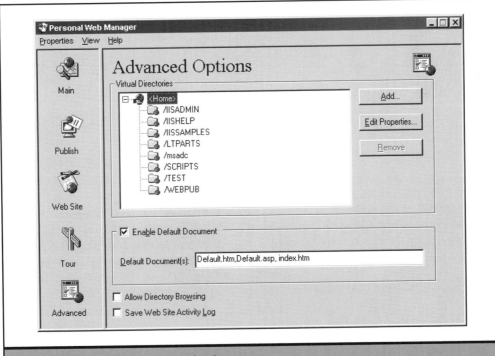

**Figure 13-10.** Accessing advanced options

you simply work through the Personal Web Manager, from which you can access any information found in these directories. The last two directories (SCRIPTS and WEBPUB) also do not require any direct intervention on your part. PWS stores server-side applications in the SCRIPTS directory and uses WEBPUB as a staging directory for the transfer of files to a remote Web server.

**SOAPBOX:**  Notice how most of these pre-installed directories start with IIS. That stands for Internet Information Server, Microsoft's heavy-duty Web server. You see, PWS is really based on IIS. The main difference is the limited number of connections PWS can support and a lack of FTP support. This will be advantageous should you choose to upgrade to Windows NT and IIS at a later date as you will already be familiar with its management and features.

Because all of these directories were created by PWS to house server-specific features, you won't need to make any security modifications in order to protect your machine.

On the lower portion of the Advanced Options view, you can tell PWS to enable default file names by checking the box entitled Enable Default Document. Doing so tells PWS to look for and then start any files with the names listed in the Default Document field whenever someone enters a URL with no file name specified. In other words, if you enable default documents, someone can enter a URL such as

```
http://musashi/test/
```

And PWS looks (by default) for files in the /TEST directory that have the names DEFAULT.HTM or DEFAULT.ASP. If it finds a file with one of those names, it returns it to the client's Web browser as a complete URL, like this:

```
http://musashi/test/default.htm
```

It is recommended that you first enable this feature. It saves your users from having to enter full URLs. However, it is also recommended that you add the two following default document names:

```
index.htm, index.html
```

Index with either .HTM or .HTML as a suffix is the most common name for a default HTML document. Most, if not all, users create HTML documents with these two suffixes. Remember, they should be separated by commas. Once you've done this, the Default Document(s) portion of the Advanced Options view should look like this:

☑ Ena̲ble Default Document

D̲efault Document(s): | Default.htm,Default.asp, index.htm |

The last two items you can configure with PWS include directory browsing and server logging. If you intend to house any documents within Web directories, which users should not see, then make sure that the check box entitled Allow Directory Browsing is deselected. Conversely, if you do not mind users browsing your Web directories with their Web browsers, then check that same box. When you enable directory browsing, users can view your Web directories as though they were file listings (see Figure 13-11).

Users can view individual pages by clicking on their file names. This is useful for corporate networks (or those behind a firewall) because it helps users locate files that may not be linked to a directory's INDEX.HTML page.

The second item concerns file logging. With PWS, you can create a log file that contains a listing of all server activity, including visits, requests, errors, and the like. To do this, click on the Save Web Site Activity Log check box. From that moment forward, PWS saves an NCSA-formatted log file.

**JARGON:**   NCSA stands for National Center for Supercomputing Applications. It was the birthplace of the graphical Web browser, NCSA Mosaic, from which Netscape produced its Navigator Web browser.

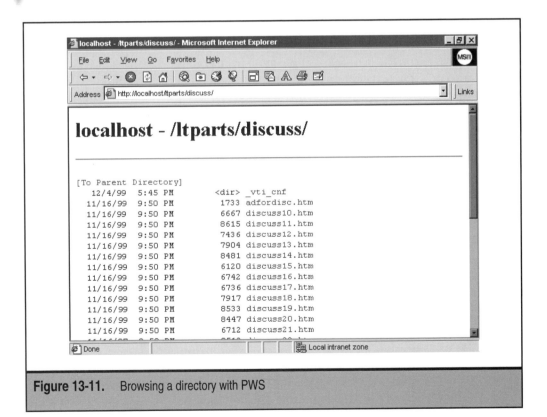

**Figure 13-11.**   Browsing a directory with PWS

Because the file is in NCSA format, you can use many different log analysis tools such as WebTrends to quickly analyze your server's performance and health. PWS creates a new file each month and stores it in the C:\WINDOWS\SYSTEM\LOGFILE\W3SPC1\ directory. Unless you are concerned with performance and stability issues, you should disable this setting as it can gobble up a lot of disk space.

> **RESOURCE:**  Looking for a log analyzer for your PWS server? Take a look through TUCOWS Interactive's online archive at http://tucows.xmission.com/log95.html.

# Creating a Web Service with PWS

Now that you've had a chance to go through all of the available server parameters, it's time to set up a Web service with PWS. It is a very quick procedure, and one that you'll find quite easy. The only catch is that you've got to have some content in order to publish it on your Web server.

## Creating Content

In the next chapter, a great deal of time is spent building content for your Web server, so this section just concentrates on creating one Web page for publication on PWS. If you already have some content created, just skip to the next section. The easiest way to build a Web page with Windows 98 is to open FrontPage Express, which is installed with Internet Explorer. You can access this application from your Start menu. Once you've got it open, just type some text such as a welcome message, adding any desired formatting. You should end up with a page that looks something like the one in Figure 13-12.

Now just click on the File menu and select Save As. This opens a Save As dialog box designed to work specifically with PWS, which should look something like this:

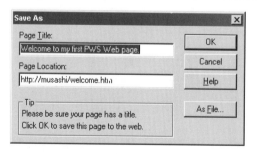

You can click on the OK button here to save this document to the root directory of your Web server. Note the page location (or URL). This root directory is where people will first go when viewing your Web server's content. In the next chapter, you'll create some sub-directories for specific content. In this example, it's http://musashi/ welcome.htm. If you click on the OK button, this is the URL you'll open in order to view the file. Or you can click on the As File button to save the file to a directory that is not a part of your Web server. For now, click on the As File button. This opens a traditional Windows Save As

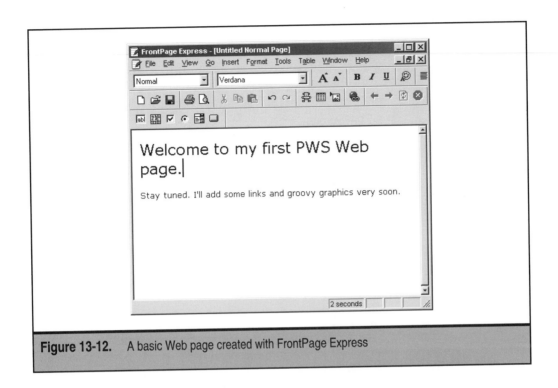

**Figure 13-12.** A basic Web page created with FrontPage Express

dialog box. To save this file to a new directory on the Web server, first make sure you're on the C:\ drive. Then double-click on the Webshare folder and double-click on the WWWROOT folder. Now, click on the New Folder button (the one with the sprite) and enter a folder name of "first." Once you've created this new folder, double-click on it and type WELCOME.HTM in the File name field. Now, click on the Save button. This saves a Web page named WELCOME.HTM to the folder first. You can now close FrontPage Express, if you wish.

## Adding Content to PWS

The last step is to add this file and folder to PWS. Open your Personal Web Manager from the System Tray and click on the home directory link from the Main view. This opens Windows 98's Explorer application (see Figure 13-13).

Notice that there's a new directory in the WWWROOT directory entitled "first." Also notice that a hand does not cradle it as with folders such as IISSAMPLES and SCRIPTS. This means that the Web server will not share this folder. If you were to try to open the file you just created, you'd receive an access denied message. To remedy this situation, right-click on the first folder and select Sharing from the resulting pop-up menu. This opens the traditional Windows 98 sharing tab within the Properties dialog box. As we

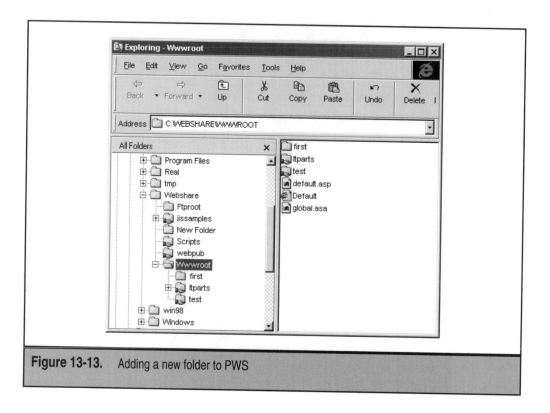

**Figure 13-13.** Adding a new folder to PWS

mentioned earlier, don't worry about the usual Sharing tab. Just click on the Web Sharing tab (see Figure 13-14).

This reveals a panel in which you can enable sharing for the first folder. To do so, click on the *Share this folder* radio button. The resulting Edit Alias dialog box should look something like this:

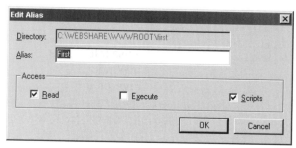

It tells PWS to create an alias for your new folder, making it a virtual folder. An alias is a name you assign to your new directory. This will be the new directory name that the

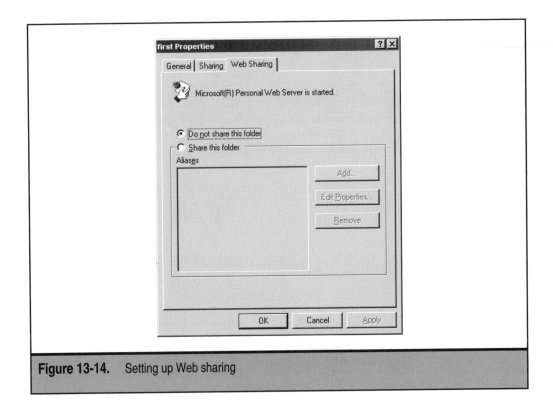

**Figure 13-14.**    Setting up Web sharing

outside world sees, and it often differs from the actual folder name. For example, you could give first the alias of myweb. In this way, instead of entering

```
http://localhost/first/welcome.htm
```

to get to your new page, users would enter

```
http://localhost/myweb/welcome.htm
```

This can be quite useful, as it allows you to use folders that reside beneath the Web server's root directory from any location on your Windows 98 file system. Because of this, you should be careful not to place any sensitive or private content in this directory structure. For more information on this aspect of virtual directories and aliases, refer to the next chapter. For now, enter a different alias for the first directory. Enter the name **myweb** in the Alias field. Before you click on the OK button, however, take a moment to set the security parameters for this new directory and its Web page. These are found at the bottom of the Alias dialog box under the Access heading. As mentioned earlier, those settings include Read, Execute, and Scripts. For this file, which is just an HTML page, you won't need to run any scripts or execute any applications, so deselect these check boxes.

However, you will need to allow users to read the contents of your new directory (namely WELCOME.HTM). So make sure the Read check box is selected before you click on the OK button.

> **SHORTCUT:**  If you need to make a change to this directory, you can do so by highlighting it from the Web Sharing tab and selecting Edit Properties. This opens the same Alias dialog box. Or you can do the same thing from the Personal Web Manager's Advanced view.

## Accessing New Content

Once you've created your Web Sharing alias, click on the OK button, which takes you back to the Windows 98 Explorer window. Just close this Window and open Internet Explorer. From here, type the following URL into the Address field and press the ENTER key:

```
http://localhost/myweb/welcome.htm
```

You should then see the Web page that you just created (see Figure 13-15).

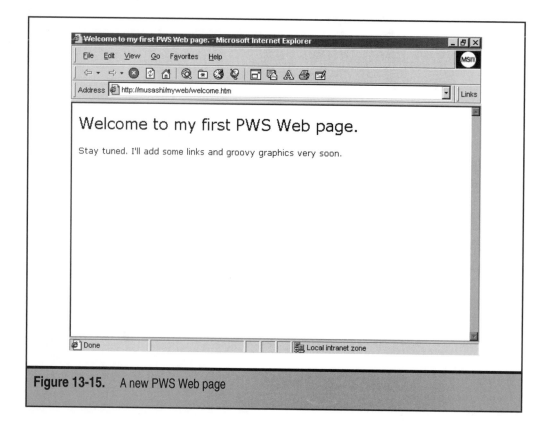

**Figure 13-15.**   A new PWS Web page

# COMING UP

That's all there is to setting up PWS and creating Web services. Of course, there are many subtleties left to master and features left to explore in publishing Web content with Windows 98. For example, with FrontPage Express, you can graphically build Web applications. With ActiveX controls and FrontPage Express Bots, you can easily add functionality to those Web pages. And the Home Page Wizard can take you step-by-step through the process of creating content and publishing it on PWS. In the next chapter, we'll dive headlong into these subjects, discussing their benefits and pitfalls, capabilities and dangers.

ETWORK
ROFESSIONAL'S
LIBRARY

# CHAPTER 14

# Publishing Information with Windows 98

**What's ahead:**

- Building Web content with the Home Page Wizard
- Building content with FrontPage Express
- Deploying content with FrontPage Express
- Deploying content with the Web Publishing Wizard

*"I am an acme of things accomplished, and I an encloser of things to be."*

—Walt Whitman, *Leaves of Grass*

In the last chapter, you learned how to set up and manage Web services on Windows 98 using Microsoft's Personal Web Server (PWS). But without content, those services are as useless as a movie projector without film. Before you or your users deploy Windows 98-based Web services, you must first create Web content, which is basically a meaningful collection of text, images, sounds, applications, and documents. This chapter is dedicated to building and deploying that content on Windows 98's PWS service. In doing so, we create individual Web pages, design and construct Web sites (which are just collections of Web pages), and deploy those Web sites. Along the way, we utilize PWS's built-in utilities, such as the Home Page Wizard, to build content; we use Windows 98's Web Publishing Wizard to deploy that content. With these tools, you learn how to set up a Web site with very little trouble. For those interested in building a Web site from the ground up, we also discuss the use of less-automated tools such as Microsoft's FrontPage Express for content creation and deployment.

Keep in mind that these tools and techniques are not designed to help you if you're working with large, enterprise-wide Web applications. They help you give Windows 98 users some direction in creating their own, simple Web services. For example, you should be able to show a user how to quickly set up either a personal or workgroup home page, containing simple content and limited interactivity. If you need to deploy a large Web application that relies upon corporate data, you should consult additional software. For example, you may want to invest in a full-powered Web server such as Netscape Communications Corporation's Enterprise Server or Microsoft Corporation's Internet Information Server (IIS). Likewise, you could purchase a high-end development tool such as Macromedia DreamWeaver or Microsoft Visual InterDev.

This chapter then is not a chapter about power Web programming or HTML techniques. This chapter is designed for those not familiar with Web development. Therefore, it gives you and your users step-by-step information on the best way to build and deploy Web content using the many tools that come with Windows 98. But it does not go into the many details of doing such. For example, we don't discuss HTML tags or non-PWS servers. You should be able to hand this chapter to a power-user or use this chapter yourself to quickly and easily get up and running with Web content on Windows 98.

# BUILDING WEB CONTENT

Although it sounds a bit obvious, the first step in publishing on the Web with Windows 98 is to create some content. It's a bit like making a phone call. Don't make a call unless you know what you want to say to the person on the other end of the line. Luckily, in today's climate of free and easy information sharing, that content is pretty easy to come by. Chances are, if you're reading this chapter, your department head or company CEO has tasked you with publishing information for a specific department or departments. For example, you may have been instructed to publish your human resources department's holiday schedule or insurance benefits. Conversely, if you are telecommuting from home, you may have been tasked with making your personal information available to your parent company at large. For example, you may have been asked to publish an office availability schedule or monthly reports. Either way, you've most likely got a good idea of what you want to publish.

You may already have a collection of Microsoft Word documents, some text files, perhaps a Microsoft Excel spreadsheet, some images, or even a database, all waiting to become a part of your Windows 98 Web site. But before you begin coding HTML or posting Web pages, however, you should first understand how Web content is organized. It's not as easy as you might think. Normally, users gain access to shared information by browsing a directory folder like the one shown in Figure 14-1.

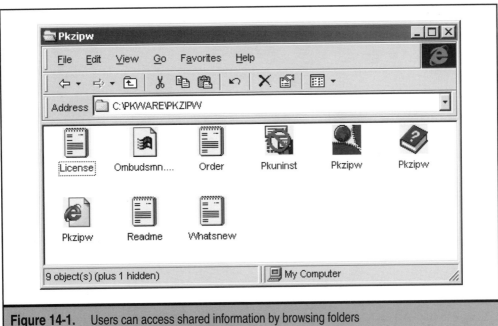

**Figure 14-1.**   Users can access shared information by browsing folders

But with the Web, users gain access to shared information through a nexus of interrelated items. Think of it as a giant spiderweb in which such items as Excel spreadsheets, text files, HTML files, images, and the like are all connected with one another. As in nature, this web can take on many different shapes and configurations. Most often, however, it looks a lot like a wagon wheel in which all (or most) items link back to a central item—the hub, you could say—as shown in Figure 14-2.

This central item is a Web page. It is often referred to as a *home page* because it is the home base for all other pages and usually the single page through which most people enter a Web site. As you might imagine, this page is built with HTML, and it links directly to other HTML pages, images, spreadsheets, and the like (see Figure 14-3). The connection between the home page and the outer pages is called a *hypertext link*. When users click on a hypertext link on the home page, they are transported to the Web page, document, image, or what have you that is connected to that hypertext link.

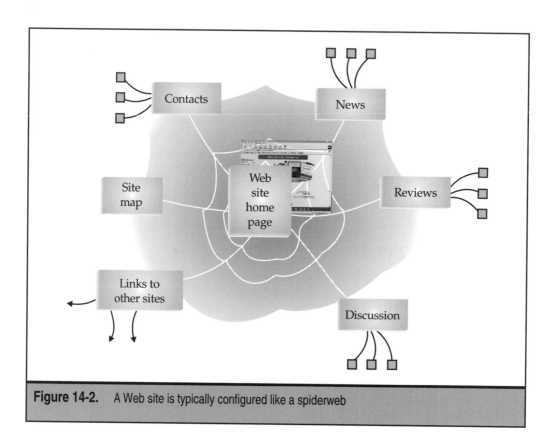

**Figure 14-2.** A Web site is typically configured like a spiderweb

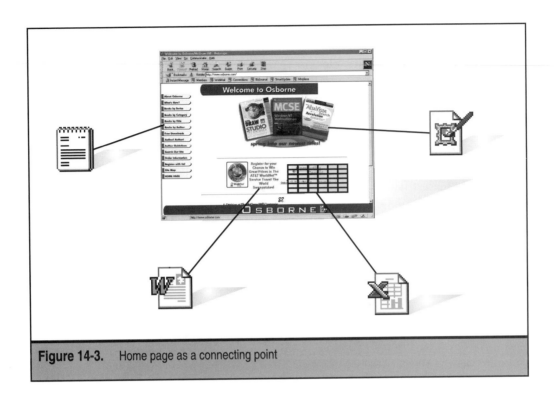

**Figure 14-3.**    Home page as a connecting point

In the remainder of this section, you'll learn how to build a home page and link it to a number of example items. With Windows 98, there are two software packages, each designed to step you through the process of creating and maintaining content. These packages are:

▼ PWS Home Page Wizard

▲ FrontPage Express

Both tools help you build a home page without having to write any HTML. The PWS Home Page Wizard comes with PWS and provides you with a menu-driven interface for creating a home page. The great thing about the Home Page Wizard is that you don't need to know anything about Web page design or hypertext links. Just follow its directions, and it creates a fully functioning Web page. Its only drawback is that the end result is not very feature-rich. It only comes with canned interactivity, such as a guest book and a drop box for e-mail messages.

FrontPage Express comes with Internet Explorer (IE) and starts where the Home Page Wizard leaves off. Like the Home Page Wizard, it helps you build a home page (or any other Web page) without requiring any HTML know-how. However, it gives you the flexibility to modify an existing Web page. It also enables you to add custom applications. For example, you can use FrontPage Express to build a Web page containing an ActiveX control that displays a graphical clock.

In the following sections, a home page is built using the Home Page Wizard. Then the page is modified with FrontPage Express, adding additional functionality.

## Using the Home Page Wizard

To get the ball rolling, we'll build a home page with PWS's Home Page Wizard. This requires, of course, that PWS be installed on your system. If you haven't already done so, read Chapter 13 before continuing. Once installed, you can access PWS from your System Tray on your desktop. The System Tray icon looks like a hand holding a page. Right-click on that icon and select Properties from the pop-up menu. The Personal Web Manager opens; it is the main management tool for PWS (see Figure 14-4).

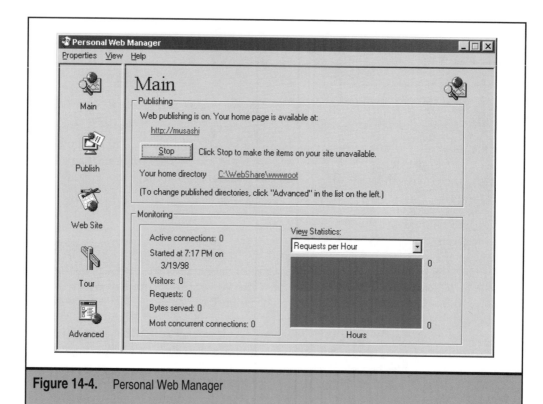

**Figure 14-4.** Personal Web Manager

You'll spend more time with Personal Web Manager later in this chapter when publishing and managing a Web site is discussed. For now, open the Home Page Wizard by clicking on the Web Site icon, which sits in the left-hand column. This opens a new window in the right pane section, as shown in Figure 14-5.

Begin creating your home page by clicking on the button containing two arrows. This replaces the current pane with the next pane, where you are asked to choose the template from which to create your home page (see Figure 14-6).

**RESOURCE:** Notice that now there is a back arrow button to go along with the forward arrow button. If you accidentally move ahead, or you find yourself needing to back up in the process, just click on this back arrow button.

The available options are:

▼  Looseleaf

■  Journal

▲  Gunmetal

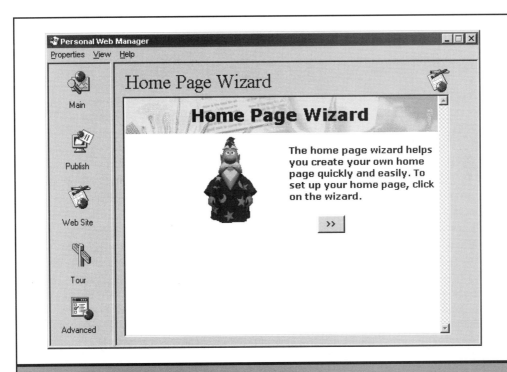

**Figure 14-5.**   Home Page Wizard in action

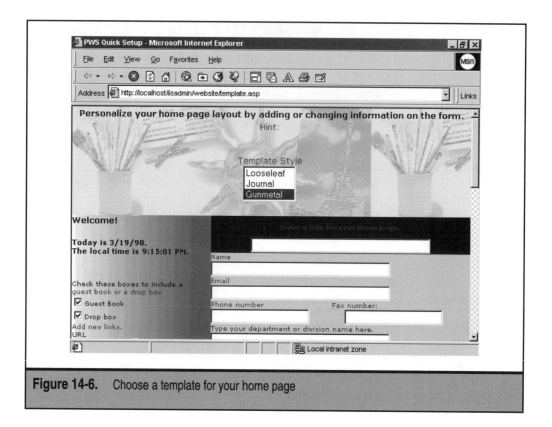

**Figure 14-6.**    Choose a template for your home page

These templates form the overall look and feel of your home page (its background color, default images, and the like). The one you choose of course depends on your personal tastes. But don't worry if you end up with something you don't like; you can always change it later. Highlight your choice and press the forward arrow button. This opens another pane where you have to choose whether or not to use a guest book. Part of PWS' allure is its ability to make interactive applications development a snap. If you select to create the guest book, PWS automatically generates the code necessary for your home page to gather personal information from your visitors and store it in an easy-to-use database. To see the Home Page Wizard's full capabilities, add the guest book to your Web site by clicking the Yes radio button on this page and then click on the forward arrow button. You won't have to do anything else in order to employ your new guest book. When you finish with the Wizard, the guest book will simply appear, ready to use.

***SOAPBOX:*** While this Wizard can help you set up Web page interactivity automatically, it can only work with Microsoft's PWS or IIS. It uses what is called Active Server Pages (ASP) in conjunction with FrontPage Server Extensions, both of which are Microsoft-only technologies. If you are building Web pages for other servers such as Netscape's Enterprise Server, you'll need to resort to more traditional, and difficult, development methods such as Common Gateway Interface (CGI) scripts, JavaScript/VB Script applications, and the like in order to create interactive Web pages.

The next pane asks for a very similar decision regarding a drop box. Like the guest book, this ready-to-run application allows your users to interact with your home page. In this case, they are able to post private messages to you directly from your home page. Again, instruct the Home Page Wizard to build in the drop box by clicking on the Yes radio button and clicking on the forward arrow button.

That's all there is to creating your home page's design. All that remains is for you to enter your personal information (the text that appears on your home page). When the next pane appears, click on the forward arrow button. This opens your Web browser (IE) containing the configuration information you just entered along with a number of form fields.

The great part about the Home Page Wizard is that from this point on, you can not only change your earlier configuration decisions, you can see the results in real time. Try it. Where you see the Template Style (templates) box toward the top of the page, click on an alternate template. The entire Web page redraws itself to reflect your change. Notice on the left side of the window that you can also change your earlier decisions regarding a guest book and drop box. If you don't want one or the other, just deselect the appropriate check box.

Just below those check boxes, also notice the field entitled Add new links. Here you can add your favorite Uniform Resource Locators (URLs). If you like LAN Times Online, for example, you can append the following to the text within the first field:

```
www.lantimes.com/
```

In the next field, you can type a description of that URL (such as "LAN Times Online"). When you're done, just click on the add link button. This clears the fields and allows you to enter more URLs in the same manner. All that remains is for you to fill in all of the fields on the right side of the window, where the wizard asks you to enter a page title, your contact information, and miscellaneous paragraph items. Don't worry about filling these out in their entirety. They are not required. Just fill them out as you see fit.

***CAUTION:*** In using the guest book and drop box and in filling out this form, bear in mind that the information you post on or gather from your home page may not be in line with your corporate security and information privacy statement. If your company has such policies, before allowing your users to fill out this form, make sure you educate them regarding what they can and cannot gather or disseminate.

## Accessing Your Home Page

When you've finished entering your information, scroll to the bottom of the window and click on the button entitled "Enter new changes," and your new home page appears inside IE (see Figure 14-7).

Pay close attention to the Address field in IE. This contains the URL for your new home page. You need to enter that URL the next time you want to access this page.

> **CAUTION:** The great thing about the Home Page Wizard is that it automatically deploys your Web page on PWS. Normally, you must build a Web page and then deploy it on the appropriate Web server. However, if you wish to add other pages to your PWS, then you must deploy those files manually. For more on this practice, jump ahead to the next section, entitled "Using FrontPage Express."

To automate the process of loading your new home page, you have two options: You can add this page to your Favorites list, or you can set it as your default Web page. To add

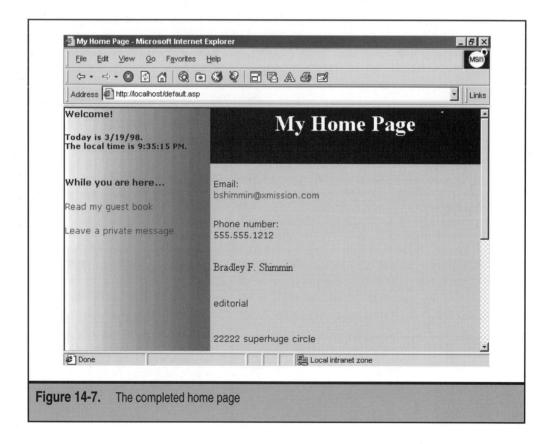

**Figure 14-7.** The completed home page

it to your Favorites list, click on the Favorites pull-down menu and select the item labeled Add to Favorites. On the ensuing dialog box, click on the OK button. The next time you want to access this page, you can select it from the lower portion of the Favorites pull-down menu (see Figure 14-8).

To make this page your default Web page (so that IE automatically opens this page each time it starts up), click on the View menu and select Internet Options. This opens IE's configuration dialog box. Here, click on the Use Current button from the home page section at the top of the dialog box. This automatically replaces the currently listed URL with that of your new home page (see Figure 14-9). When you're done, click on the OK button. Now each time you start IE, your new home page appears automatically.

In order to make your new home page visible to others, you must make this URL publicly available. How this is done depends on the protocols set in motion by your company. Some maintain mailing lists to which users can publish URLs for home pages. Others simply allow users to send company- or workgroup-wide e-mail messages

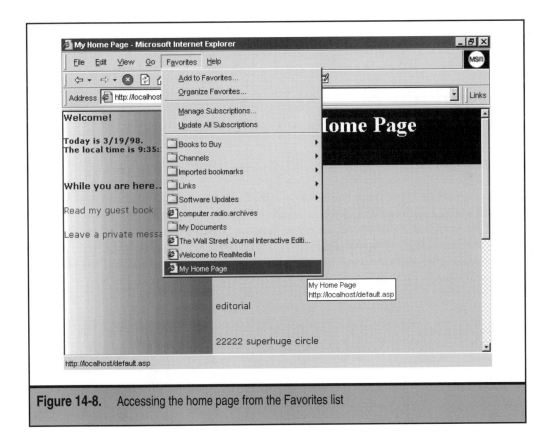

**Figure 14-8.**   Accessing the home page from the Favorites list

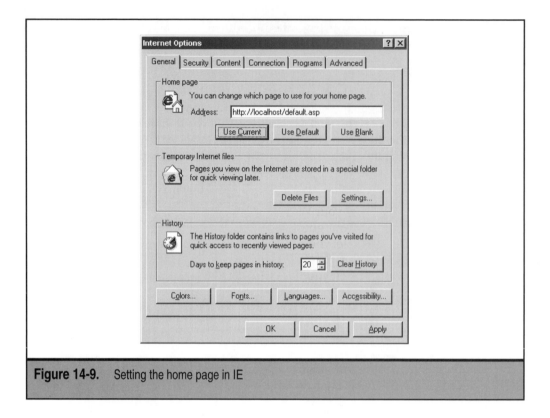

**Figure 14-9.**    Setting the home page in IE

containing the URLs. No matter how you get the URL out, you should bear in mind a few gotchas. For one, if your company is using the Dynamic Host Configuration Protocol (DHCP) to assign TCP/IP addresses in conjunction with a Domain Name System (DNS) server to resolve TCP/IP addresses with machine names, you must make sure that you publish your URL with the host name for your computer, not its TCP/IP address. For example, instead of publishing:

```
204.151.55.177
```

you could publish:

```
mycomputer.mycompany.com
```

Conversely, if your company does not use a DNS server and uses static TCP/IP addresses, you should send out your machine's static TCP/IP address, such as:

```
204.151.55.177
```

## Working with Your Home Page

Once you've created your home page, you can use the Personal Web Manager's Home Page Wizard to maintain your Web page. Basically, it lets you edit your page and interact with your guest book and drop box. Access the Home Page Wizard as you did previously. This time, instead of displaying the Microsoft Agent (wizard), you see a page with three links:

▼ Edit your home page

■ View your guest book

▲ Open your drop box

These tools let you modify your Web page, see any messages that have been left for you, and see who has signed your guest book, respectively. If you click on the "Edit your home page" button, for example, you see the same window as shown in Figure 14-6. The only difference is that all your previously entered information is available to you for editing. If you click on the "Open your drop box" button, you are confronted with a pane that looks a bit like a simple e-mail client, containing any outstanding messages (see Figure 14-10).

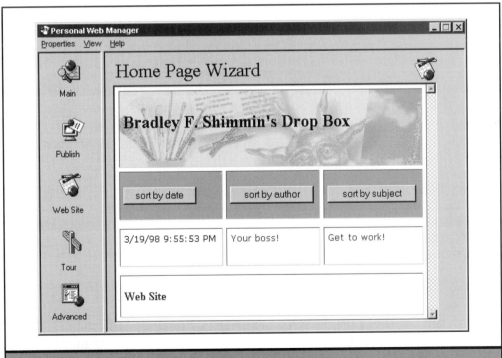

**Figure 14-10.** Reading e-mail from your drop box

By clicking on the author's name or subject line, you can view the entire message and delete or respond to it as you see fit.

# Using FrontPage Express

Although the Home Page Wizard can help users publish a personal Web page quickly and easily, it only goes so far in accommodating all of the information your organization may need to publish. That's where FrontPage Express comes in. As a rapid application development (RAD) tool for Web page construction, FrontPage Express lets users build and customize Web pages simply by dragging and dropping graphics, text, and applications. To give you an idea of FrontPage Express's capabilities, consider that FrontPage Express can:

▼ *Open and save your work directly to a Web server.* You won't need to download a Web page, edit it, and then upload it to the Web server in order to test its functionality.

■ *Manage ActiveX controls and Java applets.* You can download these small, downloadable applications and embed them in your Web pages without writing any code.

■ *Provide simplified interactivity through WebBots.* Included with FrontPage Express, these WebBots are pre-built applications such as a time stamp and search facility.

■ *Embed sounds, video clips, even PowerPoint animation.* These features can be dropped right into a Web page with no programming at all.

▲ *Simplify both Visual Basic (VB) Script and JavaScript application development.*

And it can do all of this within a *what you see is what you get* (WYSIWYG) development environment in which you get to see how your Web page looks while you work on it.

While the decision to use FrontPage Express is fairly simple (mostly because the product comes with Windows 98), be aware that there are many other Web development tool options out there. Some comparable tools include those shown in Table 14-1.

With these tools, you can create the same content you could with Microsoft's FrontPage Express. There are slight differences in feature-sets and focus (DreamWeaver, for example, targets cross-browser development), but the real difference comes in price. FrontPage Express comes as a free Windows 98 accessory, while these tools range in price from $99.00 for HoTMetaL Pro to over $400 for DreamWeaver.

## Editing Your Home Page

To get started with FrontPage Express, click on the Start menu, select Programs, Internet Explorer, and finally FrontPage Express. This starts the program (see Figure 14-11).

Notice the full cadre of toolbars? Much like Microsoft Word, you've got buttons for printing, saving, and opening documents. Likewise, you've got buttons for formatting text (e.g., setting bold, italic or underlining), changing indentation, and creating bullet or

| Vendor | Tool | Benefit |
|--------|------|---------|
| Macromedia | DreamWeaver | Powerful cross-browser with Dynamic HTML support |
| Adobe | PageMill | Simple, Mac-like interface for WYSIWYG development |
| SoftQuad | HoTMetaL Pro | Powerful HTML validation as well as strong WYSIWYG capabilities |

**Table 14-1.**    Web Development Tools

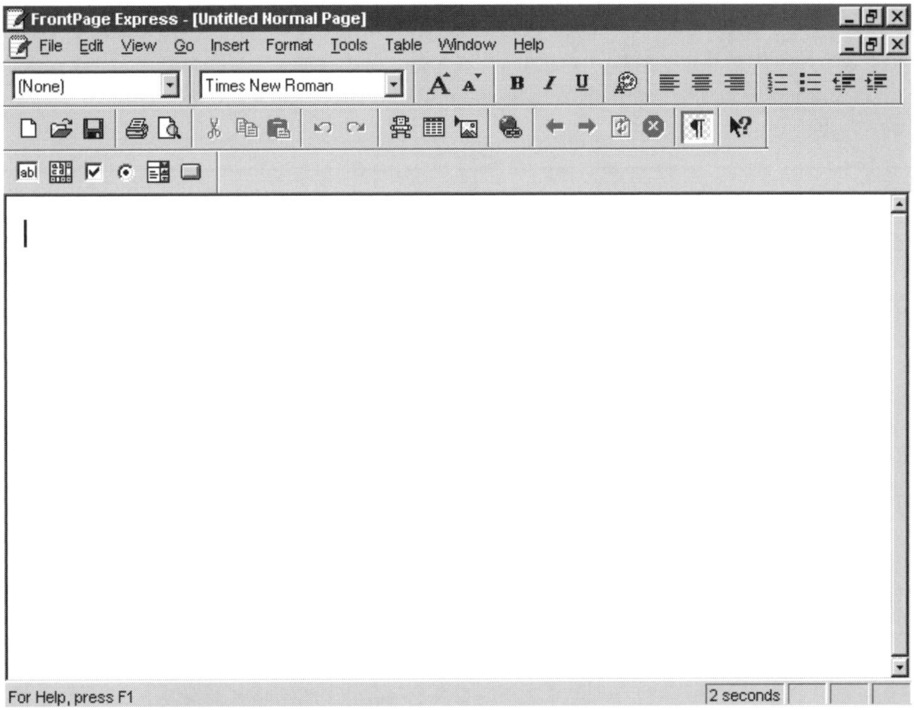

**Figure 14-11.**    FrontPage Express

numbered lists. One of the truly great Microsoft Word-esque features of the FrontPage Express toolbar is its style and font pull-down boxes. With them, you can easily select a section of text and change its style (making it a heading, address, bullet list, and so forth) and font (making it Times Roman, Verdana, etc.) like so:

Don't be surprised if your Web page does not look the same on all browsers. Though most browsers are capable of displaying the same basic set of fonts such Times Roman and Arial, not all can support unique fonts like Verdana. In these situations, the browser simply falls back to what it thinks is the closest font.

Now it's time to open your home page. Click on the File menu and select Open. This opens the Open File dialog box (see Figure 14-12), which asks you to open a Web page either from a file or from a location.

If you choose to open a Web page from a file, FrontPage Express acts just like a regular editor (such as Microsoft Word). You can open the file and save it to disk. But in order to view that page on your Web server, you have to then copy that file to your Web server. Conversely, if you open a Web page from a location, you are instructing FrontPage Express to open that file as it resides on your local Web server. This means that when you make changes and save them, those changes are automatically visible to everyone who has access to your Web server.

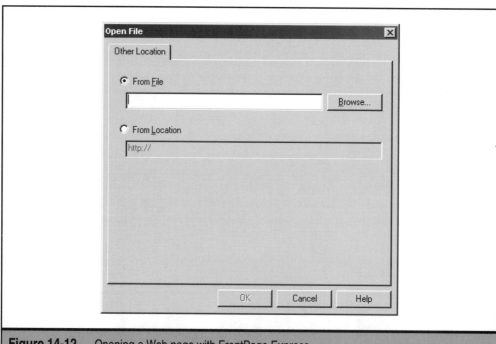

**Figure 14-12.** Opening a Web page with FrontPage Express

*SHORTCUT:* Opening a file from a location does not limit you to your local Web server. You can also open Web pages from Web servers running on other, remote machines. The only catch is that first you must have access to that Web server, and second that server must be either Microsoft Internet Information Server (IIS) or PWS.

For small Web sites that do not have a large viewing audience, opening a Web page directly from the server is optimal. It saves your users from going through additional complexities in delivering their Web content to a Web server. However, if there is a large number of people accessing your Web servers, you may want to take the extra time to show your users how to edit files locally, where they can check them for errors before uploading those files to a production Web server.

For now, open your home page right from your local Web server. To do this, just click on the From Location button on the Open File dialog box (see Figure 14-12), and enter the following URL:

```
http://localhost/default.asp
```

When you're done, click on the OK button. Your home page appears inside FrontPage Express, looking almost identical to that which you viewed through IE (see Figure 14-13).

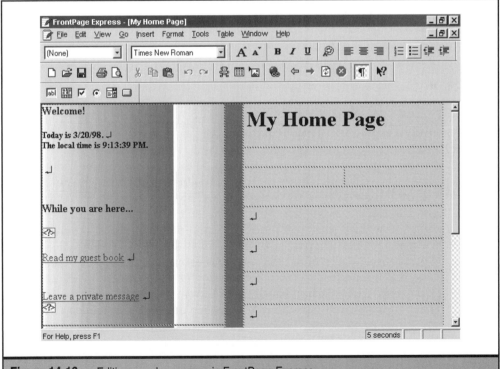

**Figure 14-13.** Editing your home page in FrontPage Express

The only difference is that here, in FrontPage Express, you can see the underlying structure of the Web page such as its paragraph marks, table borders, and HTML markup.

**JARGON:** What's HTML markup? Well, it's HTML that is not directly supported by FrontPage Express. While FrontPage Express supports HTML version 3.2, there are many non-standard and emerging standard HTML tags that you may want to use when building your Web pages. For example, where <font size=2> is acceptable to HTML 3.2, something like <font style="font-family: verdana;font-size:10pt"> is not. But as you might guess, the second of the two is preferable as it sets an absolute font size and absolute font face.

It's time to get to work on this page and add some text. Click in the first box beneath the text that reads My Home Page (see Figure 14-13). This is the first field in an HTML table. Next, type the following text:

```
Click here to see what I'm working on.
```

When you're done, highlight that text, just as you would when working in Microsoft Word, and click on the bold and italic buttons. Notice how your text changes as you press the buttons. If you don't like the highlighted text in bold, just click on the bold button again, and it will return to italics, like so:

*Click here to see what I'm working on.*

You can do virtually anything you want to this text, including changing its font. To do so, click on the down arrow button on the font pull-down menu and select something like Verdana.

## Creating a Second Web Page

When you're done experimenting with the look of this text, click elsewhere in the page to deselect it and then re-select just the words "Click here." We're going to create a hypertext link with this text that takes readers to a second page that contains a list of your current projects. With these words highlighted, click on the Insert pull-down menu and then select Hyperlink. This opens the Create Hyperlink dialog box (see Figure 14-14).

Take a good look at this dialog box. With it, you can make links to a variety of objects. For example, by changing the Hyperlink Type pull-down menu selection, you can generate an e-mail message, connect to a news server, download a file via FTP, or just open a local file (such as a Microsoft Excel spreadsheet or Word document). You can also use this dialog box to link the text to other locations on the same Web page. For the purpose of the current example, use this dialog box to create a new Web page. To do this, just click on the New Page tab. This reveals the New Page panel, which asks for a page title, URL, and target frame. Where it requests a page title, enter something like "Current Projects." Where it asks for a URL, enter the following text:

```
current.htm
```

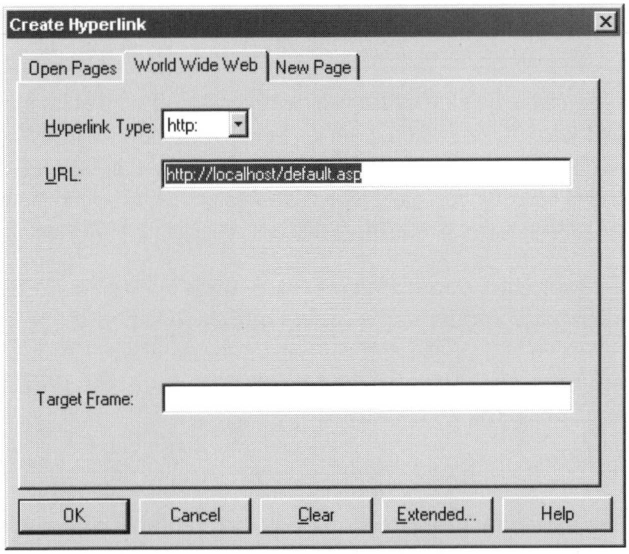

**Figure 14-14.** Creating a hypertext link

Now click on the OK button. This opens a small dialog box in which you can create your new page from existing templates. As you become adept at creating Web pages with FrontPage Express, you'll find this feature quite useful as it saves you from having to repeat many steps when creating Web pages. It also helps you create consistency across multiple Web pages. To create a plain Web page, just highlight the Normal Page selection and click on the OK button. This opens a blank document in FrontPage Express. Don't worry about your home page. It is still open. Just click on the Window pull-down menu and select it from the list of available Web pages. Now return to your new Web page and enter the following text:

```
Reading Ulysses

Playing fetch with my dogs

Watching the NCAA championships

Listening to Depeche Mode
```

Highlight this text and click on the Bullets button. Make any additional formatting changes you desire. When you're done, click on the Save button, switch back to your home page via the Window pull-down menu, and save it as well. Now you can view your handiwork directly from a Web browser.

**CAUTION:** If you receive an error message indicating that your current file cannot be saved to the Web server, don't worry. Often, when a server like PWS is busy, it cannot accommodate such requests. You can simply try again. If the problem persists, however, select Save As from the File pull-down menu and save the document to a local directory. Then skip to the next section entitled "Deploying Web Content" to see how to move those files back to the Web server.

Assuming you've set your home page as the default Web page in IE, you'll see your newly modified home page appear in the main window when you open the browser (see Figure 14-15).

If you did not set your home page as the default Web page, enter the following URL in the Address field and press the ENTER key:

```
http://localhost/default.asp
```

Notice in Figure 14-15 how the line of text you entered now appears beneath the text, "My Home Page." Also notice how the first two words appear in blue (unless you've modified IE's default settings). If you click on these words, you are transported to the Web page you just created. It's that easy.

# DEPLOYING WEB CONTENT

With FrontPage Express and the Home Page Wizard, you can help your users quickly and easily build Web content. That is their strength. But it is also their weakness. You see, the Home Page Wizard can only work with one Web page, your home page. And FrontPage Express cannot work with complex Web pages away from the Web server. That is, if you've created Wizard applications, you cannot test those applications anywhere but on the PWS server. However, there are three techniques at your disposal that can help your users get content into a Web server's file structure.

▼ Edit pages directly on the Web server with FrontPage Express and the Home Page Wizard.

■ Edit pages locally and deploy them to the Web server using FrontPage Express and the Home Page Wizard.

▲ Edit pages locally and deploy them to the Web server automatically with the Publishing Wizard.

The first technique has already been covered in this chapter. The latter two are explained here, along with a discussion of the benefits and drawbacks of each.

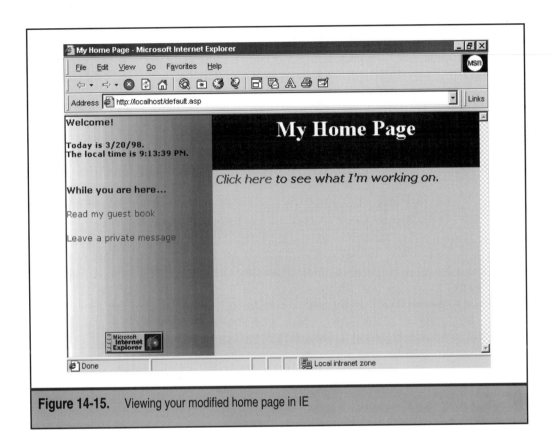

**Figure 14-15.**   Viewing your modified home page in IE

# Deploying Web Pages with FrontPage Express

A testament to FrontPage Express's flexibility is that you can use it to deploy Web pages directly to your Web server from anywhere. You simply treat them as regular files, opening them from Windows 98's file system as though they were regular files and save them to the Web server as Web pages. Why is this important? Well, in some cases, you may already have a Web page somewhere else on your file system, which you want to edit and then place on your local Web server. With this technique, you can just open a file (or create a new file) and then use the Save As option from the File pull-down menu to save that file to your Web server's file system. You can also work directly with Web pages that are already present on your Web server's file system. For example, if you have created a new Web page and saved it to the Web server, you may need to modify a file that already resides on the Web server, adding a hypertext link between the two.

## Creating and Deploying a New Web Page

To begin, create a new Web page with FrontPage Express. Click on the File pull-down menu and select New. In the resulting dialog box, highlight Normal Page and click on the OK button. This opens a blank document. Next, enter the following text:

```
Gazing out the window,

"All that meets the eye:
brown plains rising and falling,
rising and falling."

--Seishi Yamaguchi
```

You can format this text to suit your personal tastes. When you're done, click on the File menu and select Save As. This opens the Save As dialog box, which asks for a page title and page location. Forget about these and just click on the As File button in the lower right corner of the dialog box. This opens the traditional Windows Save As File dialog box. Here, navigate to the C:\webshare\wwwroot\ directory. This directory is called the root directory for your Web server. Those who access your Web server can only see documents in this directory and its subdirectories. They cannot see anything in the C:\ or C:\webshare directories.

**CAUTION:** If you have trouble locating this directory, don't worry. PWS's file system can reside anywhere on your hard disk. If it is not in C:\webshare, try C:\inetpub. If that doesn't work, manually browse your hard disk, looking for the directory called wwwroot.

Name this file GAZING.HTM and click on the Save button. That's all there is to creating a new document and publishing it to your Web server. You can view this Web page by opening Internet Explorer (IE), entering the following URL in the Address field, and pressing the RETURN key (see Figure 14-16).

```
http://localhost/gazing.htm
```

## Working with Files on Your Web Server

Although it's pretty easy to open your new Web page by entering its URL directly in IE, it's not very efficient, especially if you've got a large number of such files located on your hard disk. That's why the Web relies upon the concept of hypertext links to connect related documents. In essence, to make your new Web page more useful, you need to connect it with your existing Web content (Web pages that are already on your Web server or documents already on your PC). To accomplish this, use the same FrontPage Express technique to open an existing Web page directly and edit it, adding a hypertext link to the new document.

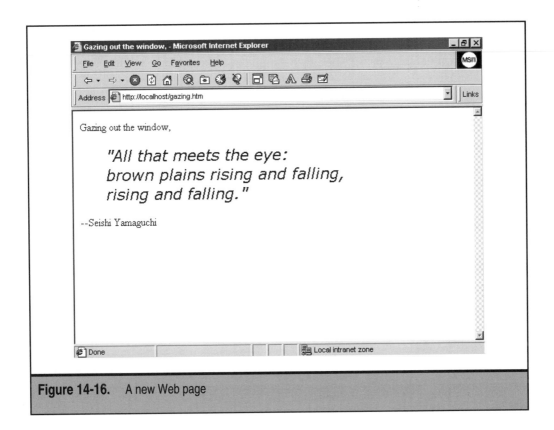

**Figure 14-16.**   A new Web page

Close all open files in FrontPage Express and click on the Open button. Instead of clicking on the From Location radio button, click on the From File radio button and click on the Browse button. This opens a traditional Windows Open File dialog box. Navigate to the C:\webshare\wwwroot\ directory and open the file named CURRENT.HTM.

Now you can work with CURRENT.HTM directly without having to save it through the Web server. To test this notion out, just add the following line of text to the end of your list of current activities.

```
Gazing out the window
```

When you're done, highlight the word Gazing and click on the Insert pull-down menu and select Hyperlink. This opens the Create Hyperlink dialog box (just as in Figure 14-14). Click on the World Wide Web tab and enter the following in the URL field:

```
gazing.htm
```

Make sure that the Hyperlink Type is set to Other, and click on the OK button to finish. This returns you to CURRENT.HTM. Notice that now the word Gazing is underlined in blue. To test the success of your new hypertext link, click on the Save button and then open IE. Just as before, from your home page, click on the Click here hypertext link. This opens your CURRENT.HTM Web page complete with the new item (see Figure 14-17).

**CAUTION:** If you don't see the Gazing hypertext link, it could be because your Web browser has cached CURRENT.HTM. This means that its contents have been stored locally in order to improve the performance of your Web browser. To clear this page from cache and load the newly modified CURRENT.HTM file, just click on the View pull-down menu and select Refresh.

Click on the Gazing hypertext link, and your new Web page (GAZING.HTM) should appear as in Figure 14-17.

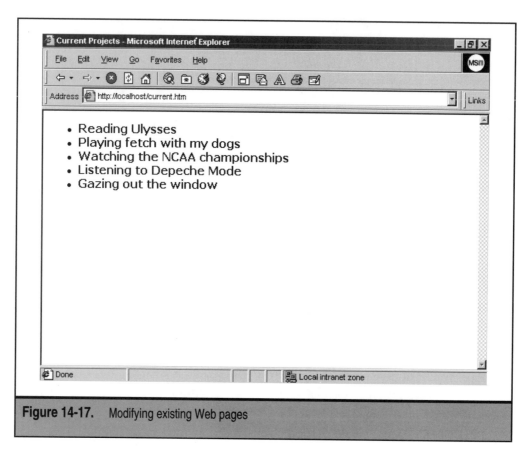

**Figure 14-17.** Modifying existing Web pages

## Limitations of FrontPage Express

The only problem with this approach is that it does not allow you to use FrontPage Express's full WSIWYG capabilities. If you have content that uses subdirectories for applications and images, then those items drop out of the FrontPage Express interface.

This happens because most Web content relies upon a directory structure similar to the following:

▼  C:\webshare\wwwroot\ (for the home page and other Web pages)

■  C:\webshare\wwwroot\images\ (for graphics files)

▲  C:\webshare\wwwroot\cgi-bin\ (for Web applications)

When your Web pages reference one of these subdirectories, it does so using the Web's document root. For example, a hypertext link to a graphic file might look like this: /images/someimages.gif. When you open a file like this outside of a Web server, FrontPage Express doesn't know where to find those files (see Figure 14-18).

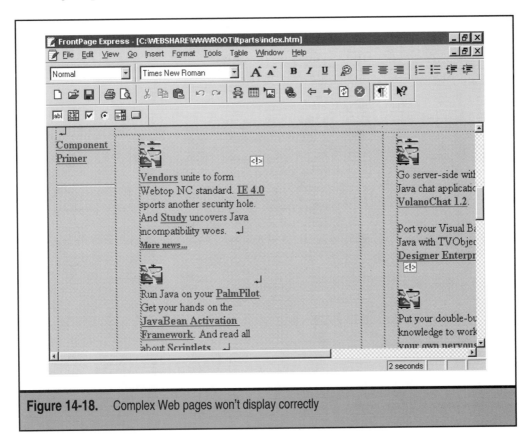

**Figure 14-18.**  Complex Web pages won't display correctly

For this reason, it is recommended that you use this technique only with small, simple Web pages. If you want to work with a file like CURRENT.HTM, for example, this approach works best simply because it is faster (at saving your changes) and more reliable (it won't give you as many errors as when you work directly with the Web server). But for large-scale projects, FrontPage Express cannot overcome its inability to work with Web pages away from the Web server.

Though not available for free with Windows 98, however, there are many tools available that will help you overcome these limitations. Table 14-2 shows a few examples, ranging in complexity and price. These tools let you edit your content away from the Web server and then automatically post that material to the Web server.

| Tool Name | Description | Availability |
|---|---|---|
| Microsoft FrontPage 98 | This is basically an upgrade from FrontPage Express. It allows you to use the same WYSIWYG environment while adding support for larger, off-line projects through link checking, and auto-deployment tools. | Price: $149 URL: http://www.microsoft.com/products/prodref/571_ov.htm |
| Macromedia DreamWeaver | This is the most advanced and most expensive tool available. It supports WYSIWYG and off-line editing, but it also automates JavaScript and VBScript development. And it can simultaneously deploy content that is tuned for multiple types of Web browser. | Price: $499 URL: http://www.macromedia.com/software/dreamweaver/ |

**Table 14-2.**   Advanced Web Development Tools

| Tool Name | Description | Availability |
|---|---|---|
| Microsoft Visual InterDev | Visual InterDev is the Cadillac of Web development tools. Supporting WYSIWYG editing, link verification, and auto-deployment tools, it can handle the largest projects. It also integrates with Microsoft's other development tools such as Visual J++ and Visual Basic. | Price: $499 URL: http://www.microsoft .com/products/prodref/ 177_ov.htm |

**Table 14-2.**   Advanced Web Development Tools (*continued*)

# Using the Web Publishing Wizard

Using FrontPage Express can help you easily add new Web files to your Web server. But it can't handle multiple document types. That is, it can't help you publish documents, spreadsheets, images, and the like. For example, suppose your boss wanted you to deploy a collection of Microsoft Word documents for others in your company to download and view. How would you get those into your Web server? You would certainly have to look beyond FrontPage Express or the Home Page Wizard.

Luckily, PWS comes with the Publishing Wizard, an easy-to-use tool designed to help you publish collections of documents to your Web server. This tool is designed to help you deploy multiple, heterogeneous documents to your local Web server. That is its strength. You can simply point it at a collection of files in one or more directories and it automatically posts copies of the files in those directories to your Web server's file system. It's great because it saves you and your users the complexities involved in manually moving files to your Web server, and the hassle and risk of manually copying the files for deployment. Note, however, that the Publishing Wizard does not change your files in moving them to the Web server. It simply posts copies of them to the Web server. If you post an Excel document, it remains an Excel document. When used in conjunction with the Home Page Wizard, it can also help you easily link these new files to your home page. Its weakness is that it only works with a local PWS service. You can't use it to deploy your content to a remote server, as you can with a more manual tool such as

FrontPage Express or the Windows Explorer. Moreover, you must select one file at a time with the Publishing Wizard. You can't simply point it at a directory to publish its entire contents.

You access and work with the Publishing Wizard just as you would with the Home Page Wizard. Open the PWS main window and click on the Publish icon in the right-hand pane. This opens an interface that looks just like the Home Page Wizard. Click on the forward arrow button to get going. This opens a new left-hand pane containing a dialog box in which you can choose which files to publish on your Web server (see Figure 14-19).

The first piece of information you must provide is the location of the files you wish to publish. You can type your path directly into the Path field (such as C:\MY DOCUMENTS\MYDOC.DOC), but it is easier to click on the Browse button. This opens a dialog box similar to Windows' File Open dialog box, but this one uses Web technologies. Instead of double-clicking on a folder or file, you single-click. All you want to accomplish here is to select the files you want to publish one at a time.

**Figure 14-19.** Adding files with the Web Publishing Wizard

> **CAUTION:** Of course, you may have multiple files and folders that are ready for deployment. This tool can handle multiple files and folders; however, as stated previously, it can only handle one file at a time. This problem is tackled in the section entitled "Manually Deploying Web Content," later in this chapter.

For each file, you simply have to follow a series of steps. Just highlight the file of your choice and click on the OK button. For our example, we chose C:\MYPROJECTS\, a folder in which we posted several documents, including a Microsoft Word document, Excel spreadsheet, PowerPoint presentation, and a text file. Then, follow these steps:

1. Once you've selected a file, add a description of this file in the field labeled Description.
2. Click on the Add button from the main Publishing Wizard pane. This transfers your selection to the large field labeled Files to publish.
3. If you would like to deploy another file, just repeat this process.
4. If you add a file erroneously, just highlight it in the File to publish field and click on the Remove button.
5. When you've selected all of the files you wish to publish, click on the forward arrow button.

The Publishing Wizard then tells you which files it published to your Web server.

## Connecting Newly Deployed Content

Getting content to your Web server is only half of the battle. Just as you discovered in creating and deploying Web pages with FrontPage Express, you must connect your new pages with hypertext links. You can do so with FrontPage Express as detailed in the earlier section called "Working with Files on Your Web Server." For example, you could open the DEFAULT.ASP Web page and manually add links to your newly deployed documents. The only drawback to this approach is that you won't be able to use the full WYSIWYG capabilities of FrontPage Express. Again, this requires a tool such as Microsoft FrontPage 98 or Macromedia DreamWeaver. We suggest that you simply use the Home Page Wizard to edit your home page.

To accomplish this task, open the Home Page Wizard and click on the hypertext link called Edit your home page. As before, this opens your Web page in an IE window, from which you can edit your home page in a WYSIWYG environment as shown back in Figure 14-6. On the left side of the window, click in the URL field within the Add new links section. Now type the name of the first file you added, appending it to the existing text, HTTP://. For example, you could type something like

```
localhost/thoughts.doc
```

In the next field labeled Description, type a quick text description of the link. When you're done, click on the Add Link button. Do the same for the remaining files. In the end, you should have a list of your file descriptions (see Figure 14-20).

If you make a mistake, or you don't like one of your entries, just highlight the suspect entry and click on the Remove Link button. When you finish, scroll to the bottom of the window and click on the button labeled Enter New Changes. Your home page appears with the newly added links (see Figure 14-21). If you click on one of these links, such as "Read my thoughts," you'll download (or open) the appropriate file.

Notice in Figure 14-20 how we've denoted the document type for each link? This is an important courtesy, as it lets those who visit your Web page know what applications they need in order to download and view these documents.

## Working with Deployed Files

Although the Publishing Wizard does have some drawbacks, it does have one very important feature. Once you deploy files to your Web server with it, you can synchronize

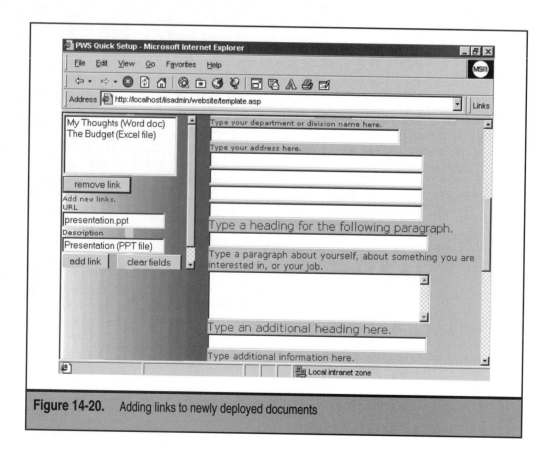

**Figure 14-20.**    Adding links to newly deployed documents

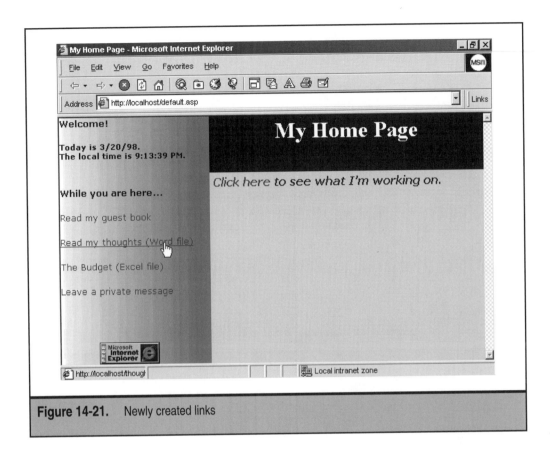

**Figure 14-21.** Newly created links

those files with the originals. In other words, if you change files that you have deployed to the Web server, you can automatically update the Web server with those new files. This works because the Publishing Wizard does not just move deployed files. It makes copies of the originals, which it creates in the Web server file structure. It then keeps track of both the original and the copies (their locations, revision status, and so forth).

If you make a change to an original file, which has a copy on the Web server, you can quickly post those changes to the Web by opening the Personal Web Manager and clicking on the Publish icon from the right pane. This opens a new window (changed from the last time you ran the Publishing Wizard) that contains a number of options (see Figure 14-22).

Click on the Refresh published files from their originals radio button, and click on the forward arrow button. This automatically moves your changes to the Web server.

## Manually Deploying Web Content

PWS's Publishing Wizard, used in conjunction with the Home Page Wizard, can help you easily and quickly deploy content to your Web server and update that content automatically.

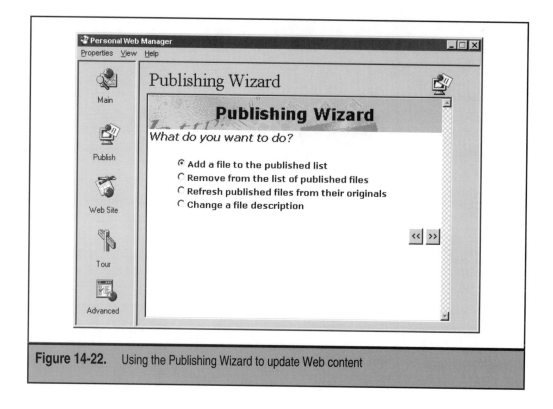

**Figure 14-22.** Using the Publishing Wizard to update Web content

However, it only does so one file at a time. If you have a large number of files you wish to deploy to your Web server, you must bite the bullet and do so by hand. You must create a new folder in which to place your new content. You must move or copy your content to that folder. And you must connect your new files to your existing content, such as your home page.

## Creating Folders

To create a folder on your Web server in which you wish to publish new content, you can use any Windows 98 method familiar to you. For instance, you can use Windows Explorer, an MS-DOS prompt, or the My Computer folder. In any case, just create the directory of your choice within the Web file system. For example, you might want to create a folder called newprojects. To do so, you would need to place it in the Web server's document root as follows:

```
C:\webshare\wwwroot\newprojects\
```

Once you've created your new folder, open the Personal Web Manager and click on the Advanced icon from the left-hand pane. This opens a new right pane, displaying a number of directories and check box items (see Figure 14-23).

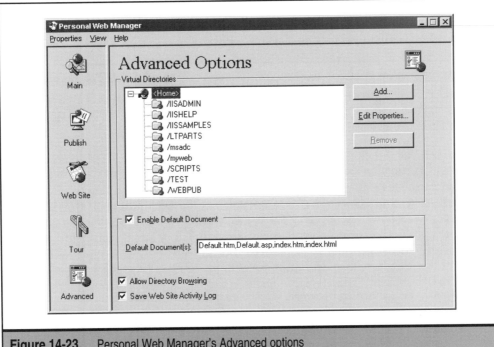

**Figure 14-23.**    Personal Web Manager's Advanced options

This is where you can manage the access to your Web server's directories and how people view your Web server's file system. For example, you can instruct PWS not to allow the execution of applications within certain directories, or you can tell PWS to allow users to browse directories themselves on your Web server.

**RESOURCE:**    For a more complete overview of PWS's Advanced options, refer to Chapter 13.

Click on the Add button. This opens an Add Directory dialog box that looks something like this:

Click on the Browse button. This opens a tree-view dialog box in which you can select your newly created directory. Just highlight the directory and click on the OK button. The next step is to give that directory an alias.

> **JARGON:** What's an alias? In Web server lingo, an alias is a name you give a real directory in your file system. It then appears in your Web server's file system under the alias name. This lets you make a folder that is not in your Web server's file system appear to the outside world as though it is a part of the Web server's file system.

The alias is the directory name users will see and Web pages will use to access your new content. For instance, if you created a physical directory named newprojects, you could create an alias for that directory named nprojs. This is especially useful if you wish to maintain a Web directory that does not fall within the traditional Web directory structure (C:\webshare\wwwroot\). The choice is entirely yours. But it is a good idea to use a name that closely corresponds to the original directory name. This helps you keep directories straight as you add new content to your site over time. Once you've chosen an alias, grant that directory the appropriate level of access. You have three choices:

▼ **Read**   This lets Web browsers load Web pages from this directory.

■ **Execute**   This lets Web browsers execute server-side applications such as Common Gateway Interface (CGI) scripts.

▲ **Scripts**   This lets Web browsers execute scripts locally that are stored in the directory's Web pages.

Selecting the first (Read) is a must. Without it, users won't be able to browse the content in your directory. The second and third depend upon the type of interactivity you're going to use in that directory. For example, if you will use a program such as a VBScript application that displays the current time in your Web pages, you'll need to enable Scripts. Likewise, if you will use a server-side application, such as a search engine, in your Web pages, you should enable Execute. When you have decided upon your level of access, click on the OK button. Don't worry if you find that you need to change these settings; you can always edit the properties for this directory from the Advanced Options pane.

## Deploying Content

Now all you need to do is move your content into this directory and link it with your existing content. Assuming you've already got some content that's just sitting around, waiting for deployment, the best way to approach this problem is to use the Windows Explorer. Remember, the Web server's file structure and the file structure of your PC are both one and the same. The only difference is that people viewing your PC through the Web server can only see directories that reside within the Web server's document root

(C:\webshare\wwwroot). Therefore, to move content into your new folder, all you need to do is copy those files into the newly created directory (see Figure 14-24).

Once you've copied your content into the new directory in the Web server's file system, all you need to do is connect it with your existing content. You can do this as discussed previously—through either FrontPage Express or the Home Page Wizard. The goal is the same either way: to link your new documents to your home page or some other Web page via hypertext links. The only catch is that because your new content is housed in a subdirectory, you need to specify that directory. For instance, as you saw previously with the Home Page Wizard, to add a new link, you must enter a URL like this:

```
http://localhost/mythoughts.doc
```

But to do the same with the same document in a subdirectory, you need to enter a URL like this:

```
http://localhost/myprojects/mythouhts.doc
```

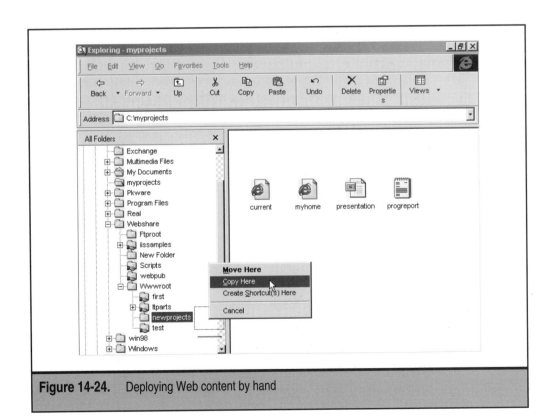

**Figure 14-24.** Deploying Web content by hand

**SHORTCUT:** Of course, you can connect with this new content directly. For example, you could use the following URL to connect to a file called PRESENTATION.PPT within the new directory called newprojects.

```
http://localhost/newprojects/presentation.ppt
```

This saves you from having to add a link to this page on your home page, but those who view your home page will have a hard time finding this file.

## Using Existing Directories

As you may have guessed from the preceding section, you don't need to copy content to your Web server. Using PWS' alias mechanism, you can actually publish material where it stands. This is possible because PWS treats each alias like a virtual directory, which means that the alias for the directory appears as though it were a part of the Web server's file system, while the actual directory may reside elsewhere on the PC's file system. This method of deployment has one huge benefit. You won't have to maintain two copies of your documents. You can simply point users toward your working files. This presents the most up-to-date content to your users, and it saves you from worrying about accidentally copying over a newer file with an older one.

**CAUTION:** The only downside is the chaos that might ensue from opening up your Web server's file system to your entire PC. For instance, if you forget that a working directory is available to the general public via the Web, you may create a subdirectory in that directory, which contains private or sensitive material. Sadly, this material would automatically become available to others within your organization. For that reason, make sure that you do not place sensitive material in these directories.

To take advantage of virtual directories, open the Advanced Options pane from the Personal Web Manager and click on the Add button. Just as before, click on the Browse button from the dialog box that opens.

But this time, instead of selecting a folder that resides within the C:\webshare\wwwroot\ directory, choose a working directory from elsewhere on your hard disk (see Figure 14-25).

Now, give this directory a new alias. Again, you can name it anything you like. But remember, this is the name of the directory that appears within your Web server's document root. Also, you should use a name that is at least close to that of the original directory in order to stave off any confusion that might creep in later. When you're done, click on the OK button. That's all there is to it. You can connect the pages in this new directory to your existing content just as before. Or you can access it directly by using a URL that appends the alias to the Web server's document root (see Figure 14-26).

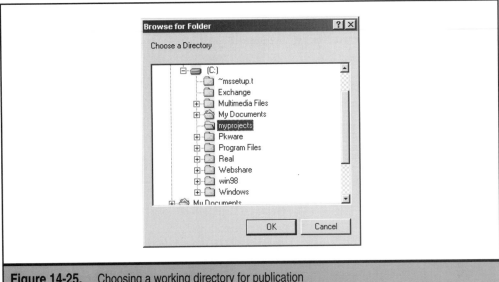

**Figure 14-25.** Choosing a working directory for publication

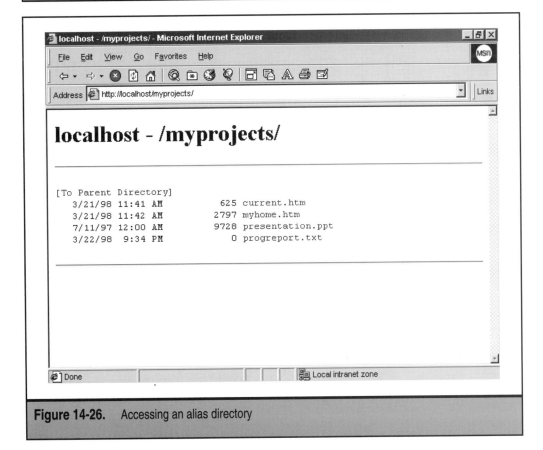

**Figure 14-26.** Accessing an alias directory

# COMING UP

In this chapter, we've covered a lot of ground, providing you with the material you'll need to help your users create their own Web content and deploy that content to a PWS service. As a matter of fact, in the last series of chapters, we've shown you how to help your users make the most of Windows 98's many features and applications. We've shown you how to install and maintain Outlook Express and PWS. We've even shown you how to work with ActiveX controls and Java applets. But how do you reign in all of this functionality? How do you manage all of these features and applications across all of the Windows 98 machines across your network? In the next three chapters, we tackle this issue head on. We show you how to manage, deploy, and secure Windows 98 and its applications (such as Internet Explorer and Outlook Express). So put on your beanie cap and prepare to get down to business managing Windows 98.

NETWORK
PROFESSIONAL'S
LIBRARY

# PART III

# Managing
# Windows 98 Clients

NETWORK
PROFESSIONAL'S
LIBRARY

# CHAPTER 15

# Managing Internet Explorer

## What's ahead:

- Introduction to the Internet Explorer Administration Kit (IEAK)

- Preparing to use the IEAK

- Using the IEAK Wizard to create customized IE distributions

- Managing browser and desktop configurations with IEAK Profile Manager

*"Let ignorance talk as it will, learning has its value."*

— J. de La Fontaine, *The Use of Knowledge, Book viii, Fable 19*

The Internet Explorer Administration Kit (IEAK) promises to simplify the task of customizing, distributing, and updating the Internet Explorer Web browser as well as certain other Windows 95 and Windows 98 user interface settings and up to 10 selected software components.

The IEAK is a very sophisticated piece of software. Entire books can and have been written about it. We won't try to explore and explain every configuration option and possible way to use the software in a single chapter. Instead, we'll discuss what it is and get you started with an overview of how to use it.

# INTRODUCTION TO THE INTERNET EXPLORER ADMINISTRATION KIT

With the IEAK, you can create, distribute, and update customized versions of the Internet Explorer (IE) Web browser. It comes in three distinctly different versions, tailored to the unique needs of the Internet content provider/developer, Internet service provider (ISP), and corporate administrator.

## Internet Service Provider

It has become increasingly difficult for ISPs to differentiate themselves from one another and build customer loyalty by virtue of what they do. Rather they must do so by providing superior customer service and by creating brand recognition. The ISP version of the IEAK can help by making it easy to create and distribute a branded version of the IE Web browser and Outlook Express e-mail client.

With this version, you have the ability to customize the following configuration points:

▼ Put your Active Channel on the user's desktop.

■ Remove any channels that are directly competitive with your own service.

■ Add your name to the IE and Outlook Express title bars.

■ Customize the Outlook Express InfoPane with your own branding, URL link, and other information of your choice.

■ Create your own Lightweight Directory Access Protocol (LDAP) directories for use in Outlook Express.

▲ Define your own welcome message to be displayed in the user's inbox after installation.

# Internet Content Provider/Developer

The Web browser has become an increasingly powerful and functional client platform for Internet and intranet applications. As the browser has been called on to perform increasingly sophisticated tasks, it has also become necessary for content providers and developers to supplement the browser's built-in functionality through plug-ins and helper applications that must be installed and configured on the end-user's computer before they can be used.

The Internet Content Provider/Developer version of IEAK can help by enabling you to create personalized IE installations that include up to 10 custom software packages that will be installed on the user's computer along with the Web browser itself. This eliminates the extra step typically required to download and install each of those packages separately.

# Corporate Administrator

Deploying, configuring, and maintaining the IE Web browser and Outlook Express e-mail client on dozens, hundreds, or even thousands of user's desktops can be a huge task for the corporate network administrator.

The IEAK Corporate Administrator edition is ideally suited for the corporate environment where you might want to take control of the user's desktop and personalize it with your own Web page or other Active content.

Customized IE configurations can be distributed using Microsoft System Management Server, e-mail, Web sites, floppy disks, or CD-ROMs. One distribution set can be created for use company-wide, or specialized installation packages with different configuration settings and options can be created for use by specific departments or groups of users.

End-user installation and setup is simplified by pre-configuring the correct values for proxy servers, security, the Active Desktop, Active Channels, and other settings. Settings that shouldn't be changed by the user can be locked down to prevent tampering. You can even specify a hands-free installation mode whereby all files will be installed into a predefined path using preselected configuration settings.

When configured to do so, the IEAK even allows you to centrally manage software updates and desktop configurations by using a utility known as the IEAK Profile Manager. Individual workstations will check for and load changes to their designated profile each time they are restarted, or based on a schedule that you define.

The Corporate Administrator version of IEAK is by far the most configurable. It enables you to customize the setup program, IE Web browser, Windows Desktop Update utility, and to manage security and content ratings, in the following ways:

▼  The Windows version supports a customizable setup program.

■  IE and other components can be bundled into a single package.

■  Active Setup can direct users to download the latest software from Internet or intranet servers.

- You can include internal programs, custom scripts, and maintenance scripts.
- You can specify which language version of IE to distribute.
- The UNIX version can be installed on a few servers instead of each workstation.
- Custom components and the IE Web browser can be bundled together as a single download package.
- Active Setup can be customized to refer users to your own Internet or intranet servers, thereby ensuring access to the latest software at all times.
- You can specify the language version to include in the package.
- You can personalize the title bar in both IE and Outlook Express.
- You can customize the links and folders in the Favorites list.
- You can customize the channels that appear on the desktop.
- You can configure the user's desktop and control which option the user can change.
- You can specify URLs for start, search, and support pages.
- The Windows version lets you control the Windows Desktop Update, including Active Desktop items, desktop toolbars, Control Panel, and My Computer.
- You can update software on the user's desktop with software update channels.
- The user's security ratings can be configured according to your own company policies.
- Security zones can be predefined.
- You can preinstall certificates and prevent users from downloading new ones.
- You can define a standard disclaimer that will be appended to all newsgroup postings.
- ▲ Proxy settings can be configured.

Because this book is intended for use by corporate administrators, the remainder of this chapter is based on this version of the IEAK. The other two versions work the same way, but their functionality is limited to those features described in the prior two sections.

# PREPARING TO USE THE IEAK

Before you can use the IEAK, there are several things you need to do. First, you must decide which version of the IEAK you need, then download it from the Microsoft Web site for free or order a copy of the CD-ROM for a small shipping and handling fee.

## Downloading the IEAK from www.microsoft.com

To download the IEAK from Microsoft's Web site, point your Web browser to the IE home page at http://www.microsoft.com/ie and follow the links from there.

The IEAK download area is password-protected. You must register before you can gain access (see Figure 15-1). Registration is pretty simple, but it is very important that you answer the required questions accurately because your access password will be sent to the e-mail address you specify on your application.

Once you receive your password, you can proceed to the next step where you will choose the license type you require, as shown here:

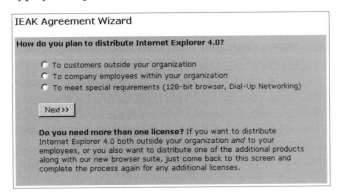

The IEAK Agreement Wizard begins by asking how you intend to use and distribute IE. It then asks if you want to modify the IE Web browser and requires you to accept the terms of its license agreement before sending you another e-mail message, this time containing an authorized IEAK customization code. The customization code will be needed later, when you actually use the IEAK. It acts as a feature key—enabling the functionality for which you have registered.

When you're ready to download the software, select the Download option from the navigation bar on the left side of the screen. The download wizard begins by confirming the language you require, as shown here:

Download IEAK

To run Setup, you must be running Internet Explorer 4.01 on Windows 95 or NT 4.0. If you aren't, <u>download Internet Explorer 4.01</u> now and return to this page.

Note: The IEAK processes for Windows 95/NT 4.0 are unchanged between versions 4.01 and 4.01a. Internet Explorer's security option must be set to **medium** before you can download the IEAK. To change the security option, go to View in the browser menu bar and choose Internet Options. Select the Security tab and then click "Medium (more secure)" from the list of security levels.

Select a language from the list below.
**Select a language**

IEAK 4.01a English for Win32, Win16, and UNIX ▼

Next >>

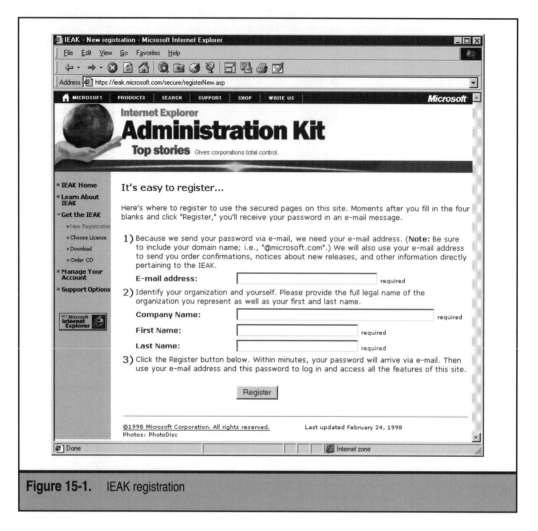

**Figure 15-1.** IEAK registration

Click on the Next button to proceed to the next screen.

On the following screen, you can choose the site from which you want to download the software:

Select the site that you believe will be the fastest and click on the Next button. The following screen lets you begin the installation:

Click on the Install Now button to begin downloading and installing the software on your computer. This step may take quite a while to complete if you are connected to the Internet via a dial-up connection.

You should also download the IEAK documentation, including the Microsoft Internet Explorer 4.0 Deployment Guide. To locate the IEAK documentation on Microsoft's Web site, select the Support option from the navigator on the left side of the IEAK home page, then follow the link titled "IEAK Documentation" to download the documentation files you are interested in. Figure 15-2 shows what the first page of the IE 4 Deployment Guide looks like.

## Decisions You Need to Make Before You Begin

There are many decisions you need to make before you use the IEAK to create a custom distribution package. The best way to become familiar with the configuration options available to you is by using the IEAK Wizard itself. In the next section, you'll see how to do just that. You might want to read through this section once first before running the Wizard yourself.

# USING THE IEAK TO CREATE CUSTOMIZED IE DISTRIBUTIONS

Now you're ready to run the IEAK Wizard to create your first distribution set. The Wizard can be found on the Windows Start menu under Programs | Microsoft IEAK | IEAK Wizard.

When you run the Wizard, the first screen you see is the Welcome screen (see Figure 15-3), which contains a short description of what we're about to do, including a

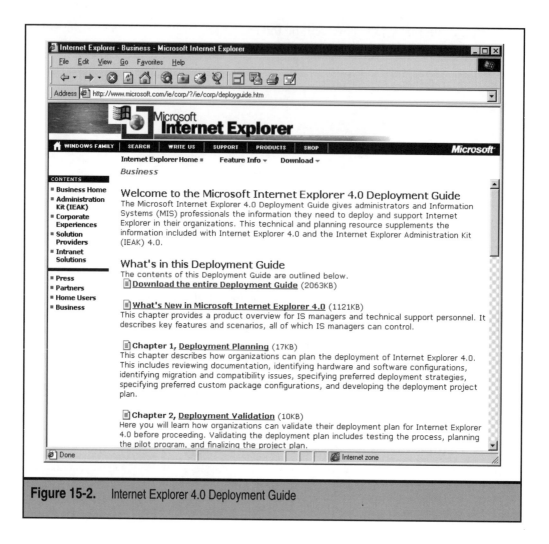

**Figure 15-2.** Internet Explorer 4.0 Deployment Guide

breakdown of the five stages involved in the process. After reading the information on your screen, click on the Next button to proceed.

The next screen is also purely informational. It describes the purpose of "Stage 1: Gathering Information." After reading the contents of this screen, click on the Next button.

Now it's time to get down to business. On this screen, shown in Figure 15-4, you need to enter your Company name, the Customization code you received via e-mail after registering on the Microsoft Web site, select the type of role that best fits your purpose, and optionally enable Automatic Version Synchronization (AVS). You will not be allowed to proceed to the next step without first entering a valid Customization code. If

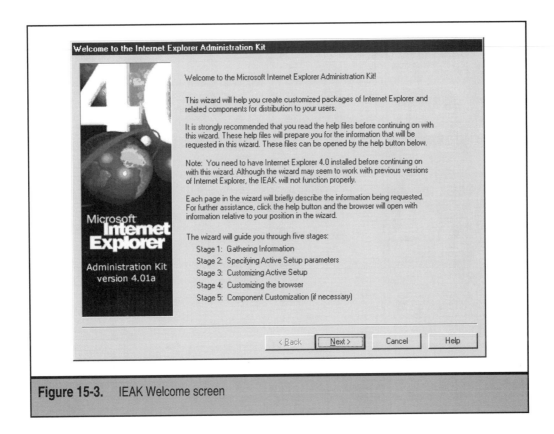

**Figure 15-3.**   IEAK Welcome screen

you do not have one, you must return to the Microsoft Web site and complete the IEAK Registration process that was described earlier in this chapter.

For our purposes, we will assume that you have selected the Corporate Administrator option. If you select Content Provider/Developer or Service Provider, some of the subsequent screens will differ from those shown and described here.

If you enable AVS, the Wizard checks the Microsoft Web site to ensure that you are using the latest version of IE and accompanying components. This is a useful option to enable if you want to ensure that your custom installation package contains the latest software available from Microsoft. However, you may want to disable the option if you are building distribution files based on an older version, are not connected to the Internet, or already know that you have the most current files on your system.

**NOTE:**   You must be connected to the Internet to use AVS. Be sure to disable AVS if you need to complete the IEAK Wizard without connecting to the Internet.

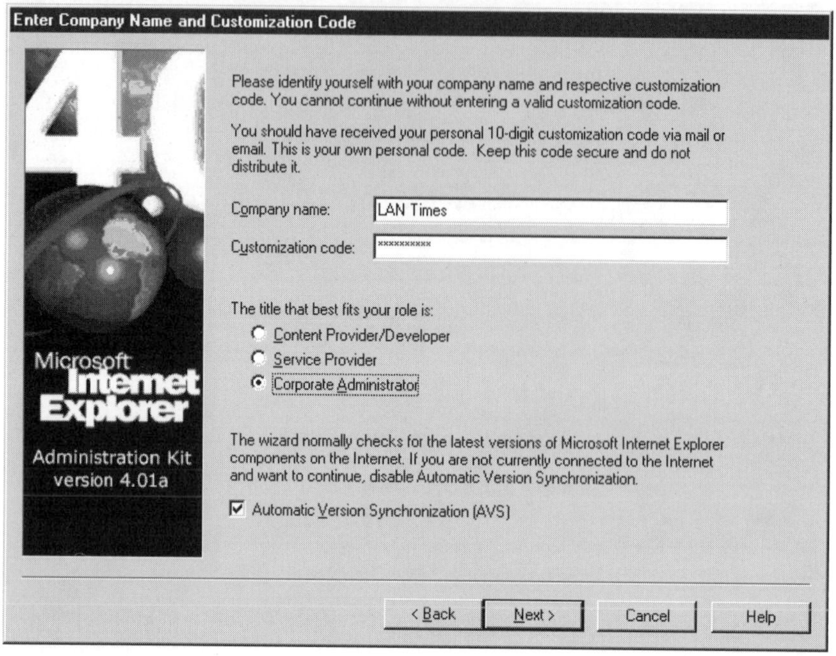

**Figure 15-4.** Enter your customization code here

Once you have completed all the answers, click on the Next button to proceed. With the IEAK, you can create distribution sets for 32-bit Windows (95/98/NT 4.0), 16-bit Windows (3.1/NT 3.51), and UNIX. But you can only create one at a time. Select the desired target platform then click on the Next button.

As with target platforms, IEAK also supports multiple languages, but only one at a time. Select the desired target language using the drop-down control, then click the Next button.

You can distribute your custom installation files via CD-ROM, floppy disk, or file download over the Internet or corporate intranet. The software requires quite a bit of disk space to complete its work and will always store a downloadable version of the installation files on your hard disk even if you enable the options for CD-ROM or floppy disk distribution. Select a path that has sufficient free disk space, enable CD-ROM and floppy disk options if desired, then click the Next button to proceed.

Stage 1 is now complete and you are ready to begin Stage 2. In this stage, you will specify where the IEAK Wizard will look for software updates and which components should be packaged with IE. After reading the instructions on the page named Stage 2: Specifying Active Setup Parameters, click the Next button to continue.

From the next screen, you can specify which download site the IEAK Wizard should use to obtain the distribution files it needs. Select a site using the pull-down menu, then click on the Next button to continue.

If AVS is enabled, the next screen, shown in Figure 15-5, will display a list of IE browser and add-on components and place a symbolic icon next to each one to signify whether you already have the most recent version of the component, have an older version of the component, or do not have the component at all.

If the display indicates that any components need to be updated, you can click on the Synchronize All button to retrieve them all or use your mouse pointer to select the specific components you wish to update, then click on the Synchronize button to update only those components that have been selected.

**SHORTCUT:**  Standard Windows conventions for selecting multiple items applies here. You can hold down the CTRL key while clicking to select multiple items or hold down the SHIFT key while clicking to select a range of items.

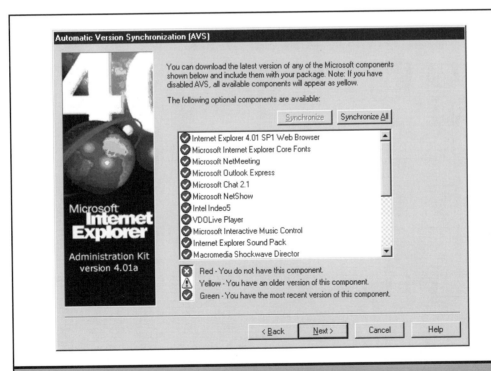

**Figure 15-5.**   A check mark means you already have the latest version

Once you have finished synchronizing all desired components, click on the Next button to continue to the next screen, Specify Custom Active Setup Components, which is shown in Figure 15-6. IEAK allows you to specify up to 10 custom components that will be distributed in the custom IE package you create, such as any browser plug-ins or corporate software applications your users require. If you wish to do so, add those components now by clicking on the Add button, then complete the remaining entries. Once you have entered all of the components you wish to distribute, click on the Next button to continue.

You should sign the custom cabinet (.CAB) files created by the IEAK before distributing them if your target platform is Windows 95 or Windows NT and the package you create will be installed via download over the Internet or intranet. Otherwise, your users may receive warning messages when they try to install it and may be prevented from installing ActiveX controls and Java packages. The IEAK Wizard can handle this task for you if you select a trusted publisher on the Specify Trusted Publisher screen. If you have one installed and wish to use it, select it with a single mouse click before clicking on the Next button to continue. If you will be distributing your custom installation files via the Internet and don't have a trusted

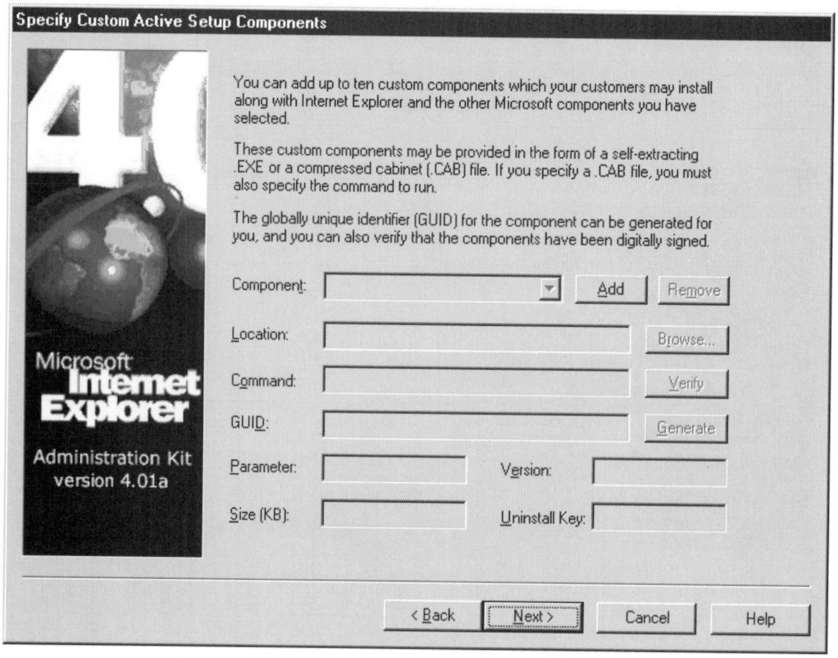

**Figure 15-6.**   You can specify up to 10 components here

publisher installed, click on the button labeled Help for detailed instructions, including the necessary Web links for securing a digital certificate.

This brings us to Stage 3, titled "Customizing Active Setup." Once again, the new stage begins with an informational screen that describes the purpose of this stage, which is to customize the look and behavior of the Active Setup installation program. Read the information on this screen carefully then click the Next button to advance to the next screen.

In this screen, shown in Figure 15-7, specify the text you want to appear in the title bar, the custom bitmap graphic to use as a background for the autorun screen, text colors, and button style to use. Click the Next button to continue.

On the Customize the Active Setup Wizard screen, you can customize the title and bitmap used by the Active Setup Wizard. If you created your own bitmap, remember that its dimensions must be $120 \times 239$ with 16 colors. You can leave these fields blank if you do not want to specify a custom message for the title bar or a custom graphic. When you're ready to continue, click the Next button to advance to the next screen.

If your installation plans call for an unattended, or "silent," installation click the box on this page. Be aware that if you enable silent installation, the end user will be unaware

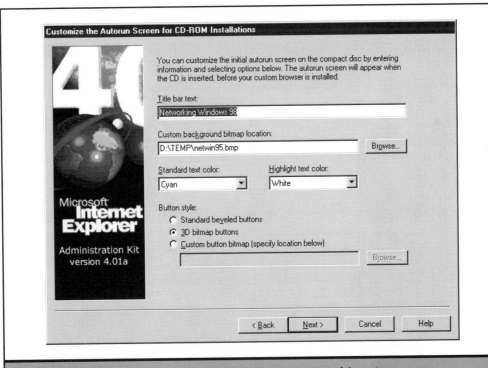

**Figure 15-7.**    On this screen, you can customize the appearance of the autorun screen

of the progress during installation and will not be able to control options such as whether to install the Active Desktop or which download site to use. If you do not specify the silent installation option, you can specify up to 10 different configurations from which the end user will be able to choose during installation. If you enable the silent installation option, you will only be able to specify one configuration set. Click the Next button to continue.

On the Select Installation Options screen, shown in Figure 15-8, you can modify configuration sets. To modify an existing configuration set, select it from the drop-down menu, then select the components you want to include or exclude by moving them between the lists of available components and components to be installed by clicking on the buttons identified by a single arrow pointing in the direction to move the item. To move all items click on the button identified by a double arrow. You can create new configuration sets by clicking on the New button, and then providing the new entry a name and description, and specifying the components to install. Once you're satisfied with the configuration sets, click on the Next button.

On the Specify Download URLs screen, shown in Figure 15-9, you can specify the sites that will be available for downloading the software. This screen works very much

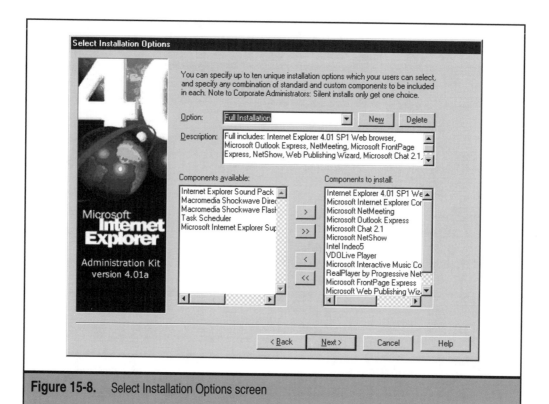

**Figure 15-8.**   Select Installation Options screen

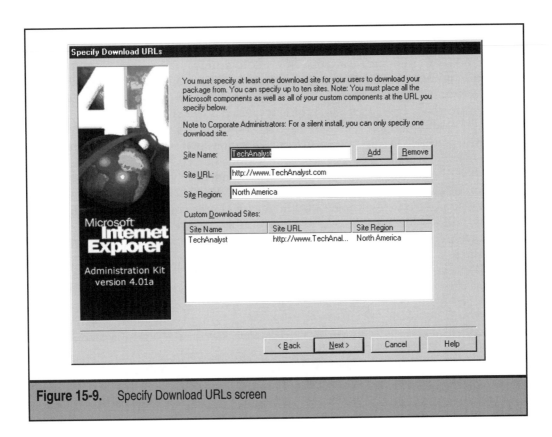

**Figure 15-9.**    Specify Download URLs screen

like the last one. If the silent option is enabled, you can only define one site; otherwise, you can define up to 10 different sites. Don't forget that after the IEAK Wizard finishes generating the installation files, those files must be copied to each server you list here. After entering all of your site information, click the Next button to continue.

On the Select Version Information screen, you can enter a unique version number so the Active Setup Wizard can determine whether or not an installation set is newer than the one currently installed. This number will automatically increment each time you use the IEAK Wizard, but you can also override that number by directly entering one of your choosing. If you have chosen to generate multiple configurations, you should enter a unique Configuration Identifier that describes this configuration set in eight characters or less. The final option on this screen allows you to customize the URL that will be used for downloading additional Add-on Components. If you leave this field blank, it will default to the file ADDON95.HTM on the current download site. When you're ready to proceed, click on the Next button.

It is customary for installation programs to prompt the user to specify or at least confirm the folder in which the installed programs will be placed. The Specify Where You

Want to Install Your Browser screen contains three options that determine how the installation program will behave in this regard. You can specify the name of a folder within the Windows folder, the name of a folder within the Program Files folder, or specify the full path desired. It is generally best to choose one of the first two options unless you know for sure that every user will have sufficient disk space available at the absolute path you specify. This path is only respected during the first time IE is installed on the user's computer. If it is already installed on the user's computer, the installation program will install the update over the existing version. Click the Next button to proceed to the next screen.

The Web Desktop Update is an optional IE component that makes the Windows 98 desktop and folders look and behave more like the Web. On the Integrating the Web Desktop Update screen, you can decide whether or not the component will be installed, but the wizard won't allow you to configure it until later. Unless you have a good reason to do otherwise, we recommend selecting the "Users choice" option. This completes Stage 3 of the IEAK Wizard. Click on the Next button when you're ready to proceed to Stage 4.

In Stage 4 you can customize the look and feel of the Web browser by defining items such as a custom title bar; start, search, and support URL's; predefined favorites and channels; and Active Desktop settings. Because we're running in Corporate Administrator mode, we will also be able to specify the browser's advanced configuration settings. You should read all of the information on this screen, then click on the Next button when you're ready to proceed.

The first thing you can customize in this stage is the text that appears in the IE title bar and the bitmap that will be displayed as a backdrop behind the toolbar buttons and drop down menus (see Figure 15-10). The text you specify will be appended to the standard IE title bar, which is generally quite long already. For this reason, we recommend that you keep your custom title bar text as short as possible. If you do not specify a new bitmap to use as a backdrop for the toolbar buttons, the standard IE backdrop will be used. When you're done entering these options, click on the Next button to continue.

With so many configuration options available, you will likely leave many of them at their default values. The options on the Customize the Start and Search Pages screen, however, are ones that you probably want to change (see Figure 15-11). You should change the default URL to point to your own Corporate Web site instead of sending the user to Microsoft's. The second entry on this screen allows you to customize the URL that will be used when the user clicks on the Search button. You can accept the default or specify another if you prefer Yahoo, Excite, or some other Internet search engine. In some intranet environments, you might even want to specify the URL to your own corporate search engine. Click on the Next button to continue.

There is a menu option titled Online Support on the IE help menu. On the Specify an Online Support Page screen, you can specify the URL that will be used when the user selects this option. If you have a corporate help desk, list of frequently asked questions (FAQ), or similar resource on your intranet, you should enter the corresponding URL on this screen. After entering the URL, you may want to click on the Test URL button to verify that you typed it in correctly before clicking the Next button to continue.

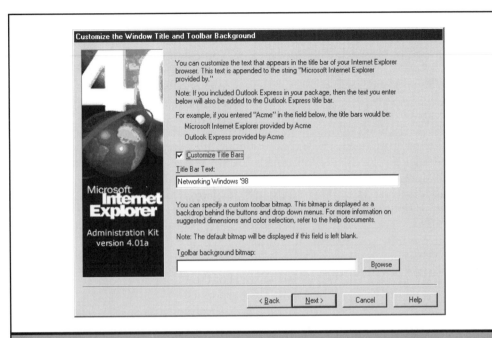

**Figure 15-10.**   In Stage 4, you can customize the IE title bar and toolbar background

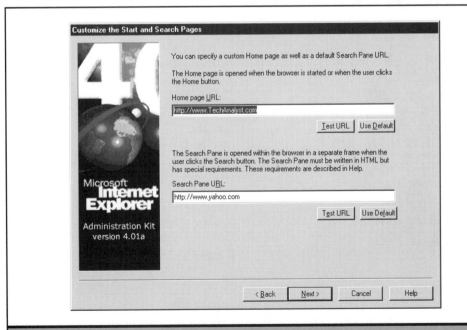

**Figure 15-11.**   It's a good idea to specify home page and search pane URLs

On the next screen (Figure 15-12), you can pre-define the contents of the Internet Explorer Favorites and Links folders. You might want to add links to your corporate intranet, business partners' Web sites industry news pages, and other sites of interest to your staff. After entering all of the desired URLs, click on the Next button to continue.

The first time IE is started after installation, it will take the user to a Welcome page instead of the home page as usual. On the next screen, you can either accept the standard Microsoft Internet Explorer 4.0 start page, disable the Welcome page, or specify your own URL, as shown in Figure 15-13. The second option on this screen allows you to disable the Microsoft Internet Explorer 4.0 Welcome window that is usually displayed on the desktop each time the user boots after installing IE, until it is disabled by them. This window is used to give the user a quick tour, explore available channels, or register online. The third option available on this screen enables you to define a custom bitmap, GIF file, or HTML file that will be used as the desktop wallpaper if desired. You can directly enter the full path and file name or click on the Browse button to locate the desired file. When you're satisfied with your entries on this screen, click on the Next button to continue.

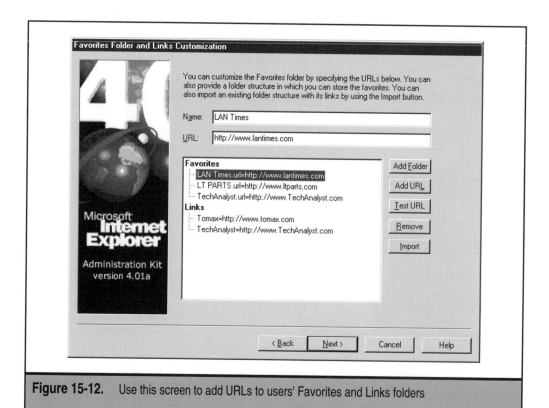

**Figure 15-12.** Use this screen to add URLs to users' Favorites and Links folders

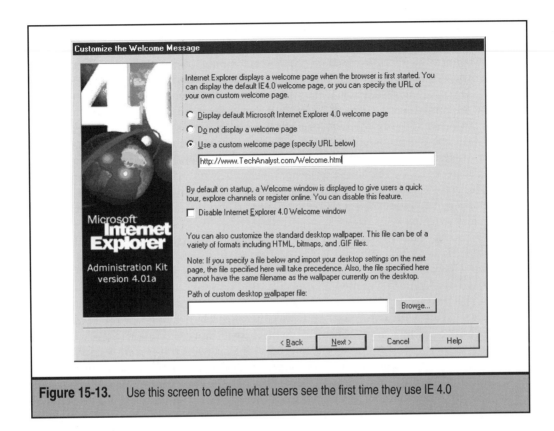

**Figure 15-13.** Use this screen to define what users see the first time they use IE 4.0

In the Corporate Administrator mode, you can customize the channels that will be distributed with and installed on the user's desktop along with the Channel Bar. You might want to remove any channels you deem competitive or otherwise inappropriate and add your own channels or those of your business partners. Unlike the rest of the IEAK setup, which is self-contained and therefore isolated from the configuration settings active on the workstation you are running it on, the only way to package custom channel definitions is to define them on your own Channel Bar then allow the IEAK to import your current active configuration. If you want to remove any channels already installed on your system, you will need to switch away from the IEAK Wizard and open the Channel Bar on your desktop. From there, you can use the right-mouse click pop-up menu to remove existing channels.

Adding channels is a little easier because this page in the IEAK Wizard includes a button that directly launches the Channel Guide. From there, you can locate and activate channels as you normally would. If you want to distribute the Channel Bar without customizing its configuration, select the option labeled "Do not customize channels." Otherwise, make sure the option labeled "Import current channel configuration" is selected before you click on the Next button to continue.

The Customize Software Update Channels screen allows you to import and distribute software update channels, which are useful for distributing updated software, such as new versions of the Web browser or other applications, to the end user. Configuring software update channels is a pretty sophisticated process and well beyond the scope of this book. If you're interested in learning more about it, click on the Help button to access the online documentation. Click the Next button to advance to the next screen.

Web browsers identify themselves each time they request a file from a server. The server might use this information to tailor its response with browser-specific content or simply to track usage by browser type. If you want to append a unique identifier to the end of IE's agent string, you can enter it on the User Agent String Customization screen. Otherwise, you should leave this field blank. Click the Next button to continue.

One of the most powerful features available in the IEAK is the ability to centrally manage and update your users configurations following deployment. This can be accomplished by enabling automatic browser configuration (see Figure 15-14). Then use the Profile Manager to alter the configuration settings as necessary. If you enable automatic browser configuration, you must also specify the URL from which to retrieve the updated configuration settings. Normally this will take the form of an INS file as generated by the Profile Manager. For more information on auto-proxy files, click on the Help button. Automatic configuration normally takes place whenever the computer is restarted, but sometimes that's not sufficient because it's not uncommon for users to leave their computers on for days or weeks at a time. If you want the system to periodically check for updates, you can also use this screen to specify how often the system should auto-configure. When you're ready to move on, click the Next button to advance.

If your corporate network is isolated from the Internet or another corporate network by a proxy server or firewall, one of your biggest support burdens can be the seemingly simple task of configuring all of your users' workstations with the proper Proxy server settings. Fortunately, the IEAK addresses this by allowing you to predefine the correct proxy settings so your end-users won't have to. On the top portion of the Specify Proxy Settings screen (Figure 15-15), you have the opportunity to enable proxy settings and specify addresses for HTTP, Secure, FTP, Gopher, and Socks proxy servers. On the lower area, you can define exceptions by listing address prefixes that will not be redirected through a proxy server. If you wish to configure the proxy settings, click on the "Enable proxy settings" check box, then enter the desired values in the remaining fields. When you're ready to proceed, click on the Next button.

IE supports the use of both Certificate Authorities and Authenticode Security. On the Certificate Settings screen, the IEAK gives you the opportunity to predefine those settings for your users by importing and modifying the current settings from your own configuration. If you wish to enable these features, change the appropriate settings from "Do not customize" to "Import current" then modify the settings as necessary. Click on the Next button to continue.

On the Security Zones and Content Ratings Customization screen, you have the option to customize Security Zones and Content Ratings. You can specify Security Zone parameters by selecting the "Customize Security Zone settings" option, then clicking on

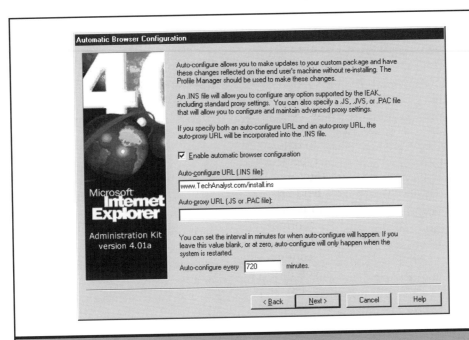

**Figure 15-14.** Use this screen to enable automatic browser configuration

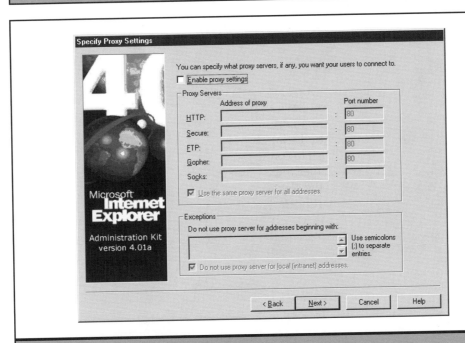

**Figure 15-15.** Use this screen to specify proxy settings

the Modify Settings button to open a dialog box identical to that used for doing the same thing within IE itself. Content Ratings work similarly, except that your current settings are imported for use as a starting point. When you're satisfied with your configuration settings, click the Next button to complete Stage 4 and continue to Stage 5 of the IEAK configuration.

You're almost done now. Stage 5 gives you the ability to customize the optional components you chose to install. Read the information found on this introduction screen then click on the Next button when you're ready to begin.

The next screen, shown in Figure 15-16, contains configuration options for Outlook Express, including the type of incoming mail server, mail and news server addresses, and whether to make Outlook Express the default client for mail and news. These settings are all pretty straightforward and will be familiar if you have ever used Outlook Express. Enter the appropriate information then click on the Next button to continue.

If you have an LDAP server on your network, you can use the next screen to configure the necessary settings so your users will be able to use it without further configuration. If you choose to configure this server, you need to enter a Friendly Name, Address of the Directory Service, home page URL, Search Page URL, and Service Bitmap, and specify

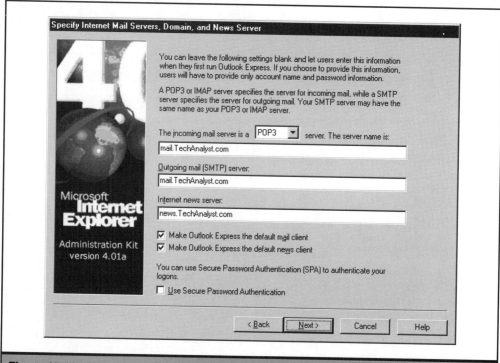

**Figure 15-16.**    Use this screen to indicate Internet mail and news server addresses

whether Outlook Express will be required to verify names against this server before sending outbound e-mail. If you don't have an LDAP server, you can leave the entries on this screen blank. Otherwise, enter the required information before clicking on the Next button.

From Outlook Express Customizations screen (see Figure 15-17), you can customize the Outlook Express InfoPane by replacing the default page with either a specified URL or local HTML file. You can also specify the contents of a custom HTML-formatted welcome message that will be added to each user's inbox the first time they open Outlook Express. If needed, you can minimize the IEAK Wizard while you create these files or leave the entry fields blank if you want Outlook Express to keep the default InfoPane and Welcome Messages, then click on the Next button to continue.

If your employees will use Outlook Express to interact with customers, vendors, and the general public via e-mail and newsgroups, you may want to append certain disclaimers or a standard corporate signature block to the end of each e-mail message and newsgroup posting. To do so, in the Include a Signature screen, click the "Append the following signature" check box and enter your message in the corresponding input field. Click the Next button when you're satisfied with your entries.

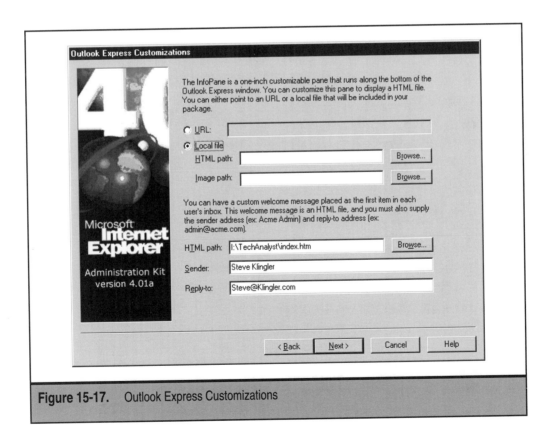

**Figure 15-17.** Outlook Express Customizations

The System Policies and Restrictions screen, shown in Figure 15-18, is used to configure specific settings for each module being installed. Most of these settings are pretty self-explanatory so each one won't be described in detail. Instead, we have listed all available options in the following sections so you can become familiar with them. Additional information about each option is available through the online help system and downloadable documentation.

# Microsoft NetMeeting

From the System Policies and Restrictions window (refer to Figure 15-18), you can control a number of NetMeeting settings to limit the ways in which the user can use the software. If you're concerned about security, you might consider disabling the use of file transfers and application sharing. If bandwidth is a concern, you should consider disabling the audio and video options.

## NetMeeting Settings

The following options are available:

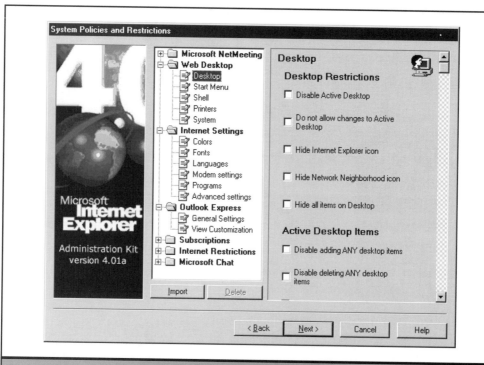

**Figure 15-18.**    The System Policies and Restrictions

▼   Restrict the use of file transfer

■   Prevent the user from sending files

■   Prevent the user from receiving files

■   Restrict the use of application sharing

■   Disable all application sharing features

■   Prevent the user from sharing the clipboard

■   Prevent the user from sharing MS-DOS windows

■   Prevent the user from sharing Explorer windows

■   Restrict the use of the Options dialog box

■   Disable the "General" options page

■   Disable the "My Information" options page

■   Disable the "Calling" options page

■   Disable the "Audio" options page

■   Disable the "Video" options page

■   Disable the "Protocols" options page

■   Prevent the user from answering calls

■   Prevent the user from using audio features

■   Restrict the use of video

■   Prevent the user from sending video

■   Prevent the user from receiving video

■   Prevent the user from using directory services

■   Set the default Directory Server

■   Set Exchange Server Property for NetMeeting Address

■   Preset User Information Category

■   Set the NetMeeting home page

▲   Set limit for audio/video throughput

## NetMeeting Protocols

Here are the NetMeeting Protocol settings:

▼   Disable TCP/IP

▲   Disable null modem

# Web Desktop

You should consider how much control you need to have over the user's desktop, if any. This is your opportunity to lock down the Active Desktop, hide or disable items on the desktop, control the contents of the Start Menu, customize the Shell, lock down printer configurations, and control which applications the user is allowed to run. If you will be using the IEAK to configure task-based workstations, this is your opportunity to control the user's experience by restricting their ability to run programs that you don't want them to and to prevent them from getting to a DOS prompt or accessing the computer's floppy drives.

## Desktop

Following is a list of the Desktop settings available to you:

▼ Desktop Restrictions
■ Disable Active Desktop
■ Do not allow changes to Active Desktop
■ Hide Internet Explorer icon
■ Hide Network Neighborhood icon
■ Hide all items on Desktop
■ Active Desktop items
■ Disable adding any desktop items
■ Disable deleting any desktop items
■ Disable editing any desktop items
■ Disable closing any desktop items
■ Desktop WallPaper
■ Disable selecting HTML as wallpaper
■ Disable changing wallpaper
■ Desktop Toolbars Settings
■ Disable adding new toolbars
▲ Disable resizing all toolbars

## Start Menu

Here are the Start Menu options you can choose from:

▼ Remove Favorites menu from Start menu
■ Remove Find menu from Start menu

- Remove Run menu from Start menu
- Remove the Active Desktop item from the Settings menu
- Disable drag and drop context menus on the Start menu
- Remove the Folder Options menu item from the Settings menu
- Remove Documents menu from Start menu
- Do not keep history of recently opened documents
- Clear history of recently opened documents
- Disable Logoff
- Disable Shut Down command
- Disable changes to Printers and Control Panel settings
- Disable changes to Taskbar and Start Menu settings
- Disable context menu for Taskbar
- Hide custom Program folders
- ▲ Remove the Windows Update item from the Settings menu

## Shell

Following are the Shell options available in the IEAK:

- ▼ Disable file menu in Shell folders
- Disable context menu in Shell folders
- Only allow approved Shell extensions
- Do not track Shell shortcuts during roaming
- Hide Floppy Drives in My Computer
- ▲ Disable net connections/disconnections

## Printers

You have two printer options:

- ▼ Disable Deletion of Printers
- ▲ Disable Addition of Printers

## System

You also have two system options:

- ▼ Run only specified Windows applications
- ▲ Do not allow computer to restart in MS-DOS mode

# Internet Settings

You might want to customize a number of the IE settings to influence the way it looks and behaves, such as colors, fonts, default language, modem settings, and each of the settings accessible through the Advanced panel of the Internet Explorer Option dialog box. Many of these settings are merely cosmetic, but you should pay particular attention to the modem dialer settings such as automatic redial and disconnect timeouts, and security settings dealing with form submissions and caching of encrypted content.

## Colors

You can modify the following settings related to colors:

- ▼ General colors
- ■ Background color
- ■ Text color
- ■ Use Windows colors
- ■ Link colors
- ■ Link color
- ▬ Visited link color
- ■ Use hover color
- ▲ Hover color

## Fonts

There are two font settings:

- ▼ Western Proportional Font
- ▲ Western Fixed Font

## Languages

You can also choose a default language preference.

## Modem Settings

The following modem settings are available:

- ▼ Connection Type
- ■ Enable Autodialing
- ■ Number of times to attempt connection
- ■ Number of seconds to wait between attempts
- ■ Connect without user intervention

- ■ Disconnect if idle after specified number of minutes
- ■ Minutes to wait before disconnecting
- ▲ Perform system security check before dialing

## Programs

You can select the following default programs:

- ▼ Program to use for Calendar
- ■ Program to use for Contacts
- ▲ Program to use for Internet call

## Advanced Settings

The following advanced settings are available:

- ▼ Browsing
- ■ Disable Script debugger
- ■ Launch channels in full screen mode
- ■ Launch browser in full screen mode
- ■ Use autocomplete
- ■ Show friendly URLs
- ■ Enable smooth scrolling
- ■ Enable page transitions
- ■ Browse in a new process
- ■ Enable page hit counting
- ■ Enable scheduled subscription updates
- ■ Underline links
- ■ Multimedia
- ■ Show pictures
- ■ Play animations
- ■ Play videos
- ■ Play sounds
- ■ Smart image dithering
- ■ Security
- ■ Enable Profile Assistant
- ■ Delete saved pages when browser closed

- Do not save encrypted pages to disk
- Warn if forms submit is being redirected
- Warn if changing between secure and insecure mode
- Cookies
- Java VM
- JIT compiler enabled
- Java logging enabled
- Printing
- Print background colors and images
- Searching
- Autoscan common root domains
- Search when URL fails
- Toolbars
- Show font button
- Small icons
- HTTP 1.1 settings
- Use HTTP 1.1
- ▲ Use HTTP 1.1 through proxy connections

# Outlook Express

When working with users who are not computer-savvy, you can often simplify employee training and support through simple means such as ensuring that the user interface on every computer is configured identically to those used for training. If you have established a standard view configuration for Outlook Express, you can instruct the IEAK to use those settings on this screen.

## General Settings

There are five settings in the General category:

- ▼ Mail and news security zones
- Put mail and news in the Restricted Sites zone (instead of the Internet zone)
- HTML mail and news composition settings
- Mail: Make plain text message composition the default for mail messages
- ▲ News: Make HTML message composition the default for news posts (instead of plain text)

### View Customization

You can customize the view in the following ways:

- ▼ Folder and Message Navigation Elements
- ■ Turn on Outlook Bar
- ■ Turn off Folder List (three view of folders)
- ■ Turn on Folder Bar
- ▲ Turn on the Tip of the Day

## Subscriptions

Subscriptions can consume massive amounts of local disk space and bandwidth if they are not kept in check through appropriate limitations on number of sites that can be subscribed to, the depth to crawl each site, and the maximum amount of content to download. You don't need to be concerned with these settings if your users have large hard drives and are capable of managing these settings on their own. However, you should preset these settings if you are configuring task stations where no one user is responsible for file maintenance on the workstation or when you want to prevent users from subscribing to additional sites on their own.

The settings are:

- ▼ Mazimum KB of site subscription
- ■ Maximum KB of channel subscription
- ■ Maximum number of sites subscriptions that can be installed
- ■ Minimum number of minutes between scheduled submission updates
- ■ Beginning of range in which to exclude scheduled subscription updates
- ■ End of range in which to exclude scheduled subscription updates
- ▲ Maximum site subscription crawlpath

## Internet Restrictions

This is the catch-all area for Internet restrictions as classified by general, security, content, connection, programs, advanced, code download, user profiles, and channels settings. Here you will find a variety of useful settings you might want to configure for enhanced security and consistency. For example, if you have a corporate intranet site and rely on it for the distribution of important information to your staff, you might want to lock down the default home page to ensure that everyone will see the latest news each time they open the IE Web browser.

## General

Here are the general settings:

- ▼ Disable changing home page settings
- ■ Disable changing cache settings
- ■ Disable changing history settings
- ■ Disable changing color settings
- ■ Disable changing link color settings
- ■ Disable changing font settings
- ■ Disable changing language settings
- ▲ Disable changing accessibility settings

## Security

You have the following security options to choose from:

- ▼ Use ONLY machine settings for secure files
- ■ Do not allow users to change policies for any other secure server
- ▲ Do not allow users to add/delete sites from a security zone

## Content

The content settings are:

- ▼ Disable changing rating settings
- ■ Disable changing certificate settings
- ■ Disable changing Profile Assistant settings
- ▲ Disable changing Microsoft Wallet settings

## Connection

With regard to the connection, you can choose from the following options:

- ▼ Disable calling Connection Wizard
- ■ Disable changing connection settings
- ■ Disable changing proxy settings
- ▲ Disable changing Automatic Configuration settings

## Programs

Here are the programs settings:

- ▼ Disable changing Messaging settings

> ■ Disable changing Calendar and Contact settings
>
> ▲ Disable changing checking if Internet Explorer is the default browser

## Advanced

Under Advanced, you can disable changing settings on the Advanced panel.

## Code Download

There is one code download option: You can set the code download path.

## User Profiles

With regard to user profiles, you can disable roaming cache.

## Channels Settings

The following options relate to channels:

> ▼ Disable Channel UI
>
> ■ Disable adding and subscribing to channels
>
> ■ Disable editing channel properties and channel subscriptions
>
> ■ Disable removing channels and subscriptions to channels
>
> ■ Disable adding site subscriptions
>
> ■ Disable editing site subscriptions
>
> ■ Disable removing site subscriptions
>
> ■ Disable channel logging
>
> ■ Disable Update Now and Update All for channels and subscriptions
>
> ■ Disable all scheduled channel and site subscriptions
>
> ■ Disable unattended dialing by subscriptions
>
> ■ Disable password caching for channel and site subscriptions
>
> ■ Disable downloading of channel subscription content—change notification will still work
>
> ■ Disable downloading of site subscription content—change notification will still work
>
> ▲ Disable editing and creating of schedule groups

# Microsoft Chat

Here you can customize a number of settings to make it easier for your users to communicate with each other using Microsoft Chat. For example, if your company operates its own chat server, you can configure it as the default chat server and define the default chat room.

Following is a list of the Chat options:

▼  Change chat server list

■  Change default chat server

■  Change default chat room

■  Change default character

■  Change default backdrop bitmap

■  Change user's profile for Microsoft Chat

▲  Turn on option to show only registered rooms in room list

## In Conclusion

When you're through setting all the desired configuration options, click on the Next button to continue. You'll see the screen shown in Figure 15-19.

You have now completed entering all the necessary information for the IEAK Wizard to generate your custom package. Click on the Finish button to instruct the IEAK Wizard to proceed. You'll see a small window tracking IEAK Wizard's progress, as shown here:

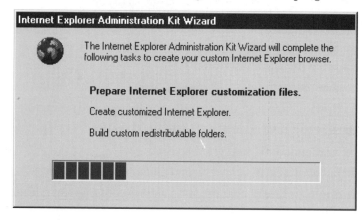

The IEAK Wizard generates your custom package in three stages. First, it prepares the necessary IE customization files. Next, it creates the customized IE. Finally, it builds the custom redistributable files. When the process is complete, the IEAK Wizard displays a

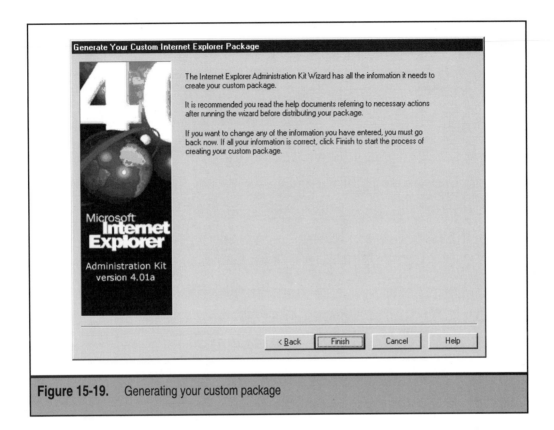

**Figure 15-19.** Generating your custom package

notification window, including a confirmation of the directory location where the customized files were placed, as shown here:

Click the OK button to exit the Wizard.

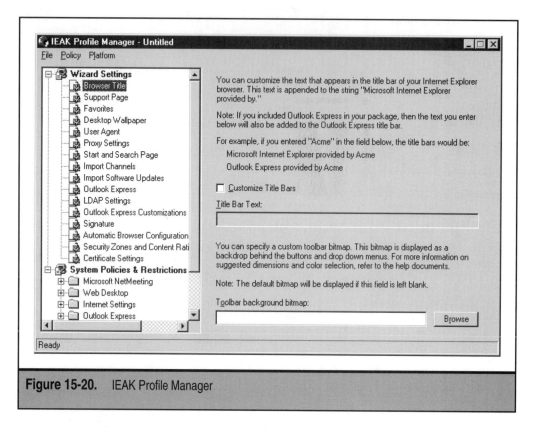

**Figure 15-20.**   IEAK Profile Manager

# MANAGING BROWSER AND DESKTOP CONFIGURATIONS WITH IEAK

A very powerful feature of the IEAK is that in a corporate network environment it allows you to centrally manage the desktop and Web browser configuration settings of your users by using the IEAK Profile Manager (see Figure 15-20).

The profile manager enables you to edit nearly all of the same configuration points that were available to us through the IEAK Wizard. Just open or create the desired INS file, change the configuration settings as desired, then save the file back to disk and copy it to the location your workstations have been configured to use for loading updated browser settings.

The IEAK Profile Manager is found in the Microsoft IEAK folder on your Start menu. It is very intuitive and easy to use, with online help available if you need it.

# COMING UP

The security of your network and all workstations connected to it is an increasingly significant concern especially in the corporate environment. In Chapter 16, we discuss security risks you should be aware of and how to make your Windows 98 workstations more secure.

NETWORK
PROFESSIONAL'S
LIBRARY

# CHAPTER 16

# Securing
# Windows 98

## What's ahead:

- Security risks
- Zones of risk
- Windows 98 security provisions
- Internet Explorer
- Software updates

> *"Our very hopes belied our fears,*
> *Our fears our hopes belied;*
> *We thought her dying when she slept,*
> *And sleeping when she died.*
>
> —Thomas Hood, *The Death-Bed*

If you use your computer to access or store valuable information or to perform important tasks, you need to take precautions to protect it. Some security breaches are nothing more than a nuisance, but others can be very costly, resulting in down-time, lost or corrupted data, or theft of confidential or competitive information.

# SECURITY RISKS

For a stand-alone computer that is never connected to a network or the Internet, the risks are few. You can secure the computer by simply controlling physical access to it and taking appropriate precautions when loading software.

Networked computers, on the other hand, even those that are only occasionally connected to a corporate network or to the Internet via dial-up connection, are at much greater risk. It's no longer sufficient to simply control physical access to your computer.

## Loss

Most of us associate a security breach with data loss. Perhaps that's because the most dramatic and newsworthy security breaches are those that result in some form of data loss. It's also true that an intrusion resulting in data loss is more likely to be detected in the first place.

Of course, if data loss is detected, everything else on your system must be considered suspect and unreliable. You should either verify the integrity of all files on your system or restore them from a reliable source—but not until after you determine how your system was compromised and take the necessary steps to secure it against future intrusions.

## Corruption

Data corruption can be more damaging than actual data loss. You can't rely on data that isn't there any more. But you could go on using and relying on corrupt data for a long time before you discover that it's been compromised.

Depending on the type of data you have and what it's used for, the consequences of using corrupt data vary greatly, ranging from harmless to embarrassing to expensive to life threatening.

# Theft

Unless your network is equipped with sophisticated monitoring, you may never know an intruder has gained access to your system. Savvy intruders will cover their tracks, so they can come and go as they please until you eventually detect the intrusion and fix the security hole.

Data theft has the potential to be the most damaging and expensive consequence of a breach in security. Some intruders may simply be curious, satisfied by looking around your hard drive and copying a few files simply for the sake of collecting trophies to prove they were there. The greater risk is from an intruder looking for files that contain confidential, competitive, or otherwise sensitive information with the intent to use it against you or sell it to your competition.

# ZONES OF RISK

There was a time when the only security risk you had to be concerned about was from direct physical access to your computer. Unfortunately, that's no longer the case. Today, it's necessary to protect your computer against intruders that might access your system locally, over the network, and through the Internet.

It's not enough to protect yourself against attack by unwelcome intruders. You also have to be concerned about infection by a virus or Trojan horse, which can be introduced to your system through any of these means.

## Direct Access (Local)

The greatest risk comes from having direct access to your system. All the firewalls, proxy servers, VPNs, and password schemes in the world don't mean a thing once someone gains local access to your system.

Windows 98, like Windows 95, does not regulate access to its file system by local users. Anyone that can turn on the computer can access every file on your system by either booting from a diskette or choosing Cancel when prompted for a login name and password.

There are steps you can take to make your Windows 98 system more secure even when it's not possible to control physical access to it. Nearly all computers allow you to configure a boot-up password in the system BIOS that will prevent unauthorized users from booting up the computer when you're not around. The Windows 98 screen saver also supports a password that will keep unauthorized users off your system when you step away from your workstation during the day.

Additionally, you can buy specialized products for use in high-security applications, such as those that encrypt the entire contents of your hard disk, requiring a non-repeatable password or hardware key before the system can be accessed.

# Network Access

If an intruder can't gain direct access to the local machine, gaining access to another computer on the network is the next best thing. In a network environment, much of the security infrastructure is focused on isolating the "trusted" private network from the "untrusted" public network. It's easier for an intruder to use such techniques as IP spoofing, session hijacking, and packet sniffing from a workstation on the trusted network than from the untrusted network.

In many corporate environments, it's not unusual to find unattended workstations that are already logged in to corporate servers and applications, with direct access to sensitive files and information. An intruder that gains access to one of these systems doesn't even have to break in.

The lesson to be learned here is that even though we talk about the internal or private network as a "trusted" network, we should always treat it with just as much caution as we do the public "untrusted" network. In many ways, the security of your Windows 98 workstations is dependent on the security of your network servers, especially if those workstations are configured for user-level access controls, as defined by your Windows NT server, or execute shared programs stored on those systems.

Some of the provisions available on various server platforms that you should be familiar with include automatic logout timers, periodic re-authentication, and execute-only file permissions.

# Internet Access

In the age of Internet connectivity, few Windows 98 computers are fully isolated from the outside world. When you connect to the Internet, even through a simple dial-up connection, you become part of the worldwide computer network.

Internet connectivity is generally a two-way street. If you can contact other systems on the Internet, your system can also be contacted. With the proper security controls in place, you can deny would-be intruders the ability to access or otherwise tamper with your system. If your corporate network is connected to the Internet, you may have firewalls, proxy servers, or other safeguards in place to isolate the entire network from unauthorized access via the Internet.

# Viruses and Trojan Horses

Even the strongest precautions against intrusion won't do any good if you or other users unwittingly download and install software infected with a virus or Trojan horse. Such programs may appear perfectly harmless when installed and used, but they have the potential to destroy or corrupt data—or even to provide unauthorized access to your otherwise secure network.

Care should be taken to scan or otherwise inspect and test *all* software that is downloaded or copied from another computer system before it is installed and run on any computer on your network.

# WINDOWS 98 SECURITY PROVISIONS

Windows 98 provides several levels of security to protect your computer and the network it is connected to from unauthorized access.

## Passwords

The most visible security measure is the password. Everyone that uses a computer understands that a password is the key that provides access to an otherwise locked resource. Windows 98 uses passwords in many different places including the Windows logon, screen savers, network shares, e-mail, the Web, and Dial-Up Networking.

### Windows Logon

When you start Windows 98, one of the first things you see is the "Enter Network Password" dialog box. This logon password is Windows' first line of defense. It is how Windows knows that you are who you say you are. It's no secret that you can respond by pressing the cancel button, or even make up a new username and password, and still gain full access to local resources, including the ability to run any local program and read, copy, modify, or delete everything on the hard disk.

The whole name and password exercise may seem irrelevant if you happen to use Windows 98 in a small office network where access to shared drives is not secured by passwords. But it plays a very important role for the rest of us who use Windows 98 on a corporate network or at home for dial-up access to an office or the Internet.

When you tell Windows to remember the passwords you use to access network drives, connect to dial-up services, or check your e-mail, it stores that information in a user-specific password file that is loaded each time you log in using the same username and password.

### Screen Savers

One of the easiest ways to break into a system doesn't require any tricky tools or hacking techniques. Instead, you simply find an authorized user that has gained access to the network by entering the necessary passwords, then watch for them to leave their computer unattended while they take a break, go to lunch, attend a meeting, or leave for the night. Then you simply sit at the keyboard and freely access the network.

A simple but effective way to prevent this is to configure your system to activate the screen saver after a few minutes of inactivity and configure Windows to password-protect the screen saver. By doing this, you reduce the window of opportunity during which anyone can access your computer after you step away from it.

### Network Shares

Whenever you access a shared network drive that is password-protected, Windows will attempt to connect using the password you used to log on to the network. If a different password is required, you will be prompted to enter one and given the option to cause Windows to remember the password so it can automatically connect to the drive the next time you log on to Windows.

**JARGON:**   Shared network drives are also known as *network shares*.

As was discussed in Chapter 3, Windows 98 supports two types of access control. With share-level access control, you can specify different passwords for read-only and full-access, but the same passwords are used by everyone that accesses the network share. User-level access control is more secure because you specify which users and groups of users will be allowed access, you have a greater level of control over the type of access they will be granted, and you never specify a password because Windows authenticates the user with the domain controller.

If you do use share-level access control, it is convenient to protect all shared drives using the same password. But it is much more secure to use a different password for each share. That way, if one password is compromised, the rest of the network is not.

## E-Mail

Many people take it for granted that their e-mail is secure and that nobody else can read it. The truth is that in most cases e-mail is not very secure. Many corporate e-mail systems facilitate management access to their employees' e-mail. Some require users to enter passwords each time they open their e-mail program. Others give you clear access to the messages that have already been downloaded from the mail server but require the user to enter a password to receive new messages from the server.

Outlook Express, the e-mail software that comes with Windows 98, falls into the latter category. Messages are stored on disk in plain-text form and can be read by anyone with access to the computer. A password is only necessary when retrieving new messages from the mail server, and you can tell Windows to remember that password so you don't have to enter it each time.

You can improve the security of your e-mail by telling Outlook Express not to remember your password. It won't protect the messages you have already downloaded, but it will prevent an intruder from downloading any new messages without first guessing your password.

## The Web

You also need to be concerned about the security of your Web browser if you use it to access sensitive information on your corporate intranet or the Internet. Internet Explorer

(IE) has the ability to cache passwords so you don't have to reenter them each time you visit a site, and it caches recently accessed content to your hard drive for quick retrieval in the event you return to the same location or request the same URL within a short period of time.

Cached passwords are easy to deal with. Simply make sure the check box labeled "Save this password in your password list" is cleared whenever you are prompted for authentication while browsing .

The file cache is a little trickier. You can disable the cache altogether but we don't recommend doing that because it will have a dramatic effect on how fast the browser displays commonly accessed files. If you are concerned about protecting the confidentiality of the files you view and download over the Internet, you can cause IE to clear both the Cache and the History folders by going into the Internet Option dialog box and selecting Delete Files under the Temporary Internet Files section and Clear History under the History section.

## Dial-Up Networking

Windows Dial-Up Networking is capable of remembering the password you use to connect. This is a handy feature to use if you want to configure Windows to automatically connect to the network as necessary or otherwise simply don't want to re-type the password each time you connect manually.

This presents little if any security threat for Dial-Up Networking entries that are used to connect your computer to the Internet. However, it can be significant if you use Dial-Up Networking to access your corporate network.

We recommend that you enter your logon password each time you use Windows Dial-Up Networking to connect to your corporate network.

# Multi-User Settings

Windows supports configuration of a single computer for use by more than one person. When configured this way, Windows will store different configuration settings for each user that logs on to the system, including desktop icons, background picture, passwords, and the locations where certain user-specific files are stored.

Multi-user settings, as shown in the following illustration, are enabled in Windows 98 by selecting the Users icon from the Windows Control Panel. If the system is not already configured for multi-user settings, you will be prompted by a wizard that will guide you through the process.

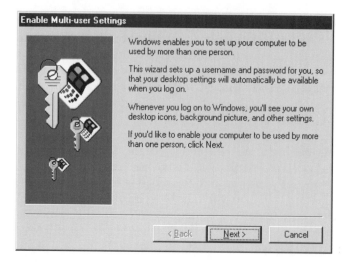

As illustrated below, the wizard allows you to specify which items will be personalized to each different user and which will be shared by all users of the computer.

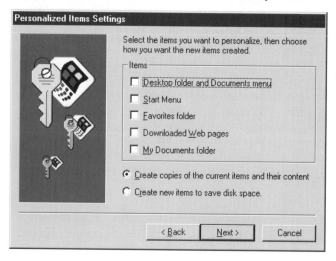

You can also specify whether the current user should inherit the current system settings and their content or start over from scratch.

## Password Properties

Password maintenance is performed through the Password Properties dialog box, which can be accessed by selecting the Password icon from the Windows Control Panel. From here, you can do such things as change your Windows and other passwords, control remote administration, and configure whether all users share the same preference and desktop settings or share a common user profile.

The dialog box contains three tabs, the first of which, labeled Change Passwords, is shown next. On this panel, there are two buttons. The first is for changing your Windows logon password. The second is for changing certain other Windows passwords, such as the one you use for clearing your screen saver and for logging on to the Windows network.

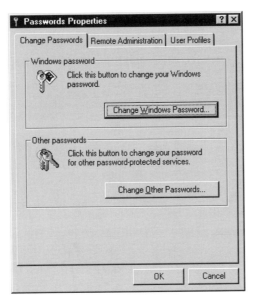

As shown in the following illustration, the second tab is labeled Remote Administration and is used to configure whether other computers will be allowed to manage your files and printers from remote locations.

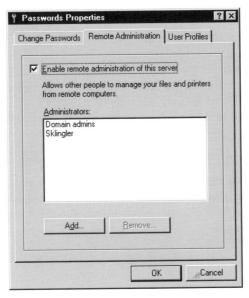

The third and final tab, shown next, provides a quick and simple way to enable personalized user profiles. Enabling personalized user profiles from this screen accomplishes the same thing as enabling multi-user settings from the Users dialog box as discussed in the last section, but without as much control over which items are personalized.

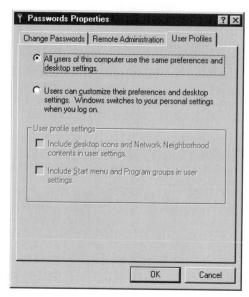

## Password List Editor

Windows 98 caches the passwords used for connecting to password-protected network resources in a password list (PWL) file. When you successfully log on to Windows with the correct password, this file is opened and its contents are read into memory so that they can be used to automatically reconnect to those resources in the future.

The Password List Editor is not installed by a standard Windows 98 installation. The easiest way to install it is to click on the Add/Remove Programs icon from the Windows Control Panel and then click on the Windows Setup tab. Clicking on the Have Disk button enables you to browse for and select the Password List Editor, which is found on your Windows 98 installation CD in the \tools\reskit\netadmin\pwledit directory.

When run, the Password List Editor contains a list of all known passwords for the currently logged on user and should look similar to the following illustration. Although you can't see the actual passwords in use, you can use this dialog to remove any passwords you don't want cached anymore, either because they are no longer needed or because you need to refresh your own cache following a password change.

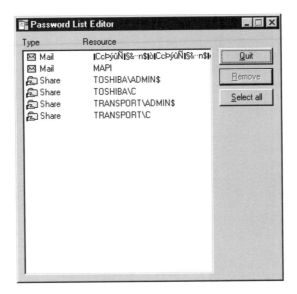

# INTERNET EXPLORER

For many users, the Web browser *is* the Internet. It is, after all, the tool they use most often to access Internet content. As such, it also has the most potential for abuse as users unknowingly access Web sites that could contain malicious ActiveX controls or Java scripts.

The Web browser has also become a popular platform for thin-client intranet applications. As the need for greater access to the local machine has driven new functionality in the Web browser, it has also created opportunity for abuse.

Microsoft has responded by providing a framework of controls and restrictions, known as Security Zones, which can be used to selectively turn off those features that can be abused. Strong encryption, digital certificates, and cookie controls also contribute to make IE more secure.

## Security Zones

Microsoft introduced Security Zones in IE 4.0. Security Zones simplify the task of configuring common security settings for related Web sites. Instead of configuring security settings for every site you visit, you configure four security zones then lump all Web sites into one of these categories. The four categories are the Internet, the intranet, trusted Web sites, and untrusted Web sites.

As shown in the following illustration, security zones contain settings that control downloading and installation of ActiveX controls, scripting, password authentication, cross frame security, and Java capabilities.

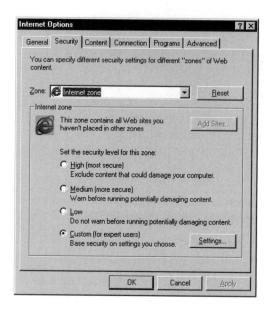

For each of the four security zones, you can specify high, medium, low, or custom security control settings. Table 16-1 lists the security controls that are affected by these settings and the effect that each setting has on the control.

If you're not satisfied by any of the three pre-defined security levels, you can select the custom option that will allow you to individually control each security option.

If you select Custom, then click on the Settings button, the Security Settings dialog box opens as illustrated below. From here, you can customize each option by clicking on the radio button next to the desired setting.

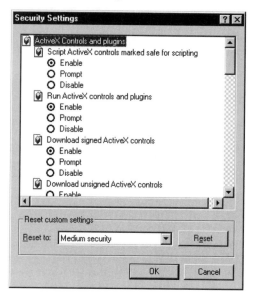

| Option | High Security | Medium Security | Low Security |
|---|---|---|---|
| **Active X Controls and Plugins** | | | |
| Script ActiveX controls marked safe for scripting | Enable | Enable | Enable |
| Run ActiveX controls and plugins | Disable | Enable | Enable |
| Download signed ActiveX controls | Disable | Prompt | Enable |
| Download unsigned ActiveX controls | Disable | Disable | Prompt |
| Initialize and script ActiveX controls not marked as safe | Disable | Prompt | Prompt |
| **Java** | | | |
| Java Permissions | High safety | High safety | Low safety |
| Scripting | | | |
| Active Scripting | Enable | Enable | Enable |
| Scripting of Java applets | Disable | Enable | Enable |
| **Downloads** | | | |
| File download | Disable | Enable | Enable |
| Font download | Prompt | Enable | Enable |
| **User Authentication** | | | |
| Logon | Prompt for user name and password | Automatic logon only in Intranet zone | Automatic logon with current username and password |
| **Miscellaneous** | | | |
| Submit non-encrypted form data | Prompt | Prompt | Enable |
| Launch applications and files in an IFRAME | Disable | Prompt | Enable |
| Installation of desktop items | Disable | Prompt | Enable |
| Drag and drop or copy and paste files | Prompt | Enable | Enable |
| Software channel permissions | High safety | Medium safety | Low safety |

**Table 16-1.**   Security control settings

If the settings you want are similar to one of the predefined security levels, you can save time by loading the predefined settings then changing the ones you don't like. You do this by selecting the desired security level in the "Reset custom settings" field near the bottom of the window and then clicking the Reset button.

# Strong Encryption/SSL

If you use your Web browser to exchange credit card information or to perform other financial and confidential transactions, a more secure version of IE, with support for Secure Sockets Layer (SSL) using 128-bit Strong Encryption, is available from Microsoft for use within the US and Canada. The easiest way to obtain the software is to visit the Microsoft Web site, where you can download it or order a copy on CD-ROM.

# Cookies

Cookies are small files of information that are passed back and forth between a Web site and your Web browser. One of the great Internet myths is that cookies somehow compromise the security of your computer or otherwise reveal personal information about you that you didn't authorize.

Many Web sites use cookies to keep track of their visitors. It allows them to collect valuable information about the number of unique visitors to a site, how those users use the site, and to deliver a personalized experience through targeted banner advertisements and other display preferences.

A good Web site designer can use cookies to recognize you as the same person that previously visited a site; to keep track of how you use the site and determine what products and services you are interested in by keeping track of the pages you request; to grant you access to secured areas without requiring you to enter a login name and password each time you visit; and to associate you with other personal information you may have voluntarily provided in the past, such as your name or shipping address.

Cookies have certainly increased the functionality of those Web sites that use them, but they really don't present a threat to the security of your computer system or to your privacy. But because it has been such a controversial subject, Microsoft has provided configuration options in IE that allow you to control how the Web browser deals with cookies.

You can control how IE handles cookies by opening the Advanced tab of the Internet Options dialog box, which is accessible through the View menu in IE. As shown in the following illustration, the Cookies section is located under the Security heading and contains three options: Always accept cookies, Prompt before accepting cookies, and Disable all cookie use.

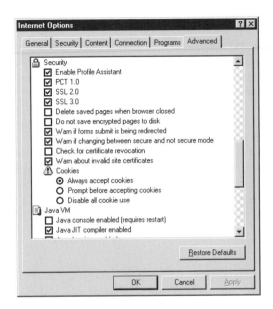

There are many Web sites and intranet applications that require cookies to function properly. Selecting the option to disable all cookie use will prevent you from accessing those sites or using those intranet applications.

If you're still nervous about cookies, select the option to prompt before accepting cookies. You will probably tire of this setting pretty quickly because many sites that use cookies also update them frequently, sometimes with every page you hit. With this setting, you will be prompted each time a new cookie is received or an existing cookie is updated.

# Digital Certificates

When exchanging information over the Internet or corporate network, it's difficult to know for sure with whom you are communicating. Internet e-mail illustrates this problem quite well because you can never trust that a message was sent by the person named in the From address field. Anyone can reconfigure their e-mail client software to pretend they are someone else and send phony e-mail.

Digital certificates were created to solve this very problem. By using digital certificates that are issued by a trusted certificate authority, you can know with a high degree of certainty that messages you receive were indeed sent by the person that claims to have sent them. Your Web browser also uses digital certificates when communicating with secure Web sites, and some Virtual Private Network (VPN) products use them for authentication and to strengthen their data encryption algorithms.

With IE, digital certificates are configured through the Content tab of the Internet Options dialog box. The Internet Options dialog box is accessible from the View menu in IE or by selecting the Internet icon from Windows Control Panel.

# SOFTWARE UPGRADES

One of the important lessons that history has taught us is that no software is perfect. Despite careful software design, programming, and testing by thousands of people, numerous bugs have turned up in Windows 95 and Windows NT, some of them security related, and it's possible that Windows 98 may contain similar vulnerabilities.

## Microsoft's Web Site

The best thing you can do to protect yourself from security holes that may be discovered in Windows 98 is to monitor Microsoft's own security advisories. The Microsoft Web site not only contains software patches that correct security holes, it also contains security advisories, tips, and a great deal of security-related information.

***RESOURCE:***   Microsoft Security Advisor at http://www.microsoft.com/security/.

## Windows Update

Another great resource is the Windows Update Web site, accessed by clicking the Windows Update icon on your Start menu. It's usually a good idea to install any software updates Microsoft makes available as soon as possible, especially if they affect the networking or Web browser components.

# OTHER SECURITY PRECAUTIONS

There are a number of other things you can do at the network level to improve the security of your Windows 98 computers.

## Security Policies

A good place to start is with the establishment of a security policy governing how and when users can connect to the network from remote locations, restricting the installation of software except from original manufacturers installation disks or CD-ROMs, and specifying how they should configure security-related settings on their local workstations, such as requiring user-level access controls and non-obvious passwords.

# Firewalls and Proxy Servers

If your network is connected to the Internet, you should use a firewall or proxy server to control the traffic that passes between your private network and the Internet. Without such a barrier, your entire network is at risk of being abused by anyone that happens to stumble across it on the Internet.

# Protocol Isolation

Protocol isolation can be used if a firewall or proxy server isn't immediately possible or as an added measure of precaution. With protocol isolation, all Windows networking is restricted to a non-TCP/IP protocol, such as IPX, and TCP/IP is only used by your Internet client software that accesses the Internet. Protocol isolation is easily accomplished by simply checking the network bindings on each computer to ensure that TCP/IP is not bound to any client, server, or file-sharing services. The weak link in this technique is that it does nothing to protect against Web or FTP servers or other gateway software that may be installed on any workstation on the network, thereby jeopardizing the security of your entire network.

# VPNs

Virtual Private Networks (VPNs) are an emerging technology that promise to provide secure access to corporate networks over the Internet. VPNs use a technique called *tunneling*, whereby all traffic is secured by passing it over the Internet in an encrypted form. The VPN server may be integrated with your firewall or may be hidden behind it on the private network.

# Net Watcher

Windows 98 comes with a utility called Net Watcher that allows you to monitor the network connection to your own computer or another server that is configured for remote administration. With Net Watcher, you can see who is connected to your computer and the shared folders and files that are in use. You can also disconnect users that you don't want connected to your system, close shared files that are in use by remote users, create additional shared folders, and modify the properties of existing shared folders. Here's what the Net Watcher interface looks like:

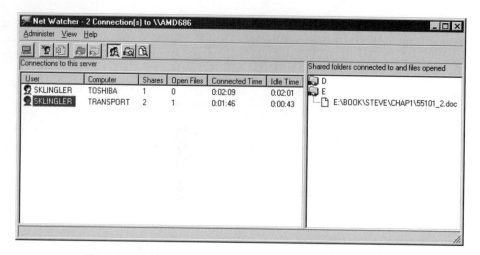

If the utility is installed, it can be found on the Start menu under Programs/ Accessories/System Tools. If it is not installed, you can do so by opening the Add/ Remove Programs dialog box from the Windows Control Panel, selecting the Windows Setup tab, and then enabling the Net Watcher option found under System Tools.

# COMING UP

No matter how well you plan or how many times you install and configure Windows 98, you're bound to run into problems every now and then. The troubleshooting guide in the next chapter will help you understand and solve some of those problems when they arise.

ETWORK
ROFESSIONAL'S
IBRARY

# CHAPTER 17

# Troubleshooting
# Windows 98

## What's ahead:

- Booting problems
- Networking troubleshooting
- General Windows 98 troubleshooting

*A child said, what is the grass? fetching it to me with full hands:*
*how could I answer the child?...I do not know what it is any more than he."*

—Walt Whitman, *Leaves of Grass*

Windows 98, as an advanced, 32-bit operating system (OS), is replete with powerful features such as built-in networking software, Plug and Play capabilities, and an integrated e-mail client. Consequently, as any complex system, it is subject to failure.

This chapter takes you through some of the potential failures (or problems) you may encounter and provides you with some practical solutions to those problems. Because many of the problems listed in this chapter refer to specific hardware and software configurations, you should first check your system for any similarities between your problem and the problem listed before making any changes. If your configuration does not match that of an example problem, please seek technical support directly from Microsoft.

Most problems listed in this chapter, however, are not prescriptive in nature and therefore can be used as templates from which you can solve many different problems. For example, instead of describing the steps required to fix a conflict between an NE2000 and a 3C509 network adapter, most examples in this chapter illustrate the basic steps required to determine similar problems between any set of adapter cards.

This section contains a large number of loosely related problems and solutions. Here's a list of the topics covered:

▼ Windows 98 installation has failed and you want to return to MS-DOS

■ Windows does not load

■ Boot failure

■ Applications do not function over more than one network segment

■ Remote Access Server (RAS) does not work

■ Internet service connection does not work properly

■ Network interface card (NIC) driver does not load

■ Windows 98 slows during disk operations

▲ Windows 98 does not work with Windows NT

# BOOTING PROBLEMS

Because your first introduction to Windows 98 occurs during installation, it is at that time you may first encounter problems. For example, when you reboot Windows 98 for the first time after installation, it may not start properly if you have selected an incorrect video adapter driver. The following solutions should help you solve these and other types of problems.

## Problem: Windows 98 installation has failed and you want to return to your previous OS

Although the Windows 98 installation process usually progresses without incident, there is a chance that you can find yourself unable to boot your new OS.

### Solution: Use Windows 98 Uninstall utility

However, you can return to your previous OS with very little trouble. If you choose to save your system files during the installation process, Windows 98 creates the following hidden files:

▼  WINUNDO.DAT

■  WINUNDO.INI

▲  WINLFN.INI

But beware: If these files are deleted, you won't be able to remove Windows 98 and return to your old OS. Also, there are some extenuating circumstances in which you can't return to your old OS, even if you've told Windows 98 to save your system files:

▼  You've installed Windows 98 on a compressed drive.

■  You're running a version of MS-DOS that predates version 5.0.

■  You've installed Windows 98 in a new directory.

▲  You didn't install Windows 98 on top of another OS.

If you're still able to start Windows 98, use the Start menu to open your Control Panel folder. From there, double-click on the Add/Remove Programs icon and select the Install/Uninstall tab. Highlight the Uninstall Windows 98 item, click on the Add/Remove button (see Figure 17-1), and Windows 98 guides you through the uninstall process. Alternatively, if you're not able to start Windows 98, hit the F8 key during the boot process, and select the Command Prompt Only item. Once the command line starts, just type UNINSTAL. Windows 98 takes care of the rest automatically. If you have trouble finding the uninstall utility, look in the C:\WINDOWS\COMMAND directory.

## Problem: Windows 98 Installation has failed and you want to return to MS-DOS

In most cases, Windows 98 should install on your workstation without a hitch. However, in some circumstances, you may not be able to complete the installation, or when you reboot your machine after installation, it fails to boot. If you have unsuccessfully attempted to fix the problem, you may want to uninstall the Windows 98 OS and return

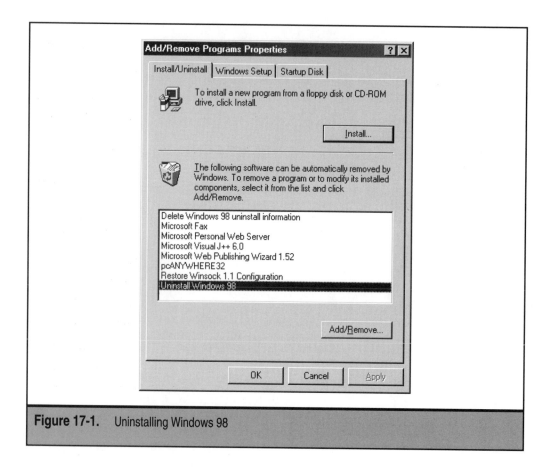

**Figure 17-1.** Uninstalling Windows 98

to MS-DOS. To uninstall Windows 98, you can insert your start-up disk, reboot your machine, and run UNINSTAL.EXE. But, because Windows 98 replaces MS-DOS, even if you delete the Windows 98 program files, your computer will not boot to MS-DOS. After installing Windows 98, if you change or delete these configuration files, you can find yourself in this situation.

## Solution: Reinstall the MS-DOS system files

In most cases, these steps can get you back to MS-DOS; however, if you are using Windows 98's built-in disk compression to make your hard disk hold more data, you should not try any of these as they will render all of your data useless. To return to MS-DOS after compressing your hard drive, you should try to boot to Windows 98's version of MS-DOS using the F4 key while booting. It loads the drivers needed to make your compressed hard disk accessible.

To return to MS-DOS, you need a bootable floppy disk containing the following files:

▼   SYS.COM

■   COMMAND.COM

■   FORMAT.COM

■   EDIT.COM

▲   ATTRIB.EXE

These files help you remove the Windows 98 system files and return your computer to normal. The file SYS.COM transfers the files required to boot MS-DOS to your hard disk. The COMMAND.COM file is the main boot file required by MS-DOS. It contains all of the internal commands you need to perform basic file and directory operations such as viewing directory contents and copying files. The FORMAT.COM file removes all files on your hard disk and makes it ready for MS-DOS. In most cases, you do not need this utility. However, it is good to have it handy in case you are unable to restore the MS-DOS OS. The EDIT.COM file is an editor you can use to edit the AUTOEXEC.BAT and CONFIG.SYS files located on your hard disk. Finally, the ATTRIB.EXE file enables you to make the hidden Windows 98 system files visible so you can delete them.

**SYS.COM**   The first thing you should try in restoring the MS-DOS OS is to install the MS-DOS system files with the SYS.COM file. To do this, boot to MS-DOS with your boot disk, and from the command line type the following:

```
SYS C:
```

Press the ENTER key. If you see a message indicating that the system has been successfully transferred, you should remove the boot diskette and reboot your workstation. If all goes well, your workstation should boot to MS-DOS.

**FORMAT.COM**   If these techniques do not restore your MS-DOS OS, you may need to reformat your hard disk. However, this will destroy all of the hard disk's information, programs, text files, directories—everything. Therefore, only use this alternative if nothing else works. To format your hard disk, boot to MS-DOS from your floppy diskette and from the command line type the following:

```
FORMAT C: /S
```

The /S option tells FORMAT.COM to transfer the files required to boot MS-DOS to your hard drive after it has finished formatting. After typing the command, press the ENTER key. You are then asked if you are sure you want to perform the requested operation. Press the Y key to continue. Once the operation has completed, you are asked to enter a volume label. Your machine should now boot to MS-DOS. You can then use the EDIT.COM file to either create or edit your AUTOEXEC.BAT and CONFIG.SYS files to ensure that your MS-DOS environment is set up correctly. For more information on how to do this, consult your MS-DOS documentation (you can also restore your files from backup).

## Problem: Windows does not load

When you boot Windows 98 for the first time, you should be presented with a login screen. However, if something has gone wrong with your configuration, you may be stuck with a blank screen. The most common reason for this type of problem concerns device drivers. For example, if you specify a NIC that conflicts with another device, such as a modem, you may not be able to boot into Windows properly.

## Solution: Boot Windows in fail-safe mode

The quickest way to remedy this problem is to boot Windows 98 in fail-safe mode. This loads the Windows 98 environment without loading any device drivers that may be creating conflicts. To boot Windows 98 in fail-safe mode, simply press the F5 key when your workstation begins the boot process. In some instances, Windows 98 detects a booting problem and presents you with the choice to boot in fail-safe mode (see Figure 17-2).

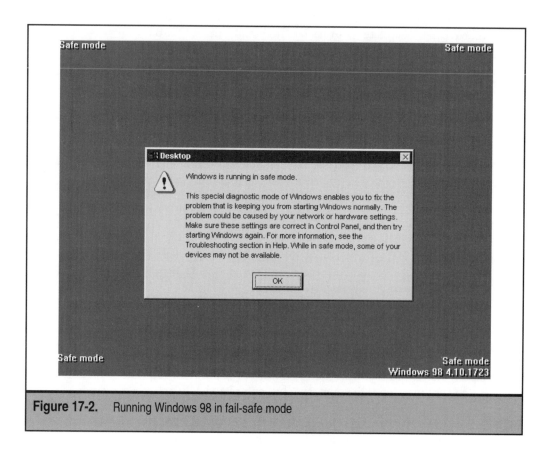

**Figure 17-2.** Running Windows 98 in fail-safe mode

It presents you with this choice whenever you reboot the workstation while it is loading Windows 98. When Windows 98 loads in this mode, you are not able to use all of your attached devices such as a NICor a modem.

However, you are able to open the Control Panel and change any of the settings that may be causing the boot trouble.

## Problem: Boot failure

In many cases, using fail-safe boot enables you to undo configuration changes that cause Windows 98 to boot improperly. However, in some instances, you may not be able to deduce the cause of your problems.

## Solution: Try alternative boot techniques

In cases where it is difficult to determine the cause of booting troubles, you should invoke the Windows 98 Startup Menu. This menu lets you choose a number of different ways to boot Windows 98. This menu should appear automatically if a previous boot process did not complete properly, but you can invoke it manually by pressing F8 while booting your workstation. Doing so opens a menu with the following options:

▼  Normal

■  Logged (\BOOTLOG.TXT)

■  Safe mode

■  Step-by-step confirmation

■  Command prompt only

▲  Safe Mode command prompt only

Each selection is designed to help you solve particular boot problems. You can therefore save a great deal of time by familiarizing yourself with the purpose and features of each.

**NORMAL**    If you suspect that a previous boot failure was merely an aberration and that it will not happen again, select this option. It simply starts Windows 98 normally.

**LOGGED (\BOOTLOG.TXT)**    This option lets you run through your AUTOEXEC.BAT and CONFIG.SYS files one line at a time, choosing whether or not to process each statement in these files. Windows 98 then creates a hidden file called BOOTLOG.TXT in the root of the boot drive (usually C:), logging the success or failure encountered during each step of the boot process. To view this file, you must first locate it using the ATTRIB command by typing the following at a command prompt:

```
ATTRIB BOOTLOG.TXT /S
```

The /S option instructs ATTRIB to look for the file in all of your hard disk's subdirectories. Once you have located the file, you can edit it with any text editor. Don't be alarmed if this file looks long and complex. It merely tracks the success of each statement executed by Windows 98 during the boot process (see Figure 17-3).

Therefore, you can use this file to locate problems simply by looking for statement failures. For example, if you notice that a video driver does not load successfully, you can reboot Windows 98 in fail-safe mode and replace that driver with one that does work properly.

If you are unable to fix a problem using this method, do not worry. Save this file to disk and contact Microsoft's technical support department for further help.

**SAFE MODE**    Similar to the fail-safe mode, this option simply bypasses all of the configuration files that might be responsible for your computer's problems. For example, it does not load any of the network drivers, modem drivers, or special Terminate and Stay Resident (TSR) drivers. You can then review your computer's settings, removing any conflicting or problematic devices manually.

**STEP-BY-STEP CONFIRMATION**    Press SHIFT-F8 to start Windows 98 in step-by-step mode. This is an excellent way for you to locate configuration problems. It allows you to review

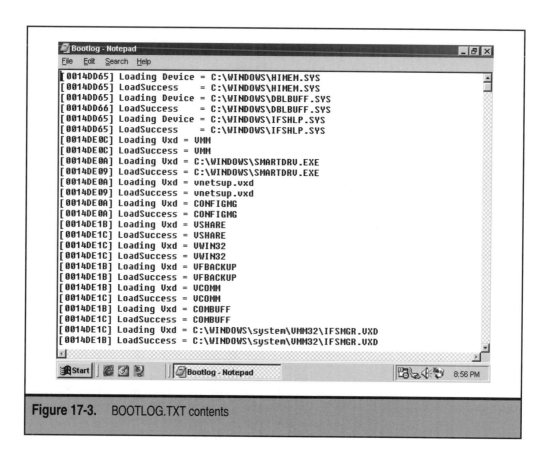

**Figure 17-3.**    BOOTLOG.TXT contents

each device statement before it is loaded, choosing whether or not Windows 98 should execute the statement. For example, if the system registry (which contains all of your user-specific information) does not appear to work properly, you can bypass it alone. This technique lets you verify that a suspect driver is at fault by process of elimination. You can also create a BOOTLOG.TXT file for further configuration review.

**COMMAND PROMPT ONLY**    Selecting to start only the command prompt lets you perform many low-level repairs that are impossible during the normal operation of Windows 98. You can press SHIFT-F5 to start this mode as well. This is a very useful tool in locating troubles because, like the previous option, it lets you select which devices to load. You can therefore quickly and easily eliminate suspect devices one by one without having to load the entire Windows 98 OS.

**SAFE MODE COMMAND MODE ONLY**    This selection gives you a quick command prompt that is very useful in situations requiring repeated boot processes punctuated with editing chores. For example, if you need to repeatedly edit your AUTOEXEC.BAT or CONFIG.SYS files, this option gives you the quickest time between boot attempts. In case you have used the Windows 98 DriveSpace application to compress your hard drive, do not worry. This option asks you if you want to load DriveSpace's disk compression driver.

# NETWORKING TROUBLESHOOTING

Despite Windows 98's Plug and Play architecture and built-in support for Internet packet exchange/sequenced packet exchange (IPX/SPX) and transport control protocol/Internet protocol (TCP/IP), you may experience problems connecting your Windows 98 workstation to other computers and online services. This section addresses the most frequently encountered networking issues using general scenarios designed to give you tools with which you can solve your particular problems.

## Problem: Applications do not function over more than one network segment

If you use applications such as the peer-to-peer talk program (called Chat), with the NetBIOS protocol, you will find that your applications function properly only while you communicate with computers that are a part of your own local network segment (subnet). This is caused because NetBIOS is unable to route across different network segments. On a Novell Inc. NetWare network, for example, utilizing Microsoft Corp.'s Windows for Workgroups client workstations (which generally rely upon NetBIOS), only machines within each segment can communicate. It is the same for Windows 98 workstations using Novell's NetBIOS Open Datalink Interface (ODI) network driver. You may be able to communicate with a workstation located on a different subnet using an application that is IPX/SPX-centric, but you cannot communicate with that same workstation using an application that is NetBIOS-centric.

## Solution: Add NetBIOS support to IPX/SPX or TCP/IP

The best way to overcome this limitation is to let a protocol that is routable transport the NetBIOS protocol from subnet to subnet. Novell's IPX/SPX protocol, for example, is able to do just that by tunneling NetBIOS packets within IPX/SPX packets. Routers that connect one subnet with another subnet see only an IPX/SPX packet's routing information, completely ignoring the NetBIOS information housed within the IPX/SPX packet. For more information about Novell's NetBIOS tunneling, please refer to Appendix B.

To enable NetBIOS to run within IPX/SPX packets, open the Control Panel window from the Settings submenu of the Start menu and double-click the Network icon. This opens the network configuration dialog box. Here, select the IPX/SPX protocol selection and click on the Properties button, which opens a dialog box containing three tabs labeled Bindings, Advanced, and NetBIOS (see Figure 17-4).

Select the NetBIOS tab and place a check mark in the box next to "I want to enable NetBIOS over IPX/SPX." This allows IPX/SPX to tunnel NetBIOS packets. Remember that this works for TCP/IP as well. Just follow the same steps, replacing IPX/SPX with TCP/IP.

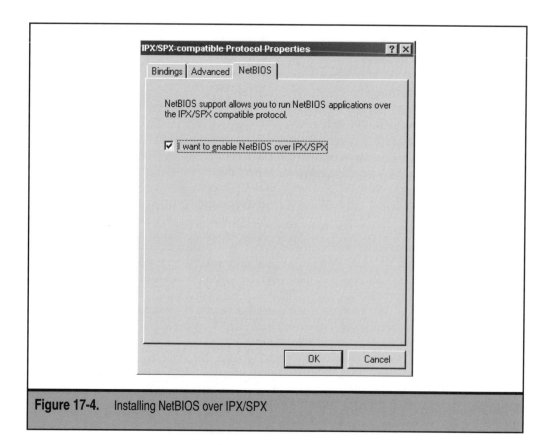

**Figure 17-4.** Installing NetBIOS over IPX/SPX

## Problem: Remote Access Server (RAS) does not work

The Windows 98 RAS allows you to securely connect with many machines, such as Windows for Workgroups, Windows NT, and other Windows 98 workstations, and it is very simple to install. However, after connecting to another machine, you may notice that although the connection seems to have been established correctly, you are unable to work on the host machine.

## Solution 1: Ensure that device-sharing is enabled on host machine

This is a very easy problem to solve. However, its cause is not apparent. This is because during the RAS installation routine, you were asked to set up every aspect required to establish a remote connection except one: sharing. If sharing is not enabled on the host machine, you will not be able to see its hard drive, printer, or network volumes from your remote access client.

To install sharing on a Windows 98 or Windows NT host machine, simply double-click the My Computer icon, highlight your hard drive, and click the right mouse button. This activates a pop-up menu. Click the Sharing option, opening the Sharing panel of the Properties dialog box. Here, you should click the radio button labeled Shared As: and enter a name for the drive as it should appear to the remote access user (see Figure 17-5).

The Access Type you choose should depend upon the amount of security you desire. If you are the only remote user, you should click the radio button labeled Full. Otherwise, choose the level of security you need (either Read-Only or Depends on Password). When you have finished, you should see a change in the icon representing your hard drive. Instead of a simple hard drive icon, you should see a box being held by an outstretched hand.

## Solution 2: Check host configuration

If you have ensured that the host machine will accept your remote connection, but you are still having connectivity problems, try checking the host configuration on your Windows 98 client. To do this, open your Dial-Up Networking folder from your Start menu, right-click on the troublesome icon, and click on the Properties item. Click on the Server Types tab and check to see if your required protocols are selected. For troublesome NetBEUI or IPX/SPX connections, all you will have to do is ensure that they are selected as Allowed network protocols.

For TCP/IP, however, there's more to check into. If you click on the TCP/IP Settings button on the Server Types panel, you'll see a window in which you must specify an IP address as well as a DNS server or WINS address (see Figure 17-6).

In the upper section, make sure that you've got the correct IP address entered. Or, if your server creates an IP address for you dynamically, ensure that you click on the radio button entitled "Server assigned IP address." In the lower section, make sure that you've entered the correct naming server (DNS or WINS) IP addresses. Often the problem here lies in an incorrect ordering of the primary and secondary naming servers.

## Problem: Internet service connection does not work properly

Once you have established a dial-up account with an Internet access provider with the protocols included with Windows 98, you can access the Internet as a Point-to-Point

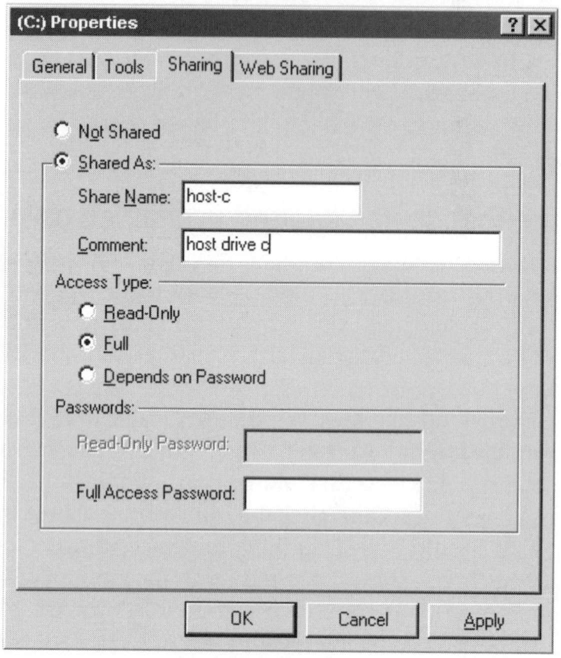

**Figure 17-5.** Checking drive sharing for remote access issues

Protocol (PPP) client. However, to set up a PPP service on your workstation, you must make a great number of modifications to your network configuration and your remote access software. If you forget any steps, your connection will not work at all.

## Solution: Follow an Internet connection check list

To install Internet support on your Windows 98 machine, use the following check list:

▼ *Gather Internet provider information.* To connect to the Internet via PPP, you must obtain information from your Internet access provider that will let your networking software communicate with the provider's host server. You should obtain your workstation's Internet protocol (IP) address (if needed), the IP address of the host machine to which you wish to connect, the IP addresses of the Domain Naming System (DNS) servers you will need, and the IP addresses of a mail server (if needed).

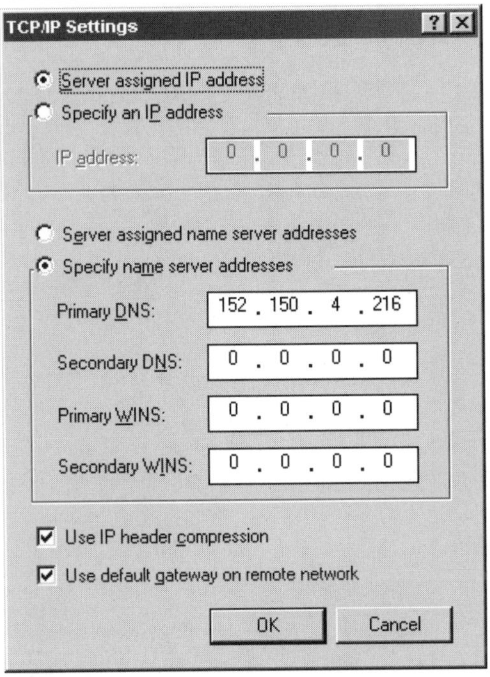

**Figure 17-6.**    Verifying TCP/IP settings for RAS connections

■ *Install dial-up adapter support.* After you have gathered the appropriate information, you must install the networking software. First, you must add a modem driver, if you have not already done so, by double-clicking the Add New Hardware icon within the Control Panel window. Follow the directions within the Hardware Installation Wizard.

When you are done, double-click the Network icon within the Control Panel window and enter the configuration information gathered in the previous step. For example, once you have opened the Network icon, highlight the Microsoft TCP/IP protocol selection and enter the Internet access provider's information (see Figure 17-7).

Once you have entered this information, all you need to do is ensure that the newly created dial-up adapter is bound to the TCP/IP protocol. To do this, select the Microsoft Dial-Up Adapter item from the Network dialog box, click

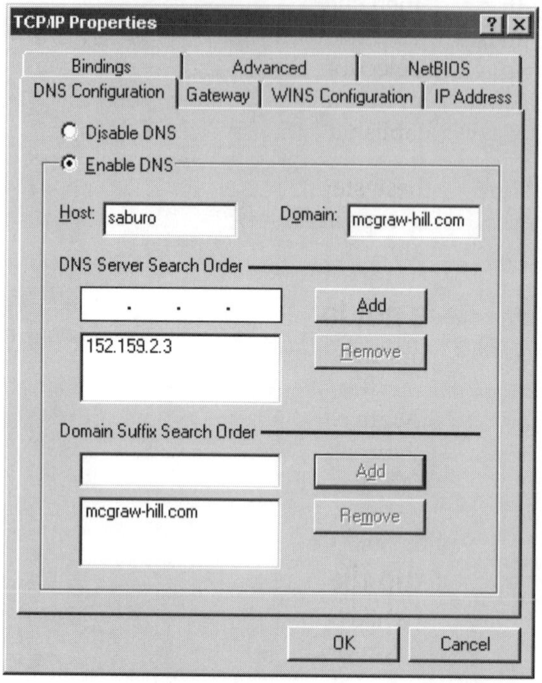

**Figure 17-7.** TCP/IP settings for PPP connections

on Properties, and select the Bindings tab. You should see an option for Microsoft TCP/IP within the box. Here, ensure that this item has a check mark next to it. If you do not bind a protocol to your dial-up adapter, you will never be able to make a connection because your modem will only try to speak over standard terminal emulation protocols, not networking protocols like PPP.

▲ *Select the proper dial-up connection type.* The only remaining items for you to check can be found within the Dial-Up Networking program. To access this service, click the Start button, the Programs item, the Accessories item, and finally on the Dial-Up Networking item. If you have not already created an Internet session, double-click the Make New Connection icon and follow the Installation Wizard, entering a name for the connection and your access provider's host telephone number. When you have finished, select the New Connection icon and then click the right mouse button, activating a pop-up menu. Here, click Properties and then click Server Types. Ensure that the type of Dial-Up server is labeled PPP: Windows 98, Windows NT 3.5, Internet. Click on the OK button and then click on the Configure button. Here, you must select the Options tab and then place a check mark next to the "Bring up terminal window after dialing" selection. This is necessary because without it, you will not be able to enter your account information such as your name and your password once you establish a connection.

Once you have followed these steps, you should be able to connect to the Internet without any problems. If you experience further difficulties, however, contact your Internet service provider directly.

## Problem: NIC driver does not load

Installing Windows 98's networking support is made simple because it comes with the drivers required to run many NICs. It can even automatically install these drivers. However, it cannot detect hardware conflicts between your interface card and any other add-on cards. Therefore, even though a network installation may appear to go smoothly, when you boot Windows 98 for the first time, you may see a command line error message indicating that the device driver for your NIC could not be loaded.

## Solution: Check the startup files and the Control Panel for conflicts

If you receive an error message while booting Windows 98, the first thing you should do is determine whether the problem lies in your software configuration or your hardware settings.

**HARDWARE CONFLICT**   If you suspect a hardware conflict, the easiest way to locate the problem is to use the Windows 98 System Properties utility. From the Control Panel folder, double-click the System Properties icon and select the Device Manager tab. From here, look for items denoted with a yellow question mark (see Figure 17-8).

If there is a conflict with any other device such as an internal modem, video adapter, or another NIC, click on the Properties button and select the Resources tab. If there is a conflict, Windows 98 tells you with which device you're having a hardware conflict (see Figure 17-9).

To fix this situation, you should try different IRQ and I/O values until Windows 98 indicates that there is no continuing conflict.

**SOFTWARE CONFLICT**   If your hardware appears to be configured correctly, the next place you should look for trouble is within the software settings for the device. For a network adapter, this means checking the protocols used by the adapter. To check for these types of issues, double-click the Network icon from the Control Panel window. Once here, ensure that you have both a NIC and a supporting protocol installed and configured. If you are not sure whether this has been done, refer to Chapter 2.

If everything appears to be in proper order, the problem most likely lies within your AUTOEXEC.BAT file. It is from here that you actually load the network drivers. To check this file, open an MS-DOS window and change to the root of your hard drive. Here, open

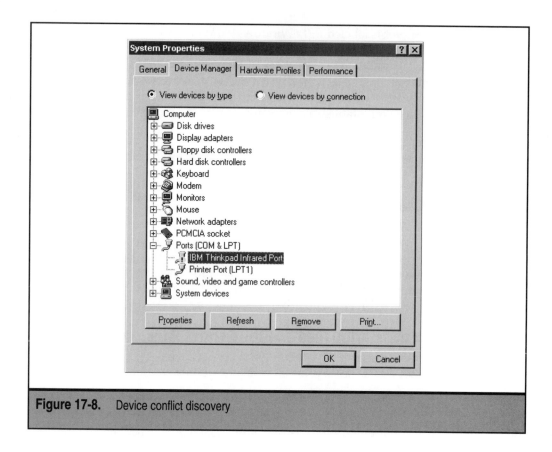

**Figure 17-8.** Device conflict discovery

the AUTOEXEC.BAT file with the MS-DOS editor that is included with Windows 98. For example, to open the file, you would type the following:

```
EDIT C:\AUTOEXEC.BAT
```

Inspect the contents of this file, paying particular attention to the statements relating to network drivers. What appears within this file depends upon a number of variables such as whether or not you have chosen ODI or Network Driver Interface Specification (NDIS) drivers, for example. If you have chosen to install ODI drivers, you should see a set of commands similar to the following:

```
LSL
NE2000
IPXODI
NETX
ODIHELP
NETSTART
```

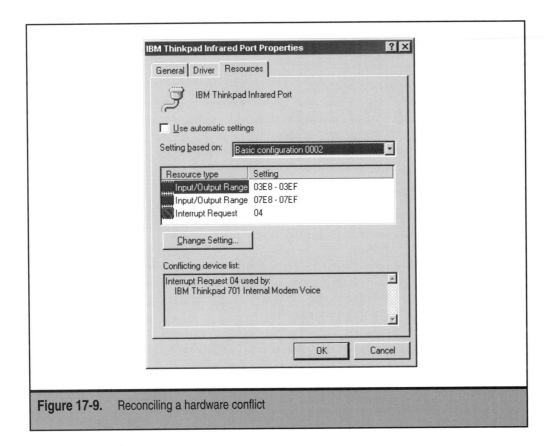

**Figure 17-9.**    Reconciling a hardware conflict

With either ODI or NDIS drivers, if you have chosen to retain your original device drivers in lieu of Windows 98's 32-bit client drivers, you should ensure that you are referring to the same NIC driver from the AUTOEXEC.BAT file as you are from the Network configuration screen.

The most common problem here stems from an incorrect reference. For example, if you have changed network adapter cards in the past and neglected to remove the old network driver, you may be referencing it instead of the new, correct driver.

# GENERAL TROUBLESHOOTING

This section covers the most troublesome topics not covered in the other areas of this chapter. Therefore, its contents are organized alphabetically rather than topically to make the varied contents more accessible. As with the other sections in this chapter, all problems and solutions act as general, deductive stratagems from which you should be able to infer solutions for your particular problems.

## Problem: Windows 98 slows during disk operations

Although Windows 98 is capable of preemptive multitasking (running more than one application simultaneously), it may appear to slow to a crawl in some situations when you run two applications at the same time. For example, if while you format a floppy disk from the Windows 98 Explorer you also open a solitaire game, you may notice that it takes an inordinate amount of time for solitaire to load and deal the cards. Because Windows 98 retains some 16-bit architecture for backward-compatibility, some simultaneous program execution combinations will slow your workstations substantially, such as the format command and the solitaire game.

## Solution: Run disk utilities from the command line

If you find this behavior unbearable, you can counter such anomalies by running file and disk utility commands from an MS-DOS box. This practice bypasses the overhead associated with the Windows 98 interface, removing one more step between the command and the OS. Of course, the only commands that can effect your general productivity within Windows 98 are those that demand a great deal of consistent processor time, such as the format command. Most commands actually complete before you are able to switch to another program.

## Problem: Windows 98 does not work with Windows NT

Although you can maintain both Windows NT and Windows 98 on the same hard drive, dual-booting between the two OSs, neither OS function properly if you install both in either the same hard disk or within a single logical disk.

## Solution: Install separately

Because the default directory for both OSs is labeled C:\WINDOWS, you must ensure that they are both installed in completely separate drives. If you do not, the currently active OS may attempt to reference programs and drivers from the other OS. This occurs because each OS contains files with identical names but incompatible content. To solve this problem, ensure that each OS has its own directory. An ideal directory structure that ensures that no cross-referencing problems occur is as follows:

C:\WINDOWS.95
D:\WINDOWS.FWG
E:\WINDOWS.NT

These drives and directories should house Windows 98, Windows for Workgroups, and Windows NT, respectively.

If you have installed or configured multiple disk drives or disk partitions, you can simply maintain each OS on separate partitions or disk drives. This is the most simple corrective technique. However, if you have only one disk or only one partition, you cannot install two partitions without destroying all of the data on your hard disk.

# SUMMARY

In this chapter, we've covered the major networking issues you're most likely to encounter when you install and configure Windows 98. As you can see, as user-friendly as Windows 98 can be, there are still many things that can go wrong. Luckily, most of these problems are easily resolved with the right know-how. If you run into any problems not listed in this chapter, you can go to your MIS manager, or you can simply point your Web browser at Microsoft's Windows 98 Web site at http://www.microsoft.com/windows98/default.asp. There you can go through online troubleshooting wizards and an online support forum maintained by Microsoft engineers.

NETWORK
PROFESSIONAL'S
LIBRARY

# PART IV

# Appendices

NETWORK
PROFESSIONAL'S
LIBRARY

# APPENDIX A

# Networking Basics

The act of sharing and obtaining information, be it the outcome of Sunday's basketball game, a drawing, holiday plans, or an interesting rumor, comprises a familiar and constant aspect of modern society. To access such information, for example, you may commonly choose to communicate over the telephone. However, the telephone (and other similar mediums such as television or radio) presents fleeting and unreliable data because it does not convey information in a permanent format and, more often, does not contain desired information. Comparatively, a *computer network*, in its most basic definition as the connection of two or more computers, is a medium through which you can obtain information that is both enduring and reliable. See Figure A-1.

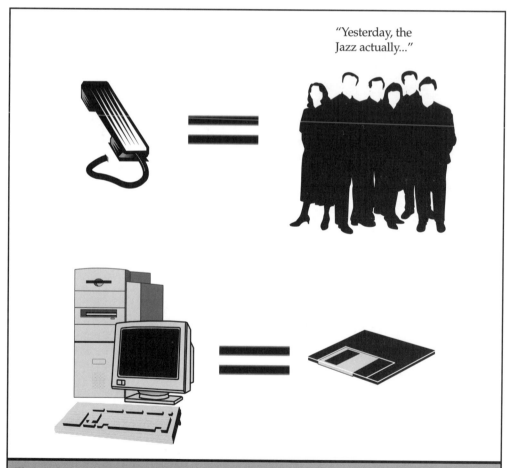

**Figure A-1.**   Computer networks convey information much like a telephone conversation; however, the data passed is more lasting and predictable

# WHAT IS A NETWORK?

Information about the basketball game mentioned previously can arrive in the form of a database of player statistics; a drawing can appear as a graphic image; holiday plans can arrive as data maintained within a scheduling program; and rumors can surface as a word processing document. Of course, because most computer networks occur within the business, educational, and research environments, databases, graphics, schedules, and documents usually contain information appropriate for such atmospheres. For example, computer networks enable you to share and access a spreadsheet containing the afternoon's stock market information, a video file containing a lecture on anthropology, and a document containing satellite trajectories and schedules.

Keep in mind that as more and more PCs connect through networks (such as the Internet) and through online services (such as CompuServe and AOL), the scope of shared information will continue to expand into all aspects of life, perhaps uniting the two worlds of personal and professional communication.

You can find excellent examples of the diversity of networks in just about every walk of life. A hospital, for example, may rely upon a wireless network of Personal Digital Assistants (PDAs), with which doctors prescribe treatment and medicine while nurses keep track of the those prescriptions, the effected patients, and numerous hospital functions. Another network could encompass a vast number of DOS or Windows workstations spread across the globe, conducting international business. Or, a network could simply contain your notebook and desktop computers. The variants are endless, but do not think that because networks are complex, they are incomprehensible. Just like an elephant, they are made up of pieces: trunk, feet, body, head, and tail. By understanding what each part does and how each part relates to the other parts, you can reconstruct an elephant, even if you've never seen one.

As with the elephant, this appendix reconstructs a network from its pieces as a mental experiment in which you can create a network from the ground up, taking into consideration each variable required to make a network work. The remainder of this appendix is dedicated to just such an experiment. We start by defining the physical items that constitute a network. The different network nomenclatures that have evolved around different network configurations, such as local area networks (LANs) and wide area networks (WANs), are then discussed. The uses of comparable network computing models such as client/server and peer-to-peer are explored. And finally, we outline the actual, physical types of networks from the cabling system to network protocols.

Networks are far more than a number of connected personal computers. The actual components can range in size and power from a digital pager to a mainframe computer. Between these two devices lie Intel and RISC-based workstations (*RISC* stands for Reduced Instruction Set Computer), multiprocessor servers, printers, PDAs, fax machines, network computers (NCs), dumb terminals, and so forth. What is important to remember is that any set of devices that enables individuals to access and share informational services comprises a network. However, regardless of the number or type of devices comprising a network, certain hardware and software features are elemental to all networks.

## Network Operating System

The network operating system (NOS) resides upon a computer (be it mainframe or PC) and makes available that computer's resources. It also provides some sort of security capabilities that control access to those resources.

**JARGON:**   Actually, NOS is becoming an antiquated term as more and more workstation operating systems (OSs) such as Microsoft Windows NT, OS/2, and of course Windows 98 become able to perform all of the functions of a NOS.

The following services are either included with a NOS or available as add-on programs:

▼ **File services**   Users can access files stored on the computer's hard disk, CD-ROM, and other storage media.

■ **E-mail services**   Users can exchange messages, graphic images, spreadsheets, text, and other files.

■ **E-mail gateway services**   Users can exchange e-mail between different mail systems.

■ **Database services**   Users can query, update, and administer databases such as Novell's btrieve and Microsoft's SQL server.

■ **Communications services**   Users can communicate with outside services and networks.

■ **Archive services**   Users can manage NOS files by backing them up to tape, optical, or other media.

■ **Print services**   Users can print documents to a large number of printers.

■ **Fax services**   Users can send and receive fax information.

■ **Telephony services**   Users can access voice mail through their workstations.

▲ **Video services**   Users can view, create, and participate in video conferencing.

## Servers

NOSs and dependent services run on computer systems called servers. Peripherals, such as printers, are often attached directly to the server. These platforms can range from an Intel single-processor 286 PC to a multiprocessor gigabyte-storage mainframe computer.

## Client Workstations

In order to utilize a NOS, individual PCs require software that enables them to communicate with the network via an internal Network Interface Card (NIC). The type of software utilized depends upon the type of network present. A UNIX network, for example, generally requires a TCP/IP protocol stack, while Novell NetWare still utilizes IPX/SPX. NetWare, however, is slowly adopting TCP/IP as its primary protocol. With NetWare 5, which is due out during the fall of 1998, almost all NetWare services should be available via TCP/IP. No matter which protocol a server uses, clients can act accordingly. Because network adapters are able to send and receive multiple protocol stacks, a workstation can contain software for both types of networks.

## Cabling System

A network cabling system simply connects workstations with NOS-based servers. Although cabling, as the name implies, usually involves physical cables, networks can be connected via satellite, broadband, and infrared wireless technologies. For the most part, though, networks are connected with coaxial, fiber, or telephone-like cable.

## Peripherals

Cabling also connects peripherals to a network. Although many peripherals are often attached directly to a network server, many are connected either to workstations or directly to the network. Printers and fax machines, for example, can be attached in either fashion. These devices do not contain a NOS, per se; however, they do contain software and hardware that enables them to advertise themselves as shareable network devices. By attaching these resources directly to the network cabling system, you can minimize the server resources required to run your network by reducing the load on your server.

# TYPES OF NETWORKS

Networks, as mentioned previously, are simply based upon connected devices, but the simplicity ends there. The scale of a network can range in size from two home computers to the millions of world-wide machines found on the Internet. These two ends of the spectrum comprise two basic types of computer networks: WANs and LANs. Within this range lie a number of interrelated network types, each arising from a specific networking need, be it geographical, financial, or populace proportional. A network can span the globe, or it can span a single room. It can support hundreds of thousands of users, or it can support a solitary individual, connecting with the Internet. As long as there are varying needs, there will be varying network types.

Generally, LANs are found in localized, geographically restricted areas such as in a single home or business building. WANs, in contrast, can connect machines between two buildings or two continents. LANs also contain a limited number of computers, while a WAN such as the Internet contains millions of machines. This dichotomy of size and distance does not mean that the two types of networks do not interrelate. Far from that, they often occur together because LANs are often a subset of a WAN. (See Figure A-2.)

From a technological viewpoint, WANs and LANs differ in the way they are connected. A LAN is usually connected by privately owned cable in a privately owned

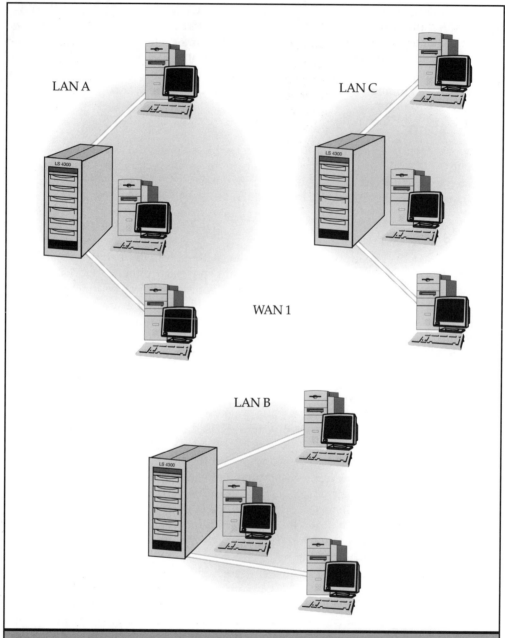

**Figure A-2.** A WAN can contain a number of interconnected LANs

building, while a WAN is usually connected by services that are not distance-dependent, such as public and private telecommunications facilities, microwaves, and satellites. For example, your corporation may use the Internet as a gateway through which it sends and receives e-mail. Or, your remote office or workgroup may connect with the main corporation via a direct, dial-up WAN connection.

Imagine a large bank with various branch offices. Within each office, people use their computers to communicate with one another, exchanging deposit and withdrawal information, sharing loan processing data, and so forth. That is a LAN. Now imagine that same bank sharing the same information with a number of other banks in other cities. That is a WAN. Between these two distinctions there are a number of interesting variants.

## Network Segment (Subnetwork)

A network segment contains a limited number of devices (workstations, servers, peripherals) that all share a specific network address. Within an Ethernet network segment, for example, all computers are able to see each other's network broadcasts. Unless connected by a bridge or router, network segments do not share information. A LAN, therefore, can be made up of interconnected network segments. This is called an *internetwork*.

**JARGON:** The Internet, being made up of thousands and thousands of LANs, is also called an internetwork. Either way, both types of networks contain smaller sub-networks.

## Campus Networks

These networks span buildings like WANs; however, unlike WANs, they do not have to rely upon outside cabling sources. Usually found on school campuses and large business facilities, these networks connect geographically separate buildings through a campus-wide, high-speed backbone such as fiber-optic cable or other high-speed media. Within each connected building, network segments or LANs exist.

## Metropolitan Area Networks

A type of network that is often confused with a WAN is the Metropolitan Area Network (MAN). This type of computer network is actually a connection of computers regulated by local or state utility commissions. A local phone company or cable company may provide LAN services in your area. Companies needing to communicate within a metropolitan area that contains public rights-of-way can rely upon a set of standards as set forth in IEEE 802.6 to obtain high-speed network connections between buildings. A MAN, therefore, is really a WAN that merely relies upon a specific set of networking standards.

## Enterprise Networks

An *enterprise network* can include LANs, MANs, or WANs. This type of network, however, interconnects network resources regardless of the NOS, geographical dispersion, cabling differences, protocol diversities, application differences, and so forth. In this way, these networks allow users transparent access to all resources. Three main connectivity strategies that enterprise networks rely upon are directory services, middleware, and e-mail switches. Directory services, often based upon CCITT X.500 standards, help network administrators organize the voluminous amounts of user and resource information found on an enterprise network. For example, Novell NetWare's NetWare Directory Services (NDS) is an X.500-like product that makes user and e-mail addresses available to every resource on the network. Middleware enables different protocols and applications to share information as though they were exactly the same. E-mail gateways, which are usually based upon the ITU X.400 standard, allow different e-mail packages to transparently transfer electronic mail.

## The Internet

Over the past two years, the Internet has become much more than a simple resource for academics and computer enthusiasts. Today, the Internet has found its way into nearly every company as both a source of communication and a platform for global applications. In order to communicate, a company might use the Internet as a communications tool for sending and receiving e-mail. The company might do this in two ways: it could use a gateway to connect its existing e-mail application with the Internet, or it could connect with an e-mail server that resides on the Internet via a direct connection through an Internet Service Provider (ISP). In order to use the Internet as an application platform, many companies are building Web-based services to sell goods directly.

**RESOURCE:** A great example of such an Internet-based application is amazon.com, an online-only bookseller. Its URL is http://www.amazon.com/. For more information on the Internet and Internet services like amazon.com, take a look through Chapters 9 and 6.

# NETWORK STRATEGIES

Two important and closely related aspects of networking that can be found in any network type involve the manner in which users access and share information. These two strategies are called client/server and peer-to-peer. Both share a common ancestry in that they evolved from a move away from the old model of computing found within mainframe and minicomputer systems, in which a centralized computer containing many processor units and massive file storage space provided processing power for a number of simple keyboard/monitor workstations (dumb terminals). Users entered information via the dumb terminal and that information was processed and stored on the centralized computer.

As PCs moved into corporations, scholastic organizations, and research institutes, the centralized processing power of the mainframe was slowly succeeded by the processing power of individual workstations. Although mainframes and minicomputers such as the IBM Corp. AS/400 are still used for their sheer processing power, the decentralization of this processing power allowed individual workstations to actively share processing, file storage, and printing services with other workstations.

# Peer-to-Peer Communication

When two machines share the services previously mentioned, the arrangement is called *peer-to-peer* networking because both machines can act upon one another in identical ways. (See Figure A-3.) Macintosh networks are an excellent example of a peer-to-peer network. First, each Macintosh computer advertises its availability on the network; then, as needs dictate, a computer can log into another computer and access that computer's information. In essence, each workstation acts as a client. One client can be a client to another client.

Many NOSs offer peer-to-peer communication. Although many of these NOSs function as client/server platforms, they all exhibit features specific to peer-to-peer networking. Some peer-to-peer OSs are described next.

## Microsoft Windows for Workgroups

This OS allows users to not only share files and peripherals (such as a printer), it also provides a platform for Microsoft's object technology, called Object Linking and Embedding (OLE). With this technology, for example, you can maintain a spreadsheet on your machine, while allowing another user to store a linked copy of it on his or her own machine in a word processing document. When you update the spreadsheet, the user holding the copy sees the update automatically. OLE does not just appear on Windows for Workgroups, however; it can be found on Microsoft Windows NT as well as Microsoft Windows 98. Other useful peer-to-peer features of Windows for Workgroups include a schedule, e-mail, calendar, chat, and terminal emulation programs.

## Microsoft Windows NT

This powerful 32-bit NOS lets you take advantage of the same features available within Windows for Workgroups. However, it also contains additional security as well as the ability to act simultaneously as a peer-to-peer and client/server platform.

## Microsoft Windows 98

By combining many of the security enhancements of Windows NT with the peer-to-peer capabilities of Windows for Workgroups, Windows 98 gains the best of both worlds through its 32-bit processing power, its integrated telephone, fax, and e-mail package, and its ability to integrate closely with many NOSs such as Windows NT and Novell NetWare.

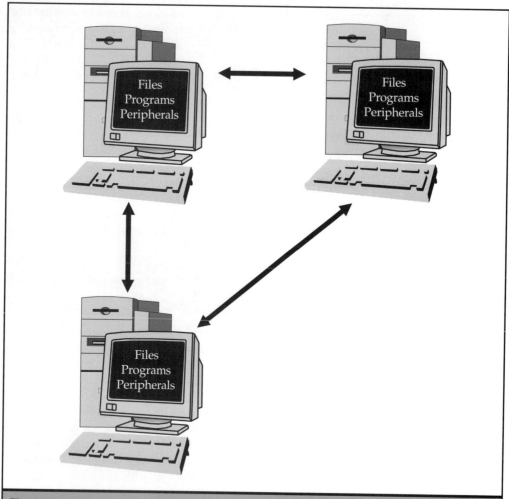

**Figure A-3.** Peer-to-peer networking lets users access resources on one another's computers in a relatively equal fashion

## Artisoft LANtastic

LANtastic, although strictly a NOS for peer-to-peer services, has recently enlisted the power of Novell NetWare to boost its file and peripheral-sharing capabilities.

## IBM LAN Server

This 32-bit NOS functions on top of IBM OS/2 as either a client/server or peer-to-peer OS. Though not as popular as it once was, IBM OS/2 is still in use as a platform for many top-notch applications such as Lotus Notes and Domino.

## Peer-to-Peer Advantages

Peer-to-peer networks offer many advantages. They are generally less expensive than client/server networks, they allow data and processing power to be distributed over a larger area, and they enable users to dynamically organize computing requirements. Information distributed across a peer-to-peer network can be broken down into related groups, such as an accounting group, a marketing group, and so forth, without necessitating the reorganization of the actual data.

There are some disadvantages to peer-to-peer networking, however. If you are a user, peer-to-peer services are functional and easy to use, but you may find it difficult to keep track of file locations as they are usually spread across many different machines. If you are a network administrator, peer-to-peer services can be difficult to govern because of this distributed data. For example, if files are continually changing from machine to machine, then how do you decide which machines, which directories, and which files to back up? Another problem occurs when too many people attempt to access a single workstation's resources. Because of the additional overhead of each client, that station's performance becomes degraded—sometimes beyond use. Additionally, maintaining security within a peer-to-peer environment is troublesome at best. With Windows 98 peer-to-peer networks, it is easy for users to set up their own network services, allowing perhaps the wrong users to gain access to sensitive data and applications.

**RESOURCE:** To find out how to secure your Windows 98 network, look through Chapter 16.

# Client/Server Communication

The client/server model of computing also grew out of the decentralization of mainframes and minicomputers. However, as a sort of hybrid, client/server retained a great number of the mainframe and minicomputer features while adding its own peer-to-peer-like capabilities. Instead of a workstation merely accessing data on a second workstation, both machines take an active role. In other words, intelligent workstations, called "front-end" systems, communicate not with another front-end as in peer-to-peer, but with a server (called a "back-end") that provides specific processor-dependent services. Your Windows 98 workstation can accommodate both peer-to-peer and client/server configurations.

An excellent example of a client/server configuration can be found in database applications. For instance, a database management system (DBMS) comprises two parts: the client that executes a series of instructional statements called Structured Query Language (SQL), and the server that houses the database. The client (front-end) initiates a directive, such as a search request, and the server (back-end) acts upon that request. At first this may not seem that much different than when a peer-to-peer workstation accesses a database file on another peer-to-peer machine. However, there are two fundamental differences that illustrate the power of client/server. First, the back-end database (called a database engine) takes care of a great deal of the processing duties. If you ask a client/server database to find a specific piece of information, it does not return with the results from each record as it passes through the database. It only reports the final results. Second, if your client workstation, which contains the database application, fails during a database transaction (such as the addition of a record), the server will automatically "roll-back" the transaction in order to maintain database integrity. No peer-to-peer database system can offer such services.

This active interaction between the front-end database application and back-end database engine constitutes a client/server relationship. Another excellent example of a client/server relationship can be found within many NOSs. These systems provide front-ends with many file- and print-related services as well as DBMS support. Some of these powerful, PC-based NOSs are described next.

**NOVELL NETWARE**    In addition to file and print services, this NOS offers a full range of features such as an e-mail system, directory and name services (similar to the X.500 standard), and a method enabling third-party developers to create additional services called NetWare Loadable Modules (NLMs). With NLMs, users gain access to fax, backup, virus protection, and many other third-party services. Recently, NetWare has developed an affinity for Sun Microsystems' extremely popular Java programming language. In order to attract Java developers to NetWare, Novell has built Java Application Programming Interfaces (APIs) into each of its network services.

**BANYAN VINES**    With its well-developed StreetTalk name and directory services, Banyan VINES is an excellent NOS for WAN-based client/server computing. Users, regardless of their location, can gain access to file, print, mail, and other services quickly and easily.

**UNIX**    The various flavors of the UNIX NOS, including SUN Solaris, SCO, and UnixWare, contain many powerful client/server features. The UNIX system was the first home, for example, to the powerful Distributed Computing Environment (DCE), in which multiple servers work in unison to provide a network service.

**WINDOWS NT**    This powerful 32-bit OS in many ways threatens the power and scalability of Novell NetWare through its preemptive multitasking, symmetric multiprocessing (the capability of using multiple microprocessors to perform tasks at the same time), and gigabyte memory addressing capabilities. This operating environment will serve as the centerpiece in many Windows 98 networks.

**IBM LAN SERVER**    LAN Server also rivals Novell NetWare's scalability and power through its newly acquired symmetrical multiprocessing. However, it is unable to dynamically acquire new network services as NetWare can through its NLM architecture.

There are many different faces of client/server computing because multiple NOSs, like those mentioned previously, can interoperate. For example, you can combine a NetWare server with a Windows NT server to give users the additional benefits of both NOSs. With such a combination, a user can use the NT server as a gateway to some of NetWare's services (such as print services), thereby adding a second layer of network security. You can also combine servers to improve performance. (See Figure A-4.)

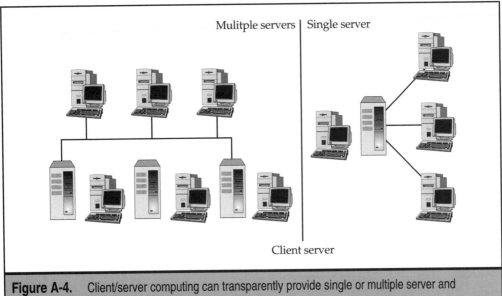

Mulitple servers | Single server

Client server

**Figure A-4.** Client/server computing can transparently provide single or multiple server and operating system support

Regardless of the configuration, client/server networking provides many advantages over peer-to-peer networking. It can help companies downsize from mainframe and minicomputer configurations. Because in a client/server network the server handles the majority of the data processing duties, network traffic between the server and the client is minimized. By centralizing data, client/server architecture promotes tighter security and facilitates data protection and recovery. And data required by every system on the network is centralized in one memory pool, thereby reducing the amount of processing required on the workstations.

## Combining Peer-to-Peer and Client/Server

Although client/server boasts many advantages over peer-to-peer networking, a combination of the two can provide excellent benefits for all members of a company or institution. For example, a network comprised of NetWare client/server OSs could provide a centralized storage solution for Windows 98 workstations, which dynamically formed peer-to-peer workgroups could use. These workgroups would then be free to share scheduling, printing, and e-mail services without disturbing those organization-wide services provided by the NetWare server. (See Figure A-5.)

# CONNECTING DEVICES AND CONFIGURING NETWORKS

Computer networks, regardless of constitution, type, or strategy, must allow NOSs, servers, workstations, and peripherals to communicate. To accomplish this, you must

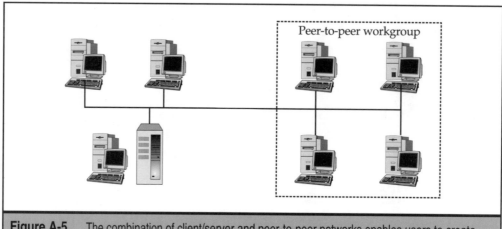

**Figure A-5.**  The combination of client/server and peer-to-peer networks enables users to create workgroups within an organization

first install a communications medium (cabling). Second, you must incorporate a cabling strategy (topology). Third, you must choose a corresponding network protocol. And lastly, you must select the appropriate hardware to connect these devices. There are no right or wrong methods to connect a network, only appropriate and inappropriate. For example, you can wire a WAN with coaxial, twisted-pair, fiber-optic, or wireless technologies; however, depending upon the current situation, only one would be the most appropriate. If your wide area link will transport time-sensitive video images, you may want to consider a T1 line running a high-speed network such as Asynchronous Transfer Mode (ATM). But if your wide area link will transport only e-mail, you may want to use either a dial-up router running TCP/IP, or an e-mail gateway based upon a standard telephone line.

# Cabling

The first required connectivity component is cabling. It is the lowest common denominator to all networks, and there are four basic types: coaxial, twisted-pair, fiber-optic, and wireless (no cable at all). Each type evolved out of specific network needs, and each solves a specific networking problem. Each cabling type has certain limits in speed and distance. All cabling types have one thing in common, however. Their speed and distance capabilities are directly proportional to their cost. Fiber-optic cable, for example, can transmit data at rates exceeding 155 megabits per second (Mbps) over great distances. However, it exacts higher costs than a twisted-pair cable, which can transmit data at speeds reaching 100Mbps over relatively short distances (100 meters or less).

## Coaxial

Coaxial cable consists of a solid copper core surrounded by an insulating layer and a shielding layer of finely woven wire, as shown in Figure A-6. Thus, it is highly resistant to

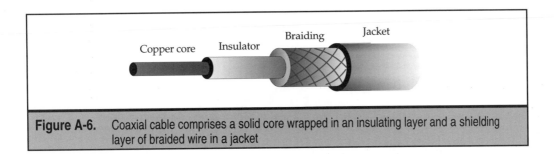

| **Figure A-6.** | Coaxial cable comprises a solid core wrapped in an insulating layer and a shielding layer of braided wire in a jacket |
|---|---|

external interference. If you have ever connected a television set to a video recording device, you have worked with coaxial cable. It can transmit data at rates reaching 100Mbps; however, it is usually found in 10Mbps Ethernet and 2.5Mbps ARCNET installations. In these environments, it functions usually as a bus topology.

Coaxial cable has an advantage over twisted-pair cable: It can transmit data over greater distances. When used in an ARCNET environment, it can transmit data up to 2,500 feet. In an Ethernet environment, it can transmit data 607 feet. But with coaxial cable, as with many other cable types, to obtain greater distances, you must sacrifice transmission speed.

For small Ethernet installations, you may want to choose coaxial cable over the popular twisted-pair cable for two simple reasons. First, you can spread up to 30 nodes (workstations) across 3,035 feet with only four inexpensive repeaters over Ethernet 10base-2. With a twisted-pair 10base-T cabling system, you must use additional hardware (concentrators as well as repeaters, which work to extend the reach of 10base-T networks beyond the usual limits of a single length of cable). However, because this 10base-2 cabling scheme functions as a linear topology, a break in the cable could bring the entire network down. The 10base-T network, on the other hand, uses a star topology that is immune to such disasters because if one cable length breaks, only the directly attached workstation/server fails.

*JARGON:*   What are 10base-T or 10base-2 cabling schemes? They represent different types of networking cables. 10base-T networks are the most prevalent, as they can support a wide range of network architectures such as Fast Ethernet and ATM.

## Twisted-Pair

Twisted-pair cabling is very popular in LAN environments because of its low cost, high speed, and reliability. (See Figure A-7.) Twisted pair cabling comes in two basic formats: unshielded twisted-pair (UTP) and shielded twisted-pair (STP). Both consist of a pair of twisted wires that form a circuit. They are twisted in order to prevent interference problems. More than one pair of wires can be bundled together within a twisted-pair cable. The only difference between the two is that STP contains braided metal shielding much like coaxial cable. This helps to prevent external crosstalk. For example, if you are planning to wire a network in an area containing florescent lights, you may want to choose STP in order to prevent signal interference.

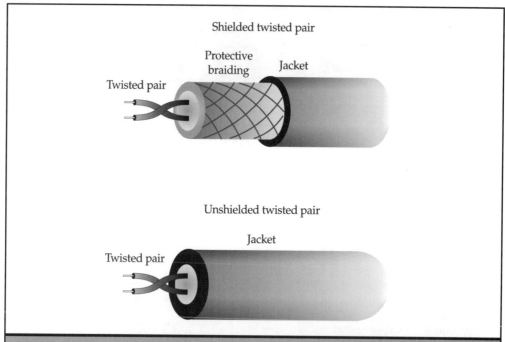

**Figure A-7.** Twisted-pair cables comprise twisted pairs of wires housed in a protective coating. UTP cable and STP cable differ in the fact that STP cable contains a braided wire coating to prevent cable interference

This cable type is quite prevalent in Ethernet and token ring networks as either a bus or star topology. Ethernet cable, in comparison with coaxial and fiber-optic cable, is very inexpensive. Moreover, it already exists in many buildings as telephone wiring. And yet Ethernet cabling can support transmission speeds as great as 100Mbps. This scalability directly relates to the manner in which you wire your Ethernet network. There are five basic cabling types with which you can wire an Ethernet network, as described in the EIA/TIA 586 Commercial Building Wiring Standard:

▼ **Category 1** If your telephone system was installed before 1983, this is the cable type you use every day when you place a telephone call. It is valid for voice transmissions but not for data.

■ **Category 2** Consisting of four twisted pairs, category 2 cable can transmit data at rates reaching 4Mbps. It is the least expensive data-quality twisted-pair network cable.

■ **Category 3** This twisted-pair wiring scheme can transmit data at 10Mbps. It is very prevalent within older Ethernet networks and 4Mbps token ring networks. Category 3 wire contains four pairs of wires twisted three times per foot.

■ **Category 4**   By transmitting data at 16Mbps, category 4 cable can handle both Ethernet and 16Mbps token ring networks. This cable also contains four pairs of twisted wire.

▲ **Category 5**   The most expensive and the most powerful, category 5 cable is ideal for many networking situations. For example, not only can it transmit all of the data handled by the preceding category cables, but it can support newer high-speed technologies such as Fast Ethernet (which travels at 100Mbps), Gigabit Ethernet (which travels at nearly 1,000Mbps), and ATM. Actually, according to AT&T Paradyne, UTP category 5 cable can transmit data at 950Mbps.

Which category of cabling you choose should depend upon your network's immediate and future needs in conjunction with the amount of money you are able to expend for cabling. Category 1 is no longer an option because it cannot support any of the newer, faster architectures such as Fast Ethernet. In many instances, companies choose category 3 or 4 cables because of their price and their ability to transmit data at high rates of speed (10Mbps and 16Mbps respectively).

No matter which category you choose, twisted pair wiring is an excellent choice simply because it is so adaptable. Of course, category 5 is the most compatible in that its component parts (connectors, faceplates, hub connections, and so forth) can support voice, ISDN, token ring, Ethernet 10base-T, Ethernet 100VG-Any LAN, Gigabit Ethernet, and future ATM applications.

## Fiber-Optic

An excellent choice for networks requiring reliable, high transmission speeds over great distances, fiber-optic cable can function effectively in many networking venues. Because of its high rate of speed (100Mbps), it is perfect as a backbone technology. In this way, it can connect many devices that require a consistent high transmission rate such as video servers and video conferencing workstations. The manner in which fiber-optic cable relays information is not through electrical signals, but through photons (basically, flashes of light). Because fiber-optic cable is made of glass, it is not subject to the following copper cabling problems:

▼ **Attenuation**   This is basically a loss of signal that occurs as data moves across large distances. This is why twisted pair and coaxial cable require repeaters, and why Ethernet requires both repeaters and concentrators.

■ **Capacitance**   This is simply a distortion of the signal traveling over a copper cable that increases with the length of the cable. Light is not subject to distortion (only interference from other sources of light).

▲ **Crosstalk**   This occurs when the signal on one wire interferes with the signal on another wire. Because light does not produce an electrical field, it does not interfere with other fiber-optic cables.

Although Ethernet can transmit over fiber-optic cabling systems, you will most likely see Fiber Distributed Data Interface (FDDI) as the medium of choice (See Figure A-8.) This is because with FDDI, there are not as many distance restrictions as with Ethernet. For example, a single Fast Ethernet packet traveling over a fiber-optic segment can only reach 450 meters. This is much farther than the 100 meters with copper wire Ethernet 10base-T. However, it pales in comparison with the more than 2 kilometers available to FDDI over fiber-optic cable.

In addition to these features, fiber-optic cable is the best alternative in many instances because of its ability to last. A laser for fiber-optic media (which is simply a high-powered transmission device) has a Mean Time Between Failures (MTBF) of 114 years. Also with the laser transmitter, you can obtain transmission distances of up to 160 kilometers.

Because fiber-optic cable transmissions are made up solely of light, there is no radiation outside of the fiber-optic cable. This means that it is virtually impossible to "hack," or monitor, transmissions.

## Wireless

An intriguing alternative to coaxial, twisted pair, and fiber-optic cabling systems does not involve a wiring system at all. Instead, it revolves around either radio or infrared

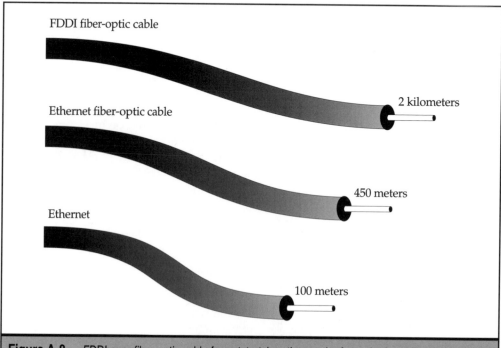

FDDI fiber-optic cable

2 kilometers

Ethernet fiber-optic cable

450 meters

Ethernet

100 meters

**Figure A-8.** FDDI over fiber-optic cable far outstretches the reach of standard and Fast Ethernet

transmissions. This quickly evolving format allows you to connect networks without laying any cables. Called wireless communications, it comprises two distinct networking issues: mobile and wireless LAN networking. With LAN networking, machines are connected via transmitters and receivers. With mobile networking, machines are connected via cellular communications provided by telecommunications providers.

The types of machines you can connect in this manner are varied, including PCs, PDAs, pagers, or notebook computers. Accordingly, wireless networking can solve a varied number of networking problems in situations forbidding standard wiring practices—though wireless networks fall prey to interference from fluorescent lights and other wireless communication services. For example, it can be used in a building of historic value, an electronically noisy area, closely situated buildings, or any situation requiring a non-intrusive network link, be it for disaster recovery or simply for backup measures.

For wireless LANs, there are mainly the following three different communication methods:

▼ **Infrared light** This technique offers the fastest transmission rates (up to 10Mbps) over the infrared spectrum of light. Although initially infrared was subject to line-of-sight transmissions, in which the transmitter and receiver must be able to "see" each other, newer, diffused infrared communication can work out of the line of site. Thus, an infrared wireless network can function around corners, over cubicles, and across hallways. However, even diffused infrared cannot communicate in an environment filled with bright and changing light sources.

■ **Narrowband radio** This method does not require line of sight because, like a radio station signal, you can receive it through walls. It is therefore ideal at sites where infrared cannot function. However, it, like the radio station signal, must be regulated by the FCC. This means that if you want to use narrowband radio networks, you must purchase a network with a specific frequency from either the FCC or the wireless network manufacturer. This type of network operates at speeds around 4,800Kbps (kilobits per second). See Figure A-9.

▲ **Spread-spectrum radio** To avoid the problems associated with obtaining a narrowband wireless network, you can turn to spread-spectrum technology, which transmits information over a wide range of frequencies. To accomplish this, a spread-spectrum receiver and transmitter utilize identical frequency jumping algorithms. When the receiver jumps to a new frequency, the transmitter does the same. Because its radio frequencies are not as high as narrowband radio, it does not interfere with standard radio transmissions. Its speed is around 250Kbps.

Mobile wireless networking accomplishes what wireless LANs do, but it does it over wide area links. For example, you can purchase a pager from a wireless company called SkyTel, which gives you an Internet address. With this address, you can receive e-mail from anyone who is connected to the Internet, regardless of your location. You can also

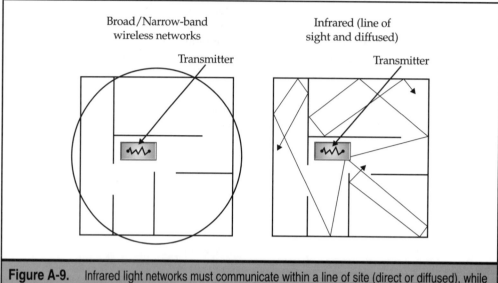

**Figure A-9.** Infrared light networks must communicate within a line of site (direct or diffused), while spread-spectrum and narrowband networks can transmit through objects like walls and around corners

use a modem attached to the modem of your notebook computer to remotely dial into your office as though you were directly connected to a telephone line.

Do not believe that wireless communications are a panacea of networking solutions. They are expensive, slower than standard cabling, poorly managed, subject to interference, and unsecured. However, as they increase in popularity, these issues will subside. There is an Institute of Electrical and Electronic Engineers (IEEE) committee hard at work on a communications standard for wireless computing, called 802.11. Transmission speeds are increasing over infrared links, and Data Encryption Standard (DES) security is available for some networks.

## Network Topologies

For workstations, printers, fax machines, servers, and the like to communicate effectively, they must be connected in a standardized fashion to accommodate future adds, moves, and changes, as well as possible connections with other networks. The standards used to connect devices in a network are called *network topologies,* and they are concerned with the type of cable used in the network.

The physical manner in which you cable a network defines its topology. This depends heavily upon the network's cabling, protocol system, and network type. To understand network topology, then, the place to begin is with either the subnetwork or connection of subnetworks, called an internetwork or LAN. You can cable each subnetwork in an internetwork as a different topology. However, each topology corresponds to the immediate wiring and protocol scheme. For example, a twisted-pair Ethernet subnetwork will most likely be wired as a star topology, in which all workstations and peripherals radiate from one or more central locations.

## LAN Topologies

Basically, there are four types of LAN topologies: star configuration, star-configured ring, star/bus configuration, and bus configuration, as shown in Figure A-10. Notice how each of the following topologies corresponds to specific cabling and protocol schemes.

▼ **Star Configuration**   This configuration is used almost exclusively by Ethernet twisted-pair networks, including IEEE 802.2 and IEEE 802.3. Because each workstation connects directly to a hub, any line breaks effect only the attached workstation. Thus, star configuration networks tend to be highly resistant to total network failure. Moreover, adds, moves, and changes are made simple through the easily expandable nature of the star topology. For each cable emanating from a server, you can attach up to four concentrators and/or repeater hubs. If you need to add another 10 to 12 people, simply pop on an additional hub. When one station transmits a signal, every other station attached to that segment (subnetwork) sees the packet; however, only the intended station acts upon that packet. This is called a Carrier Sense Multiple Access with Collision Detection (CSMA/CD) cable access method. This type of broadcast method of communication is what allows you to install workstations, servers, and any other peripheral at any point upon a subnetwork.

■ **Star-Configured Ring**   This is used primarily by IEEE 802.5 token ring networks. Here, a token is passed around a cabling circle. Attached to this ring are all of the workstations, servers, and peripherals for a single subnetwork. An attached device can pick up the token and transmit a message. Compare this with the broadcast topology of Ethernet in which stations may attempt to simultaneously transmit. The benefits of this sort of configuration, until recently, were mainly related to speed because IEEE 802.5 token ring allowed 16Mbps transmission rates. Although this is only 6Mbps faster than standard Ethernet, because Ethernet's CSMA/CD carries a great deal of overhead (roughly 30 percent of the available bandwidth), the 16Mbps of token ring far outperform Ethernet. With the advent of high-speed Ethernet, however, this advantage has been somewhat nullified. Another problem with this topology rests in its susceptibility to complete failure. For example, if a break occurs in a ring, every device attached to that ring will fail. There is a second protocol, however, that takes advantage of the star-configured ring topology, provides even faster transmission rates, and boasts cable failure protection. It is called FDDI. This protocol can transmit at speeds reaching 100Mbps, and if a ring is broken, the protocol simply reroutes data back through the unbroken portion of the cable to re-create the ring.

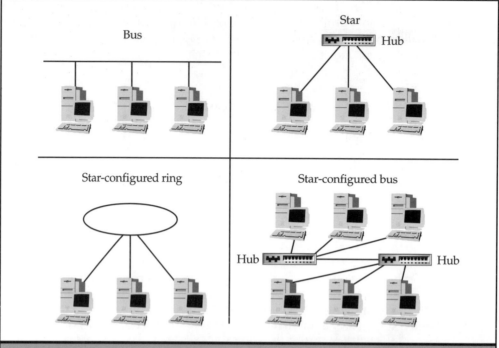

**Figure A-10.** The star, star-configured ring, star-configured bus, and bus subnetwork topologies

- ■ **Star/Bus Configuration** A combination of the star and star-bus configuration topologies, this method connects groups of star wired devices via one or more linear bus trunks. By combining the two topologies, you can more easily configure and reconfigure network devices. As with star topologies, this method caters mostly to the twisted-pair Ethernet subnetwork. A 10base-5 or 10base-2 linear bus can be used to connect 10base-T hubs, from which devices radiate in the star topology.

- ▲ **Bus Configuration** Ideal for smaller subnetworks, or subnetworks in which each device resides directly in line with the next, the bus topology attracts Ethernet 10base-5 and 10base-2 cabling schemes. The bus topology basically connects all devices to a central cable. However, if a break occurs anywhere along that cable, the entire subnetwork will fail. This is a drawback to the star/bus configuration as well.

## Internetwork Topologies

The manner in which you connect subnetworks and groups of subnetworks (LANs) is called internetwork topologies. Where hubs, concentrators, and repeaters connect devices within a subnetwork, bridges and routers and superhubs connect subnetworks and LANs. For example, a bridge is used to connect two or more subnetworks, while a router is used to connect two or more LANs. Based upon these pieces of hardware, there are three different types of internetwork topologies: meshed network, backbone network, and interlink star network.

**MESH NETWORK**    When large networks need to be connected over long distances via telecommunication links, this is by far the best topology. By connecting routers to routers, you enable the network to choose the fastest route for a given transmission. The way this occurs is quite ingenious. Because each router learns the addresses of all network devices to which it is attached, when a packet enters a given router, that router estimates the amount of time the packet will need to reach its destination along all possible paths. When it finds the quickest path, it sends the packet in that direction. This allows the network to automatically adjust both to changes in network utilization (percent of bandwidth occupied by traffic) as well as any router/cable failures. If a connection fails, all other routers automatically route packets around the failed line of communication.

**BACKBONE NETWORK**    To connect campus and office networks, it is often prudent to utilize a single bus or ring topology to connect various subnetworks or LANs through bridges or routers. This backbone usually functions over a high-speed cabling system such as fiber-optic cable. The protocol of choice is usually FDDI, as it can span the distance required to connect the disparately located subnetworks and LANs while providing the bandwidth and fault tolerance necessary to handle a large organization's entire flow of information.

**INTERLINK STAR NETWORK**    New to the scene of internetwork topology, interlink star networks take advantage of a new breed of superhubs to connect a structured wiring system as set forward by the EIA/TIA 568 wiring standard. These hubs act like a backbone network in miniature. They contain a very fast medium, called a backplane, to move the organization's data from the centralized hub out to distributed hubs and vice versa. Because it is based upon the EIA/TIA 568 wiring standard, this topology is very easy to administer. Each floor (subnetwork) contains a centralized hub (which could also be a superhub), which connects directly to the centralized hub in a star topology fashion. Thus, any breaks in the cabling structure will be easy to detect and correct without fear of the entire internetwork or WAN collapsing.

# Network Protocols

To understand how hardware and software combine to form a network, you need to be familiar with the protocols used by hardware to communicate. Protocols, like wild creatures, come in all shapes, sizes, and temperaments. Novell NetWare, Banyan VINES, UNIX, Apple, and LAN Manager all utilize completely different protocols to connect their services to the outside world. Although you may wonder how these OSs could ever coexist, do not worry. There is a template from which all protocols derive their individual traits. This template is a methodology developed by both industries and consortiums as an information standard. With a standard, different protocol animals are able to get along peacefully and even work together.

Created by the International Organization for Standardization (ISO), this template, called the Open Systems Interconnection (OSI) model (as shown in Figure A-11), acts as a mold from which protocol development teams can create interoperable hardware. By creating a model of layers (OSI layers one through seven), ISO enables two devices to map corresponding device and application functions to an OSI layer because each layer represents a different function. The layers are physical, data-link, network, transport, session, presentation, and application. As an example of how these layers work, consider that the physical layer carries coded electrical signals, while the data-link layer carries data that is hardware-specific (such as NIC driver information). If you study the OSI model, you will understand all of the different protocols available under different NOSs.

**LAYER 1: THE PHYSICAL LAYER**    This is the lowest layer in the protocol stack. It is responsible for linking a computer's software with its hardware, such as a NIC or even a serial port. As such, it handles all the low-level characteristics of the NIC. For example, it specifies voltages and binary values. It is also responsible for creating, maintaining, and terminating the physical link, which means that it opens and closes the door between your workstation and the network.

**LAYER 2: THE DATA-LINK LAYER**    This layer creates a set of rules that the sending and receiving workstations must follow in order to communicate. It also provides error-detection. This is also where bridges function. When a packet travels from one subnetwork to another, it must pass through a bridge. If the subnetwork address matches the current subnetwork address, the packet is forwarded to the appropriate network. The data-link layer also supports the software drivers used by the workstation's NIC.

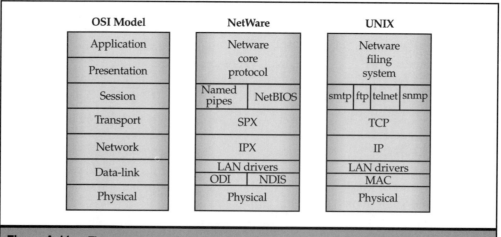

**Figure A-11.**    The open systems interconnection model can be directly compared to the protocols used by NetWare and UNIX

**LAYER 3: THE NETWORK LAYER**   This layer defines protocols used by NOSs for basic communication. It also defines device addressing information. This is why routers operate upon this level. When a packet arrives at a router and contains a network or device address not found in the current network, the packet is forwarded to the appropriate network. Some important protocols specific to this layer are the deeply entrenched Internet Protocol (IP), Novell's Internet Packet Exchange (IPX), Banyan VINES Internet Protocol (VIP), and the wide area connectivity protocol, X.25.

**LAYER 4: THE TRANSPORT LAYER**   Providing improved error-handling capabilities and security features, the transport layer provides connection-oriented services between two network devices. Common packets found in this layer include Microsoft NetBIOS/NetBEUI, Banyan VINES Interprocess Communication Protocol (VIPC), Internet Transmission Control Protocol (TCP), Internet User Datagram Protocol (UDP), and Novell's Sequenced Packet Exchange (SPX).

**LAYER 5: THE SESSION LAYER**   This layer simply provides a method for network applications to restart a failed transmission if a connection is temporarily lost. It also includes techniques designed to let these applications know when one set of data has finished transmission and when another set has begun.

**LAYER 6: THE PRESENTATION LAYER**   Within this layer, data is encoded for proper presentation when it arrives at its destination. For example, the presentation layer formats a print job differently than a screen dump, even though they both contain the same data. Here, you can find protocols such as NetWare's NetWare Core Protocol (NCP), UNIX-centric Network Filing System (NFS), Apple Computer's AppleTalk Filing Protocol (AFP), and LAN Manager's Server Messaging Blocks (SMBs).

**LAYER 7: THE APPLICATION LAYER**   This layer handles file transfers, e-mail transports (X.400), transaction processing, and directory services (X.500). Applications talk directly to this layer to accomplish tasks. For example, to log into a NetWare file server, the application layer carries your request to and returns the response from the server.

# IN CONCLUSION

The combination of the elements presented in this appendix should give you a good idea of the manner in which networks operate, how they are constructed, how they process information, and how they communicate. Your installation and use of Microsoft Windows 98 will involve most of these concepts. For example, you may want to connect your workstation to a Microsoft Windows NT network; you may want to connect to a separate subnetwork; you may even want to set up your Windows 98 workstation as a file and print server. Whatever the case, knowing the type of environment you and your Windows 98 workstation will encounter will make the installation far more pleasant and productive.

NETWORK
PROFESSIONAL'S
LIBRARY

# APPENDIX B

## Networking Protocols

Understanding how your Windows 98 workstation communicates with and takes advantage of network services such as file, print, and application services relies upon understanding the concept of network protocols. Without protocols, you cannot print a file on a network printer or open a file on a file server.

This appendix discusses protocols from the ground up to show you the benefits of each type of protocol. We begin by addressing a core concept that will make a protocol's purpose much more clear. It is a model, called the *open systems interconnection model* (or *OSI model*), from which each protocol can be broken down into understandable parts. We then apply this model to the IPX/SPX protocol in order to illustrate how a protocol works in reference to the OSI model.

# WHAT ARE PROTOCOLS?

*Protocols* allow you to perform many tasks because they, in their most basic sense, are rules. They dictate the manner in which two machines communicate over a network. When a computer requests a file from a file server, for example, both computers must agree upon a great number of rules such as the amount of data to be passed between the workstation and the file server, the addressing information for the packet carrying the information, the error-checking routine used to ensure the information arrived successfully, and the timing procedures sent to ensure that the packets carrying the information arrived in the right order.

In a manner of speaking, a protocol helps applications communicate with Network Interface Cards (NICs) as well. This forms a two-tier connectivity model: one level defines the connection between NICs; the second level defines the connection between applications.

Because many network operating systems (NOSs) utilize different protocols, you may find yourself in a position to decide which protocol to use on your Windows 98 workstation. Each protocol grew out of a different need; therefore, each is designed to function within different networking environments. For example, there are some protocols that work better in a wide area network (WAN) environment, and there are those that function better in a local area network (LAN) environment. Network Basic Input Output System (NetBIOS), as an example of a LAN protocol, originally provided connectivity for IBM and Microsoft networks as a stand-alone protocol. Currently, however, it is commonly used within other protocols such as IPX/SPX to provide compatibility and additional features to its host protocol. IPX/SPX, which performs equally well in both WAN and LAN environments, evolved in the opposite direction, beginning life as a foundation technology behind what is today's world-wide collection of connected networks, the Internet.

# WHAT DO PROTOCOLS DO?

As mentioned previously, protocols help network hardware (NICs) and software (applications) work together in harmony. To do this, a protocol must provide three services:

▼   Timing

■   Semantics

▲   Syntax

These items may sound at first like grammatical terms for a language. In a way they are grammatical terms, but instead of describing the manner in which words are combined within a sentence, they describe the way informational elements are combined within a network connection. The basic building block for this communication is a *packet*, which is basically a single chunk of information that is transferred between two connected computers. When a computer asks for a file, it receives the file not as one chunk of data, but as a vast number of small packets of information. (See Figure B-1.)

Packet-based communication accomplishes two things. First, it ensures that in cases where a large file's information is corrupted as it crosses the wire, only a very small

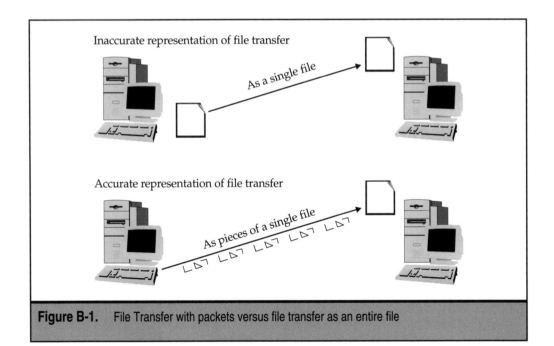

**Figure B-1.**   File Transfer with packets versus file transfer as an entire file

portion of the file is corrupted. This means that instead of resending the entire file, a computer need only send the corrupted packet(s). Second, it allows greater amounts of network traffic from greater numbers of workstations to traverse the same section of cable. Otherwise, if a workstation had to send an entire request (such as a login request) and that request failed, the workstation would have to retransmit the entire request. In its most basic sense, this really keeps a workstation from having to wait for a large packet to pass across its cable before sending or receiving its own information.

A consequence of sending a file over the network as a large number of packets, however, is that it becomes very confusing for a receiving NIC to reconstruct a file from the myriad of packets that pass across its section of cable. For example, what happens when a packet is lost? What happens if a packet arrives out of sequence? And what happens if a packet arrives in an unreadable format?

## Timing

A protocol answers these questions through timing. Although timing can have many meanings within a protocol, its basic function is to ensure that NICs agree to a time factor in sending and receiving packets. For example, when an IPX/SPX packet leaves a machine, it is given a certain amount of time (called *time to live*) in which it must reach its destination. Once a packet leaves a machine, it is marked with a time stamp that indicates its life expectancy. If it reaches its destination after exceeding its life expectancy, it is ignored. This ensures that a workstation does not listen for a missing packet forever.

When a station receives a packet, it generally sends off a reply indicating that the packet was received all right. If a packet reply does not return to the sending station within a certain amount of time, the sending station assumes that the packet was lost. It then resends the packet. This is why the time-to-live ratio is so important: If a packet arrived late at a workstation, and it were accepted as a valid packet, what would the receiving station do with the second, duplicate packet sent from the originating station that assumed the original packet had been lost?

## Semantics

In grammar, *semantics* defines the meanings behind words. For example, the word "romantic" can have the semantic meaning of one who is demonstrative in his or her feelings of love. Like language, protocols have words that contain a specific meaning. These words, however, are called *fields*. A typical protocol packet contains a number of fields, each one housing a particular piece of information required for successful communication. For example, each packet contains source address and destination address fields. These fields tell the receiving station, for example, where to send a successfully received packet reply. (See Figure B-2.)

There are many fields in addition to these, including total packet length, checksum number, type of service of the packet, version of the protocol, and packet identification.

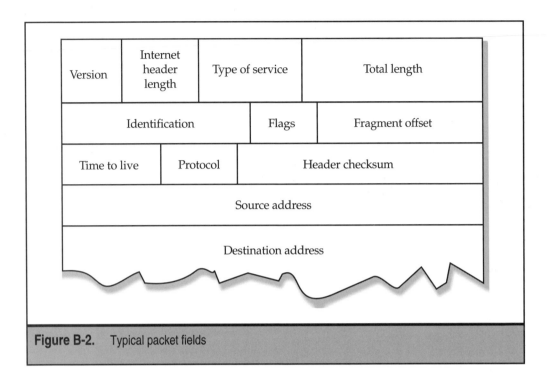

**Figure B-2.**    Typical packet fields

Therefore, as you might imagine, it is vitally important for both machines to agree upon which fields contain what information, or which words contain which meanings. Because packets arrive as binary 1s and 0s, this agreement on field semantics is crucial; without the agreement, one machine might mistake a destination address for a source address and thereby render further communication impossible.

## Syntax

*Syntax*, another grammatical term, defines the order and length of the fields within each protocol packet. This works in conjunction with semantics to provide a meaningful packet structure by ensuring that each field starts at a certain position within a packet, and that each field means the same thing over time. For example, within an IP packet's header information, the source and destination addresses must appear at the same location within the packet, and they must mean the same thing from one packet to the next. This feature closely corresponds to semantics in that each relies upon the other. Without proper syntax, the meanings of the individual fields within a packet would be worthless. Without proper semantics, the order in which the fields appeared within a packet would also be worthless.

# OSI MODEL

To better understand how semantics, syntax, and timing enable your Windows 98 workstation to communicate over a network, you should consider the International Standards Organization (ISO) Open Systems Interconnection (OSI) model. This model, which was introduced in 1983, defines a generalized model describing all of the functions required for network communications. It describes how NICs interact with each other, how applications and NICs interact, and how applications interact with each other. Beyond this, the OSI model is meant to help software manufacturers create network software that is *open*—in other words, software that can operate across heterogeneous network adapters and across heterogeneous OSs regardless of the network hardware/software manufacturer. For example, through current network protocol drivers, you can simultaneously load two or more protocols on any NIC, regardless of vendor. The TCP/IP protocol could be made by the Santa Cruz Operation, Inc.; the network adapter could be made by Intel Corp.; and the IPX/SPX protocol could be made by Novell, Inc. All can coexist without modification.

# OSI LAYERS

The model is comprised of seven layers. All of the layers together form an entire packet. Each layer represents a different point of interaction between two network devices such as computers, printers, file servers, and so forth. The seventh layer, the application layer, defines the manner in which two network applications interact. When two e-mail applications (such as X.400-compliant applications) communicate over the network, they exchange program-specific information over the seventh layer. Similarly, the first layer defines the manner in which two network adapters interact. It handles the electrical specifications of the wall sockets, wiring, and other hardware required for networking. The seven layers of the OSI model are:

- ▼ Application
- ■ Presentation
- ■ Session
- ■ Transport
- ■ Network
- ■ Data link
- ▲ Physical

Each layer provides services to the layer directly above it. And all layers provide support for one another. Although each defines a separate function, layers four through seven are primarily responsible for the interoperability mentioned previously, while layers one through three create the physical connection between two network devices.

Because all OSI model layers work with one another and with corresponding layers on other machines, they are called *protocol layers* and make up what is called a *protocol stack*.

This naming convention causes some confusion because a protocol layer and a protocol, such as TCP/IP, do not completely make up the communication between network machines. Novell NetWare's primary protocol, IPX/SPX, for example, is actually a combination of many protocols. SPX resides within the transport layer, while IPX resides within the network layer. This takes up only two of the seven layers. The remaining layers are made up of different NetWare-specific protocols such as the NetWare Core Protocol (NCP), which actually resides within the transport, session, presentation, and application layers simultaneously. Other layers contain protocols such as the Logical Link Control (LLC) protocol (data link layer) and the NetBIOS protocol (session and transport layers). Therefore, to say that a network's protocol is IPX/SPX is accurate yet incomplete, as there are many other protocols contained within this protocol suite.

Even more confusing, not all network protocols adhere to the OSI model standard. In a perfect OSI world, each layer exists in isolation. That is, each layer functions without affecting the surrounding layers. Although each communicates with its neighbor, no layer is dependent upon another. If a specific protocol manufacturer changes a layer—such as the Internet protocol within the TCP/IP stack—no other layers would require any changes in order to continue functioning with the new protocol. If Novell decides to change IPX/SPX, network adapter card manufacturers should not have to change any of their software in turn.

This modularization works in most situations. However, some protocols, such as NCP, NetBIOS, and the UNIX-based File Transfer Protocol (FTP), refuse to reside within one layer. Such protocols as NCP, which expand over more than one layer, break the OSI model's idyllic structure by not providing modularity at the layer level. This does not imply that NCP is flawed, or that the OSI model is flawed. It simply means that Novell, in orchestrating its network communication protocols, chose to give one protocol multiple responsibilities as they are defined within the OSI model.

In many cases, these renegade protocols act as single modules because they do not affect any of the other protocols. For example, the UNIX-based protocol, Telnet, which provides remote control of one machine by another, spans the application, presentation, and session layers. But neither it nor the lower layers are dependent upon each other. You could replace the standard Telnet application and protocol at any time with a different version without repercussions.

# Application Layer

The application layer, as mentioned previously, is responsible for allowing network applications to work together. This is where the most meaningful information is passed. Applications such as e-mail, databases, schedulers, and so forth all use the application layer to transfer information.

## NCP

An example of a network protocol that defies the OSI model standard by handling the duties of more than one layer is Novell's NCP. It is responsible for a vast number of network services ranging from simple file transfer to user authentication and network security. When you copy a file from a NetWare file server to your Windows 98 workstation, the XCOPY.EXE program that you use to copy the files carries on a complicated discussion with the file server over NCP. First, it asks if the requested file exists. Packets containing NCP information are then bandied back and forth as yes-or-no questions concerning the whereabouts of the file, your rights to access the file, and availability of the file (whether or not it is in use by someone else). When your Windows 98 workstation receives the "all clear" for the file transfer, the file is sent one piece at a time over NCP packets.

NetWare-specific management applications such as NWADMIN.EXE and FILER.EXE also take full advantage of the NCP protocol in obtaining network data and providing a means for network administrators to manage all aspects of a NetWare network. Using NWADMIN.EXE you can, for example, add and delete users from any workstation.

## X.400

Another illustration of an application layer protocol is the X.400 standard. Used as an application interface for e-mail compatibility, X.400 defines the way in which an e-mail message passes from one computer to another. Regardless of whether or not you are using TCP/IP, IPX/SPX, or NetBEUI, X.400 applications pass through the application layer. (See Figure B-3.)

## X.500

An application layer protocol vitally important to X.400 connectivity is the directory services protocol known as X.500. Also created by the ITU, X.500 allows workstations to access and share network resource information such as user names, file server addresses, e-mail addresses, and printer locations. Like the White Pages, X.500 is really just a list of useful information. However, instead of being organized linearly, it is organized in a tree structure with each branch, or level, corresponding to a domain. (See Figure B-4.) The common X.500 domains are:

▼ Organization

■ Division

■ Department

■ Workgroup

▲ Object

The levels are nested: Each level contains the following level, starting with Organization. Therefore, an organization can house divisions, a division can house

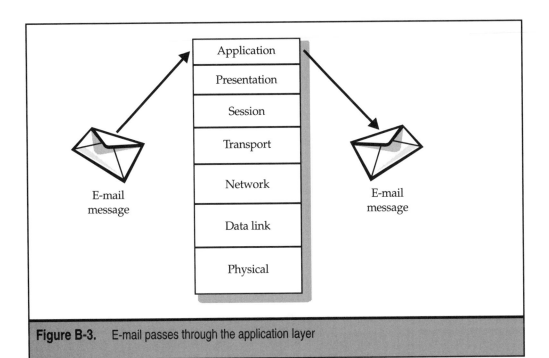

**Figure B-3.**  E-mail passes through the application layer

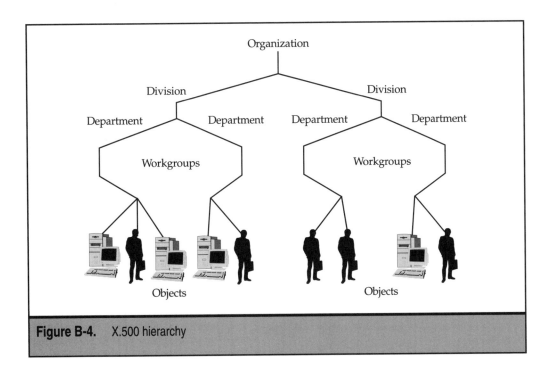

**Figure B-4.**  X.500 hierarchy

departments, and so forth. This hierarchy makes it easy for your Windows 98 workstation to find network resources because it provides a unique location name for every resource on the network. If your Windows 98 workstation is attached to a Novell Inc. NetWare 4.*x* network, for example, you can use its NetWare Directory Services (NDS) to find any other user's e-mail address on the NetWare network, regardless of that user's geographical location.

Although not truly X.500 compliant, Internet applications provide other application-layer services that can help you find information. If you connect your Windows 98 workstation to an Internet UNIX host via a TCP/IP, PPP, or SLIP connection, for example, you can enter the command **whois** at the UNIX command prompt, followed by the name of a user you wish to locate; you'll receive a list of names and e-mail addresses of all users matching your search. This information is housed on a number of X.500-like directory name servers belonging to the Defense Data Network (DDN) Network Information Center. The **whois** command establishes a session between your workstation and a DDN server.

# Presentation Layer

The presentation layer houses protocols that handle the format of the network application data. Residing beneath the application layer and above the session layer, the presentation layer takes data from the application layer and formats it for network communication. This layer provides the protocol syntax previously mentioned. The presentation layer orders the application data into a meaningful format for the session layer, which sends it across the network.

Many popular LAN protocols incorporate this layer into the application layer. For example, NetWare's IPX/SPX utilizes the NetWare core protocol for both layers. The predominantly UNIX-based TCP/IP utilizes the Network Filing System (NFS) protocol for both layers as well.

One protocol, however, that fully complies with the OSI model is Apple Computers Inc.'s AppleTalk. This protocol utilizes the Apple Filing Protocol (AFP) to format application-layer data. (See Figure B-5.)

This layer is contained within the workstation's OS and resident applications. For example, your Windows 98 OS works in conjunction with your network applications to format special characters such as tabs and graphic images, among others. Additionally, this layer is responsible for any encryption techniques applied to application data.

# Session Layer

The first OSI element beneath application-specific layers, the session layer provides the upper-most level of transport reliability by creating and closing communication sessions between the sending and receiving machines. When you request that a file be sent from a

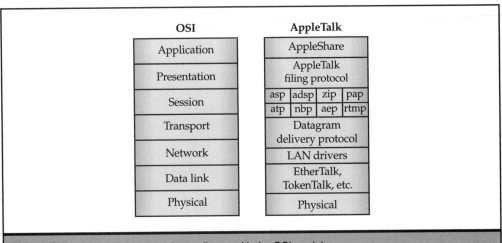

**Figure B-5.**    AppleTalk protocol compliance with the OSI model

NetWare file server to your Windows 98 workstation, for example, the session layer initiates a communication session that lasts for the duration of the request.

In creating a communication session, the session layer lays out the terms and agreements to be withheld during the session, such as the size of the packets to be exchanged and whether or not to transport data at full- or half-duplex speeds (for Ethernet networks). If something goes wrong with the transmission, this layer passes information along to the remaining layers, indicating the action required to remedy the problem.

# Transport Layer

The transport layer ensures that communications established in the session layer take place correctly. In this way, it ensures point-to-point communication between two machines. If a packet arrives at its destination in an incorrect order, for example, the transport layer is responsible for notifying the station that the packet was received incorrectly. This layer also manages network traffic rates. If the network is too congested, the transport layer throttles back the rate of packet transmittal to reduce the number of lost—and subsequently re-sent—packets.

The most common network protocols found at this level in the OSI reference model are TCP/IP's Transmission Control Protocol (TCP), Novell's Sequenced Packet Exchange (SPX), and NetBIOS/NetBEUI.

## Network Layer

The network layer is a very important layer for larger networks because it manages connectionless communication between machines. In other words, it contains information about the sending and receiving machine's home network. When machines on separate networks—different physical segments of a network, called *subnets*—wish to communicate, the information housed in the network layer allows packets from one network to travel to another network through a mechanism known as *routing*.

Routers, which connect subnets together, rely upon the network layer to route traffic between subnets. When a packet leaves your Windows 98 workstation on its way toward a distant subnet across the Internet, for example, it is handed off from router to router on the way to its destination. These routers do not know much about the actual destination of your packet, however. They simply know about the subnets to which they are connected. (See Figure B-6.)

This capability to forward only outbound traffic from one subnet to another is very important for larger networks such as the Internet because it eliminates unnecessary traffic passing from subnet to subnet. The protocols that reside at this level in the OSI reference model are TCP/IP's Internet Protocol (IP) and Novell's Internetwork Packet Exchange (IPX).

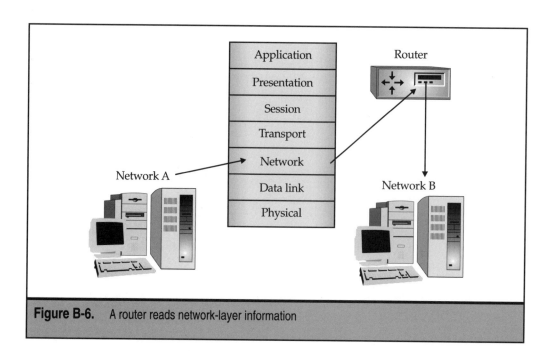

**Figure B-6.**    A router reads network-layer information

# Data Link Layer

This is a very important layer in the OSI reference model because it actually forms the data sent down through the protocol stack into packets to be sent out over the network through the next, and final, layer—the physical layer. The data link layer is responsible for forming packets that conform to a specific network access method. If you have attached your Windows 98 workstation to a token ring network, for example, the data link layer forms the data into a format recognizable to a token ring network. Other access methods include Ethernet, Fiber Distributed Data Interface (FDDI), Asynchronous Transfer Mode (ATM), and ARCNET.

It is at this layer that your Windows 98 OS talks to the hardware in your computer. Assuming you are connected to a network via the Ethernet access method, when you installed Windows 98, you chose to install either a Network Driver Interface Specification (NDIS) or an Open Data-link Interface (ODI) to communicate with your NIC.

These driver specifications, developed around 1989, allow you to load more than one protocol on your Windows 98 workstation. For example, if you wanted to simultaneously communicate with the TCP/IP-based Internet and an IPX/SPX-based NetWare LAN, you could choose to install both protocols either during installation or afterward through the protocol configuration menu.

You are able to choose both protocols because each protocol layer is very well-defined. Therefore, if you installed Windows 98 with NetWare ODI drivers, each time you boot up, you will automatically load a number of drivers:

```
LSL.COM
NE2000.EXE
IPXODI.COM
TCPIP.EXE
NETX.EXE
```

This sequence of commands loads the network software necessary for your Windows 98 workstation to communicate using both TCP/IP and IPX/SPX. Interestingly, these commands span the second through the fourth layers of the OSI reference model. The LSL.COM command loads the Link Support Layer (LSL) software that manages the ODI connection at the data link layer. The NE2000.EXE command loads the driver that enables your software to talk to the NIC. It also resides in the data link layer. The IPXODI.EXE command loads the ODI software responsible for accommodating more than one protocol as well as the IPX portion of the NetWare protocol stack. Therefore, this command represents both the data link layer and the network layer. The TCPIP.EXE and NETX.EXE commands load the remaining software for the TCP/IP and SPX protocol stacks. They represent the transport layer (SPX and TCP) as well as the network layer (IP).

# Physical Layer

This layer, as previously mentioned, represents the actual connection between your software and your hardware. It really does not have anything to do with protocols, except that it defines the access method used by the data link layer. It is handled differently for each type of access method, FDDI, ATM, token ring, and Ethernet. In defining this connection, it is the initial reporter of network errors to the higher levels; it is the first layer to monitor network performance; and it is the first layer to synchronize network packets.

# OSI BENEFITS

As mentioned previously, the benefits of the OSI layered model are twofold. First, they help users and vendors visualize and compartmentalize network communication procedures. Second, the OSI model gives vendors a hierarchical method to produce hardware and software that is interpretable with other vendors' hardware and software. This gives vendors the opportunity to concentrate on one or more layers of the OSI model without having to worry about the other layers.

For example, an e-mail vendor can write an e-mail package that can send and receive messages across the network without having to write the communication software responsible for such connectivity. Likewise, a hardware vendor can create a NIC without worrying about the manner in which an e-mail application must communicate with their hardware.

# EXAMPLE OF PROTOCOL LAYERS IN ACTION

The best way to understand how these OSI reference layers operate in connecting your Windows 98 workstation to the network is to chart the course of a network command as it is sent from your workstation to a network service provider such as a NetWare file server.

This demonstrates the manner in which data passes down the protocol stack (from layer seven to layer one) on the sending workstation and up the protocol stack (from layer one to layer seven) on the receiving workstation. For this demonstration, imagine using the IPX/SPX protocol to open a file from the Explorer program in Windows 98.

Open your Explorer program in Windows 98, double-click the Network Neighborhood icon, double-click on a NetWare volume folder, and then double-click on a text file such as a Microsoft Word document. This action invokes a number of communication sessions between your Windows 98 workstation and the NetWare file server. The Windows 98 OS sends the command to a NetWare file server.

## Redirection

In most cases, you will not have to enter a command like **open** or **print** at a command prompt with Windows 98's graphical user interface (GUI) Explorer application. Without the GUI of Windows 98, you would have to enter a command at the MS-DOS command prompt, such as WP myfile.doc to open the MS-DOS version of WordPerfect with the MYFILE.DOC file as the initial document. (See Figure B-7.) However, the point is that in

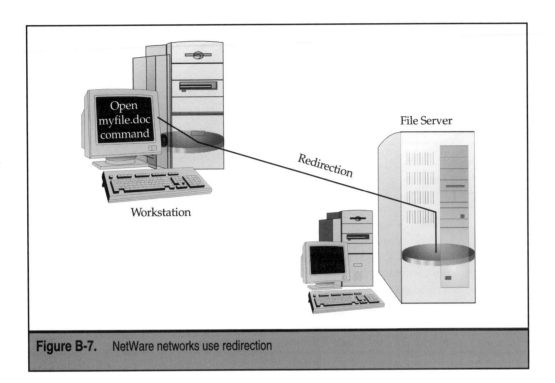

**Figure B-7.** NetWare networks use redirection

both cases, the same commands are sent across the network; all network commands on a NetWare network, for example, rely upon the resident protocol such as IPX/SPX.

The way Windows 98's GUI and the DOS command line work is simple. Assuming that you've included your network drive in your workstation's PATH statement, when you enter a command, the command processor on your workstation searches the local hard disk for the command. If it cannot find the command, it transfers control to the network software, which then searches the NetWare file server's hard disk for the desired program. At the point where the command ceases to search the workstation's hard disk and begins to search the file server, the IPX/SPX protocol stack goes into action, wrapping the command into a package that is able to traverse the network to the NetWare file server.

## OSI Reference Model Stack

Once the data is placed into the hands of the IPX/SPX protocol stack, it is passed down through the OSI reference model stack on its way from the Explorer program to the network cable. As the data passes from one layer to the next, each layer adds its own information to the data. Each layer also formats the data to accommodate the next layer.

Although each bit of information destined for a networked computer passes through each protocol level as defined in the OSI reference model, each protocol suite contains a family of protocols that corresponds to different layers. Some protocols overlap layers, while others occupy only a portion of a layer.

In the IPX/SPX protocol suite, all network packets are encapsulated in the connectionless IPX protocol, but within that packet, other protocols can reside in order to carry out specific functions. This means that when you issue the network command **Open file**, your data travels across the network always as an IPX packet, but that packet can contain NCP information, SPX information, or NetBIOS information. (See Figure B-8.)

## Application Layer

The command **Open file** is first redirected to the application layer of the protocol stack. There, it is translated into a language that NetWare can understand, namely NCPs.

Novell's NetWare core protocol represents a proprietary set of commands used to access and manipulate a NetWare file server. These commands let you make and break connections between your Windows 98 workstation and the file server. They let you find and open files residing on a NetWare file server. They also let you print to a network printer. Virtually all communication between a client and server on a NetWare network occurs over NCP packets.

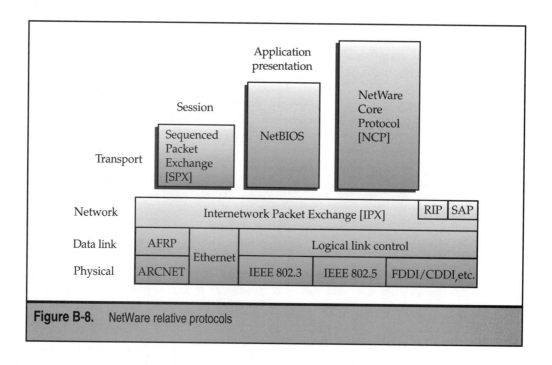

**Figure B-8.** NetWare relative protocols

Although the NCP protocol technically spans both the application and presentation layers of the ODI reference model, its practical abilities reach beyond these two layers and into the transport and session layers. This is possible because the NCP protocol, as a member of the IPX/SPX protocol suite, contains some of the session-control and sequencing mechanisms normally found in the SPX protocol. Therefore, by tightly integrating the NCP and the IPX protocols, NetWare can forego the overhead associated with a "thicker" protocol stack fully utilizing NCP, SPX, and IPX.

Normally, however, only the first two layers of the ODI reference model are collapsed into the NCP protocol. Once your data passes into the NCP layer, it is translated into a command the NetWare file server can understand and then passed directly to the session layer.

## Session Layer

Having skipped the presentation layer, the NCP information is passed to the session layer, which is controlled by two special protocols, NetBIOS and Named Pipes. NetBIOS, for the most part, is a compatibility protocol originally designed to provide peer-to-peer communication between applications written specifically for IBM's NetBIOS protocol. It is not a fully functioning NetBIOS protocol stack, however. It is simply a translation routine that provides interoperability between NetBIOS-specific applications and a NetWare network.

Named Pipes support provides a similar level of compatibility as NetBIOS. It can, however, be used to create a full range of network services such as logging in and out from a network machine. For example, some application server software packages reside on a NetWare network but do not contain any built-in NetWare networking capabilities. These applications must allow users to log in and authenticate with the application server. They therefore use Named Pipes support to let users attach to their services. (See Figure B-9.)

If the data requires support for these two protocols, the appropriate information is added to the network packet and then passed down from the application and presentation layers.

## Transport Layer

When the command information passes through the transport layer of the OSI reference model, it is given the information required to ensure that once it arrives at its destination, it will be recompiled into its greater whole in the right order. It is here that the information can be given this sort of help from the SPX protocol. SPX is a connection-oriented protocol. It does not assume that the receiving station actually received any packets. Like NCPs, NetBIOS, and Named Pipes, SPX packets utilize the services of the IPX protocol to obtain the initial connectivity between your Windows 98 workstation and the NetWare file server. However, the SPX protocol adds a service capable of maintaining a virtual connection between the two machines. It does this by listening for a response from each packet, indicating whether or not the transmission went all right.

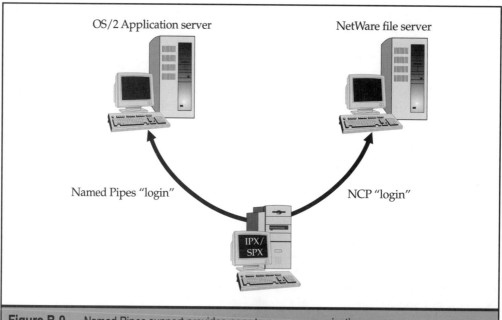

**Figure B-9.** Named Pipes support provides peer-to-peer communications

## Network Layer

Once the **Open file** data that has passed through the application, presentation, session, and transport layers has been correctly formatted and given the information needed to reach its destination, it passes into the network layer. It is subsequently encapsulated into a packet capable of actually traveling over a network cable. For the IPX/SPX network, the information is encapsulated into an IPX packet. IPX packets, unlike connection-oriented SPX-enhanced packets, do not guarantee that your command will reach its destination. It simply sends out information and assumes that it will arrive at its destination. In working this way, IPX can deliver at rapid transport speeds because it only uses approximately half as much bandwidth as connection-oriented protocols.

To ward off the chaos that can ensue without proper assurances of packet delivery, the IPX protocol builds into each packet a cyclic redundancy check (CRC). If the receiving machine looks at the CRC and discovers that there has been a problem, it notifies the sending station of the error, which then resends the packet. Conversely, if the sending workstation does not receive an acknowledgment that the destination workstation received the packet, it resends the packet.

## Data Link Layer

Now in the shape of an actual packet of data, your command enters the data link layer of the OSI reference model. At this point, it is formatted into a frame type that can accommodate your network cable type, such as Ethernet, ARCNET, FDDI, and token ring. It is also here that your data is formatted to accommodate the ODI or NDIS specifications.

## Physical Layer

Once past the data link layer, your newly formed packet enters the physical layer, its last stop on its way to the network cable. At this point, the IPX/SPX protocol no longer controls the way your packet traverses the network. It is up to the physical layer to ensure that your packet reaches the NIC to subsequently travel across the network cable. It is this same process that lets you utilize a modem through the RS232 port on your Windows 98 workstation.

# Reverse Communication Process

Once your newly formed NCP packet containing the **Open file** command passes through the NIC, it finds its way to its destination. Actually, in most network environments such as Ethernet, your packets are simply sent to all machines attached to your subnet. Only the workstations with a NIC number that matches the destination address within your packet actually act upon the command. All other workstations simply ignore the packet.

As the packet passes into the NIC, the information added to your command data is stripped away in the opposite order in which it was applied. That is, what was added at the network layer is analyzed before data added at the application layer. This gives the receiving workstation a chance to resolve lower-level problems such as a faulty network connection before spending a great deal of time processing the higher levels of the protocol stack. In this way, if it spots a problem (such as a bad CRC), it can simply not respond if the packet does not use the SPX protocol, or respond that a problem occurred if the packet contains the SPX protocol. (See Figure B-10.)

After moving up through the protocol stack, your **Open file** command is passed along to the NetWare file system as an NCP request to open the desired file. If your user name has been granted the rights to access that file, the file server then sends an NCP response indicating that it is okay to open that file. The response then goes through the same formatting stages as your request to open the file.

# IN CONCLUSION

The act of sending and receiving a sequence of two packets to determine whether or not you have access rights to a desired file is just a small part of the entire process involved in locating, verifying, authenticating, opening, sending, acknowledging, closing, and terminating the communication session. Each of these events requires at least one series

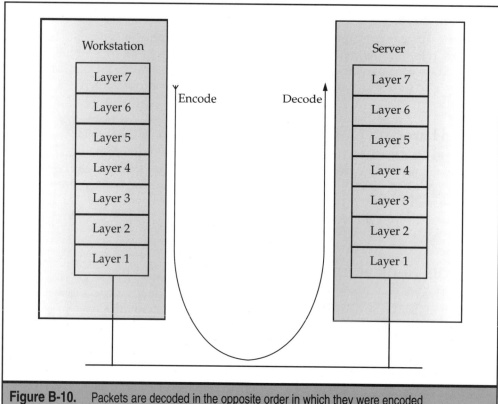

**Figure B-10.** Packets are decoded in the opposite order in which they were encoded

of two packets. In general, requesting that a file be opened and its contents retrieved from a file server can require virtually thousands of packets.

In this appendix, we discussed the nature of networking protocols from two standpoints: the OSI reference model, which defines a series of seven layers required for two networked machines to communicate effectively; and an example of the OSI reference model at work in the NetWare-centric IPX/SPX protocol.

NETWORK
PROFESSIONAL'S
LIBRARY

# APPENDIX C

# Windows 98
# Resources

W indows 98, together with its predecessor, Windows 95, is the most popular operating system (OS) in history. With such a huge installed base, it's not surprising that there are a lot of resources available.

# ONLINE HELP

In the age of Internet connectivity, it's easy to forget about the resources already installed on your computer, like online help. The Windows 98 online help system was installed automatically when you loaded the OS. Additionally, the Welcome to Windows 98 Tour, provided on the Windows 98 CD-ROM, also contains a great deal of helpful information.

## Windows Help

On the Windows 98 Start Menu, you will find a menu option titled Help. Selecting this option opens the Windows online help system, as shown in Figure C-1. If the Contents

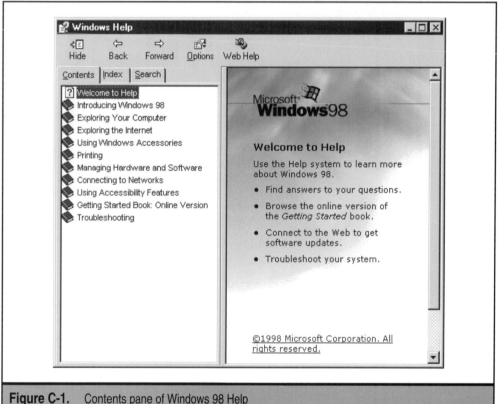

**Figure C-1.** Contents pane of Windows 98 Help

tab is not selected by default, select it now by clicking on the tab labeled Contents. To the left of each item listed in the window you will see one of two icons. The icon that resembles a piece of paper with a blue question mark on it signifies that the item is a help document. The purple book icon signifies that the item contains links to other documents or books, in much the same way that file folders work in Windows Explorer.

The Index tab, shown in Figure C-2, provides direct access to an index of important terms found in the help system. It can be searched quickly by first clicking in the entry field above the list, then typing the word or term you are interested in. The help system performs a progressive search as you type, automatically advancing to the first entry that matches your input.

There are three ways to select and display the desired help topic. You can double-click on the desired help topic. Click on the desired help topic once, to select it, then click the Display button at the bottom of the window. Or, if you select a help category using either technique, you are presented with a dialog box from which to choose the help topics that belong in that category. The third tab, labeled Search, does exactly that (see Figure C-3). It provides an interface in which to search for keywords and is most helpful when the term you are looking for is not found in the index.

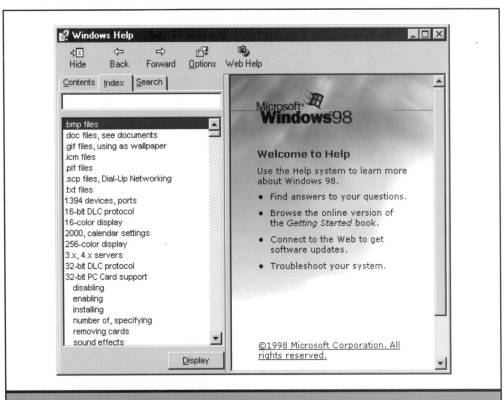

**Figure C-2.**   Index pane of Windows 98 Help

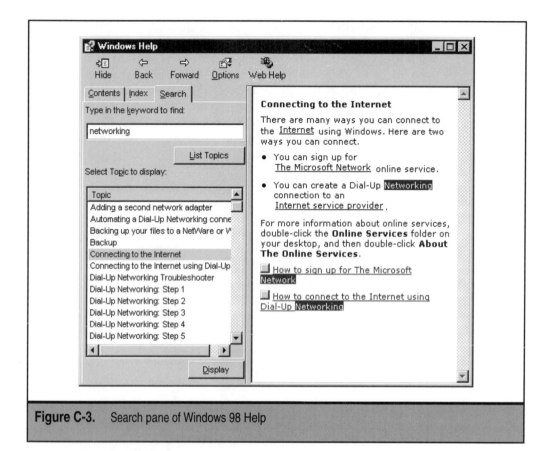

**Figure C-3.** Search pane of Windows 98 Help

Searching is pretty simple. Just click in the entry field labeled "Type in the keyword to find," type the word or phrase you're looking for, then click on the List Topics button. This causes Windows Help to search for all entries in the help system that contain the word or phrase you entered, and display them in the Topic window. From there, you can select and display any desired topics just as we did before—by double-clicking on the desired entry or selecting the entry with a single mouse click then clicking on the Display button.

## Welcome to Windows 98 Tour

The first time you start up Windows 98 after installing it, you are greeted with a "Welcome to Windows 98" dialog box that offers you a tour of some key OS features (see Figure C-4). You can also access this program from the Start Menu by selecting Programs | Accessories | System Tools, and then choosing Welcome to Windows.

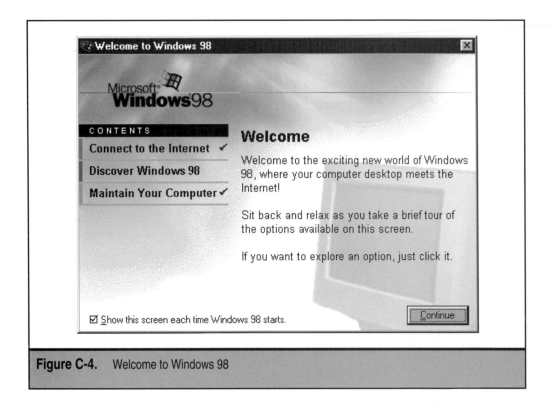

**Figure C-4.**   Welcome to Windows 98

There are three menu options on the left side of the window:

- ▼ **Connect to the Internet**   Launches the Internet Connection Wizard
- ■ **Discover Windows 98**   Contains three Windows 98 introductions/tutorials
- ▲ **Maintain Your Computer**   Launches the Maintenance Wizard

The first and last options launch Wizards that have already been discussed earlier in this book. The second option, titled Discover Windows 98, is your gateway to more information about Windows 98. Selecting this option leads to a full-screen display that contains a series of three tutorials and a link to more information about Microsoft Press publications, as shown in Figure C-5.

## Computer Essentials

The first option in Discover Windows 98 is titled Computer Essentials and is for new computer users. From here, you can learn about how to use your keyboard and mouse in Windows 98 and get basic instruction on the Windows Desktop, Start Menu, and Windows.

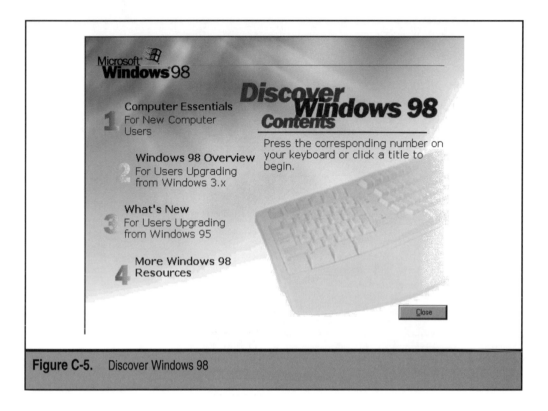

**Figure C-5.** Discover Windows 98

## Windows 98 Overview

The second option, Windows 98 Overview, is for more advanced computer users. Users that are upgrading from Windows 3.x will appreciate this tutorial, which explains key differences in Windows 98 (see Figure C-6).

The tutorial contains six topics: Starting a Program, Exploring Files and Folders, Finding Information, Managing Open Windows, Connecting to the Internet, and Exploring the Active Desktop.

## What's New

The third tutorial, What's New, is for users who are upgrading from Windows 95 rather than Windows 3.x (see Figure C-7). The topics in this tutorial are classified and grouped into five categories: Easier to Use, More Reliable, Faster, Web Integration, and More Entertaining.

## More Windows 98 Resources

For users who want to learn more about Windows 98, the Microsoft Press Resources area is a pretty good place to look for more information (see Figure C-8). Unlike the other three

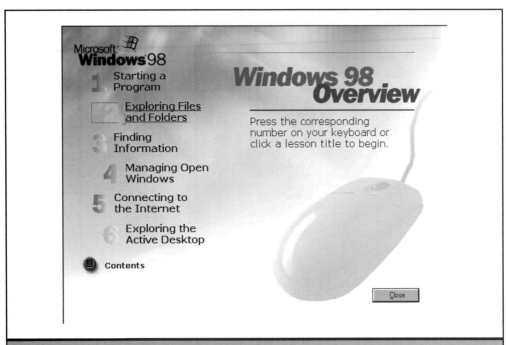

**Figure C-6.**   Windows 98 Overview tutorial

**Figure C-7.**   What's New tutorial

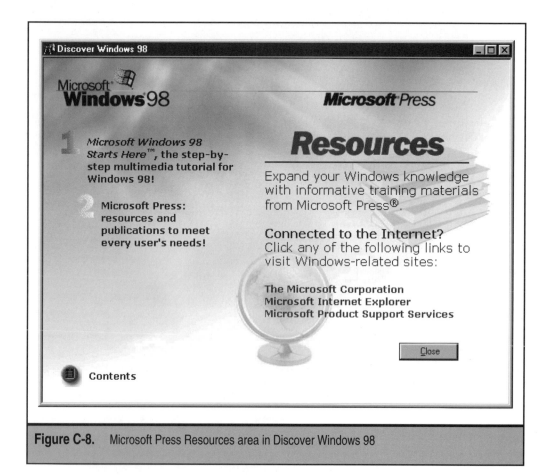

**Figure C-8.** Microsoft Press Resources area in Discover Windows 98

areas, which all contain instructional tutorials, this is more like an advertisement for products you can buy, such as the "Microsoft Windows 98 Starts Here" multimedia tutorial and books from Microsoft Press.

If you have an Internet connection, you can also take advantage of the three Web links found in the lower right portion of the window, each of which takes you to a different area of the Microsoft Web site: the Microsoft home page, Microsoft Internet Explorer home page, and Microsoft product support page.

# KEYBOARD SHORTCUTS

As difficult as it may sound, you can actually run Windows 98 entirely from the keyboard, without ever using the mouse. No, it isn't always easy or even appropriate to do so all the time, but there are several keyboard shortcuts you should know about because they can really boost your productivity versus reaching for, positioning, and clicking with the mouse all the time.

# The Windows Key

Many keyboards now have a key known as the Windows Key. It is typically situated on the bottom row, near the left side, between the CTRL and ALT keys. Most Windows users quickly learn that pressing and releasing this key activates the Windows Start Menu, but there's actually more to it than that:

▼   ⊞   Activates the Windows Start menu

■   ⊞+E   Opens Windows Explorer

■   ⊞+F   Opens Windows Find Files dialog box

■   ⊞+M   Minimizes all open windows

■   ⊞+R   Opens Windows Run dialog box

▲   ⊞+D   Switches to the Windows Desktop (same as ⊞+M)

Any other combinations of ⊞+keystroke will respond as if you had simply pressed the keystroke alone without the ⊞ key.

# Other Special Windows Keyboard Commands

The following is a list of other special keyboard commands you should know:

▼   CTRL+ESC   Activates the Windows Start menu (like ⊞ in the preceding section)

■   ALT+TAB   Selects the most recently used Window (pressing TAB multiple times while holding ALT cycles through all open programs)

■   ALT+SHIFT+TAB   Works like ALT+TAB, in reverse order

■   ALT+ESC   Cycles through all open Windows in sequence

■   ALT+SPACEBAR   Activates the control menu for the selected Window (allows keyboard control of Restore, Move, Size, Minimize, Maximize, and Close options)

■   ALT+F4   Closes the current Window (exits the application)

▲   CTRL+F4   Closes the current child window or document in the selected Window (does not close the application)

# User-Defined Keyboard Shortcuts

One of the best-kept secrets in Windows is that you can define your own keyboard shortcuts. All programs defined on the Windows Start menu can be assigned to a unique keyboard sequence, which will immediately run the program when pressed. For example, if you open DOS windows a lot, you might consider assigning the key sequence CTRL+ALT+D to it, or CTRL+ALT+W for Microsoft Word, CTRL+ALT+E for Internet Explorer and CTRL+ALT+M for your Internet Mail.

To assign a keyboard shortcut, open the properties dialog for the desired program icon and look for the field labeled "Shortcut key," which can be found on either the Program or Shortcut tabs, depending on whether it is a DOS or native Windows program. To define the key, click once in this field then press the keyboard combination you desire to use. If the combination is already in use, Windows launches the program associated with it. If it is available, the key sequence is entered into the field. Your newly defined keyboard shortcut will be active and ready for use after you close the dialog box.

# WINDOWS UPDATE

In the past, if Microsoft updated the Windows OS to fix a known bug or add new functionality, you had to seek out and download the necessary files over the Internet or somehow get your hands on a new Windows CD-ROM. Locating the most current drivers for your peripherals was even more complicated, often involving a more extensive Internet search or endless telephone calls and hold-time waiting to talk to someone who could tell you where to download the latest driver files from.

Fortunately, Microsoft has made this a whole lot easier in Windows 98 by creating a special Internet site specifically for this purpose and providing a link, titled Windows Update, right on the Windows Start Menu when you install Windows 98.

Selecting this menu option launches Internet Explorer and directs it to the Windows Update site (see Figure C-9), where you can choose to check for new and updated software programs and device drivers.

The Product Updates option retrieves a list of new and updated components that are available for download from the Microsoft Windows Update Web site. Using this option, you can compare the downloadable files to the files installed on your system, as shown here:

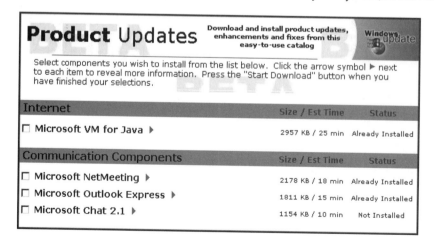

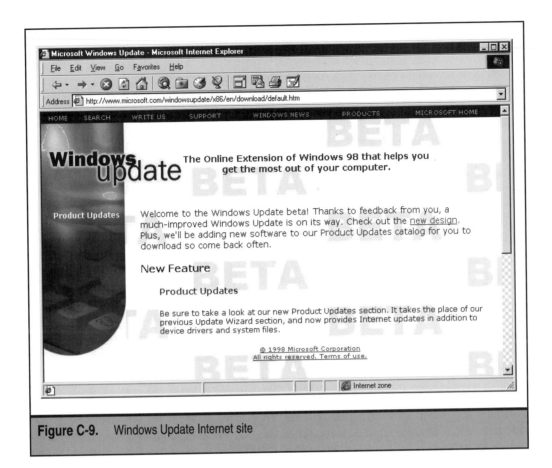

**Figure C-9.**    Windows Update Internet site

Installing a new component on your system is as easy as clicking the check boxes next to the items you are interested in then clicking the Start Downloading button at the bottom of the screen.

# MICROSOFT PLUS

Microsoft Plus is another great resource for Windows 98. This collection of add-on components, utilities, and games is usually sold separately but is sometimes bundled along with Windows 98 itself when you buy a new computer.

Microsoft Plus for Windows 98 includes the following components:

▼   Desktop Themes

■   3-D Screen Savers

- Windows 98 Maintenance Wizard Updates
- Disk Cleanup
- Compressed Folders
- Deluxe CD Player
- Picture It! Express
- Microsoft Golf 1998 Lite
- Spider Solitaire
- Lose Your Marbles
- ▲ McAffe VirusScan

# WORLD WIDE WEB

The Internet, specifically the Web, is a great source for Windows 98 information and software. There are thousands of Web sites dedicated to Windows software and usage tips.

## Microsoft's Web Site

Microsoft's own Web site is a great place to start. It's full of product information, usage tips, technical bulletins, troubleshooting advice, and free downloadable software.

The Microsoft Web site can be accessed at http://www.Microsoft.com. You can go directly to the Windows 98 page at http://www.Microsoft.com/Windows98.

The Microsoft Web site is well organized and easy to navigate or search, but the look and feel and menu structure does change from time to time, so we won't bother to document how to navigate the site in this book. You shouldn't have any trouble finding your way around.

## Other Web Sites

There are many Web sites available on the Internet that are useful to Windows 98 users. Here we list a few select sites, followed by the URLs for the most popular Internet search engines that will help you locate sites that contain the specific information you may be looking for.

| Web Site | URL |
| --- | --- |
| LAN Times Online | www.LanTimes.com |
| LAN Times PARTS | www.LTParts.com |
| BYTE Magazine | www.Byte.com |
| Osborne McGraw-Hill | www.Osborne.com |
| Shareware.com | www.Shareware.com |
| Download.com | www.Download.com |

| Web Site | URL |
|----------|-----|
| CNET | www.CNet.com |
| ZDNet | www.zdnet.com |
| Yahoo | www.Yahoo.com |
| Excite | www.Excite.com |
| Alta-Vista | www.AltaVista.com |
| Infoseek | www.InfoSeek.com |
| Lycos | www.Lycos.com |

# PERIODICALS

Magazines and trade journals are another great resource for Windows 98 users who are looking for more information about the OS, application software, networking, general usage tips, and software development.

| Web Site | URL |
|----------|-----|
| Microsoft Personal Computing Magazine | www.microsoft.com/magazine |
| PC Computing Magazine | www.zdnet.com/pccomp |
| Windows 95 Magazine | www.win95mag.com |
| Windows Magazine | www.winmag.com |
| WinUser Magazine | www.WinUser.com |
| Windows Sources Magazine | www.zdnet.com/wsources |
| Computer Life Magazine | www.zdnet.com/complife |
| PC Week | www.zdnet.com/pcweek |
| PC Magazine | www.zdnet.com/pcmag |
| Family PC Magazine | www.zdnet.com/familypc |
| BYTE Magazine | www.byte.com |
| LAN Times | www.lantimes.com |
| Microsoft Certified Professional Magazine | www.mcpmag.com |
| InfoWorld Magazine | www.infoworld.com |
| Internet World Magazine | www.iw.com |
| Network Computing Magazine | www.networkcomputing.com |
| Windows Magazine | www.cmp.com/domesticpubs /windowsfiles/windows.htm |

# BOOKS

There are lots of books about Windows 95 and Windows 98. Osborne/McGraw-Hill is a great place to start. Online bookstores such as Amazon.com and Barnes & Noble are also great resources.

| Web Site | URL |
| --- | --- |
| Osborne/McGraw-Hill | www.osborne.com |
| Amazon.com Web site | www.amazon.com |
| Barnes & Noble booksellers | www.barnesandnoble.com |

# Index

**B**

# I

**T**

**X**

 **Y**

 **Z**